DESIGN THROUGH DISCOVERY

Reproduced on the cover:
Dale Chihuly. *Green Cobalt Sea Form
Set with Red Lip Wraps.* 1985.
1′9½″ × 4′ × 2′5¼″ (5.5 × 12.2 × 7.7 m).
Photo Dick Busher.

DESIGN THROUGH DISCOVERY

An Introduction to Art and Design

Fifth Edition

Marjorie Elliott Bevlin

Holt, Rinehart and Winston, Inc.
Fort Worth   Chicago   San Francisco   Philadelphia
Montreal   Toronto   London   Sydney   Tokyo

Publisher: Charlyce Jones Owen
Acquiring Editor: Karen Dubno
Picture Research: Marion Geisinger
Special Projects Editor: Jeanette Ninas Johnson
Production Manager: Annette Mayeski
Composition and camera work: York Graphic Services
Color separations: The Lehigh Press, Inc.
Printing and binding: Rand McNally Book Manufacturing Co.

Photographic credits appear on pages 379 and 380.

Printed in the United States of America

ISBN 0-03-026303-4

Library of Congress Cataloging in Publication Data

Bevlin, Marjorie Elliott.
   Design through discovery.

   Bibliography: p. 375
   Includes index.
   1. Design. I. Title.
NK1510.B53   1989   745.4   89-2143

Holt, Rinehart and Winston, Inc.
The Dryden Press
Saunders College Publishing

9012   045   9876543

Preface

The original purpose of DESIGN THROUGH DISCOVERY was to provide a supplement to studio classes in design. The student searching for a solution to an assigned project would be led to *discover* the treasure of inspiration to be found in nature, a threshold leading into a realization that the elements and principles inherent in the natural world are the basis for effective design as well.

With every succeeding edition, this purpose has taken on new meaning. Each few years between editions has seen enormous change, not only in the forms of contemporary design but in the attitudes of a world striving to keep pace with the technology of space and the computer, with the issues of human rights, and with the awareness that the nature which serves so abundantly as inspiration for the designer demands responsibility for its protection and preservation. A new edition of a college textbook on design becomes as much a revelation to those who formulate it as to those who read it, for it is in essence a summary of the tremendous changes that take place in the contemporary world in an astonishingly short time.

Underlying all the transformations in social patterns and technology, however, the elements and principles of design—and of human life—remain constant. There are rhythms and texture in the progression toward human rights, and there must be balance and proportion in the adaptation of the computer to human living. In the emphasis on this universal structure, the continuing patterns and rhythms governing the world since its beginning, lies the fundamental value of *Design Through Discovery*. The discovery for the student expands from a means of creating a design to a basis for establishing an individual life in a constantly changing world. By enlightened selection as well as creation, we design our environment, our lives, and the products that enhance them. By surrounding ourselves with objects we appreciate and love, we find our sense of home.

Like its predecessors, the fifth edition is a totally rewritten text, with a new alignment and new emphases. Part One concentrates on the role of design in the universe and in human life, exploring the reasons why people create art. It analyzes the creative process as a problem-solving procedure, citing examples of different kinds of design problems carried through to an effective solution. Of particular importance is the clarification of the distinction between design and art, a continuing stumbling block in the teaching of design. By stressing the fact that *purpose* can be aesthetic as well as utilitarian and by giving varied examples, the book attempts to strengthen the fine line of difference while at the same time emphasizing the genetic relationship that makes the distinction a detail rather than an issue.

Part Two is devoted entirely to the elements of design and Part Three to the principles. Since the elements and principles are considered by most professors using the book to be the heart of the material offered, the separation into two parts has been made for the sake of clarity and distinction, not for isolation. Students sometimes have difficulty in distinguishing the difference between an element and a principle; it is hoped that grouping them in this way will offer clarification. At the same time, special effort has been made to emphasize the interrelationships of all the elements and principles as a recurrent theme throughout the book.

The addition of suggested class projects following each chapter on an element or principle of design is the result of specific requests by some of the professors who use the book. Such suggestions are in no way meant to be conclusive or comprehensive, nor are they intended as a reflection on the wisdom and judgment of experienced faculty who have their own philosophy, methods, and course of study for studio work. It is very simply a rather reluctant response to requests, and it is hoped that for those who wish such suggestions, these may offer an opening into broader and more specialized applications of their own creation.

Part Four concentrates on the materials and processes of design, and on their logical progression into structure and decoration. In this way, the technical aspects of materials and processes are concentrated in one section. Although an earlier edition devoted a separate chapter to each material, making for easy reference, such extensive coverage tended toward tedious reading. With clear headings for each process and material, the essential information should be readily accessible in a more concise form.

In considering design as communication, Part Five concentrates on widely divergent techniques, ranging from painting to the computer. Although there is usually an element of self-expression in any creative technique, these areas all center on an implicit sense of communication, whether of sharing an aesthetic experience or a computerized corporate communiqué. This relationship to a viewer grafts them into a logical, though diversified, kinship.

Finally, Part Six brings all the previously cited material into focus as a setting for human life. This section discusses those areas that touch and influence our lives, from the intimacy of our wardrobe to the unknown limits of the universe. It stresses the role of selection as well as of creation and emphasizes the importance of personal awareness and involvement in such matters as city rehabilitation, restoration of natural landscape, and concern for the future of the planet and the universe.

The final chapters are followed by a glossary of design terms for easy reference, and an updated bibliography for further exploration in specific fields. Each chapter of the book concludes with a brief summary to identify crucial points and help the student to retain the basic framework of the material covered.

Acknowledgments

It would be impossible to express the impact on the present edition of the diversified group of professors who have taken the time and effort to review the manuscript in the light of their own students' needs. My sincere appreciation goes to: Mary Ann Baird, University of Wisconsin–Stevens Point; Diane Davis, Purdue University; Pete Engle, Indiana State University; Martha Horvay, University of Nebraska–Lincoln; Ramona Kellam, Langston University; Diane Massey, Georgia Southern College; Patricia Mitchell, Western Washington University; LuAnn Nissen, University of Nevada–Reno; Esther Williams, Idaho State University.

I am indebted to Robert Rollins for his professional eye in reading the section on computers and for his suggestions for bringing the material to a state current at the time of publication.

My thanks go to Karen Dubno, Acquisitions Editor at Holt, Rinehart and Winston, who guided the production of the book, and to Marion Geisinger, who worked tirelessly to secure the illustrations, as well as to Jeanette Ninas Johnson, Special Projects Editor, who directed the emergence of the book into its final form.

Finally, I am grateful to Jill Poyourow for her photographic skills and to S. Max Jones for her cheerful fortitude in presiding over the copy machine. As always my thanks go to my family for their support and encouragement, and to the friends who bore with me in my preoccupation. Most of all, I appreciate the understanding and collaboration of my husband, Robert O. Nichols, who shared the entire experience.

M. E. B.

Cragbourne
Orcas Island, Washington

Contents

Preface *v*

Part One   Design as Universal Reality   1

1   The Essence of Design   3

The Nature of Design   *Art and Aesthetics   Art and Design*
Design Through Selection   *The Individual as Critic*   The
Psychology of Seeing   *The Eye and the Brain   Perception and the
Individual   The Gestalt Principle   Closure*   Imagery
Definition of Visual Design   *A Plan for Order   Expression of the
Material   Form   Fulfillment of Purpose*

2   The Design Process   25

Inspiration   Craftsmanship   *Media and Materials   Art and
Craft*   Problem Solving   *Concept   Decision Making
Definition   Creativity   Analysis   Production   Clarification*
Aesthetic Problem Solving   Integrity   *Integrity of Materials
Integrity of Form   Integrity of Function*   Evaluation

Part Two   The Elements of Design   43

3   Line   45

The Quality of Line   Symbolic Line   Line as Modeling
Line as Form   Line as Direction and Emphasis   Line as
Pattern and Texture

4   Shape and Mass   61

Shape   *Natural Shapes   Geometric Shapes   Abstract Shapes
Nonobjective Shapes*   Shape Relationships   Mass   *Natural
Masses   Geometric Masses*   Abstract Masses   *Nonobjective
Masses*   Mass and Movement

5   Space   82

Pictorial Space   *Implied Space*   Illusionistic Space
Overlapping   Tiering   Size   Perspective   Actual Space
Space, Time, and Motion   Contemporary Concepts of Space

6 Texture 99

Tactile Textures   Visual Textures   Texture Through Structure   Texture Through Light   Textural Symbolism   Texture and Pattern   *Pattern as Repetition*   *Pattern as Surface Design*   *Interacting Patterns*

7 Color 114

Color and Light   Additive and Subtractive Color   *Refraction and Diffraction*   *Light and Pigment*   Color Theory   Color Properties   Color Relationships   Color Harmonies   *Monochromatic*   *Neutrals*   *Analogous*   *Complementary*   *Split Complementary*   Color Interaction   *Interaction of Complements*   *Simultaneous Contrast*   *Interaction of Analogous Colors*   Color Interaction and Tonality   *The Psychology of Color*   Color and Space   *Balance of Color*

Part Three   The Principles of Design   137

8 Rhythm 139

The Nature of Rhythm   Varieties of Rhythm   *Metric Rhythm*   *Flowing Rhythm*   *Swirling Rhythm*   *Climactic Rhythm*   Rhythm, Time, and Motion   Rhythm as a Unifying Force

9 Emphasis 150

Emphasis by Location   Emphasis Through Drama   Emphasis Through Light   Emphasis Through Shape   Emphasis Through Contrast   Subdued Emphasis

10 Balance 160

Structural Balance   *Horizontal Balance*   *Vertical Balance*   Visual Balance   *Symmetrical Balance*   *Radial Symmetry*   *Asymmetrical Balance*

11 Proportion and Scale 171

Proportion   Definition of Proportion   The Greek Concept   *The Golden Mean*   *The Artistic Application*   *The Spiral*   The Fibonacci Series   Dynamic Symmetry   The Contemporary View   Scale   Scale as Symbol   Monumental Scale   *Human Ego*   *Devotion*   *Security*   *Elegance*   Diminutive Scale   Scale as Perception   Scale for Emphasis

12 Variety and Unity 190

Variety   *Contrast*   *Originality*   *Variety Through Structure*   Unity   *Opposition and Transition*   *Unity Through Color*   *Unity Through Value*   *Unity Through Line*   *Unity Through Shape*   *Unity Through Repetition*   The Illusion of Motion   Symbolic Unity

Part Four   Design in Action   205

13   The Influence of Materials on Design   207

Characteristics of Materials   Materials as Components of
Design   *Wood   Metal   Stone   Concrete   Clay   Glass
Fiber   Plastics*

14   Forming Techniques   224

Additive and Subtractive Techniques   Forming Techniques for
Metal   Forming Techniques for Glass   Forming Techniques
for Clay   Forming Techniques for Fibers

15   Structure and Decoration   235

Structure as Decoration   Perception of Structural Design   The
Importance of Space and Time   Materials as Structural
Design   Decoration as Structure   Composition   Decorative
Design   *Symbolism*   Decorative Processes   *Metal   Clay
Glass   Fabrics*

Part Five   Design for Visual
                       Communication   253

16   Painting and Sculpture   255

Attributes of Painting and Sculpture   The Materials of
Painting   *Painting Media*   Directions in Contemporary
Painting   *Les Fauves   Impressionism   Cubism   Abstraction
German Expressionism   Surrealism   Abstract Expressionism   Op
Art   Minimal Art*   Current Trends in Painting   Sculpture
*Categories of Sculpture   Casting Methods   Sculpture and Space
Sculpture and Light   Directions in Sculpture   Contemporary Trends*

17   Graphic Design and the Computer   277

Printmaking   Printmaking Processes   *Relief   Intaglio
Lithography   Serigraphy*   Mechanical Reproduction
Monoprint   Book Design   Magazines and Periodicals
Advertising   Package Design   The Computer   *Computer
Graphics   The Computer and the Designer   The Computer and Art*

18   Photography and the Performing Arts   300

The Camera   Attributes of a Photograph   The Photograph as
Symbol   The Photograph as Document   Commercial
Photography   The Photograph as Design   Special Effects
Special Techniques   Television   The Performing Arts   *Set
Design   Design with Lighting*   Contemporary Trends

Part Six   Design for Environment   317

19   Fashion and Industrial Design   319

Fashion Design   *The Role of Clothing   The Fashion Industry
Haute Couture   Costume Design   Space Apparel*   Industrial

Design   *Categories of Industrial Design*   *The Industrial Designer*
Design and Manufacture   *Contemporary Trends in Industrial Design*

20   Furniture and Interiors   331

The Manipulation of Space   Furniture   *The English
Cabinetmakers*   *Contemporary Furniture Design*   The Elements
and Principles of Interior Design   *Color   Texture   Balance
and Rhythm   Proportion and Scale*   Public Interiors   Time,
Motion, and Light   Contemporary Trends in Interior Design

21   Architecture and the Environment   348

Structural Design in Architecture   Attributes of Architectural
Design   Elements and Principles in Architectural Design
Development of Contemporary Architecture   Contemporary
Trends   *Vernacular Architecture   Post-modern Architecture   The
Revival of Modernism*   The Environment   *The Environment and
the City   Rehabilitation*   Environmental Design   *Landscape
Design*   Design for the Future

Glossary   368
Bibliography   375
Photographic Credits   379
Index   381

PART 1
Design as Universal Reality

The Essence of Design

The concept of design is as old as the universe. Although we think of it as a human expression, design actually encompasses every process of selection and evolution by which the universe is continually being formed. Planets with their moons, stars in their galaxies, and our own earth, with its complexities of structure and environment, are all part of an underlying order that reveals itself increasingly to the scientific mind, while ultimately defying total comprehension.

Even the human patterns imposed upon the earth are actually a development of the underlying structure. Areas of fertility yield patches of growth that become farms (Fig. 1), rivers and natural harbors form obvious sites for the construction of cities, and mountain ranges, rivers, and other bodies of water mark the boundaries between nations. At the same time, deserts, dense jungles, and towering

1. Aerial photo of terraced farms in Central Peru.

mountains defy the possibility of any lasting human imprint (Fig. 2). Seacoasts, pounded by surf, retain a stark beauty that triumphs over the most persistent human intrusion. Eroding rock and ebbing tides react to nature's rhythms, revealing patterns and configurations far beyond the capability of human designers, yet with the potential of offering limitless inspiration to them (Fig. 3).

The Nature of Design

The quest for inspiration can be a lifelong adventure in discovery. Our purpose is to explore the ways in which designers utilize their discoveries, transforming perceptions into uniquely personal expressions. First, however, it is intriguing to consider why artists and designers find such expression necessary. *Why do people create art?*

Art and Aesthetics

Since the days of ancient Greece, art has been associated with aesthetics, a derivation of the Greek *aisthetikos*, pertaining to sense perception. For centuries artists considered beauty to be the ultimate good, and the contemplation of a work of art led the viewer to an awareness of the perfection to which human form and character could aspire

2. Moraine Lake, near Banff, Alberta, Canada.

3. Victor B. Scheffer. Green sea anemone, *Anthopleura xanthogrammica,* Olympic seacoast, Washington. Photograph.

4. Venus de Medici (3rd century B.C.?). 5' high. Uffizi, Florence.

5. Joan Snyder. *Mourning/Oh Morning.* 1983. Oil, acrylic, papier mâché, cloth, on canvas; 6'6" × 12' (1.98 × 3.66 m). Nielson Gallery, Boston.

(Fig. 4). This expectation was in itself sufficient reason for the creation of a work of art. The artist, experiencing an often brutal world, sought out and cherished the heroic aspects, creating a personal world of order and harmony. The visual expressions of this ideal became an inspiration for all who viewed them, forming an integral component of Greek religion and continuing as the basis for art well into the twentieth century. Although even in Greek times the subjects for depiction were not always pleasant, the association of aesthetics with a pleasurable reaction has through the centuries been bound up with the conception of what constitutes a work of art.

The Contemporary View Contemporary art extends the range of expression to include the entire gamut of human activity and emotion. Many beautifully presented films, novels, and television documentaries emphasize the sordid side of life. Drawings and paintings often memorialize an atrocity. Still others become a cathartic for the artist, lifting an emotional burden by articulating a personal trauma. Psychologists and psychiatrists often ask a patient to paint what he or she feels, in an effort to release the patient from a sense of guilt or grief. The painting in Figure 5 was a kind of summing up of a tragic period in the artist's life, making it possible for her to go forward eased of the pain of the past. She states: "That painting is all about loss: the abortion, the miscarriage, the loss of my home, my marriage, everything." Most contemporary artists feel that art must represent the wholeness of life in order to be valid, and that whatever response is evoked, it is ultimately aesthetic, a reaction to sensory perception.

The Purpose of Art Interviews with artists concerning their motivation invariably bring out some interpretation of the idea of *wholeness*, of being at one with the universe. Sometimes the idea is expressed as losing oneself in the totality; at other times it is a matter of finding oneself, of pulling everything together in *inner* wholeness. In any

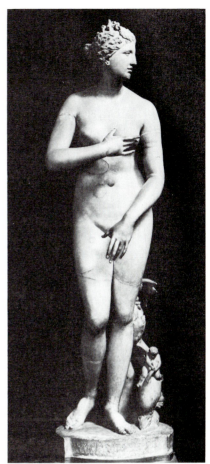

4

5

6

event, the act of creation is essentially a rebellion against having to consume oneself within the confines of a single life. It is a leap toward *freedom* and *meaning*, freedom to enter a dimension larger than one's self, meaning implicit in creating something more important, and perhaps more lasting, than its creator.

Any experience important enough to be expressed calls out to be shared. The degree to which expression thus becomes communication between artist and audience is variable, depending upon the background, associations, and receptivity of the viewer. A work that is meaningless to one viewer may be vibrating with significance to another. The message conveyed may be baffling or repugnant, or it may provide a glimpse of the nobility of the human spirit. Even a rendition of a landscape may elicit a wide range of responses, varying from simple visual appreciation to a complex network of memories and emotions arising from having visited the scene or from being reminded of someplace similar (Fig. 6).

More important than any individual message, however, is the fact that in this moment of personal expression the artist becomes a part of humanity, a voice not only of one place and time but of all the sufferings and aspirations of the human spirit throughout history. This is the essence of wholeness, the ultimate reason for creating art.

Art and Design

It is almost impossible in a book of this kind not to use the terms "art" and "design" interchangeably, for the distinction between the two is subtle and variable, and the similarity is basic. First, let us consider the difference.

Art is skilled and original work that arouses an aesthetic response. Whatever that response may be, it is usually accepted as the reason for the

6. Bill Sullivan. *Niagara Sunset.* 1986. Oil on canvas, 4′10″ × 6′6″ (1.47 × 1.98 m). G. W. Einstein.

7. Howard Buchwald. *Masquerade.* 1986. Oil on canvas, 7′ × 6′1¼″ (2.14 × 1.84 m). Nancy Hoffman Gallery, New York.

8. James D. Makins. Pitcher/tumblers/tray. 1982–83. Black porcelain, 10½ × 22 × 23″ (26.6 × 55.8 × 58.4 cm).

7

work. When we speak of design, however, we usually think of de-  signed *objects*. The earliest decorations were applied to tools and weapons, embellishments on implements vital to survival. In general, then, we tend to consider that *a design has an explicit practical purpose*. This purpose may range from household efficiency, as with an iron or a television set, to the encouragement of self-esteem, as in the case of clothing design. In any event, an effective design also has an aesthetic aspect. What we do not always realize is that *this aesthetic aspect may be the sole purpose of the design*. Perhaps the point will be clearer if we make a comparison.

The painting in Figure 7 is *nonobjective*, meaning that it does not attempt to represent any recognizable object. The artist expects us to react to the lines, shapes, and textures, all of which are elements of design. The appearance of the work, with its feeling of motion and tension, and the artist's experience in creating it, are its reason for being.

The pitcher in Figure 8 also has line, shape, and texture. It is attractive, capable of evoking an aesthetic response. Being an effective design, it also holds liquids and pours easily. However, if we were to

8

fill it with water and a puddle formed at its base, we would know that it leaked and therefore was faulty. If it swung out of control or cramped our fingers when we tried to pour from it, we would know that the handle was poorly placed. If the spout did not deliver a full even stream, we would reject it as not practical. If any of these faults existed, the pitcher would *not* be good design.

It is too simple a distinction to say that more is required of a design than of a work of art. A design may be a wall hanging or a panel of mosaic on a building. In such cases, the work can be classified as either art or design or, more accurately, as both. This interrelationship is not accidental. It is the result of a body of specific elements and principles governing the creation of both. The elements—*line, shape, and mass, space, texture, and color*—are the ingredients with which both the artist and the designer work. The principles—*unity and variety, balance, emphasis, rhythm, proportion, and scale*—provide the means by which the elements can be combined in an aesthetic way. Consequently, while in some cases the distinction between art and design is discernible, there are many times when it cannot be conclusively drawn.

Design Through Selection

We are all designers. We design when we plan our days with a balance of work and recreation. We design again when we organize the contents of a desk or dresser, arrange furniture, or place books on a shelf in orderly fashion. An excellent example of design is a workshop arranged with an assemblage of tools neatly placed for convenience and accessibility.

The Individual as Critic

We are also continual critics of design. Every time we make a purchase from among a selection of items we exercise judgment in matters of appearance and function. The professional designer chooses from a world filled with *sensations* and *concepts,* but the consumer chooses from a world filled with *things.* For fifty thousand years people have used a sharp edge for cutting. Today we select our cutting edges from hundreds of varieties of scissors and knives. The knives differ in width and length of blade, in size, shape, and material of handle, and in the potential for retaining a keen cutting edge without continual sharpening. Even the choice of a knife for kitchen use may present a formidable exercise in selection (Fig. 9).

A Basis for Selection In order to select any object intelligently, we must know what kinds are available, what specific purposes each is designed for, what styles and colors are offered, and frequently what sizes. Clothes must fit, and a car must be able to serve our needs whether we live in the city or on top of a mountain with narrow icy roads. The more we are aware of the needs and possibilities, the more intelligent will be our final selection. This is true of nearly every object we choose. If we are aware of the processes and materials involved in manufacture, we will be aided in our selection. Perhaps even more important is an awareness of the requirements of effective design.

9

The Creation of Our Personal World When we select home furnishings, clothes, or a car, we do not make a simple choice of an individual object. Consciously or not, we are choosing an element of our personal world, a symbol of who we are and how we want to live. Every selection contributes to the design of our life style, from the lines of furniture to the colors or patterns on the walls. The relative emphasis we place on *appearance* or *practicality* provides a clue to our personality and our financial resources. Even more intimately, our clothes indicate a personal style, a declaration of self-esteem. Here again, durability and ease of upkeep are indicative considerations, depending upon our needs, or financial capabilities, and our outlook. In the selection of a car the priorities may be reversed. Most people hope first for maximum dependability and economy of operation, yet want a model and color they can enjoy. In every choice we make we are exercising design preferences.

The Psychology of Seeing

Fundamental to either creating or appreciating a visual design is the process of *seeing*. Sensations enter the human eye through the lens, a flattened sphere constructed of numerous transparent fibers, which flattens or becomes more spherical depending upon its distance from the object to be viewed. The lens brings *images* of such objects to the light-sensitive retina where the images are registered; in fact, the retina of an eye removed from either a human being or an animal will frequently show a complete image of the world toward which the eye had been turned.

The Eye and the Brain

What happens after the image reaches the retina has long been a subject of philosophical and psychological debate. Experiments have proved that perception is not a simple mirroring but a process involving selective acts. Scientists still are not certain which aspects of perception take place in the physical eye and which are the result of reactions within the brain, reactions conditioned by heredity, culture, and personal associations. Painters striving for *abstraction*, in which recognizable objects have been developed (*abstracted*) into nonrealistic forms, are continually frustrated by viewers who insist upon seeing images in their works, much as we see animal forms in rocks and woolly lambs in shapes of clouds. The eye will link almost any abstract shape to past associations, associations that are present in the brain.

Perception and the Individual

Although such association is often highly personal, much is also the result of geographical and cultural background. People from the mountains think of landscape in terms of jagged lines, while people from the plains think of the earth as horizontal as far as the eye can see.

10

10. Chapter House at Maulbronn Abbey. Würtemberg, Germany. 1147.

11. Four lines demonstrating the principle of closure. The human eye tends to join them into a square.

12. Four dots and three possible figures into which the human eye may join them according to the principle of closure.

Geography also has an influence on the perception of cultural events. In the northern hemisphere Easter is the essence of spring flowers, new clothes, and a renewal of life generally, while Christmas brings visions of skiing and family gatherings by the fire. In the southern hemisphere, on the other hand, Easter is celebrated in the midst of falling leaves and winter closing in, and Christmas arrives in the heat of summer. While Americans dressed in woolens eat turkey and cranberry sauce, Australians sunbathe at the beach, with Christmas beer and barbecue.

Religious background has a significant effect on perception generally. Native Americans see gods in birds, animals, and sea life, and the ancient Chinese imbued every flower, tree, blade of grass, and insect with traits of human character. History also plays a part. The three-leaved shamrock has been a symbol of the Trinity to Christians since St. Patrick's time, later becoming a familiar feature of ecclesiastical architecture in the form of the *trefoil* (Fig. 10). Today the shamrock is primarily a secular symbol, denoting all things Irish.

When variations in geographical, religious, cultural, and familial background are combined with personal associations, the resultant perception of any sight or experience can only be individual, if not unique.

The Gestalt Principle

Gestalt is the German word meaning "form," a term applied to a school of psychological thought first formulated in 1912. It emphasized the importance of studying entire patterns of behavior rather than isolated mental phenomena. The idea arose from experiments in perception which showed that perception of form does not depend upon seeing individual elements making up the form but tends to grasp the form *in its entirety*. For example, in Figure 11 we see four lines. Conceivably, these lines could represent four straws floating on the surface of a pond, ready to drift in opposite directions with the first ripple. However, to the mind surrounded from early childhood with building blocks, geometric buildings, doors, books, rectangular pictures, and sheets of paper, the four lines immediately designate a square. Now look at the four dots in Figure 12. These dots are unrelated, each a unit in space. Seen in this particular position, however, they indicate a square. Why? If lines were drawn connecting them in a certain way, a square would result, but connecting lines could also produce an X or a Z. In any case, the eye does not see them in their unrelated actuality but insists upon *closure*, supplying lines that will create a total shape. The most familiar shape is the square; therefore the human eye tends to see the four dots simply as the corners of a complete form.

Closure

The fact that the human mind and eye exercise closure frees the artist to work with more subtlety than would otherwise be possible. In the sculpture in Figure 13, the circle is employed as a never-ending symbol of strength and solidarity, denoting the complete happiness experienced by mother and child. If it were a total circle, it would be less effective, almost contrived. By relying upon *closure*, with which the

11

12

13

13. Esther Wertheimer.
Madre con Bambino in Circolo.
1985. Polished bronze,
24 × 20″ (60.9 × 50.8 cm).
Collection, Dominion Gallery,
Montreal, Canada.

14. Tim Lovejoy.
*The Thirumalai Naick Palace,
Madurai.* 1986. Watercolor,
16½ × 18¼″ (41.9 × 46.4 cm).
Courtesy Coe Kerr Gallery.

viewer perceives the symbolism of the circle, the artist has achieved a sense of joy and freedom implicit in the meaning of the work.

The same principle is employed in rendering drawings and paintings. Primitive artists and beginners usually depict every detail of what they see—each stone or shingle or leaf on a tree. Such works are related to scientific diagrams, providing factual information. The watercolor in Figure 14 is a sensitive rendition of a romantic subject. All the architectural details are there, but they are represented by carefully chosen examples placed where they will give us the essence of the palace without providing a complete inventory. The subtle fading away or *vignetting* of the architecture allows us to enter into the setting in a personal way, with our eye and mind providing the missing details.

14

Imagery

Imagery is the raw material of any artist or designer. Composed of an intangible combination of memory, imagination, dreams, and fantasy, it, like perception, is both extremely personal and the product of its time and place. Although imagery is vital to music and literature as well as to the visual arts, our use of the term will refer to *visual imagery.*

Traditionally, visual imagery has been characterized as either *perceptual,* referring to things actually seen and represented, or *conceptual,* relating to images existing only in the mind. The two categories are obviously not clear-cut, as no image springs from a vacuum, and visions from the mind frequently have their origins in actual things seen, however they may be distorted. Dream imagery is a good example. It is difficult to describe our dreams because of the illogical way in which familiar images are associated, yet the images do indeed arise from past experience.

Such dual imagery characterizes the fantasies of M. C. Escher, which are represented in Figure 15. Escher himself would hardly identify them as fantasies, for he writes that his works bear witness to his amazement and wonder at the *laws of nature* that operate in the world around us; he considers himself more closely allied to the mathematician than to his fellow artists. Nevertheless, his works abound with an imagery that is immediately recognizable to anyone familiar with his style. Stairways going nowhere, interlacing rings and gears, and imaginative creatures of earth and sea form only a portion of his

15

16

15. M. C. Escher.
Concave and Convex.
1955. Lithograph,
10⅞ × 13⅛″ (27.5 × 33.5 cm).
Haagsgemuntemuseum,
The Hague.

16. John Marin. *Woolworth
Building, New York, No. 3.*
1913. Etching,
12⅞ × 10½″ (33.02 × 26.6 cm).
Brooklyn Museum
(Dick S. Ramsay Fund).

17. Joseph Stella.
Skyscrapers. 1922.
Mixed media on canvas,
8′3¾″ × 4′6″ (2.53 × 1.37 m).
Newark Museum, N. J.

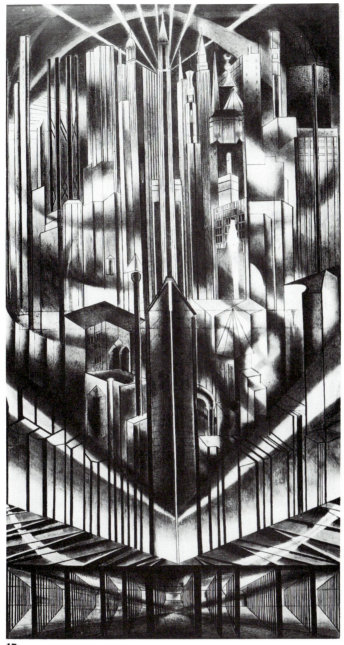

17

rich configurations. It becomes obvious, then, that imagery cannot be divided into categories but must be recognized as the result of a lifetime of interweaving *perceptions* and *associations*.

Figures 16 and 17 compare the imagery with which two artists depict a single subject, the skyscrapers of New York City. John Marin, an early 20th-century watercolorist, was sensitive to atmospheric effect, having done much of his work along a misty seacoast. In his etching of the Woolworth Building he shows the skyscraper being tossed about in the wind, implying that the structures of human beings are not impervious to the forces of nature. Joseph Stella, on the other hand, has placed the Woolworth Building as part of a cityscape replete with tall buildings and a bridge, and has invested the whole with geometric precision and lines that are solid and soaring. Stella's spires would never bend in the wind. They are like the spires of a cathedral, perhaps signaling the brash new religion of technology. These artists are using similar visual elements but treating them according to their unique personal imagery. In doing so, they are achieving *originality,* a keynote of any work of art.

Definition of Visual Design

We have noted the order underlying the universe and the affinity of the designer and artist to this order and its manifestations. Before we move into an examination of the many ways in which the designer expresses this affinity, it would be well to analyze exactly what constitutes an effective visual design.

Stated concisely, *a design is the organization of materials and forms in such a way as to fulfill a specific purpose.* This definition encompasses four aspects of design, each of which we will examine: (1) organization or order, (2) materials, (3) form, and (4) fulfillment of a purpose.

A Plan for Order

Much of the underlying order of the natural world is related to survival. From the most delicate flower to the towering mountains, the features of our environment exist because they have survived cataclysms or gradual attrition that has taken its toll of less hardy species. Many human designs have also had their origins in the instinct for survival. One of the earliest and most effective is the walled city (Fig. 18). Clustered together for survival, Europeans of the Middle Ages surrounded themselves with a mighty wall, thick enough to withstand attack, wide enough to walk on, and topped with round towers affording a 360-degree lookout against approaching danger. The wall itself was a masterful *design for order* and protection, yet the city within was no less so. Here houses and shops huddled together along narrow streets, supportive and self-contained, designed to sustain life even under siege. When the populace expanded beyond its capacity, a new wall was built beyond the first one, allowing room for shops and houses between the two walls, in the *faubourg.*

Less complex and two-dimensional, the paintings of Dutch artist Piet Mondrian present another aspect of planned order. Mondrian began his career by painting landscapes, then did a series of trees in which he became increasingly impressed by the idea of abstraction. In the end he devoted himself to exploring the essential relationship between two straight lines meeting at a right angle. In the painting in Figure 19 no two areas are of exactly the same size and shape. This is a *meticulously planned* aspect of the work, as is his sparing use of a bright accent of color among dark lines and light background. Every painting is designed in one way or other, but Mondrian's work is an eloquent testimony to his emphasis on order.

18. Carcassonne, a fortified medieval city in southern France.

19. Piet Mondrian. *Composition with Red, Yellow, and Blue.* 1939–42. Oil on canvas, 28⅝ × 27¼" (72.4 × 69.2 cm). Tate Gallery, London.

18

19

The Essence of Design** **17

Expression of the Material

Much of the impact of a design depends upon the way in which specific materials are used. Oil paints can be brushed on in transparent glazes, or they can be applied with a palette knife in a single thick layer. Wood can be finished to a high polish or left rough in the manner of driftwood.

The two sculptures in Figures 20 and 21 are the work of a single artist, Auguste Rodin. The strikingly different treatment of forms, surface, and modeling can be attributed at least in part to Rodin's feeling about *two different materials*, marble and bronze. In the marble Danaïd we see a smoothly polished, luminous interpretation of the nude. Every bone and muscle is beautifully expressed, and the figure's flesh seems almost as though it would be warm to the touch. Rodin was clearly responding to the pure sensuousness of the *marble* in designing this work. The bronze Balzac (Fig. 21) is quite another matter. Here the artist wished to create an impression of overwhelming monumentality, of sheer power, in the personality of the French writer. Physical characteristics yield to the dynamic flow of Balzac's cloak, a movement culminating in a head whose features are highly stylized. The character's essential dynamism is depicted through the inherent strength and force of the *bronze* itself.

Designers approach their work in different ways. Some *plan* a specific object with its purpose in mind, and all other considerations are secondary. Many designers, however, visualize first in terms of form. They have an idea, and they choose a medium in which to express it. The selection of the material is a major decision in terms of how the specific form will best be realized.

Form

The world around us is composed of *physical* forms, from the pebble we hold in our hand to the mountain of similar substance that requires days to climb. Trees that at a distance are flatly silhouetted against the

20. Auguste Rodin. *The Danaïd,*
1885. Marble.
13¾ × 28½ × 22½″
(34.9 × 72.4 × 57.2 cm).
Rodin Museum, Paris.

21. Auguste Rodin.
Monument to Balzac. 1897–98.
Bronze (cast 1954),
height 8′10″ (2.69 m),
at base 48¼ × 41″ (1.23 × 1.04 m).
The Museum of Modern Art, New York
(presented in memory of
Curt Valentin by his friends).

20

21

sky become at close range three-dimensional forms that can be walked around and viewed from all sides. Form, however, is not a synonym for mass or volume. A two-dimensional object can have form just as a three-dimensional one does. When shape is governed by structural considerations, it becomes form. In other words, the silhouetted tree is still a form because its shape is determined by the structure of the tree,

22

22. *The Creation of the World.*
13th century. Vault mosaic.
St. Mark's Cathedral, Venice.

not by the conditions of our perception. *Form, then, is the actual shape and structure of an object.*

The term *form* is also used in reference to medium or subject matter in a work of art. A sculptor's work may be in the form of stone, or a painter's canvases may be in the form of landscapes. There are other uses of the term. For instance, form may be the physical being of an object, as the female form, or it may refer to physical composition, as a solid or vaporous form.

From the standpoint of the designer, form is the particular combination of sizes, shapes, and masses that compose a work and cause that work to exist in the space around it. The designer organizes these elements into an integrated whole. The form may spring entirely from imagination, or it may be governed by other factors. The mosaic in Figure 22 was governed by two overriding factors: it had to be applied to the interior of a dome, which posed a tremendous challenge in the matter of composition and perspective, particularly as the nearest viewer would be many feet below it; and it had to be a Christian subject since it would adorn one of the great cathedrals of Christendom. For seven centuries the finished design has provided the world with the story of creation executed in one of the most difficult

Plate 1. Oskar Kokoschka. *Montana Landschaft*. 1947. Oil on linen,
35½ × 47″ (90 × 120 cm). Kunsthaus Zürich.

Plate 2. Helen Frankenthaler. *Nature Abhors a Vacuum.* 1973.
Acrylic on canvas, 8′7½″ × 9′4½″ (2.63 × 2.86 m).
Courtesy Andre Emmerich Gallery, New York.

of materials, tiny pieces of glass fitted together and held to the surface of a ceiling. In this case, form was predetermined and the artists and crafts workers who executed it rose magnificently to the challenge.

Fulfillment of Purpose

Form is greatly influenced by the purpose the designed object must serve. In utilitarian objects—home furnishings, utensils, clothing—this purpose is clear, yet there are many ways in which a design challenge can be handled. An example of the possibilities can be seen in the two typewriters shown in Figures 23 and 24. Both are electric, designed for the same purpose, yet the span of three-quarters of a century separating the designs has resulted in dramatic refinements, not only in function but also in appearance. In creating the 1902 model, the designer was obviously concentrating on the technical aspects of an invention that was less than thirty years old. Seventy-five years later, the designer could take function for granted, freeing attention to consider such elements as proportion, color, line, and texture. This need not imply that the earlier machine is necessarily an inferior design; each is a product of its time.

Fulfillment of purpose is not restricted to those works that have a primarily mechanical or practical function. As we have noted, art and design are closely interwoven, and a painting or sculpture can fulfill a purpose just as surely as a piece of office equipment. In the work in Plate 1 (p. 21) the purpose was to communicate an emotional state through visual means. After years of artistic struggle as he witnessed the Nazi domination of European life, Austrian-born Oskar Kokoschka returned to Switzerland at the end of World War II, free at last to travel and to express the pent-up energies of ten years of self-imposed exile in England. He painted the mountains, always among his favorite subjects, but with a sweep and emotional grandeur more powerful than any of his previous works. This is not merely a landscape painting; it is the *jubilation of a liberated spirit*, filled with singing color and expressive line. In this expression it fulfills its purpose. Years later, viewers who know nothing of Kokoschka's life continue to respond to the vitality of his painting, a fact that completes and ratifies the fulfillment of purpose.

23. Blickensderfer electric typewriter. 1902. Courtesy British Typewriter Museum, Bournemouth, England.

24. The IBM Quietwriter 8 Typewriter. 1987. © IBM Corporation, 1987.

23

24

This, then, is the essence of design: inspiration from the world around us, an individual way of seeing, and the organization of our impressions into an integrated whole.

Summary

The universe is based on an underlying order, providing human designers with limitless material for inspiration. People create works of art in order to find wholeness with the universe, to seek order and meaning within themselves, and to share their inner experiences with others.

Art and design are inextricably interwoven. Although a design is usually considered to have an explicit practical purpose, that purpose may very well be purely aesthetic. Both art and design are based on the same elements: *line, shape and mass, space, texture, and color*; and the same principles: *unity and variety, balance, emphasis, rhythm, proportion, and scale*. The principles provide the means by which the elements can be combined in an *aesthetic* way, arousing a sensory response. A knowledge of design is as essential to discriminating *selection* of products as it is to the creation of an effective design.

CHAPTER TWO

The Design Process

The most original designs are conceived intuitively, yet the design process is more conscious than unconscious. The idea of a design springing into being in a moment of brilliant inspiration is appealing, but few designers would lay claim to such an experience. The *idea* for a work may certainly come suddenly with exciting assurance and with a vision of the finished product, but its successful fulfillment is possible only in the hands of a designer or artist trained in a craft capable of expressing it.

Designs in nature are formed as the result of instincts and laws governing their creation. A spiderweb, for instance, often materializes within minutes, complete in its intricate geometry and with no tools obvious beyond the moving body of the spider (Fig. 25). The human designer, however, transforms nature into new forms and materials according to a personal vision and with specially designed tools. The vision or plan is in the mind before the process of creation is begun, and the process takes place as the result of skills unique to the human designer. The first of these skills is a specialized perception.

25

25. David Cavagnaro. *Orb Weaver Spider Web.* 1970. Photograph.

26

27

Inspiration

Almost everyone can appreciate the beauty of a spiderweb or a tree, but their potential application to human design may not be readily apparent. The inspired designer observes the universe with sensitivity, absorbing impressions from every experience. These impressions enter into the subconscious mind like cells that divide and re-combine to form new entities that could never be constructed through conscious effort. Often when least expecting it, the designer becomes aware of new relationships and, seeing them in unique terms, works to give them a form that will make them apparent to others. This, in essence, is the phenomenon we call *inspiration*.

Such inspiration is usually derived from a particular skill or process that the designer finds personally satisfying. The potter will look at a plant with the idea of interpreting its forms in clay, whereas the weaver will see the same forms as color and texture that may be translated into fiber. In Figure 26 we see a copper bowl. Knowing nothing of the personal experiences of the designer, we can see at once that the pearly iridescent quality of the inside of the bowl and the roughness of the outside are similar to the composition of many varieties of seashell (Fig. 27). However, the interior has a fluted effect that also resembles a toadstool (Fig. 28). The work does not *imitate* either object, but it does indicate that the designer has seen them and found them intriguing. The rest could have been largely unconscious.

Since inspiration is nourished by impressions, the *conscious* groundwork for the designer is to absorb through the senses as much

26. June Schwarcz.
Electroformed enamel bowl 571.
1970. Cooper enamel;
diameter 11″ (28 cm),
height 2¾″ (7 cm).
Courtesy Mrs. K. Reichert,
San Diego, California.

27. *Haliotis fulgens,*
a shell found on the beaches
of California.

28. *Clitocybe sudorifica
(Clitocybe dealbata).*

29. David Cavagnaro.
Dew-Covered Dry Grasses.
1970. Photograph.

30. Microscopic view
of crown gall.

28

of the world as possible. Many designers find motivation in travel to other lands, others in films of outer space, still others in the sights and sounds of a small area of earth studied in minute detail to reveal the intricate beauty of insects and grasses (Fig. 29). Even further treasures are to be found in the world of the microscope (Fig. 30).

These areas provide a variety of perceptions to artists and designers in particular. While appreciating the innate character of the sub-

29

30

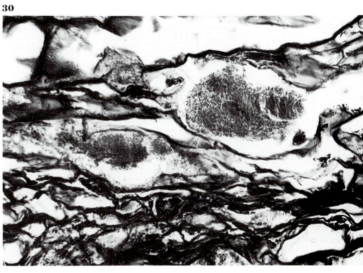

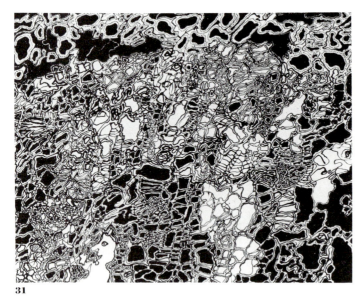

31   32

ject, artistic perception adds the dimension of *creative possibility*. Perception is formed by heredity and past associations, but inspiration is concerned with the potential for a new aesthetic entity. Thus, even a microscopic slide of crown gall could conceivably inspire a scintillating drawing (Fig. 31). or an acrylic screen (Fig. 32).

Craftsmanship

Media and Materials

Every design is executed in a *medium*. The term medium is related to materials but is not limited by them. For instance, architecture is a medium for design but the possible materials are extensive and diverse. In a more specific example, oil painting is a medium and the term stipulates the use of oil paints, but the *materials* extend to a wide variety of brushes, painting knives, thinners, varnishes, and supports such as canvas, wooden panel, or paper. A medium is a means a conveying something, as in the expression "news media," or, in the world of the occult, of getting in communication with spirits. In the world of design and the arts, a medium is a *channel for expression*.

Much of the success of any creative work results from the "feel" the artist has for the material involved. Some sculptors enjoy the manipulation of clay in the hands, the sensuous forming of a shapeless mass into an object of beauty or interest. Others prefer to chip away with tools at wood or stone, freeing the form within by cutting away

31. Jean Dubuffet. *Radieux Météore, from Ferres Radieuses.* 1952. Brush and pen drawing, 19¾ × 25½" (50 × 65 cm). Courtesy Pierre Matisse Gallery, New York.

32. Ted Hallman. *Acrylic Screen.* 1960.

33. Philip Pearlstein. *Model with Minstrel Marionettes.* 1986. Watercolor, 42 × 30" (106.7 × 76.2 cm). Courtesy Hirschl & Adler Modern, New York.

33

the excess. Painters may thrill to the free flow of washes and the excitement of being unable fully to predict the results (Pl. 2, p. 22), or they may prefer to lay paint on precisely, anticipating accurately the final effect (Fig. 33).

The designer's affinity for his or her tools can be just as compelling an element in the success of the work. A painter has favorite brushes, the carver a knife or chisel that will do exactly what is required. When work does not go well, the designer can often find the answer in a fresh approach to materials. We will consider the properties and possibilities of specific materials in detail in Chapter 13.

Art and Craft

The term "artsy-craftsy" has become part of our jargon, usually designating a person who dips into diverse areas of the visual arts, with no single-minded pursuit of excellence. The term "craft" is now widely used for those activities that can be pursued as hobbies, with no intense devotion to the result. Numerous "how-to" books on the market are published for people who work in the so-called crafts of the present day.

Craftsmanship, however, is a fundamental and extremely important aspect of design. It means total dedication to a medium, exploring its properties, getting its "feel," finding one's own affinity to it and how it can be exploited. It describes the dedication of the musician who practices eight hours a day on an instrument. A potter, writing of his art, has stated that one must practice on the potter's wheel for six hours a day for at least six months before hoping for satisfactory results. The legendary craft worker of past centuries has almost disappeared, due to the restrictions and demands of modern industry and consumerism, but the concept of spending a lifetime in dedication and learning remains the keynote of the true professional.

Creating any specific design is largely a matter of problem solving, but behind each individual experience there must be the skill to manipulate materials and tools. Only through the possession of such skill can the designer concentrate fully on the aesthetic and technical problems of the design itself.

Problem Solving

Once a project has been determined upon, the mind enters the process by sorting out the possible approaches. The designer may have felt a surge of inspiration or have been given an assignment in class or by an employer. In any case, even the most seemingly straightforward design may present a wide range of possibilities. From the moment of confronting the possibilities to the evaluation of the end product, the designer is involved in the process of problem solving. This consists of five stages: *definition*, *creativity*, *analysis*, *production*, and *clarification*.

If the object to be designed is a teapot, one might think there are few decisions to be made. Over the centuries, the teapot shape has assumed a fairly standard form, determined by the requirements of brewing and serving tea. The *concept* of a teapot is that of a hollow container with a lid and a spout for pouring, perhaps with a strainer for the tea leaves. The aim of a new *design*, however, is to create something quite different from what has existed before—a more beautiful or interesting appearance, a more functional shape.

Concept

Design begins with concept. The wheel may well have begun to take form in the human mind when people noticed that round stones turned underfoot, propelling the body forward. The realization that a heavy load could be moved by rolling it on logs imbued the phenomenon with practical application in everyday life. The slicing of logs into disks carried the concept into the realm of earth-shaking design. The wheel was in itself a design, but it embodied a concept giving rise to thousands of other designs and endless refinements, ultimately making possible sophisticated machinery for every conceivable purpose. A design makes use of concepts in a new and original way; thus a clock uses the wheel as gears in a design for recording time, and an airplane uses it as components of a machine that enables people to fly.

Decision Making

Problem solving is in essence a series of decisions determining the direction a work will take at any stage of its development. One of the first decisions in designing a teapot must concern the material. Traditionally, most teapots are ceramic, which holds the heat well (Fig. 34). Some are glass, allowing one to watch the brewing process. A teapot can also be metal, as many fine teapots have been through the centuries. The spout should pour without dripping or spilling: a straight or curved spout could do this equally well if properly proportioned and placed. Sometimes the handle reaches across the top of the pot; frequently it is placed on the side opposite the spout. Teapots generally have flat bottoms, but there are other possibilities. A built-in stand to insulate the table against heat could be a practical innovation. Many fine old teapots have short curved legs, sometimes ornately decorated in the style of the period in which they were created. A contemporary design could also have legs. There remains the potential for decoration, in which the choices are even wider.

34

34. Anne Currier.
Teapot with Two Cups. 1975.
Slip-cast earthenware with slab-built handles and spout, luster glaze. Height 9″ (22.86 cm).
Courtesy the artist.

The stages of problem solving do not necessarily follow a fixed sequence. They represent a mental attitude at a specific point in the development of a piece of work and are akin to the orderly processes pursued by scientists and engineers, which are often based on mathematics. Although art is considered to be more intuitive, the objective remains the same: the development of a solution.

Definition

There are many ways of approaching the definition of a problem. Some people use diagrams and sketches, laying out aspects of the problem in visual symbols. In designing the teapot, for example, one might sketch the essential elements simply as diagrams: possible shapes, spouts, handles, bases. Next, one would visualize the working process, the finished object in use and the demands that would be made upon it. These could be set down in a few phrases beside the sketches. Problem solvers often make two lists, one headed "Given" and the other labeled "Find."

In the case of the teapot, the first item under "Given" would undoubtedly be the capacity. Is this a pot for the daily use of one or two people, or is it for entertaining, possibly at large receptions? The answer to this question could in itself define the problem, indicating aspects of material and design, since a teapot handled continually at a reception must protect the hands against burning when filled with very hot tea, and it must be easily refilled. As a starting point, the definition of the problem can be reassuring, helping the solver to maintain a cool and logical attitude that leads to a confident and creative approach to subsequent decisions. Two interior designers make statements that can help us to understand what is involved here. Tonny Foy says: "The kind of contemporary design I do is changing the function of space . . . rearranging rooms to suit the rhythms of a person's life."[1] Designer Jay Spectre states: "Most of my interiors seem to work best at night, because they are apartments in the city and the residents are usually out most of the day."[2] Each of these designers has arrived at a specific definition of his work in general. Every commission is then given a specific definition within the broader framework.

Creativity

Creativity describes the stage at which the imagination soars. Some designers fantasize to the extreme, pushing originality beyond the obvious solutions to discover surprising results. The construction in Figure 35 is an excellent example. What might have begun as a wall hanging evolved through imaginative use of materials and forms into a unique work, one that does not simply decorate a wall but forms a dynamic wall in itself. The teapot created by an imaginative designer could very well look like the one in Figure 36.

[1] Paige Rense, "People Are the Issue," *Architectural Digest*, May 1981, p. 24.
[2] Paige Rense, "People Are the Issue," *Architectural Digest*, September 1980, p. 24.

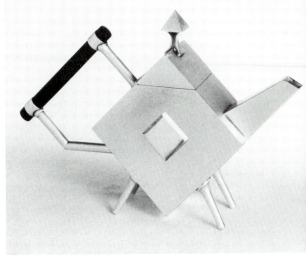

36

35

Analysis

Analysis is the direct opposite. It means applying preset rules of judgment and taking into account constraints of time, economy, and purpose. Analysis employs logic, integrity, and the consideration of potential problems. If some aspect of the project appears to be an insurmountable problem, isolating it can be helpful. Perhaps the spout for the teapot does not pour properly when it is attached to the body of the pot. Possibly the handle is not comfortable, throwing the "feel" of the pot out of balance. Dissecting the problem and viewing it from various angles can be the solution, making the problem disappear. If a different shape of handle or spout is considered, or either is placed a bit higher or lower on the pot, the problem may vanish. If not, this is the stage at which adjustments can be made in the shape or size of the pot, or even in the total design if necessary.

35. Patricia Campbell.
Constructed Light Wall 11.
1979. Shellacked fabric,
paper, cord, fabricated;
8′ × 6′6″ × 1′6″ (2.44 × 1.98 × .46 m).
Collection the artist.

36. Christopher Dresser.
Silverplated teapot.
© 1879.
James Dixon & Sons, Mfr.

Production

Throughout the production of a work, the designer must remain flexible in order to take advantage of unexpected implications in the material or in the evolving form. If the teapot is being thrown on the potter's wheel, it is possible that it will not take exactly the form originally intended. The clay may become too wet or too heavy, and small adjustments will be made. The potter cannot fight the clay successfully under such conditions, but he or she can accept the new form and use it imaginatively. It is the degree of imagination with which necessary choices are made that determines the ultimate character of a work. Remaining flexible can be the means of discovering an entirely new technique.

Clarification

The design process is a continuous unfolding in which each step determines those that follow, culminating in clarification. Regardless of the designer's methods, there comes a moment when the work is complete, and the effort to appraise the results must be made. Occasionally, the designer is elated with the results. Frequently, the reality does not measure up to the original vision. This is the stage at which real growth takes place within the artist, who becomes critic and objective appraiser of an intensely personal effort. This is not easy, but it is the key to improvement. It is also the mark of the professional designer.

Aesthetic Problem Solving

Many aspects of designing the teapot were concerned with aesthetics, but the principal considerations necessarily had to do with a very practical matter, the brewing and pouring of tea. To expand our understanding of the creative process, let us now consider the steps as they apply to painting a watercolor, specifically the one in Plate 3 (p. 55).

The definition of the problem is to paint, on a 15 × 17″ sheet of paper, a depiction of the Grand Canyon, one of the most grandiose and awesome subjects possible. Without presuming to document the thought processes of this artist, we can assume that the words stated under "Given" might approximate *grandeur, wildness,* and *forces of nature.* Under "Find," one could list *distance, depth,* and *natural rhythms.*

Foregoing the usual warm earthy tones of the Grand Canyon, the artist has relied on the softer tones of approaching evening, cool colors that recede, immediately contributing to the sense of distance. Earth forms grow smaller, and there is less detail in the furthermost hills and mesas. Depth is obvious by the deepening of color that forms chasms behind highlighted edges. These are preset rules of the craft of painting, but this is a spectacular subject and routine measures may not be sufficient to portray it. The problem of achieving greater depth might be isolated and approached from different angles. To have depth one must have height, but the tops of the mesas are already close to the upper edge of the painting. Deeper color in the canyons might contrast too sharply, disturbing the sense of flowing distance. The artist has chosen a dramatic solution. By placing a steep cliff immediately in the foreground, he has plunged its vertical lines into infinity, carrying the depths of the canyon with them. By articulating details of rock and vegetation in the foreground, he has established a clearly defined focal point from which the natural rhythms of the earth carry our eye into a sweep and vastness that flows beyond the limits of the painting.

Integrity

The quality that makes a design a unique expression of its time and of its creator can be termed *integrity*. Stemming from the Latin *integritas*, the word integrity has as one of its meanings the quality or state of being whole. In design, this means a unity of conception that makes a design an original statement.

Integrity of Materials

Before any design can be attempted, the designer should be aware of what materials are available and should be familiar with their advantages and disadvantages. The architect must know which materials are strong in compression (when pressed under weight) and which have more strength in tension (when stretched). A designer must be aware of the potential for wear and longevity of any material considered for a specific work. A painting whose surface cracks or flakes after a few months of hanging on a wall is no better than a building that collapses or a piece of weaving that ravels.

Selecting materials for suitability includes a willingness to accept and even exploit their visual qualities. When steel was introduced as a building material, architects, while welcoming its advantages, sheathed it in brick or stone to enable their buildings to resemble their predecessors. The contemporary cityscape, however, is defined by expanses of steel, glass, aluminum, and concrete, the building materials of our time. Plastic has been subjected to a long apprenticeship as an imitator of other materials before finally coming into its own in contemporary design (Fig. 37).

37

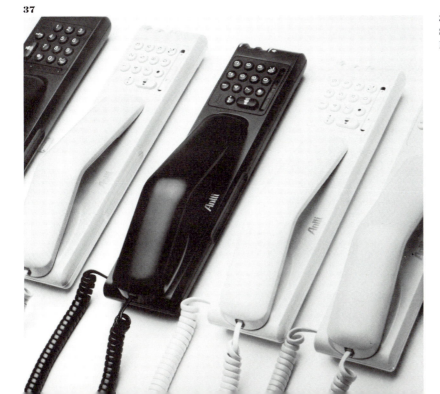

37. Antti Nurmesniemi.
Slim-line push-button telephone.
Manufacturer: Fujitsu, Japan.

38

39

Marcel Breuer. *Club Armchair*.
Chrome-plated tubular steel with
canvas slings, 28⅛ × 30 × 27¾"
(71 × 76 × 70 cm). Collection,
The Museum of Modern Art, New York
(gift of Herbert Bayer).

39. Gad-dam stilt tree house.
Luzon Island, Philippines.

40. Stephen A. Foley.
Spinning wheel.
Black walnut, lignum vitae,
with brass and steel hardware;
35¼ × 17 × 24" (89 × 43 × 61 cm).
Renwick Gallery of the National
Collection of Fine Arts,
Smithsonian Institution,
Washington, D. C.

Integrity of Form

During much of the twentieth century, the idea of integrity in form
has been summed up in the phrase "form follows function." Emerging
from the writings of the 19th-century sculptor Horatio Greenough,
this phrase is generally attributed to the American architect Louis
Sullivan. The concept has long been associated with the Bauhaus, a
school of design founded in Weimar, Germany, in 1919. Among the
major aims of the Bauhaus program was the development of designs
suitable to machine production. Wishing to effect a transition between
centuries of handcrafted products and the Industrial Revolution, the
Bauhaus faculty and staff worked with architecture, textiles, furniture, and household items, paring them down to an essential form
that would be expressive of their function as well as of the material
and the machine processes responsible for them. Consumers accustomed to heavy carved oak and mahogany furniture must have found
the chair in Figure 38 startling when it appeared in 1925; however,
the fact that it could fit into contemporary settings today attests to the
integrity of its design.

Nature provides limitless designs that adhere to the principle of
form following function. Birds build nests from materials that blend
with their surroundings, offering protection against predators. Bea-
vers build lodges from sticks and small logs under water, making it
possible for them to move in and out freely without detection. Many
people living close to nature follow the same principle. Deep in the
Philippine jungle, in an area plagued by high humidity, floods, insects, and dangerous animals, the inhabitants build tree houses forty

feet above the ground (Fig. 39). This elevation allows cooling breezes to flow under the house, while minimum walls provide maximum ventilation, and a steeply pitched roof sheds torrential rains. The form in this case not only follows the function of human survival but makes it possible.

Integrity of Function

If form follows function, form and function are inextricably interwoven, and a successful design incorporates integrity in both. In Figure 40 Stephen Foley has chosen one of the most time-honored of functional objects, the spinning wheel, and, in an innovative leap, has given it a totally contemporary design while retaining the efficiency of its original function. For centuries spinning was done by hand, holding in one hand a distaff, or staff, with a bunch of wool, cotton, or flax, with the other hand twisting from the bunch individual fibers that could be used for weaving, knitting, or sewing. The 18th century brought the traditional spinning wheel with foot pedal and spindles, which transformed spinning into a smooth operation accomplished by sitting at a sizable three-legged piece of equipment. Foley's version is a delicately balanced form that conserves space while providing flowing lines that seem a part of the act of spinning. The wheel and spindles, both circular, are the focal point, as always, but the form holding them is also curved throughout, even where supports meet at right angles. Design and function become one.

40

Many of the irritations of contemporary life stem from objects that lack integrity of function. Furniture with drawers that do not run smoothly, automobiles that require a contortionist's skill to inject oneself into the back seat, umbrellas that turn inside out under the slightest breeze—these are commonplace nuisances. Such faults in function almost invariably stem from a fault in the form, often one inherited from a previous prototype. Irons, vacuum cleaners, and washing machines all evolved gradually from more arduous models of previous years, in which the operator bore down or scrubbed lustily to make the equipment work. The light models of today expand function and simplify effort at the same time, providing successful designs for busy and complex lives.

Some of the best designs today are found in products that are uniquely of our own time. When a designer undertakes the creation of something that has never existed before, function is necessarily the first consideration since there can be no preconceived idea of how the object should look. The computer is perhaps the most dramatic example of how evolution in design takes place. The first computers for personal use involved nearly filling a room with equipment. Twenty years later, a comprehensive personal computer program can be accomplished in less space than that consumed by an office desk and the computer itself has become compactly portable (Fig. 41).

Function, like purpose, is not limited to the design of strictly utilitarian objects. Through the centuries painters, sculptors, musicians, and writers have rebelled against the existing order, creating furor by their controversial innovations. The avant-garde (advance guard) has become a presence in every generation, referring to those who charge ahead, feeling the accepted methods and forms no longer express the

41

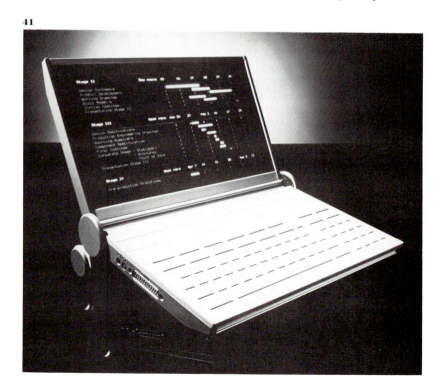

41. Portable computer. *Exect 100.*
1½″ × 11¾″ × 9″ (3.8 × 29.8 × 22.9 cm).
Manufacturer: Dawn Systems,
England.

spirit of the time in which they live. The seeking for new forms represents a search for integrity, not only in form and function but, in many cases, in materials as well.

Perhaps the most urgent need for integrity in design concerns the earth and the well-being of the people who live upon it, both now and in the future. In recent years we have become aware that countless designs that make life easier or more stimulating are dangerous, even life-threatening. Some are the result of dangerous materials, such as the ubiquitous aerosol spray cans that we now suspect contribute to the gradually enlarging hole in the ozone over the South Pole which could ultimately develop into an untenable situation for life on earth. Asbestos, used for generations as insulation in buildings, has proven fatal to many of the workers who installed it and continues to pose a threat to people living and working in buildings where it remains. Allergies have increased dramatically throughout the population of the world, some related to materials used in homebuilding—synthetics in carpets and draperies, glues, paints, and fabricated building materials—and some to foods, many of which are sprayed or injected with substances to preserve them or make them more visually appealing. Other designs are faulty in form. We frequently hear of automobiles that have been recalled by the manufacturer because some fault in construction has become obvious. These are areas in which a designer's knowledge of materials and methods of manufacture can be of vital importance. Consumers must share the responsibility, for awareness of these matters is a fundamental area of consumer evaluation.

Evaluation

One of the most vital areas of design is consumer evaluation. There are many criteria for such evaluation and many levels of judgment, from the simple "I like it" to the detailed analysis that will be possible after we have explored the elements and principles of design in succeeding chapters. However, in Chapter 1 we stated four attributes of a successful design: a plan for order, expression of the material, form, and fulfillment of function. Now that we are aware of the considerations that enter into the *process* of design, these attributes can be applied to specific objects as criteria of their effectiveness. Together the four attributes sum up the essence of a good design; a lack in any one of them can cause the design to be considered flawed.

Let us first analyze a design that has proven highly successful. Hundreds of thousands of people in the world are chronically confined to wheelchairs, a situation causing two major problems: balance (especially when the lower part of the body is paralyzed), and pressures on limbs forced to stay in the same position. Painful skin ulcers may arise from improperly fitted equipment, and at worst, pressures could result in amputation or even death. Faced with these problems, a team of designers set out with *a plan for order* that would alleviate the sufferings of people confined to wheelchairs. Using chromium for strength and appearance and rubber for tires and footrests, they made use of a newer and particularly appropriate material, foam in the form of beads that would conform to the contours of the individual body. Thus each chair becomes custom designed for the patient who will use it. The *materials* are aptly expressed, the *form* is personally adapted to its use, and the *fulfillment of the purpose* of the design has brought relief to thousands of people. This is design at its best (Fig. 42).

Quite a different plan for order determined the design of the Tacoma Narrows Bridge at the lower end of Puget Sound in Washington state. The plan of the designing engineers was to produce a graceful, aesthetically pleasing bridge, and as a result they succeeded in building the third longest bridge in the country which, for its length, was the narrowest suspension bridge ever built. The steel cables and roadbed were beautifully expressed and the form was impressive for its delicacy. However, the bridge was so flexible that even light winds twisted the roadway in waves that rolled along its length, causing it to

42

42. Frank Low and Robert Burridge, for Contourpedic. Custom wheelchair. 1975. Chair was designed with plastic bags filled with foam beads to conform to the contours of the body.

43. Tacoma Narrows Bridge, Puget Sound, Washington. Destroyed by violent winds, 1940.

44. Pottery bud vase.

be nicknamed "Galloping Gertie." The engineers had designed the
bridge to withstand winds of up to 120 miles per hour but they had
overlooked one factor. When there is vibration, there is also resonance, a phenomenon that increases the force of the vibration in direct ratio to the length of time it persists. On November 7, 1940, a
prolonged 42-mile-per-hour wind set the roadway to twisting with
increasing violence. After four hours of wrenching, the bridge ripped
itself apart and fell into the waters of Puget Sound 600 feet below (Fig.
43). The entire world of structural design took notice. In time a totally
different design was created and constructed.

Fortunately, not all designs fail so dramatically as Galloping
Gertie, yet faulty designs often have one point in common—a single
error in judgment, sometimes seemingly minor. The plan for the vase
in Figure 44 was for the holder of a single flower that would be different from the classic narrow "bud vase." The material was well-handled
on the potter's wheel, the glaze unusual, and the form pleasing to the
eye. However, when one turns the vase upside down to empty it, the
water does not run out. Only when it is laid on its side does the water
gurgle out drop by drop. The reason? The neck is pinched at its base,
impeding a free flow. By a matter of a fraction of an inch, the design
fails to fulfill its function.

When the consumer is involved in evaluation, the personal element inevitably enters in, and rightly so. A professional artist moves
through a gallery assessing works by the way the artist has handled the
medium or developed an individual technique. The casual viewer is
more apt to dismiss a work with a comment such as "I couldn't live

43

44

with it," or perhaps "That would look nice above the sofa." Somewhere in between lies the technique of informed evaluation. As we explore the elements and principles of design, new insights will develop, enabling the consumer or the potential designer to view the world and its products with a knowledgeable and discerning eye.

Summary

Inspiration is the phenomenon by which an artist observes the universe, becomes aware of unique relationships, and gives them a form that will be apparent to others. A *medium* is the means the artist uses to express inspiration; *materials* are influenced by the medium but independent of it. Oil painting is a medium; brushes, knives, and canvas are materials. *Craftsmanship* is fundamental to any design and requires long periods of dedication. The creation of a design is a matter of *problem solving*, consisting of five stages: *definition, creativity, analysis, production*, and *clarification*. The quality that makes a design a unique expression of its time is *integrity*. A successful design will have integrity of *materials, form*, and *function*. Evaluation is an important aspect of the field of design. Both designers and consumers need a sound background of knowledge to be discerning judges.

The Elements of Design

CHAPTER THREE

Line

As we begin our exploration of the elements and principles of design, one fact must be thoroughly understood. No element or principle works alone. We separate them purely for purposes of identification and analysis, in order to understand exactly what is meant by each and what its potential is for creating a design. By such understanding we are enabled better to analyze the interactions that take place among them in any given work.

Line is at once the most illusory and the most fundamental of the design elements. In nature, line is entirely a matter of human perception. What we see as lines are actually cylindrical twigs or branches (Fig. 45), veins in leaves, cracks in cliffs, or the horizon line where earth and sky appear to meet but never do. Often what appears as a

45. David Cavagnaro. *Valley Oak,* Quercus lobata, *in a Winter Morning Ground Fog, near El Verano, California.* Photograph.

45

sharp line is actually the joining of two surfaces (Fig. 46). Nature is rich in linear design but the lines are symbolic of structure and function.

In the hands of the artist or designer, however, line is a basic tool. When we commit a design to paper we place a drawing instrument at a *point* on the paper, extend the point into a line, and, by means of additional lines, give shape to our vision. In the process our lines join to become *shapes,* at the same time delineating the *space* around them. When the design is complete, we refer to its lines as expressive of its essential quality, as in the flowing lines of a costume, or the dynamic lines of a motorcycle, which hint at its possible speed and power (Fig. 47). Line is fundamental to design, and its uses and qualities are virtually limitless.

46

46. Charles Moore. *Death Valley.* 1970. Photograph.

47. Honda Hurricane. American Honda Motor Corp. Gardena, CA.

48. Hokusai. *A Sake Bout.* Late 18th or early 19th century. Ink on paper, 10½ × 15″ (26 × 38 cm). Freer Gallery of Art, Smithsonian Institution, Washington, D. C.

47

The Quality of Line

Lines can be powerful or delicate, soothing or jarring. One of the masters in the use of line was Katsushika Hokusai, a Japanese artist who lived at the turn of the eighteenth century. Known widely for his color woodcuts, in which the image is carved into a block of wood with a small knife, Hokusai also produced an impressive group of drawings in which he used line in a manner reminiscent of the woodcut technique. In Figure 48, for example, his line, though always strong, varies in character from a fine curved line, giving a humorous twist to a foot, to a broad angular one, which depicts descriptively the fold of a garment. These folds and shadows delineate his figures within, transmitting, through the carefree disarray of clothing, their state of utter relaxation.

48

49. Ronaldo de Juan. *Gate #6.* 1976.
Charcoal, 6'3" × 3'10" (1.9 × 1.16 m).

50. Amédée Ozenfant. *Fugue.* 1925.
Pencil, 18 × 22" (45.72 × 55.88 cm).
Collection, The Museum of Modern Art,
New York (gift of the artist).

49

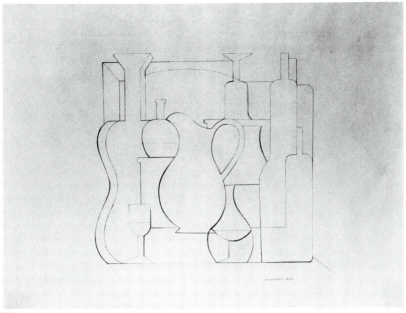

50

Vigorous, ragged, curving lines may imply terror or turbulent emotions. In the drawing in Figure 49 the heavy charcoal lines in the upper center seem to loom menacingly, and the texture of crossed lines suggests barbed wire. In titling this work "Gate," the artist was obviously not thinking of a quiet peaceful spot but of an obstacle to be overcome before passing into another area of experience. The frenetic curved lines at the bottom hint at whiplash strokes. The work is a powerful design laden with emotional overtones.

In contrast, the drawing in Figure 50 is almost serene in its smooth delicate line. The swelling and tapering widths encourage the eye to follow the lines throughout the drawing. Although the group is self-contained well within the borders of its rectangular format, our eyes move continuously, exploring the shapes, but even more led through the rhythms created by their flowing and interaction.

Symbolic Line

A line becomes a *symbol* when a specific meaning is attached to it. As a symbol, it may delineate a shape that has meaning to the viewer, or it may express the reaction of the artist to the shapes, forms, and rhythms of the environment. Many lines do both. When two or more people agree about the meaning, the symbol can serve as a method of communication.

Sometimes the shortest lines have the most comprehensive symbolism. The lines that form letters and numbers can, in combination, represent all the knowlege that humanity has ever recorded. The symbolism of line encompasses not only the alphabets of the world but mathematical formulas and musical scores as well (Fig. 51). Such symbols make possible the continuity of knowledge and culture throughout the centuries.

51

With its branches,

trunk,

and roots,

here is–

一

A TREE;
WOOD

木

"One tree does not make a forest."

A FOREST;
A GROVE

林

DENSE;
THICK WITH TREES

森

Man plucked with his hand

two leafy branches.

52

Nearly all civilizations have practiced a form of *calligraphy* (from the Greek for "beautiful writing"). Some of the most decorative calligraphy exists in the highly stylized brush strokes of Oriental characters, many of which are *ideographic*. This means that, instead of simply being assigned to certain sounds as is the case with the Roman alphabet, the Oriental characters are actually abstracted images of the things they represent; for example, the character that stands for "tree" is based on the form of a tree (Fig. 52).

Line used as a symbol becomes a powerful tool for the designer, for it communicates abstract ideas or immensely complicated associations with just a few strokes. The fiberwork in Figure 53 uses cotton and rayon filaments as strokes, to impart an image filled with both symbolism and visual impact.

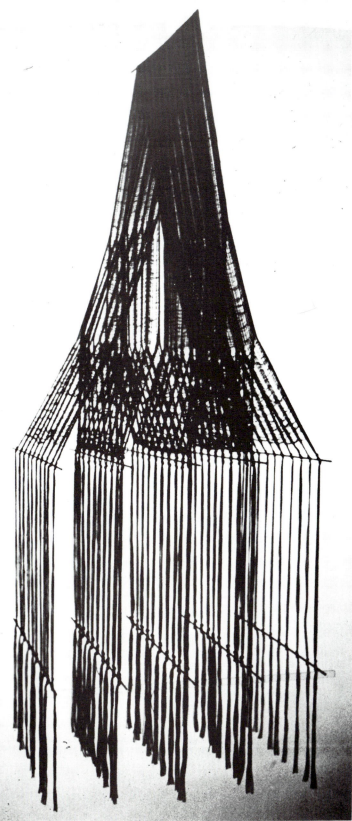

51. Facsimile of autographed manuscript of Ludwig van Beethoven's *Missa Solemnis,* page 25. Published by Hans Schneider (Tutzing).

52. Evolution of Chinese written characters from symbolic representations of actual objects.

53. Charlotte Lindgren. *Mooring.* 1965. Black cotton and rayon, 21 × 21 × 46″ (53.3 × 53.3 × 116.8 cm). Courtesy of the artist.

54

Line as Modeling

A contour line is a line that traces outline or overall shape. Existing on a two-dimensional surface, it does no more than carve that surface into two-dimensional shapes. However, a contour line *can* give a distinct sense of three-dimensional volume. Sometimes this is done by a *modeled* line, subtly shaded to indicate hollows or shadows, or it can be achieved with closely spaced parallel lines (hatchings) or intersecting parallel lines (cross-hatchings). In the pen-and-ink drawing in Figure 54 both methods are used. There is width between cap and forehead to convey shadow but the facial features and bone structure are articulated completely with a variety of hatchings.

Line as Form

Sometimes line not only conveys form but actually *is* form. We see this most readily in three-dimensional works such as sculpture or constructions, where wires or fibers are the means of building form. The construction in Figure 55 is a simple composition of flowing lines drawn in stainless steel.

The lines in Figure 56, on the other hand, are drawn in sucker shoots of willow and wild plum. Concerned with the universal life force and its expression in the rhythms of the environment, Carol

54. Pavel Tchelitchew. *Africa.*
1932. Pen and ink,
10½ × 8¼" (26.7 × 20.9 cm).
Collection, The Museum of Modern Art,
New York.
John S. Newberry Collection.

55. Jose De Rivera.
Brussels Construction. 1958.
Stainless steel. Courtesy Art
Institute of Chicago (gift from
Mr. and Mrs. R. Howard Goldsmith).

56. Carol Shaw-Sutton.
Dusk River Crossing. 1981.
Fruitwood, linen, paint;
1'8" × 7'10" × 4"
(50.8 × 238.76 × 10.16 cm).

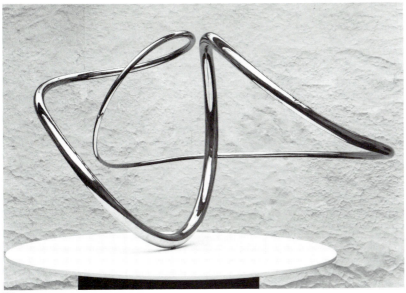

55

Shaw-Sutton constructed a series of "space drawings" in which the shoots build a linear construction composed of layers suggesting depths and ripples with which she intersperses linen threads and washes of color. In *Dusk River Crossing* she seeks to express a personal experience by means of an intricate construction of lines.

56

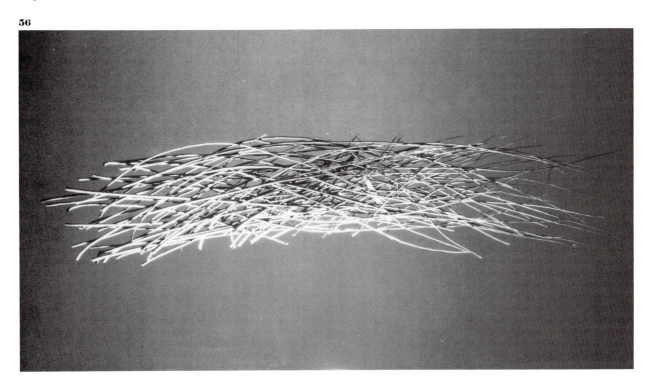

We mentioned above that a contour line simply carves a surface into two-dimensional shapes. Sometimes a contour line does more. In his drawing in Figure 57, Gustav Klimt has used no shading except at the model's hairline, yet by breaking the line on the legs into short strokes and by converting the contour line into circles and "scribbles" throughout the costume, he has achieved, by clear simple line, a solid figure in a fluffy dress.

Line as Direction and Emphasis

In any design, line can perform the important function of leading the eye to create emphasis. Such use of line is an important part of *composition, the total organization of any work of art*. At the same time, line is often responsible for the prevailing emotional quality of a work. In the work in Figure 58 the composition converges, and we see and hear the throbbing of the city as we look down on it from the top of the Woolworth Tower. The focal point was actually cut out and sewn on to represent the gold leaf on the dome of the Old World Building as seen from above. This was New York many years ago, yet the effect is a dizzying scene of large buildings and small, car-choked streets, the old elevated railroad, and zigzag perspectives of buildings as the eye plunges downward into the turmoil. The converging lines, some jagged, some not, provide a dynamic sense of great forces at work, constantly moving in tension.

In contrast, the painting in Figure 59 is predominantly horizontal. It is a peaceful subject, a quiet time of day, but if represented in vertical or diagonal lines, the emotional quality would be quite different. Even the clouds drift horizontally, and the only verticals, a gentle

57. Gustav Klimt.
*Standing Woman Looking to
the Right. 1917.* Pencil,
2 × 1¼″ (5 × 3 cm).
Albertina Gallery, Vienna.

58. John Marin. *Lower Manhattan.*
1920. Watercolor, 21⅞ × 26¾″
(56 × 68 cm). Collection,
The Museum of Modern Art, New York.
Philip L. Goodwin Collection.

58

Plate 3. Gunnar Widforss. *The Grand Canyon*. Watercolor, 17 × 15″ (43.2 × 38.1 cm). Dr. and Mrs. Charles D. Campbell.

Plate 4. Thornton Willis. *Break Dancer*. 1986. Acrylic on canvas, 7′ × 9′8″ (2.14 × 2.95 m). Courtesy Oscarsson Siegeltuch Gallery, New York.

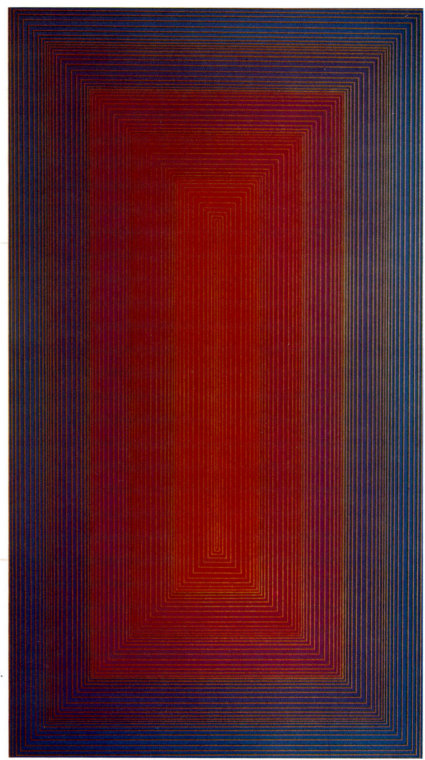

Plate 5. Richard Anuszkiewicz.
Blue to Red Portal. 1977.
Screenprint on Masonite,
7 × 4′ (2.1 × 1.2 m).
Courtesy Editions
Lassiter-Meisel, New York.
Collection of the artist.

59

contrast to the prevailing lines, are the three human figures, echoing the church steeples and the lines of Lombardy poplars in the distance. Invisible horizontal lines mark the tops of the figures and the steeples, and the poplars form a dark horizontal band of vertical strokes.

Curving lines often denote a flowing rhythm, but circular ones can suggest force, as in a whirlwind. There is nothing soothing about the work in Figure 60. The tumbled disarray of books implies dis-

60

order, even violence, but without the circular lines the books might simply be falling off a shelf. The lines pull them into a vortex that whirls and dramatizes their confusion, providing at the same time an excellent example of *closure*.

Line as Pattern and Texture

When lines are repeated to form an area of pattern, they become texture. The texture may be both visual and *tactile*, capable of being felt with the fingers, as is the case with the glasses designed by Michael Boehm (Fig. 61). One could not touch these glasses without being aware of the texture. The texture on the pottery bowl in Figure 62 is

61

62

61. Michael Boehm. *Glasses.* 1973. Designed in the "twist" pattern for Rosenthal Studio-Linie.

62. Wayne L. Bates. *Complex Cut Geometric.* 15″ wide × 4″ deep, at sign of the Swan Gallery. Philadelphia, PA.

63. Steven Weiss. "Infinity" table. Plexiglass.

64. Otto Peine. *Manned Helium Sculpture from Citything Sky Ballet.* 1970. Helium-filled polyethylene tubing. Courtesy the artist.

no less tactile, but its primary interest lies in the visual pattern formed by imaginative use of line swirling and radiating to accentuate and reinforce the form of the bowl.

The table by Steven Weiss (Fig. 63) uses line in a unique manner, one that relies on *light* for its effectiveness. While we do not treat light as a separate element of design, there can be no doubt of its importance in the success of many designs, ranging from the way a painting is lighted when hanging on a wall to designs that are composed entirely of light beams (Fig. 64). In Weiss' table the lines in the design are actually the perimeters of sheets of Plexiglas cut in such a way that their edges catch the light. This could be considered one of the instances in which lines do not exist except in human perception. Under certain conditions there would be no sense of linear design at all, but

63

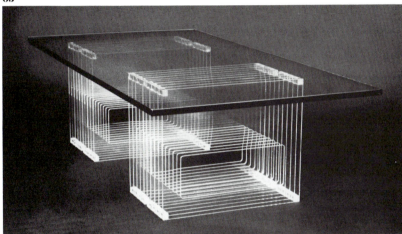

64

with proper lighting everything disappears except the tabletop and the composition of lines supporting it, producing the dramatic illusion of a form that is purely linear.

The importance of line lies in its ability not only to convey shape but also, by its very quality, to express or arouse a mood, a strong emotion, or an impression. As an element of design, then, line is not only fundamental; it carries unlimited potential for versatility.

Summary

Line is the most fundamental of design elements. Lines joined together form *shapes* and at the same time they delineate the *space* around the shapes. Lines vary widely in character, making it possible to convey a range of emotions through use of line alone. *Symbolic* lines are used in writing, musical scores, and mathematical formulas. Line can be used in different kinds of hatching to give a three-dimensional quality to a drawing. Line can also govern the composition of a work, leading the eye, providing emotional quality, and resulting in a unifying continuity. Line is an effective means of achieving texture in nearly any medium.

For Further Exploration

1. *Achieving form through outline.* On a 9 × 12" sheet of drawing paper, using a 4B pencil, draw *in outline only* a simple spray of leaves or flowers. Vary the outline to achieve form, broadening the line for shadows, narrowing it for lights, leaving it out entirely where highlights appear. Use no shading. (Refer to Fig. 50.)

2. *Achieving form through hatching.* Using pen and ink on a sheet of 9 × 12" drawing paper, repeat the drawing in Project #1 but keep the outline uniform in width. This time use hatching to indicate form, parallel lines of varying widths and spacing, curving where necessary to describe a surface. Do not allow the lines to run together—individual lines should be obvious throughout the drawing. (Refer to Fig. 54.)

3. Using charcoal on a large sheet of newsprint, draw lines *expressing emotion*. Try to feel the emotion as you draw, then analyze why the lines express it. Dissect the results, asking yourself if, as is often assumed, horizontal lines are peaceful, jagged lines violent, curving lines tempestuous. Label the lines according to the way they make *you* feel.

4. Selecting a reproduction of a painting in a book or magazine, lay a piece of tracing paper over it and trace the dominant *lines of the composition*. Darken the lines that you feel establish the primary feeling of the work, or that give it unity. Remove the tracing and compare your analysis with the original work to see if the two are giving the same message.

Shape and Mass

As elements of design, shape and mass are inseparable since they are frequently different human perceptions of the same thing. Mass is generally considered to be the three-dimensional extension of shape. A tree is a flat black silhouette against a moonlit sky, but the tree is actually there in all its mass, so the two-dimensional aspect of the silhouette is merely a matter of perception. When the light changes or the human eye moves its position, what has been seen as a shape is revealed as a mass, disclosing surfaces and bulk that were originally not perceived (Fig. 65).

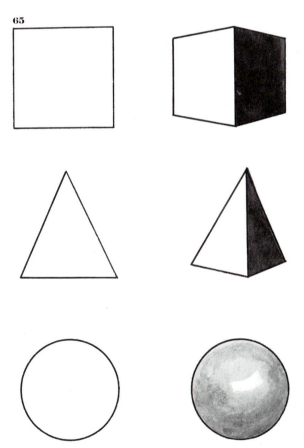

65. A shape often becomes a mass through a change in viewpoint or in lighting.

61

In everyday usage, form and volume are often used as synonyms for mass. As we saw in Chapter 1, however, *form* has a much broader meaning in the field of design. Volume, too, has a meaning of its own, being defined as the amount of space occupied by a three-dimensional object as measured in cubic units. When we speak of mass, we may refer to the mass of a mountain, an earth mass in geographic time, or the mass of a crashing wave that changes form with every second. We may also speak of the mass of a building or a piece of sculpture.

Shape

Shape is formed in many ways. In *nature* a patch of growth provides a shape, as does sunlight striking a facet of a cliff, or pools left by a receding tide (Fig. 66). Each of these shapes, of course, implies a mass: even a patch of moss has depth, a cliff has enormous mass beneath the sunlight, and pools have depth and the water has volume. The designer, working on a two-dimensional surface, does not have to consider these complexities of terminology. A simple continuous line encloses space and creates a shape (Fig. 67). Shapes can also be formed by flat areas of texture, of value (light and dark) or by blocks of color (Pl. 4 p. 55).

66

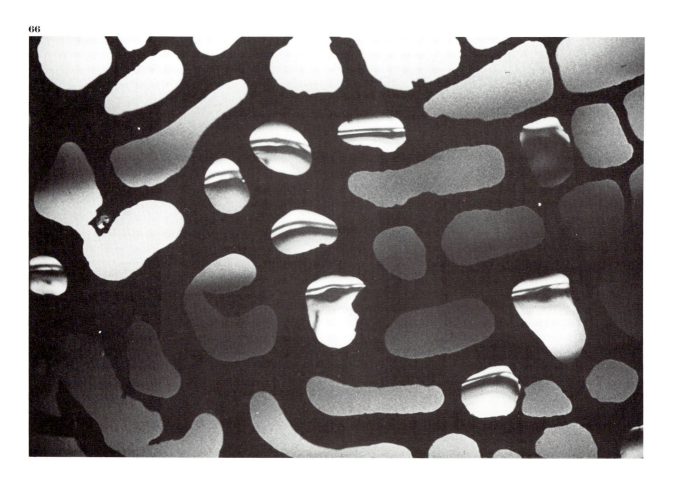

66. Ernst Haas. Water left in the crevasses of a coral after it has been washed by a wave. 1963. Photograph.

67. Paul Klee. *Angstausbruch III.* 1936. Oil on cardboard, 25 × 19″ (63.5 × 48.1 cm). Kunstmuseum, Bern.

67

Considering pure shape, then, we find four general categories into which shapes may be divided: *natural, geometric, abstract,* and *non-objective.*

Natural Shapes

Natural shapes are understood to derive from anything in the natural environment, including the human figure. Although many of the sources are actually three-dimensional, the two-dimensional shape or outline provides the designer with endless possibilities for creativity. The Japanese silk design in Figure 68 could have been derived from either flowers or snowflakes or both; its charm lies in the originality that brings both shapes together in a new and decorative design. The design of the cotton print from Finland (Fig. 69) looks like a huge

68

69

flower shape, even though its title suggests that the artist had something else in mind as well.

Any landscape painting is composed almost entirely of natural shapes, with the exception, of course, of the presence of buildings. Animal shapes have been used by artists for more than fifteen thousand years—as paintings on cave walls and skins, and as carvings, often with a touch of humor. Contemporary artist Tak Kwong Chan,

70

68. Japanese stencil used to decorate silk. c. 1680–1750, Tokugawa period. Slater Memorial Museum, Norwich Free Academy, Norwich, Conn., Vanderpoel Collection.

69. Maija Isola. *Medusa.* Screened cotton print designed for Marimekko, Helsinki, Finland.

70. Tak Kwong Chan. *The Horse—Away He Goes.* 1980. Brush and ink 40 × 24″ (1.02 × .61 m). Collection the artist.

with a few masterful strokes, creates horses that are full of action and beauty, yet are striking designs as well (Fig. 70).

Natural shapes are often *geometric,* providing transition between the two categories. One of the most important of these shapes is the hexagon, part square and part circle, found in honeycombs, turtles' shells, mineral deposits, snow crystals, and biological tissues (Fig. 71). Used by ancient Egyptian mathematicians, it was given a name by the

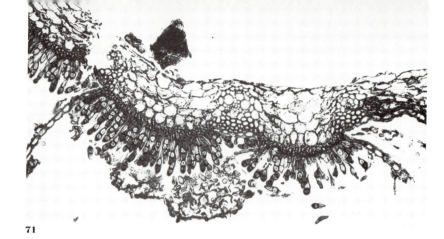

71

71. Microscopic photograph showing cellular structure of black stem wheat rust.

72. Stonehenge. 1800–1400 B.C. Height of stones above ground 13′6″ (4.1 m). Salisbury Plain, Wiltshire, England.

73. Victor Vasarely. Design based on circles. 31.1 × 31.1″ (84 × 84 cm). The Vasarely Center, New York.

74. Harijan patchwork quilt. Embroidered and pieced cotton, 6′9¼″ square (2.06 m). N.D. From Kutch district of India. UCLA Museum of Cultural History. Gift of Mr. and Mrs. Richard B. Rogers.

72

Greeks, and is today a familiar shape to chemists who use it to designate molecular structure. Shapes flow through the universe in a thousand guises, relating all life and all periods of time.

Geometric Shapes

Human construction is dominated by geometric shapes. Basic *post-and-lintel* construction sets a horizontal crosspiece over two separated uprights, creating a square or rectangle of space between them. The solidity of this shape has permitted the structures at Stonehenge to remain in position for 3500 years, despite the fact that they were erected by primitive means with no mortar of any kind to hold them together (Fig. 72). Of course, the massive stones themselves are responsible for the durability of Stonehenge, but the equilibrium of the square must be given credit for their age-long stability.

The regularity of circular shapes relates them to industrial design in which they can be turned out in quantity by machinery designed for

the purpose. Gears are only one form in which geometric shapes have become fundamental to our everyday life. On the other hand, geometric shapes can be varied in imaginative ways to create designs far more decorative than mechanical. In Figure 73 Victor Vasarely has used the circle in an allover pattern so lively that one does not realize at first glance that it is composed entirely of circles and their parts. The patchwork quilt in Figure 74, on the other hand, is composed entirely of the components of the square.

Many 20th-century artists see in geometric shapes and masses a symbolic expression of the highly mechanized and technological char-

73

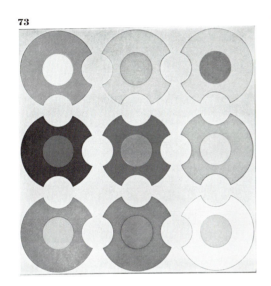

74

acter of contemporary civilization. Richard Anuszkiewicz executed a series of prints based on the rectangle, of which the example in Plate 5 (p. 56) could be considered as the ultimate geometric expression, consisting simply of linear rectangles in a concentric configuration. However, the result is far from cold or mechanical. The distances between the rectangles are subtly varied to provide a sense of radiation from the center, and the color emanates and shimmers to intensify the effect.

Abstract Shapes

When a natural shape is altered in such a way as to reduce it to its essence, we say that it has been *abstracted*. Another term for this is *stylization*. Some of the most beautiful abstract designs are those created by Native American potters, in which religious symbols and earth forms are interrelated in distinctive abstract entities. The pottery in Figure 75 is stylized and geometric, but every element has symbolic meaning, dominated by the eagle feathers that cover jar and bowl. Even the most casual observer can appreciate the design, but to the artists who created the jar, each abstract shape had symbolic meaning.

Abstraction is the essence of any written language, and a contemporary language of abstract shapes has become familiar to automobile travelers (Fig. 76). Originating in Europe to simplify travel through countries with different languages, pictorial highway signs are now commonplace in the United States as well, bringing instantaneous recognition of warnings and notices when seen from a moving vehicle.

75. Maria and Julian Martinez.
Pottery (earthenware).
Museum of New Mexico, Santa Fe.
Cat Plate, 13″ dia., c. 1925.
Feather Plate, 11½″ dia.,
Maria & Popovi Da, "⁵⁄₆₉."
Feather Jar, c. 11″ dia. 8″ H,
Maria & Popovi Da, c. 1965.

76. West German traffic sign.

77. Pablo Picasso.
Les Deux Femmes Nues.
(Two Nude Women.) 1945–46.
Lithographs, eighteen states,
each c. 10⅛ × 10⁵⁄₁₆″
(25.65 × 34.04 cm).
Cleveland Museum of Art
(J. H. Wade Fund). State V.

78. State X.

79. State XVII.

75

76

The process by which abstraction evolves can be seen clearly in a series of lithographs by Picasso. We will refer to three from an edition of eighteen, choosing examples that will best exemplify the evolution from natural shape to abstraction. The fifth print (Fig. 77) shows a relatively natural representation of two female nudes, with normal shapes and masses. The tenth state (Fig. 78) has eliminated much of the shading, flattening the figures into simplified versions drawn in outline. The dark background has become a decorative screen and the space has less depth. By the seventeenth state (Fig. 79) the similarity to female figures has become remote. The origin of the shapes is obvious but the development into abstraction stresses the shapes themselves rather than any association with models. The third example would be difficult to comprehend if seen alone, but in context with its predecessors it gives us a clear idea of the artist's investigation into shapes, planes, and outlines, revealing a systematic progression from representational drawing to abstraction.

77

78

79

Nonobjective Shapes

Nonobjective shapes are those that do not originate in any recognizable shape or object. As we mentioned earlier, artists who work in a nonobjective manner find it difficult to create a work in which viewers will not see something recognizable; therefore the term becomes more a matter of the artist's intent than of the work itself. Wassily Kandinsky stated that as his career progressed he found the presence of objects harmed his paintings (Fig. 80).

Henri Matisse spent the latter years of his life working with shape for its own sake, cutting shapes from colored paper and experimenting with various arrangements to observe their interaction. In *The Swimming Pool* (Fig. 81) he created a nine-panel mural around cut-

80.

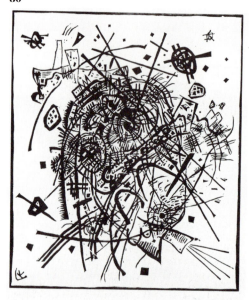

80. Wassily Kandinsky. *Small Worlds VIII.* 1922. Woodcut. Solomon R. Guggenheim Museum, New York (The Hilla Rebay Collection).

81. Henri Matisse. Three panels from *The Swimming Pool,* a nine-panel mural in two parts. 1952. Gouache on cut-and-pasted paper mounted on burlap, 7'6⅝" × 27'9½" (2.3 × 8.47 m) and 7'6⅝" × 26'1½" (2.3 × 7.96 m). Collection, The Museum of Modern Art, New York (Mrs. Bernard F. Gimbel Fund).

82. Jasper Johns. *Cups 4 Picasso.* 1972. Lithograph, 22 × 32" (56 × 81 cm). Universal Limited Art Editions. Courtesy Leo Castelli Gallery, New York.

81

and-pasted paper shapes that would show the movement and flow of swimmers interacting with water. In some cases, the images appear as abstracted human figures but this was not the artist's primary intent. His consuming interest in these years was in shape and space relationships.

Shape Relationships

No shape exists in a vacuum. We usually see shape on a two-dimensional surface, which means that the shape carves a second shape from the space on which it is placed. The shape itself is known as a *positive* shape, while the shape around it is known as *negative*. Depending upon our viewpoint, these entities may also be known as positive or negative *space*.

Jasper Johns has made the phenomenon of positive and negative shapes obvious in his work in Figure 82. If we look at this picture in one way we see a vase or urn. However, if we look again we see two profiles of Pablo Picasso, facing each other nose to nose. Looking at it for any length of time, we find that the two images reverse repeatedly. This trick of perception is known as *figure-ground ambiguity*, the term "ground" referring to the background or so-called negative shape. In this case, of course, figure and ground become interchangeable.

While the negative space, or shape, is not always of equal interest with the positive figure, it is an important part of any composition. It is often the negative space that provides an illusion of depth, achieved by shading or the devices of perspective (see Chapter 5). In Figure 83 there is a sense of overlapping because of the strong vertical line that seems to shave off the edge of the dark form at right. This line serves

82

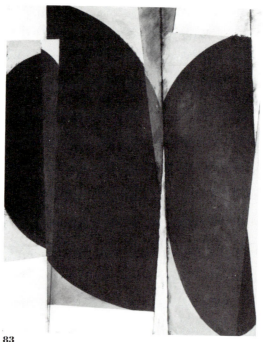

83

another important purpose. By dividing the total rectangle of the canvas into two related rectangles, *it relates the composition to the ground upon which it is painted*. Four smaller rectangles throughout the composition elaborate upon the theme, just as a musician relates variations in a composition to a basic theme.

By now it is obvious that the four categories of shape overlap and interact; this, too, is an important aspect of shape relationships. When a shape echoes shapes found in nature without actually representing them, it is called *biomorphic* (from the Greek "life" and "form"). The shapes in the *Medusa* (Fig. 69) and the shapes in Matisse's swimming pool (Fig. 81) could be considered biomorphic shapes. It is a term that could describe puddles and patterns of oil on water, configurations in clouds, and the shapes of glaciers. Such shapes are actually natural shapes but, out of context, would not necessarily be recognized as such. They might be classified as abstractions of natural shapes or even as nonobjective. Like the geometric shapes in nature, they become a part of the interrelationships that make both nature and art an organic continually changing process. Categories can only be considered as guides to identifying the stages in the process.

Mass

The categories applying to shape apply to mass as well. Mass in its actual three-dimensional entity is one of the most important elements of design.

Natural Masses

Probably the natural mass most widely used by artists has been the human figure. Beginning with stiff symbolic representations more

83. Robert Rector. *Charmed Dance.* 1986. Acrylic on canvas, 7′ × 5′7″ (2.14 × 1.71 m). Collection of Gremillion & Co. Fine Art Houston.

84. Michelangelo. *David.* 1501–04. Marble, height 18′ (5.48 m). Academy, Florence.

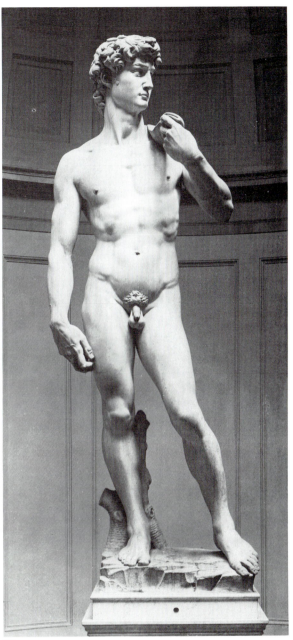

84

than four thousand years ago, it has flourished as a favorite subject through the centuries, reaching a pinnacle in the hands of Greek sculptors in the 4th century B.C. and, under their influence, culminating in the masterpieces of the Renaissance (Fig. 84). Sculptures of birds and animals have also played an important part in human expression, from the sacred cat of the Egyptians to the brass eagles topping many American flagpoles.

Natural masses are the raw materials of the gardener and landscape architect, who utilize the myriad shapes, colors, and textures of

85

plants and trees to create both natural and geometric designs. The proliferation of cities with their masses of metal and glass has brought new importance to small gardens and accent plantings that modify an otherwise austere environment with softened contours, bright colors, and the shapes and scents of nature (Fig. 85).

Geometric Masses

If the square is basic to construction because of its equilibrium, the *cube* must be considered the most stable of all masses. This is no doubt why sculptor Isamu Noguchi chose to stand it on its corner in his work in Figure 86. Placed foursquare in a plaza surrounded by tall rectangular buildings, a cube, even with a circle on one side, would hardly have attracted attention as a piece of sculpture. Tipped, it becomes a composition in diagonals that not only contrasts with its surroundings but intrigues the viewer with its challenge to gravity.

The cube is stable, but the *circle* is satisfying, symbolizing wholeness and eternity. The glass sculpture in Figure 87 shimmers with light, echoing the mass of the earth in its role as satellite. Even though it rests on a pedestal, it expresses the fundamental character of the sphere—ever mobile, always turning, never static.

85. Centennial Square, Victoria, B. C., Canada.

86. Isamu Noguchi. *Cube.* 1969. Steel and aluminum, painted and welded, height 28′ (8.53 m). Located in front of 140 Broadway, New York.

87. Pavel Hlava (in cooperation with the workshop of Miroslav Lenc, Czechoslovakia). *Satellite.* 1972. Blown crystal hemispheres, joined by welding, diameter 13¼″ (34.93 cm). Courtesy the artist.

86

87

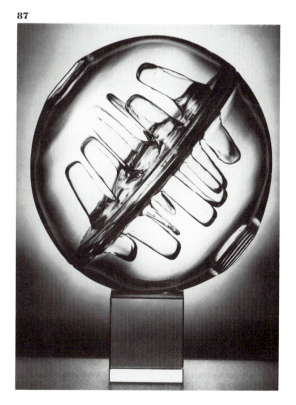

88

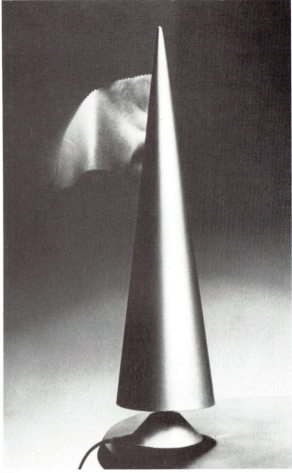

89

88. Magician's Pyramid,
Uxmal, Yucatán, Mexico.

89. Denis Santachiara.
Table lamp, *Maestrale*. 1986.
Sculptured, cone-shaped object;
the fan flutters a fabric flag,
illuminated by an internal light.
height 22″ (56 cm).
Mfr. Tribu, France.

90. Lino Sabattini.
Silverplated flower vases
designed for Argentina Sabattini,
Italy. 1974. Heights 14″ and 10½″
(35.56 and 26.67 cm).

91. Quartz crystals.

92. Peter Aldridge. *Arcus.*
Height 3½″ (8.9 cm);
width and depth 5″ (12.7 cm).
Steuben Glass, New York.

The *pyramid* has a long history as a monumental structure of religious significance. While in Egypt the pyramids were tombs for the pharoahs, civilizations from Southeast Asia to pre-Columbian America have built them as altars. Immensely stable from an engineering point of view, pyramids are fitting structures for monuments to eternity (Fig. 88).

We began our consideration of shape with three geometric shapes that expand to mass under varying conditions of perception: the square expanding to the cube, the triangle evolving into the pyramid, and the circle becoming a sphere. We now translate angles into curves and discover two more basic masses: the *cone*, the curvilinear counterpart of the triangle, and the *cylinder*, deriving from the square or rectangle.

Variations on the cone are often found in glass or pottery since it provides a solidly based form for fragile materials. Conversely, some of the finest old cut-glass goblets are inverted cones suspended on slim stems with solid bases. The table lamp in Figure 89 exploits the grace of the cone form in striking purity, varied only by the fluttering fabric flag, which is illuminated by an internal light.

The cylinder is so much a part of contemporary life that it would be difficult to identify all of its guises. From tree trunks to the loaded shelves of the supermarket, the cylinder is a medium for serving human needs. The so-called tin can, which is actually primarily of zinc, serves us soup and drinks, houses cleaning fluid and furniture polish. The simplicity of the silverplated vases in Figure 90 reminds us of the actual beauty of the form when lifted above our mundane acceptance of its utility.

Beyond the basic geometrical forms, nature offers, through crystallization, a rich system of masses whose facets may be square, triangular, or pentagonal (five-sided). Garnets, coal, and diamonds are only a few of the chemical elements and compounds that form in this way. Quartz, for instance, crystallizes in hexagonal prisms with intriguing and complex variations modifying the crystal form. (Fig. 91). This system by which separate masses, or *modules*, are joined together in nature in a rhythmic and unified manner offers a treasure of possibilities to the human designer (Fig. 92). The ancient Greeks found deep philosophical connotations in the fundamental relationship of solid geometrical forms to universal structure; in fact, Plato inscribed over the door of his school of philosophy the injunction: "Let no one unacquainted with geometry enter here."

90

91

92

93

93. Matisse.
Heads of Jeannette. 1910–13.
Bronze, heights 10⅜ to 24⅛"
(26.42 to 61.2 cm). Los Angeles
County Museum of Art (gift of the
Art Museum Council in memory of
Penelope Rigby, 1968).

94. Dale Chihuly.
Cobalt green macchia
with Cadillac yellow
lip wrap. 1986.
16 × 44 × 39⅓"
(41 × 112 × 99 cm).

Abstract Masses

Many contemporary sculptors work in abstract masses, simplifying and stylizing subjects into new forms. We can follow the abstraction process in three dimensions by studying a series of five heads by Henri Matisse (Fig. 93). The head at the far left is probably the most realistic interpretation. As the heads develop, the nose becomes larger, the forehead narrower, and the hair progresses from three ovoid masses to a simple cap perched above a large ear. The artist has gradually intensified certain features, probably because the relationships of the masses interested him, but also perhaps because in this way he captured the essence of the model, as he saw her, or possibly the essence of Woman.

Nonobjective Masses

Blown glass is a natural medium for nonobjective masses, being organic by its very nature, changing with each breath and twist of the blowpipe, being shaped by its own weight and colored by its substance. The skilled glassblower forces the material to assume specific shapes and masses, but of itself it relates to all manner of mythical or imagined creatures. In Figure 94 Dale Chihuly has utilized this natural quality to form a nonobjective mass that he gives a specific title, a title that in itself suggests nonobjective natural masses. Without the title, the viewer might easily see some entirely different connotation. In this

78 *The Elements of Design*

94

fact lies the importance of nonobjective or biomorphic shapes and masses: the viewer experiences an aesthetic reaction directed by his or her personal experiences and associations.

Mass and Movement

Movement is indigenous to mass. Mountains change with storms and avalanches, masses of foliage move with every breeze, altering in form and color as the seasons pass. Designers who work in mass allow for movement with sculptures meant to be climbed upon, and buildings whose entire reason for being is the continual movement of life that passes through them. Theater and the dance consist of moving masses changing form continuously throughout a production. Landscape design is one of the most organic fields of design in mass, planning for the growth and replacement of plants from season to season.

    Among the most impressive natural masses are the crashing waves of the ocean, which have inspired generations of painters to attempt to capture their power. A wave is a definite mass, yet a second after the image in Figure 95 was captured, no single molecule of water would still have been in the same place and the wave would have taken an entirely different form. Thus mass, like shape, is continually changing, forming new relationships and often unexpected patterns. Shape and mass are a carving of space, another vital element of design that we will now consider.

95

Summary

In design, shape and mass are inseparable, for mass is the three-dimensional manifestation of shape. Both can be considered as falling into one of four categories: *natural*, *geometric*, *abstract*, and *nonobjective*. Shape is actually a carving of space. This creates positive shape and negative shape, which together may result in *figure-ground ambiguity*. Movement is indigenous to both shape and mass, whose very character implies change and life and an organic relationship with space.

For Further Exploration

95. Russell Dixon Lamb. *Rising Wave*. Photograph.

1. From bright-colored construction paper cut two identical natural shapes approximately 4 to 5″ in length or diameter. Ar-

range one of them on a 9 × 12″ sheet of black construction paper, studying the negative shape created around it. Now add the second shape and move the two about until you have arrived at the most interesting negative shapes around them. Paste in place.

2. From colored construction paper cut 6 identical geometric shapes approximately 1″ in diameter or length. Arrange them in as many ways as possible on a 9 × 12″ sheet of black construction paper. Fit them together to form larger shapes, then separate them to create negative shapes between and around the positive shapes. Experiment in every way possible, paying special attention to the interaction of positive and negative shapes. When you feel you have arrived at the most interesting arrangement, paste the positive shapes in place. (Refer to Fig. 73.)

3. Cut two abstract shapes from construction paper, each shape approximately 4 or 5″ in length. Move them about on a 9 × 12″ sheet of *white* drawing paper, but also try overlapping them, noticing the new shapes that are created. Paste them in place in an overlapped position in which they form the most interesting shapes.

4. From a magazine cut out four images—a person, a piece of furniture, a car, book, and so on. Now turn them over and arrange them in different ways on a 9 × 12″ sheet of black construction paper, seeing them as abstract or nonobjective shapes and not as their original images. When you have arrived at an interesting composition, draw around the clippings on colored construction paper, forming their shapes without association to the original images. Paste in place on the black construction paper.

CHAPTER FIVE

Space

All physical things exist in space. The character of space has engaged thinkers from Euclid to Einstein, and many theories have been advanced as to its reality and extent. For the visual designer, space is not only the vehicle in which shapes and masses exist; it is also a determining element in their aesthetic form. In many cases, space working in and through a design establishes its essential character.

Visual design is concerned primarily with three types of space: *pictorial*, *illusionistic*, and *actual*.

Pictorial Space

Pictorial design is design related to a flat surface, as in the cutout paper silhouette in Figure 96. The space here is a matter of width and height; although we do not see borders, the design itself is contained within obvious dimensions. The design could lie flat or it could be mounted on a stiff backing for hanging, but the dimensions would remain the same—there is no attempt at depth or thickness. Although at first glance the formal pattern appears to be entirely a silhouette, closer observation reveals scattered accents in which the white background is allowed to become a part of a flower, a pattern in a leaf, or the texture on the urn. This, of course, is closely related to our discussion in Chapter 4 of positive and negative shapes, for the flow of space throughout a design takes on shapes that can be characterized as shape or space, and in reality are both. The complexity of the design in Figure 96 makes the actual negative shapes less important than the sense of space flowing throughout the positive pictorial space.

We have mentioned Henri Matisse's fascination with shapes in connection with his *Swimming Pool* but his approach to the matter of shape and space bears further examination. After a long and successful career as a painter, when he became too ill to stand at an easel, Matisse devoted his time entirely to the matter of space relationships. Choosing colors he wanted to use, he would have an assistant paint sheets of paper, after which he would cut, arrange, and finally paste the varied shapes on colored backgrounds, having rearranged them endlessly until the spatial relationships were exactly as he wanted them. The result was a series of striking designs, some of which were later interpreted in walls of ceramic tile. For Matisse, however, the importance lay in the experimentation, which he called "sculpting with color," cutting the paper away much as a sculptor chisels away

96. C. Schwizgebel.
Cut-paper silhouette from
Switzerland. c. 1950.
11½ × 7⅔″ (29 × 19.5 cm).
Schweizerisches Museum für
Volkskunde, Basel.

97. Henri Matisse.
The Parakeet and the Mermaid.
1952–53. Paper cutout with gouache,
11½″ × 25′4¼″ (3.37 × 7.73 m).
Six parts. Stedelijk Museum,
Amsterdam.

96

97

stone, until the shapes and the space flowing through them produced a unified result (Fig. 97).

Implied Space

The cut paper design in Figure 96 is self-contained, without borders. However, when a design is planned for a specified area, as in the case of a poster or book cover, designers sometimes break through the restrictions of the area by *implying* the use of space beyond. Let us consider the possibilities of the catalogue cover in Figure 98. Assuming that a standard size has been determined for the catalogue, the designer could approach the project in various ways. The size of the catalogue is the pictorial space allotted, and the message is a simple one consisting of four words. The designer has selected a shape from the exhibit to serve as a representative form. The problem now is

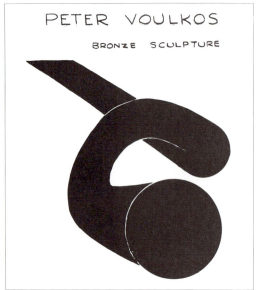

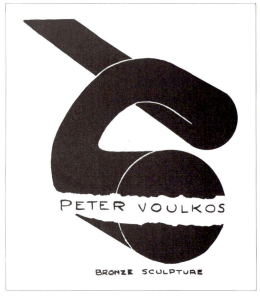

98

98. Three possible space
relationships for the design
of a catalogue cover for the
Peter Voulkos Sculpture Exhibition
at the San Francisco Museum of
Modern Art in 1973.

99. Harry Murphy. *Catalogue Cover.*
1973. Printed graphics,
10 × 10″ (25.4 × 25.4 cm).

simply a matter of space relationships. The words can be shaped into a vertical ribbon, a block, or a broad horizontal band. The sculptural form can be placed at any point within the allotted space. Three possibilities are explored in Figure 98, any one of which would have fulfilled the purpose of the design. However, designer Harry Murphy leaped beyond these possibilities by carrying the predominant shape to the very edge of the catalogue cover, and therefore, we assume, beyond (Fig. 99). This assumption piques our curiosity. What does the sculpture really look like and how far does it extend beyond our vision? The cover leads us into the exhibit because we are curious, not only about this one piece but because we know there is an entire ex-

Peter Voulkos

Bronze Sculpture

99

hibit of similar pieces to be seen. We want to see what is in the space beyond our vision. This treatment of space is known as *implied space*.

The uses of implied space reach far beyond the field of poster design. Auguste Renoir has made masterly use of it in his painting *La Première Sortie* (The First Evening Out) in Plate 6 (p. 121). Renoir's interpretation of space was one of the ways in which he expressed the influence of the French Impressionists, whose most notable rebellion was obvious in their use of color to imply diffraction of light. The refusal to contain the subject matter of a painting within the conventional four borders was another startling innovation. In Plate 6 the action is not contained at all but is simply a vignette of a world that

100. *Geese of Medum.*
Egyptian, c. 2700 B.C.
National Museum, Cairo.

101. *Harold Swearing Oath,*
detail of Bayeux Tapestry.
c. 1073–88.
Wool embroidery on linen;
height 20″ (51 cm),
overall length 231′ (70.4 m).
Former Palace of Bishops,
Bayeux, France.

glitters beyond, a part of the larger space that is *implied*. Our attention is focused on the young girl, the central character, who is experiencing her first evening at the theater, and we sense her excitement and suspense as she watches something that we cannot see. Sitting erect, holding her bunch of violets, she is fully realized pictorially, but the rest of the audience and indeed the theater itself are implied by blurred outlines just as they would be if we were present at the scene and focusing our vision on the girl.

Illusionistic Space

Pictorial space is concerned with shapes and space interacting on a flat surface with no sense of depth implied. Such space relationships work beautifully for allover patterns on fabric and wallpaper and for decorative panels in various media. However, when artists began portraying *scenes* on a flat surface there arose the question of depicting depth, of establishing one vertical plane behind another. This has been accomplished in several ingenious ways.

Overlapping

Artists discovered early that placing one figure in front of another immediately pushed the one behind back into space. There are indica-

100

101

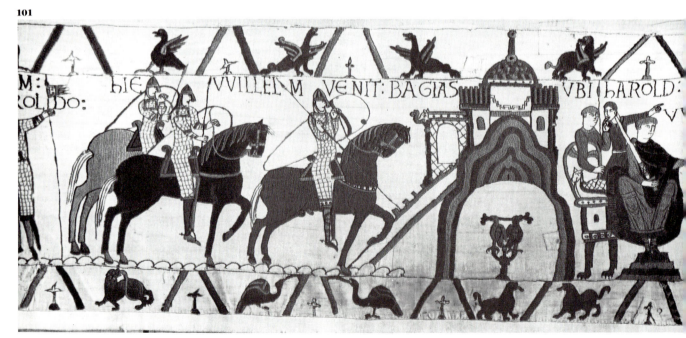

tions of this discovery as far back as 10,000 B.C. when Paleolithic cave drawings of running animals placed the legs of one deer or bison overlapping the animal behind it. By 2700 B.C. the Egyptians had mastered the technique to the point of using it regularly in their wall paintings and carvings. In Figure 100 the overlapping geese seem perfectly natural, even modern, in treatment.

One of the most charming examples of overlapping occurs throughout the Bayeux Tapestry (Fig. 101). Actually an embroidered cloth banner, this historic document depicts the Norman invasion of England, portraying episodes leading up to the Battle of Hastings and its aftermath, all arranged *sequentially*, so that the visitor walking around the gallery where it is mounted on the wall, can "read" the story. Said to be the work of the ladies of the court of William the Conqueror, it is rich in detail, from the loading of boats on the French side of the English Channel to the flight of the English at the end of the battle. With so much activity, the use of overlapping was the only possible way to include all the necessary elements, establishing vertical planes.

Tiering

Looking closely at the Bayeux Tapestry, we note another interesting characteristic. The main action of the banner takes place in the wide band in the center, but at top and bottom there are narrower bands, both filled with figures. In these bands are birds and cats and dogs of various types. However, in the bottom band below the battle scenes (not shown in Fig. 101) are fallen bodies. Here the top band represents objects in the sky or behind the line of battle, whereas the bottom band shows the fallen victims who would be in the foreground. Thus, degrees of distance are indicated by tiers or layers, in which the fore-

102

103

ground action is at the bottom and the distance recedes as the eye travels upward.

Tiering or *layering* is not actually a primitive method for denoting distance. It follows the natural sequence by which we focus our eyes on the ground where we are standing, and raise them gradually to take in the immediate surroundings, or *foreground*, the *middle distance*, and finally the far horizon. Children find this a logical way to depict distance as do many adult artists all over the world (Fig. 102). Even more deliberate is the use of layers by Persian artists. The miniature in Figure 103 is a sophisticated design in which the figures are beautifully executed, and the many areas of ornamentation are rich in intricate pattern. If there is no feeling of a third-dimensional depth it is not from lack of ability to depict it. Western conceptions of space depiction are the outgrowth of the Renaissance in Europe; other parts of the world use different methods, which they find entirely satisfactory. The Islamic artist who painted the scene in Figure 103 made no effort to show the paving blocks receding toward the rear. To the Western eye they appear vertical, as does the rug upon which the upper figures are sitting. Still, we know that the lower figures are in front of the Turquoise Palace, while the higher ones sit in a recess within it. The use of tiers tells us exactly what the artist wants us to know.

Size

The Bayeux Tapestry (Fig. 101) and the painting by Nauja (Fig. 102) use still another means of depicting distance, the apparent diminution

102. Nauja of Rankin Inlet. Painting. 1966. Hudson's Bay Company Library, Winnipeg, Manitoba.

103. Mahmud Muzahib or Follower. *Bahram Gur in the Turquoise Palace on Wednesday,* page from the Khamsa of Nizami. 16th century. Illuminated manuscript. Metropolitan Museum of Art. New York (gift of Alexander Smith Cochran, 1913).

104. Denison Cash Stockman. Cover design from *Urban Spaces,* by D. K. Specter (New York Graphic Society Books, 1974).

104

of size as objects move farther from the viewer. In the center portion of the segment of the tapestry shown, the two conferring men are considerably smaller than the figure of William the Conqueror seated on his ceremonial chair, sword in hand. This could be the conventional symbolism of artists in all ages in which the important figure is larger than the rest. However, we note that the men in the boat pushing away from shore are also smaller than the figures surrounding William and smaller than the men on horseback at the left. There can be little doubt that the figures are growing smaller as they recede into the distance. It is because of this same diminution of size that the painting by Nauja is so convincing. Even with the use of tiering, this landscape lies flat and stretches into the distance because the reindeer and the people in the foreground are larger than the ones in the middle distance, where the much smaller dogs contribute to the illusion. More important, there is a gradual progression of size in the hills or islands, which leads the eye quite naturally from front to back.

Lest we think of the various devices mentioned above as predecessors to the use of perspective (which we will examine shortly), let us look now at the cover design by Dennis Stockman in Figure 104. This is a contemporary design of considerable impact and certainly one with an original approach. The vantage point above the crowd adds to the effect of three-dimensional space, as does the way the figures seem to move across the cover in front of the type. However, Stockman also uses tiering for indicating space. The figures at the bottom of the design seem to be directly under us, since we are practically looking at the tops of their heads. As the eye moves toward the upper edge of the composition, the figures move farther away simply because we see them from the side, in greater length. Actually, this is a reversal of the usual diminution of size as figures move into the distance. In this case, the closer figures are smaller because of *foreshortening*, the phenomenon by which objects tend to diminish in length when they are tipped toward the observer.

Perspective

Perspective is attributed to the Italian Renaissance architect Filippo Brunelleschi, who worked out a mathematical system for creating three-dimensional space on a two-dimensional surface. His contemporaries became devoted to the system, and the Western eye has accepted it for more than five centuries as the logical way to depict distance.

Linear Perspective As practiced in the Renaissance, linear perspective became an extremely involved mathematical science, yet the basic assumptions are simple. First, they took note of the apparently diminishing size of objects as they recede into the distance. Second, they considered the illusion that parallel lines receding into the distance seem to meet at some point. We have all noted this phenomenon in rows of telephone poles or fenceposts or in looking down a straight stretch of railroad track. The Renaissance artists termed the point of apparent meeting the *vanishing point*, and actually constructed vanishing points and lines receding to them as they laid out their paintings.

We can see the evolution of linear perspective by studying two Renaissance paintings. Giotto, considered by many to be the first great painter of the Renaissance, was seeking a way to depict depth in his work in Figure 105. He has mastered the idea of parallel lines slanting

105

105. Giotto. *Annunciation to Anna.* c. 1305–10. Fresco. Arena Chapel, Padua.

106. Piero della Francesca and Luciano Laurana. *View of an Ideal City* (detail). c. 1460. Tempera on panel, 1'11" × 6'6¾" (0.58 × 2 m). Galleria Nazionale delle Marche, Palazzo Durale, Urbino.

107. Perspective drawing analyzing composition of *View of an Ideal City.*

106

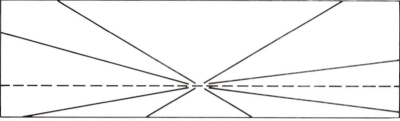

107

into the distance and has managed to place his figures in space with walls behind them. However, the space ends there, and the effect is one of figures in a box or on a stage set. A hundred and fifty years later Italian painters were producing elaborate studies like the one in Figure 106, in which involved series of buildings and arches, towers and cupolas, colonnades and paving blocks, were deliberately constructed to demonstrate the artist's mastery of perspective. The diagram in Figure 107, though simple, shows the kind of framework on which such works were based. Lines converging on the vanishing point formed the basis for every kind of architectural elaboration.

Space and Light The relationships inherent between space and light are sometimes placed under the heading of *atmospheric* or *aerial* perspective. This aspect considers only one of the ways in which space and light are related—the manner in which human perception sees objects in the distance in less detail and in more muted colors than objects that are close. This effect is caused by two factors: the softening quality of the body of air intervening between object and viewer, and the inability of the human eye to distinguish clearly forms and colors at a distance. Atmospheric perspective is employed by artists' attempts to duplicate this reality by a progressive graying and blurring as the composition recedes into the distance. This means colors are softened by lightening the value and are grayed by modifying the hue (see Chap. 7). The quality of lightness or darkness, brightness or grayness, is known as *tonality*, and it is a particularly effective tool for the landscape painter (Fig. 108).

Space can be depicted in the opposite way as well, however, by highlighting a center of interest and implying receding distance by surrounding areas of darkness. Rembrandt has made this an effective

108

109

108. J. M. William Turner.
Dido Building Carthage. 1815.
5′1½″ × 7′5½″ (1.54 × 2.28 m).
National Gallery, London.

109. Rembrandt.
The Presentation in the Temple.
1631. Panel,
24 × 18⅞″ (60.96 × 47.94 cm).
Royal Cabinet of Paintings,
Mauritshuis, The Hague.

110. Pieter de Hooch.
Interior with Card Players.
1638. Oil.
30″ × 26½″ (76.20 × 67.31 cm).
Buckingham Palace.

110

means in many of his works. In Figure 109 he uses it for religious drama. The central figures are bathed in a mystical glow while the less important figures blend into a background rich in deep color. Here great *physical* space is not necessary, but the lighting creates *symbolic* space, not only behind the figures but also above them, where, in the original work, the arches of the temple are barely discernible.

Still another means of relating space and light was employed by the Dutch painters of the 17th century. Instead of highlighting the center of interest, they flooded the entire room with sunlight, even conveying the feeling of sunshine pouring in through doors and windows (Fig. 110). The people who become the focal point are rendered partially sunlit and partially in shadow, providing dark accents to contrast with the pervading feeling of air and light.

Actual Space

Pictorial space implies space that is the product of the skill of the artist, in relating shape and space with an aesthetic or pictorial result. *Illusionistic* space tells us clearly that the artist has provided the sense of space and motion through various devices, some subtle and some highly scientific, but creating perceptual illusions nonetheless. *Actual*

111

space is concerned with three-dimensional works, in which space is a real and tangible part of the design. This may mean pottery, in which the inner space is often the main reason for its being; or jewelry, in which an airy sense of space is integral to the design; or it may concern sculpture, in which positive and negative space interact to create the form of the work. It may also mean architecture, in which existing space is enclosed in such a way that it serves the needs of the people who live and work within it.

In the sculpture in Figure 111 we are aware at once of the negative spaces because of the circles that dominate the design. From the circles the observer's eye follows the winglike forms, soaring up and dipping down, interpreting in a personal way the title the sculptor has given to the work. It is the figure leaning against the sculpture that provides us with the ultimate realization of what the sculptor had in mind. This is not a work to be viewed from a distance. One walks up to it and through it, sits on it and *feels* it; only then does the viewer experience the full meaning of the space flowing through and around it.

Space, Time, and Motion

If all things exist in space, we must expect them to move about within it. We experience this in parks and plazas, where spaces are designed for human enjoyment with ponds and flower beds, paths and sweeping lawns. These spaces require time for appreciation; they are planned for the pleasant expenditure of time. It also takes time to walk through a building. Visitors to the great European cathedrals find themselves returning again and again in order to experience the

111. Hans Van DeBovenkamp. *Mariner's Gateway.* 1986. White epoxy paint on Cor-ten steel. Height, width, depth 30′ (9.15 m). Haverstraw Marina, New York, Circle No. 11.

112. Staircase and foyer of Metropolitan Opera House, Lincoln Center, New York City.

113. Augustin Hernandez. Hernandez House. Mexico City.

112

113

full impact of the impressive spaces with their woodcarving, stone
sculpture, stained glass, and other treasures. A business building also
requires time.

 Perhaps the most exciting experience of public space comes in a
major opera house. Such a building is designed to heighten the sense
of anticipation by providing glamour and an aura of luxury from the
moment one enters (Fig. 112). Especially at night, with crystal chandeliers sparkling and lighted fountains shimmering, one lingers, climb-
ing the richly carpeted staircase slowly, absorbing this eloquent stage
setting in which the viewer, as a member of the audience, is about to
become a living part of the performance.

 Smaller-scale architecture can also stimulate anticipation. The
house in Figure 113 seems to have been sculpted rather than built,
and it gives the viewer a feeling of curiosity as to what the interior
spaces will reveal. Its complex of shapes, curves, spaces, and hollows
would offer a fascinating adventure to anyone walking through.
Looking at this particular view, we can realize that if the photographer

114

had stood just a few feet to either side of the present vantage point, the spaces might be entirely different. The house was designed for a woman who collects shells as a hobby, and its swooping curves and interesting arcs seem to echo the configuration of a shell (Fig. 114). The element of time is important in appreciating such a house and certainly movement is a vital part of the experience. The viewer must linger and *experience* the spaces, feeling their flow and rhythm rather than merely viewing them.

Contemporary Concepts of Space

We have explored devices for conveying space and distance that have been used over thousands of years in all parts of the world. If we were to make a survey of the last century we would find just as many concepts, ideas, and experiments developed by artists seeking new ways of expressing age-old realities. For centuries the linear perspective of the Renaissance was considered to be the ultimate solution to conveying three dimensions on a two-dimensional surface, but in the 20th century artists began to question whether this was even ethical, much less the ultimate goal of the artist. If one is going to work on a two-dimensional surface, why violate the integrity of the surface by creating illusions, even deceptions? Such reasoning has led to many approaches and innovations.

Ellen K. Levy is one contemporary painter who has found a personal area in which to work and has invented appropriate forms for it. Intrigued by outer space, she studied astronomy, visited observatories, and was commissioned as a painter by NASA, where she was captivated by the aspiring spirit of the space program. In Figure 115 we see her work entitled *January 28, 1986*, the date of the explosion of *Challenger*. In this personal expression of a national tragedy, she uses geometric masses and other forms, painted according to the laws of perspective but seemingly weightless, falling through space in confused disorder. She states that the forms she uses have multiple identities, their shapes emerge and later dissolve like passing thoughts. Still, one cannot help noticing the giant question mark that slices through the composition and the rigid vertical form that could be a launching tower. In painting outer space, she has used two-dimensional space in a personal way, exemplifying the contemporary attitude of exploiting traditional devices as a means to individual experimentation.

Summary

Visual design is concerned with three types of space: *pictorial, illusionistic,* and *actual.* Pictorial space is related to a flat surface in which space flows through positive and negative areas with no effort to depict depth or distance. *Illusionistic space* attempts to create the illusion of three dimensions on a two-dimensional surface. Devices used for this purpose are *overlapping, tiering, diminishing size,* and *perspective.* Space and light are closely allied in the work of painters. *Actual space* concerns three-dimensional works such as pottery, sculpture, and architecture. Space, time, and motion are all closely related in three-dimensional works.

114. Trumpet shell from the Philippine Islands.

115. Ellen K. Levy. *January 28, 1986.* 1986. Casein on panel, 5′ × 2′6″ (1.53 × 0.76 m). NASA Collection.

115

For Further Exploration

1. From gray construction paper, cut 12 shapes resembling flying
    birds, all identical and about 1½″ long. Place before you a
    9 x 12″ sheet of white paper and look at it for several minutes,
    thinking of it as space, infinite space, outer space, whatever
    connotations come to mind. Now arrange the bird shapes in
    this space, singly, in groups, thinking of them as soaring with
    space circulating about them. When you have arrived at the
    arrangement that signifies movement through space in your
    own mind, paste them on.

2. Cut similar shapes from white paper but make some of them larger and some smaller so that there are at least four different sizes. On a 9 x 12″ sheet of gray construction paper, move the bird forms about in the same way as in Project #1 but be aware of the diminishing sizes and the effect it has on the overall sense of space. The small ones should give you a feeling of being higher and farther away. Spend plenty of time studying the effect, then paste them on in the way that seems to achieve the desired sense of distance. (Refer to Figure 97.)

3. On a 9 x 12″ sheet of white paper, draw a horizontal line from side to side and three inches down from the top edge. Label the line "horizon line." Two inches in from the right side make a dot and label it "vanishing point." At the lower left, 2″ from the bottom of the page and 2″ in from the side, draw a fencepost extending upward 2″ high. From the top and bottom of the post draw slanting lines that converge at the vanishing point. Now draw a second post an inch further along the converging lines. Establish a point halfway up its height and draw a slanting line from the top of the first post through this midpoint of the second post. The diagonal will strike the bottom converging line. At this point draw a third upright fencepost. Square off the tops and bottoms of the posts to make them look like fenceposts, then continue with the exercise, drawing short slanting lines from the top of each succeeding post through the midpoint of its neighbor until you have a row of posts extending to the horizon line. You will now have demonstrated one of the fundamental exercises in linear perspective: the posts diminish in size and grow closer together with mathematical precision as they approach the horizon line.

CHAPTER SIX

Texture

Texture involves the tactile sense, the sense of touch. As infants we touch before we see, and through the years the role of texture in our lives remains a vital one. People react to textures in different ways and much of the interest and livability of our environment results from its variety of texture.

Texture and pattern are inevitably intertwined. A pinecone has a distinct pattern and also a texture that *feels* rough to the hand. A patterned fabric gives us a *visual* sense of texture, making us "feel" surface variations even when none exist to the touch. In a design sense, pattern is created when a unit is repeated, whether the unit is felt or seen (Fig. 116). A unit thus repeated as a thematic element becomes a *motif.*

116

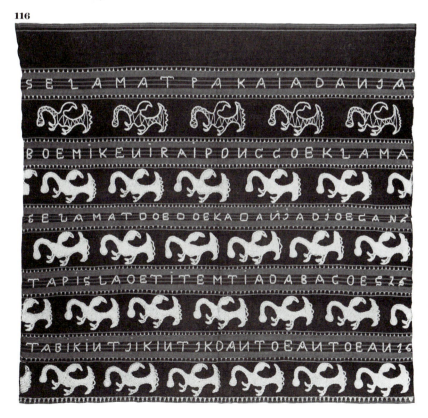

116. Tapis (ceremonial skirt), c. 1900–1925. Lampong District, Sumatra, Indonesia. Silk and cotton ground with couched metallic embroidery, 3′10″ × 4′1½″ (1.17 × 1.26 m). Atlantic Richfield Corporate Art Collection.

117

Numerous adjectives describe textures—rough, smooth, prickly, fuzzy, grooved, bumpy, and so on. Because of the psychological element that makes us "feel" textures that we cannot actually sense with our fingers, we make a major distinction between *tactile* and *visual* textures. All other descriptions of surface quality fall within these two main categories.

Actual changes in plane that can be felt by the fingers result in *tactile textures,* whereas variations in light and dark on smooth *or* unsmooth surfaces produce *visual textures.* A chunk of porous lava rock has definite tactile texture; if we pass our fingers over it, we can feel bumps and hollows. A smooth granite pebble also has texture, but it is more a visual texture resulting from flecks in the composition of the stone. Similarly, a glaze on pottery may be smooth to the touch yet be textured to the eye by fragments of chemical oxides suspended in the glaze (Fig. 117).

Textures are so much a part of our environment that we generally take them for granted. The clothes we wear, the homes in which we live, and the world in which we move are all a collection of textures. The textures of different foods add immeasurably to the pleasure of eating, and good cooks make use of that fact, adding crisp croutons to soups and salads, smooth sauces to fibrous vegetables, and crunchy nuts as toppings for desserts.

Tactile Textures

Tactile textures in nature have long been a matter of survival. Scales, whether on dinosaurs or fish, provide protection while allowing for movement, much as the wearing of chain mail fortified centuries of warriors. The mountaineer's life depends literally on the projections of rough rock with which he or she can gain a foot- or handhold. The grooved bark of trees provides sustenance for birds through the insects that inhabit the crevices, and the roughness of root and hollow log make it possible for small animals to construct shelters.

Few human textures are as rugged as those found in nature, but Figure 118 demonstrates an extremely rough texture that has become

117. David Shaner.
Pillow Pot. 1985. Stoneware, crystalline glaze, handbuilt; 5 × 11 × 11″ (12.7 × 27.9 × 27.9 cm).

118. Cesar (Cesar Baldaccini).
The Yellow Buick. 1961. Compressed automobile, 4′11½″ × 2′6¾″ × 2⅞″ (1.51 × .78 × .8 m). Collection, The Museum of Modern Art, New York (gift of Mr. and Mrs. John Rewald).

a part of contemporary human life. The crushing of obsolete automobiles into disposable blocks of metal has solved a problem that reached major proportions as junk car lots proliferated on the perimeters of cities and towns all over the United States. This particular example was displayed as a work of art in the 1960s but its counterparts are no longer novel. What *is* novel is that the texture is not actually as rough as it appears. Running one's fingers over it would inevitably result in a feeling of smooth metal in some areas, a *tactile* smoothness, to be sure, but not what one would expect from the appearance of the piece. It is not the metal itself that actually creates the texture but the deep shadows of the crevices resulting from the crushing process. The visual element thus becomes as powerful as the tactile one, though psychologically we feel that the texture is unmistakably tactile.

Tactile textures are nearly always visual as well. Irregularities in a surface cast shadows, and roughness becomes immediately obvious. There are exceptions, however. A piece of marble may look smooth

118

119. Nobuo Sekine.
Phases of Nothingness—Cone
1972. Black granite,
height 11¼″ (30 cm).
Courtesy Tokyo Gallery.

120. Philip Cornelius.
Covered Jar. 1981.
Charcoal-glazed stoneware,
height 12″ (30.48 cm). Courtesy
Marcia Rodell Gallery, Los Angeles.

121. Fragment of *salalua*,
tapa cloth skirt from the
Futuna Islands. Bark cloth,
paper mulberry. Collected by
E. G. Burrows, 1932. Bishop Museum
(Division of Ethnology), Honolulu.

until we run our fingers over it, discovering ridges and hollows undiscernible to the naked eye. Similarly, some textiles *feel* more interesting than they look. Weavers rely heavily on the textures of fibers for the design quality of their work, speaking of the "hand" of a textile, which may have considerably more character than a casual glance reveals.

Japanese sculptor Nobuo Sekine created several works dramatizing contrast in texture, of which Figure 119 is an excellent example. Here a perfectly smooth cone of black granite rises from a base of roughness suggesting the raw material from which the cone emerged. The two sections blend, at the same time deriving greater interest from their contrast.

Handcrafted objects are particularly appreciated for the variety and warmth of their texture. The stoneware jar in Figure 120 has an individual quality that could not be duplicated. Its charm is partly the result of the material, but it emerges even more from the way in which the hands of the potter have worked. In addition, the glaze reminds us of geological formations after long weathering, and we feel the affinity of clay to the other materials of the earth.

119

121

120

122

123

People who live close to the earth are masters at producing fascinating textures. Native Americans of the Pacific Northwest wove textiles from the shredded bark of native cedar trees, using them for clothing, rugs, and blankets. People in the Pacific islands beat and steep the bark of the paper mulberry tree, dyeing it in distinctive patterns of tapa cloth (Fig. 121). The Incas of Peru made garments of brightly colored feathers (Fig. 122), and the Navajo rugs woven by natives of the American Southwest have become collectors' items for their distinctive patterns and earthy textures (Fig. 123).

Contemporary artists, on the other hand, create their own textures, often from unlikely materials. In Figure 124 the texture was the work of the artist in every sense, since it originated as ordinary phonograph records.

122. Inca feather tunic from Peru. c. 1100–1400. Feathers knotted on cords stitched to plain-weave cotton ground 5'11" × 2'9" (1.81 × .84 m). Los Angeles County Museum of Art (gift of Mr. and Mrs. William T. Sesnon, Jr., 1974).

123. Navajo rug. Garland's Navajo Rugs, Sedona, Arizona.

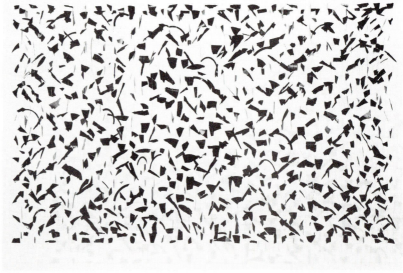

124

Visual Textures

The smoothness and frequent superb finish of visual textures makes them a natural choice for elegance. Palaces and impressive public buildings are replete with gleaming marble and inlaid floors, whose innate patterns and textures seem even more impressive when combined with satin-smooth surfaces. Cabinetmakers of the 17th and 18th centuries spared neither time nor effort in their painstaking efforts to create masterpieces, inlaying woods imported from all over the world for their decorative qualities.

Many of the most famous paintings of the Italian Renaissance are actually *frescoes*, wall paintings in churches or castles, in which the pigment is applied in a solution of lime water directly to the wet plaster of the wall. When the plaster has set, the painting is thus a part of the structure, and any tactile quality results from the structural surface of the wall itself (Fig. 125).

There are, of course, innumerable examples of visual texture that were not designed for lavish effect. The *batiks* of Indonesia have been a symbolic and cultural medium for more than four hundred years

125

126

and only recently have come to be appreciated by western eyes for the beauty of their patterns, achieved by applying wax to certain areas of cotton through successive baths of dye (Fig. 126).

Texture Through Structure

Many of the textures we have mentioned are a result of irregularities in material or surface application; others are deliberately planned for interesting effect. Some of the most fascinating textures result from structure, which in turn derives from imaginative use of certain materials.

Weavers use this knowledge as the keynote of their work. Fibers and yarns provide a vast assortment of widths, thickness, color, variations in "feel," and weight, and it is the manner in which the weaver combines them, seeing imaginative possibilities, that results in the ultimate textural quality of a work. The same may be said of stitchery. There is an entire repertoire of possible stitches, fibers, threads, and materials for backing, but the combination of these, perhaps with quilting or appliqué, forms the actual textural quality through its very structure. The tapa cloth in Figure 121 has distinctive visual texture but the tactile texture is also unique, the result of the mulberry bark and the structural beating that formed the fabric before it was dyed. Thus texture is often determined to a large degree by the designer's original choice of material and method of construction.

Texture Through Light

Although light obviously facilitates perception of any kind, the quality of tactile texture depends to a large extent upon its role in casting shadows. The Greeks developed this knowledge into consummate skill, enriching their temples with ornaments and moldings carefully

124. Mattie Berhang.
Costello Ferry (detail). 1985.
Broken record pieces suspended on monofilament, 5′9″ × 9′3″ × 1′2″ (1.76 × 2.83 × 0.36 m).
Carlo Lamagna Gallery,
New York.

125. Michelangelo.
Sistine Chapel, Rome.
The Creation of Man.
Fresco. 1508–12, restored 1987.

126. *Wadasan.* c. 1850.
Handdrawn batik on cotton.
Museum for Ethnology,
Rotterdam.

127

128

designed to capture the brilliant Mediterranean sunlight and drama-
tize it by casting deep shadows (Fig. 127). Even the fluting of columns
was a device for playing light against shadow (Fig. 128).

The architects of the Middle Ages installed magnificent stained-
glass windows in their cathedrals not only as agents of light but of
color. The panes, created by melting certain minerals and cooling
them to colorful solidity, poured a mosaic of brilliance into the dark
stone interiors, infusing the entire structure with a mystical quality. A
20th-century adaptation was used by Le Corbusier when he designed
his chapel of Notre-Dame-du-Haut at Ronchamp (Fig. 129). Both exterior and interior walls are rich in tactile texture, but even more interesting is the visual texture provided by the light admitted through

129

127. Epidaurus, Tholos,
Corinthian capital.
2′1½″ (64.8 cm) high.

128. Propylaea, Athens. West side.

129. Le Corbusier.
Notre-Dame-du-Haut.
Interior view of the south wall.
Ronchamp, France. 1950–55.

130. A "Minimal" all-white
living room designed by
Bill Ehrlich is nearly all smooth
in texture except for one
visual accent.

131. Hugh Hardy, designer.
Both visual and tactile textures
contribute to a feeling of warmth
and informality in this New York
City living room.

windows of varying size, shape, and placement. The windows themselves, set deep into thick walls, add interest to the surface and, throughout the day, as the light changes, texture the interior with mottled light. Some of the windows are painted with casual designs and inscriptions in red and blue, hinting at the effect of stained glass but in no way imitating it.

Textural Symbolism

Our associations with texture are never more personal than in interior design. Here they have acquired their own symbolism, which has much to do with our physical and emotional comfort. Generally speaking, smooth textures in an interior can seem cold, and when they predominate, as in a hospital, they may feel not only chilly but impersonal and ominous. Rough textures, on the other hand, seem close to the earth, and they have a warmth about them that makes most people feel at ease. The rooms in Figures 130 and 131 show extremes of textural treatment. In the first room everything is smooth, uncluttered, even impersonal. In the second room, what could be a bare loftlike room has been made warm and personal almost entirely through the use of tactile textures in brick, rattan chairs, plants, and the visual textures of bare wood and textiles brought to a focal point in a large dramatic painting. The variety of texture is as important as any specific texture, for the environment is enhanced by the changing sensations offered to the eye and hand.

For centuries the criterion of expert painting was the smoothness with which the artist rendered the subject of the work. There have been exceptions, however. Rembrandt was accused of crudeness when he laid paint on thickly to convey emotional impact and the suffering of his models, many of whom were Jews who had walked to Holland from Spain to escape the Inquisition. He found thick paint necessary to catch light that would contrast with the throbbing darkness that is characteristic of so much of his work (see again Fig. 109). Vincent van Gogh painted with concentrated frenzy, covering his canvases with

130

131

132   **133**

thick swirling strokes in an *impasto* that approximated three dimensions, not only to express his subject matter but to release the furious energy within himself (Fig. 132). (See also Fig. 291, p. 258.)

Twentieth-century artists have added textures to their work by actually imbedding materials in the paint. One of the best-known methods is known as *collage*, the French term for pasting. Beginning with playing cards and bits of paper, collage has evolved into a technique by which artists use all kinds of visual symbols (Fig. 133). Some artists even incorporate three-dimensional objects into their work, obscuring the dividing line between painting and sculpture. Such works are often referred to as *constructions*.

We have learned to appreciate as works of art many of the useful objects of other people around the world, some of which originated as symbolic artifacts. Violet Moore learned to make baskets from her grandmother and mother, and continues to gather, cure, sort, and dye the original materials, such as black or red fern, porcupine quills, and yellow moss (Fig. 134). Used for every sort of receptacle, the baskets of these Native Americans are also considered to have a soul, which is

132. Vincent van Gogh.
Cypresses (detail).
1889. Oil on canvas,
36¾″ × 29⅛″ (1.01 × 0.74 m).
Metropolitan Museum of Art,
New York (Rogers Fund, 1949).

133. Thomas Gruenebaum.
Soho Wall Series #9. 1986.
Mixed media on wood,
29½″ × 31½″ (74.9 × 80.0 cm).
Ingher Gallery, New York.

134. Baskets by Violet Moore.
Northwest California Yurok
basketry.

135. Detail drawing of
Ahir skirt. Embroidered cotton,
mirrors; 33″ (83.3 cm).
Kutch region of India.
UCLA Museum of Cultural History,
Los Angeles.

136. Ahir skirt.
Embroidered cotton, mirrors;
33″ (83.3 cm).
Kutch region of India.
Gift of William Lloyd Davis and
Mr. and Mrs. Richard B. Rogers.

134

expressed in the intricate patterns and magnificent textures incorporated into their making. "Baskets stay with you from the dawn of light until the last light touches you," according to tribal belief. "Immediately after you are born, you are placed in a basket. At death, a basket is put on your grave and a stake is driven into it in order to release the spirit."[3] Here, then, we see the ultimate symbolism of texture, in which the textures of the earth and of human life become inseparable.

Texture and Pattern

A single brick is textured, but a wall of textured bricks creates a pattern. This does not mean that repetition is a requisite of pattern. It is only one of the means by which pattern is created.

Pattern as Repetition

The design motif in Figure 135 was embroidered by Ahir women in northern India and displays diverse shapes and symbols. Alone, it is an interesting design. Repeated around the border of a skirt, however, it becomes an entirely different entity, a border pattern (Fig. 136).

[3] Pam Mendelsohn, "Northwest California Basketry," *Southwest Art*, June, 1983, pp. 57–63.

135

136

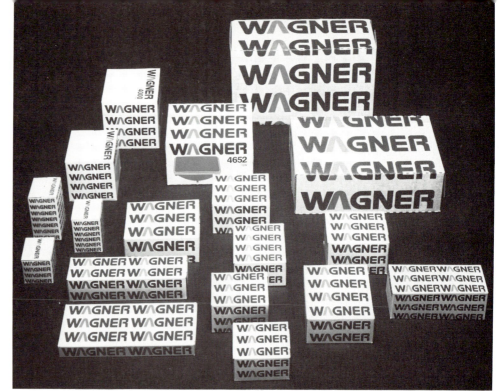

137

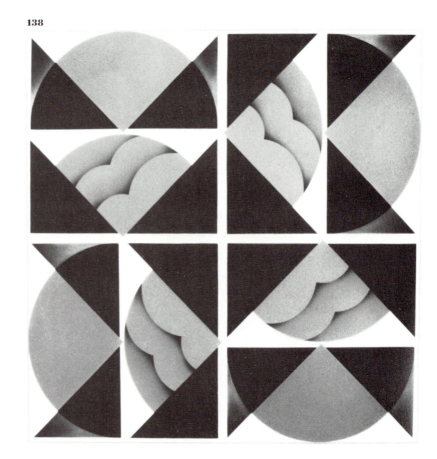

137. Package designs for marketing automotive and brake products for Wagner Division of McGraw Edison. Red and blue on a white background; measurements vary. Design: Ko Noda.

138. Shuji Asada. *Form-B.* 1980. Stencil dyeing (cotton), 7′2½″ × 7′2½″ (2.2 × 2.2 m).

139. Jane Hamilton-Merritt. *Norway Street.* 1976. Photograph.

140. Constantino Nivola. Mural façade of Covenant Mutual Insurance Building, Hartford, Conn. 1958. Sand-cast concrete relief, 30 × 110′ (9.14 × 33.53 m).

In an allover design, no single feature predominates. For that reason a repeated pattern lends itself to backgrounds such as wallpaper, fabrics, and decorative wrappings. It can also be effective as package design. Using only the name of the product in a distinctive type style with color contrast, such a pattern can fulfill two requirements: improving the appearance of the merchandise and impressing the name of the product on the mind of the buyer (Fig. 137).

An allover pattern gains interest when the motif is varied. The stencil-dyed cotton in Figure 138 uses a strong geometric unit but has changed the position of each of the four units shown, placing them in a clockwise rotation. Not only does this variation add interest; it also creates new design elements, such as the strong diagonals throughout and the diamond shape that forms a central focal point.

Many of the streets of Europe are patterned with cobblestones, carefully chosen as to size, shape, and color to produce intriguing patterns (Fig. 139). Drainage gulleys may be outlined in one size and shape of stone and sewer covers lie like the center of a flower in a radiating pattern. The basic units, the stones, are similar, and many of the motifs are repeated in different places, as in the stripes of different size and color of stones composing the streets outlining the buildings. Here again, there is repetition, but it is so varied that it could never be considered mechanical.

Pattern as Surface Design

Although 20th-century cities seldom exert such effort on their busy thoroughfares, texture and pattern are being appreciated increasingly for their ability to relieve stark walls of concrete, metal, and glass. In Figure 140 panels of relief sculpture (sculpture that is attached to a background) have been cast by pouring wet concrete into molds

139

140

formed by sand. The play of light over the textured surface, casting shadows wherever the texture protrudes, provides a lively pattern as well as a sense of kinship to the materials of the earth.

Interacting Patterns

Frequently there is an element of surprise in pattern. Units placed in repetition or in combination with other units over a large area inevitably create new units that even the designer may not have foreseen. Often these are the result of unpredicted negative space playing through the pattern. The wrought-iron screen in Figure 141 is composed of identical units fastened on vertical iron poles, and the shapes of the units are interesting. However, within the allover pattern, new shapes become apparent between the units, becoming ovoid shapes that change with the viewpoint. Seen in the illustration, against a light background, the pattern seems almost dominated by the negative shapes or spaces. Any artist who creates an allover design is, in fact, making two designs: the individual motif and the design that results from its repetition or combination with other motifs. Often the placement of motifs in relation to one another is a major decision of the designer. Any of the allover patterns shown above would change character if the motifs were placed at different angles or different distances from one another.

Texture and pattern are actually two aspects of the same element. Their variations and relationships represent one of the most basic

141. Wrought-iron lattice.
Werkkunstschule, Aachen, Germany.

human impulses, the need to decorate objects, the human body, and the environment in which we live.

Summary

There are two kinds of texture: *tactile,* which can be felt by the fingers, and *visual,* which is seen by the eye. Both overlap in many instances. A *motif* is a unit that is repeated to form a visual texture or *pattern.* Textures are created in many ways: by the use of textured materials; by the use of light, which casts shadows; and by the ways in which human hands manipulate materials. Textures have symbolism for us in the way we decorate our homes and in the ways we interpret textured surfaces such as paintings. Pattern and texture differ only in degree. A texture may be a pattern and pattern becomes visual texture. Pattern can be used as design in *repetition,* as *surface design,* and in *interacting patterns* that create new designs.

For Further Exploration

1. In a 3″ square, design a motif to be used in an allover design, based on either a natural or a geometric shape. Mark off a 9 x 12″ sheet of drawing paper into twelve 3″ squares and transfer the motif to each one, each in the same position. Outline with black drawing ink and a medium-heavy pen, filling in areas to add to the design quality. Study the effects and particularly the surprises arising from the combining of the same shape in an allover pattern.

2. Follow the instructions in #1 but place the motif in alternate rows upside down; in other words, in rows 1 and 3 place it as above but in rows 2 and 4 turn the motif upside down. Outline as before and fill in certain areas to emphasize lines and shapes that add to the design. If different solid areas are indicated as a result of the different arrangement, emphasize these. Compare the two allover designs, studying the variations and analyzing the differences. (Refer to Fig. 138.)

3. Cut a piece of 3-ply wood 15 x 36″ and edge it on all four sides with a 1″ strip of wood. Stain the board and trim a dark brown. On a piece of newsprint or other paper the same size as the wood, block out a nonobjective design, thinking in terms of textures as well as shapes. Visualize each shape as small pebbles or crushed gravel, sand, bits of bark, or seashells. Gather whatever materials are available and arrange them on the board according to your drawing, noting contrasts in color as well as in size of materials. When the design is well-balanced, with smooth areas balancing rough ones and a distribution of color and texture, glue the materials in place, using a water-proof glue.

4. Repeat #3 but use heavy poster board or matboard and create the composition entirely from visual textures: cloth, tissue paper (crinkled or otherwise), playing cards, and so on.

CHAPTER SEVEN

Color

Of all the design elements, color undoubtedly elicits the greatest emotional response. Although it is not necessary for the creation of a great work of art, color suggests a mood and depth of experience that cannot be achieved in any other way. We speak of the color wheel in the visual arts in much the way that we speak of the tonal scale in music. Like the basic notes of the musical scale that can be expanded into symphonies, colors can be combined in an unlimited number of ways and have great capacity to manipulate our emotions. Undoubtedly, color is one of the most powerful tools of the designer.

Color is both art and science. Physicists explain the abstract theories of color and its relationship to light, as well as the optical principles involved in color sensation. Chemists formulate rules for mixing and applying colors. Psychologists study emotional responses to specific colors. The artist needs to understand all these factors before developing a personal color symbolism with which to fulfill an aesthetic purpose.

Color and Light

Without light there can be no color. Things that we identify as being red, green, or orange are not innately those colors; we perceive them as such because of the action of light upon their surface.

What we call light represents only a small portion of the electromagnetic field, the part that is visible. The entire electromagnetic

142. This diagram of the electromagnetic field shows the portion of the spectrum that is visible to the human eye—in other words, what we call "light." A millicron is one thousandth of a micron which, in turn, is one millionth of a meter.

143. A ray of white light projected through a prism separates into the hues of the rainbow.

142

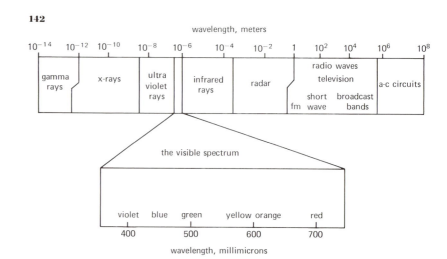

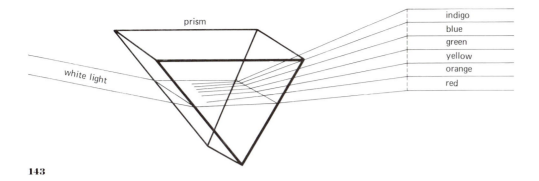

143

spectrum includes many frequencies, as shown in the diagram in Figure 142. The small segment that we see as light vibrates in varying wavelengths that cause the human eye to perceive different colors. The longest wavelength is seen as red, the shortest as violet or purple.

Although ancient Greek philosophers asserted that color is not a physical property but a matter of perception, it was not until 1666 that Isaac Newton produced scientific evidence of the fact. As an experiment, Newton directed a beam of sunlight into a glass prism. Since glass is denser than air, the light was refracted, or bent, as it passed through the prism. Newton expected this, but he did not expect the light to be dispersed into colors as it left the prism. The short waves in the light were refracted more and the long waves less, and as they emerged from the prism they arranged themselves systematically into the colors of the rainbow: indigo, blue, green, yellow, orange, and red (Fig. 143). There is no purple in the natural spectrum of color, but where the first and last colors, red and indigo, combine or overlap, the result is purple or violet. Realizing this, Newton joined the colors into a circle so the flow from tone to tone would be continuous, thus creating the first color wheel. After separating sunlight into its color components with the first prism, he used a second prism to reverse the action, and found that all the colors combined back again into white light. This established beyond doubt the fact that color is basically white light and further, that *in light*, all colors mixed together result in white.

Long before we are aware of color theory, most of us marvel at the sudden appearance of a rainbow, arching transparently across the sky in a full range of color (Pl. 7, p. 121). The appearance of a *double* rainbow is enough to send an entire neighborhood into a state of high excitement. Usually seen immediately after a shower, and in the quarter of the sky opposite to the sun, a rainbow is the result of the refraction, reflection, and dispersion of light in drops of water falling through the air. When only one rainbow is seen, the colors are arranged with red on the outside. This single bow is known as the brightest or primary bow. A double bow is known as the perfect rainbow, and the second arch, which is concentric with the first but above it, is called the secondary bow and has the colors arranged in reverse order and dimmer, due to a double reflection within the drops. Under certain conditions, a rainbow can be seen arching across a waterfall, reflecting the action of light upon the spray above the water.

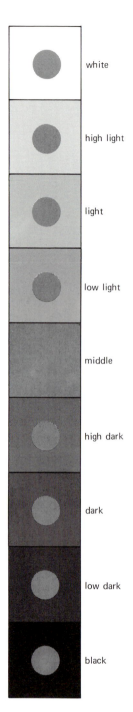

white

high light

light

low light

middle

high dark

dark

low dark

black

144

144. The gray scale shows variations in value from white to black. The circles in the centers are all middle value, although they seem different against lighter or darker backgrounds.

Additive and Subtractive Color

The mechanism by which surfaces produce color is not thoroughly understood, but it can be assumed that it has to do with the molecular structure of the surface, since inorganic compounds are generally colorless in solution and the hue of organic compounds can be changed by altering them chemically. Most colors seen in everyday life are caused by the partial absorption of white light. A surface we call red will absorb all the rays except those from the wavelength that produces red, so we perceive red. When light is totally absorbed by a surface we see black.

Refraction and Diffraction

Many factors influence the way in which light is absorbed or reflected. Light waves passing through the prism are *re*fracted, or bent, from their original course. Colors in a soap bubble or raindrop result from *dif*fraction, in which a wave of light, after passing the edge of an opaque or solid object, breaks or spreads out instead of continuing in a straight line. The blue of the sky is the result of the scattering of short-wavelength blue components of sunlight by tiny particles suspended in the atmosphere. A tree in the sunlight seems a different color on its shaded side, and its leaves display a tremendous variation in color, depending upon the way in which the light strikes them.

Light and Pigment

Additive color is color in direct light. This is a scientific theory and becomes highly complex, particularly when pursued with computerization, in which one color can be given thousands of variations and color relationships are altered and intensified.

Subtractive color is color in relation to pigment, or to any surface that absorbs wavelengths of color; in other words, to *reflected* light. This is the area that concerns the artist. It may be helpful to note a few distinctions between the two.

Plate 8, page 122, demonstrates the additive principle. In light, three colors are considered to be primary in that all other colors are derived from them. The three primaries in light are *red, blue,* and *green.* When these colors are combined, or overlapped, they form *secondary* colors: magenta from red and blue, cyan (a turquoise blue) from blue and green, and yellow from red and green. When all six of these colors are combined, as in the center of the rectangle, they add up to white light.

We see at once the difference between this approach and the experiences we have had with color in school projects. For one thing, red and green would never form yellow in paint or crayon. For another, no amount of paint mixed together, whatever its colors, is going to produce white paint. The most likely result would be a muddy gray or brown.

Plate 9, page 122, demonstrates the subtractive principle in which the process is reversed, and which comes closer to the reactions with which we are familiar. In this case, *yellow, cyan,* and *magenta* are considered primary colors. When they are overlapped, they do not add color, but *subtract* those wavelengths that we do not see. The result is that the overlapping colors look like the primary colors with which we began in Pl. 8. The process of subtraction is completed when all six of the colors are combined in the central rectangle. Here we do not have white, but black, which is actually the *absence* of all color.

The field of color experimentation is still very much alive, with possibilities enormously expanded by the computer. People who work professionally with color have strong personal feelings on the subject and many have developed individual theories and formulas to serve their needs. The history of painting is enlivened by groups of painters with innovative color theories, or with distinctive ways of seeing and using color.

Color Theory

For many years, students learned color theory on the basis of studies begun in the eighteenth century and culminating in the work of Herbert E. Ives. Ives devised a color wheel based on *red, yellow,* and *blue* as the *primary* colors (Pl. 10, p. 122), from which all other colors were derived. In mixing the primaries on Ives' wheel, one arrived at the *secondary* colors: green from yellow and blue, orange from yellow and red, violet from blue and red. Going a step further, one could mix a primary and a secondary color to produce a third group, known as *tertiary* colors: yellow-orange, orange-red, red-violet, violet-blue, blue-green, and yellow-green. When all of these colors are placed in such a way that they *modulate* into one another, the basic color wheel results.

Any color wheel is to some extent arbitrary. Ives designed another wheel for use in mixing dyes and pigments, and there are wheels that concern themselves with human vision and the sequence in which we see colors. There are wheels that use eight colors and others that use more than a hundred. There are also variations in the names given the same color. Orange on one wheel becomes yellow-red on another, or violet may become purple.

In 1912 Albert Munsell devised a color system that has been generally accepted as the most scientific of the systems in use. It has become a standard method of designating color for government agencies such as the National Bureau of Standards, as well as for systems of standards in Japan, Great Britain, and Germany. In this system, color is described in terms of three attributes: *hue, value,* and *chroma* (or intensity). There are five key hues: *red, yellow, green, blue,* and *purple* (Pl. 11, p. 122). Secondary hues thus become yellow-red, green-yellow, blue-green, purple-blue, and red-purple. Munsell's unique contribution lay in using a numerical scale to designate variations in value or lightness, and chroma or brightness, so any given color can be defined with precision. Because of the scientific accuracy of this system, we will focus our attention on the Munsell theory.

Color Properties

The color tree in Plate 12 (p. 123) demonstrates visually the properties of color, hue, value, and chroma, as Munsell understood them, and their interrelationships.

Hue is the name by which we identify a color. It refers to the pure state of the color, unmixed and unmodified as it is found in the spectrum. The hue red means pure red with no white, black, or other colors added. Hue is the basis for all color properties.

Value refers to the relative lightness or darkness of a color. It can best be understood by a study of the *gray scale* (Fig. 144). We show the scale with a center circle of the same value in each of nine blocks ranging from white to black. The average person can distinguish perhaps 30 or 40 gradations between white and black, although a person with high acuity (visual sharpness) might be able to see as many as 150 gradations. The colors on the gray scale have no hue and are therefore termed *achromatic*. The differences in the center circles are illusory, the result of the changes in background.

Every color has what is termed a *normal* value. This is the value of the hue when it is seen at its highest intensity. For instance, yellow is always very light when it is most intense and purple is always quite dark when it is most intense. Therefore the normal value of yellow is lighter than the normal value of purple. Normal values of red, green, and blue are closer to the middle value scale. The hues are represented in their normal values on the color wheel; however, hues at their normal value can themselves be arranged in gradations of value corresponding to the gray scale (Pl. 13, p. 123).

The reverse process, the conversion of colors into values of gray, occurs in black-and-white photography (Fig. 145). In general, values are less noticeable in color photographs and color reproductions of paintings than they are in black-and-white reproductions of a work, since intensity and hue are more diverting to the human eye.

145.

145. Art Malik, Tim Piggott-Smith, and Susan Wooldridge in a scene from the television production of *The Jewel in the Crown*.

Color values that are lighter than normal value are called *tints*. Those darker than normal value are *shades*. Thus, pink is a tint of red, and maroon is a shade of red. In mixing paints, the addition of white will lighten value and black will darken it; however since neither black nor white is actually a color, the addition of either to a color will lessen the chromatic value of that color.

Chroma, also known as intensity, indicates the brightness or dullness of a color. Colors that are not grayed, that are at their ultimate degree of vividness, are said to exhibit *full intensity*, as shown in Plate 14, page 123. Chroma is often the most difficult of the color properties for students to understand. One way of visualizing chroma is to imagine a jar of powdered pigment in any hue and a saucer of oil into which the pigment will be ground. The oil is poured into a *mortar*, a small sturdy jar such as chemists use, and the pigment is added to it, and ground thoroughly with a *pestle*, a small clublike implement, until it becomes a thin paste. When the first portion of color is added, the chroma is weak and dilute, but as the amount of pigment is increased, the hue becomes more intense. The oil becomes *saturated* with pigment and, therefore, with color. In this sense, *intensity, chroma,* and *saturation* may be considered to be synonymous. If, however, the pure pigment is altered when being added to the oil, the intensity is affected. The term *low intensity* means that the pigment has been grayed by the addition of another color or of black or white, and therefore its character has been altered from the original pure hue. Low-intensity colors are often referred to as *tones*, and they include some of the most useful and subtle ranges of color.

Many dark colors are not only low in value but low in intensity. Maroon, in addition to being a shade of red, is also a low-intensity version of it. Browns are generally low-intensity, low-value yellow-red. Tan is a low-intensity, high value yellow-red.

Color theory is the beginning of understanding color. With the properties of color clearly in mind, it is now possible to consider how these properties can be put to use through the relationships of colors to each other.

Color Relationships

The modulated flow of color around the color wheel has a far greater impact than the aesthetic one in which the wheel resembles a circular rainbow. In actual fact, the position of each color on the wheel has a genetic influence on its role and possibilities.

We naturally assume that any two colors next to each other on the wheel have traits in common: their names establish that fact, such as blue and blue-purple, or green and green-yellow. Adjacent colors are close relatives and can be expected to blend and harmonize with one another. The term for such colors is *analogous. Any two colors adjacent on the color wheel are analogous colors.*

Experiments with all the basic color wheels have shown another interesting fact: colors diametrically opposite one another on the wheel are as different from one another as is possible, for example, yellow and purple-blue, or red and blue-green. This fact has far-reaching implications for working with color harmonies, and we will explore them shortly. For the moment, however, it is enough to know that such colors are known as *complementary. Any two colors opposite each other on the color wheel are known as complementary colors.*

For purposes of creating color harmonies, another distinction is frequently made. A color on the color wheel has not only its direct complement as a possible partner in creating color harmonies, but it has *split complements: the two colors on either side of its complement on the wheel.* The split complements of purple-blue, therefore, will be yellow-red and green-yellow, and the split complements of red will be green and blue. These relationships are of fundamental use in formulating and analyzing color harmonies.

Color Harmonies

A color harmony is a combining of colors into an aesthetically pleasing composition. This may refer to a great painting, a piece of folk art, the decoration of a bathroom, the choice of clothing, or the arrangement of food upon a plate.

Monochromatic

A monochromatic color harmony is based on a single hue and it can be one of the most ingenious, varied, and pleasing of color harmonies. The idea of selecting one hue and developing all its possible values, with tints and shades and tones, its full range of intensity, and its possibilities for modulation through slight additions of its analogous neighbors, can be one of the most challenging of design projects.

Neutrals

Technically, a neutral is defined as a color that has no color quality but that simply reflects light. The scientific explanation is that such colors reflect *all* the color waves in light, leaving none for the human eye to see. Under this definition, white, of course, is the ultimate neutral. However, black reflects *none* of the color waves in light, so it, too, has no color quality. With black and white both classified as neutrals, it follows that any mixture of the two would produce modified neutrals, in other words, an entire range of grays. However, from the artist's standpoint, a more satisfactory range of neutrals is formed by mixing complements, which, when combined in equal parts, also produce gray. The mixture of any two complements provides a spectrum of *chromatic neutrals,* bordering on gray, or on beige, depending upon the hues used and on the proportion of each that is added. The room in Plate 15 (p. 124) appears at first glance to be all white. When we compare the whites, however, we find a subtle variation. Upholstery and carpet have a faintly rosy tinge, seeming to echo the warmth of the wood in the cabinet against the wall. The walls and ceiling, on the other hand, flooded with light and of a harder surface, reflect a cooler white, one that seems a continuation of the cool colors in the painting that provides the striking focal point at the extreme right. The granite floor beyond the carpet provides a soft gray bridge between the painting and its dramatically understated background. This is monochromatic color harmony at its most effective, carrying neutrality to an extreme and then exploding it with a single exciting blast of color.

Plate 6. Auguste Renoir.
La Première Sortie.
(The First Outing.)
c. 1875–1876. Oil on canvas,
25½ × 19¾″ (65 × 50 cm).
The National Gallery, London.

Plate 7. Ernst Haas.
Rainbow Rock. 1965.
Photograph, Iceland.

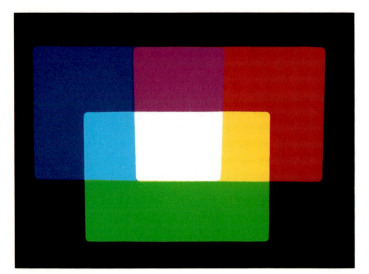

Plate 8. According to the additive principle in light, the three primary colors, red, blue, and green, when overlapped, create the secondary colors of yellow, cyan, and magenta. When combined, they add up to white light.

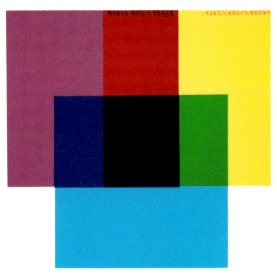

Plate 9. In the subtractive principle, the process is reversed. Yellow, cyan, and magenta are considered the primary colors, and when they are overlapped they produce red, blue, and green. When combined, they add up to black.

Plate 10. The traditional color wheel by Herbert Ives begins with primary colors of red, yellow, and blue. From these three hues are formed the secondary colors orange, green, and violet. Tertiary colors result from combining a primary with a secondary.

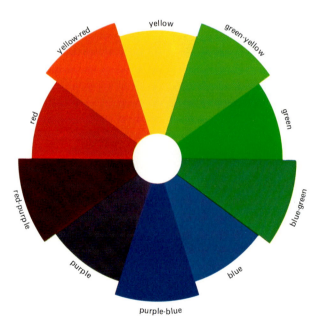

Plate 11. The Munsell color wheel is based on five key hues: red, yellow, blue, green, and purple. From these primaries are formed secondaries of yellow-red, green-yellow, blue-green, purple-blue, and red-purple. Although the terminology differs slightly and the Munsell wheel has ten colors to Ives' twelve, the colors themselves are essentially the same.

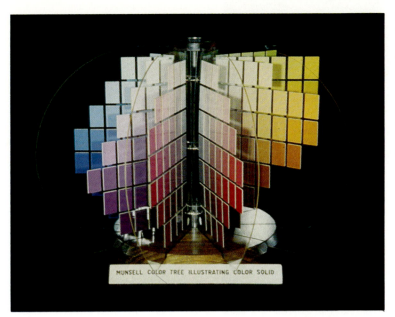

Plate 12. The Munsell system in three dimensions, known as the Munsell Color Tree. The center trunk changes only from light to dark, but the colors change in hue as they move around the tree. The value of each panel changes as it moves from top to bottom of the tree. The greatest intensity of each hue is found in the color panel or "vane" farthest from the center trunk. Courtesy Macbeth, a division of Kollmorgen Corporation, Baltimore, Maryland.

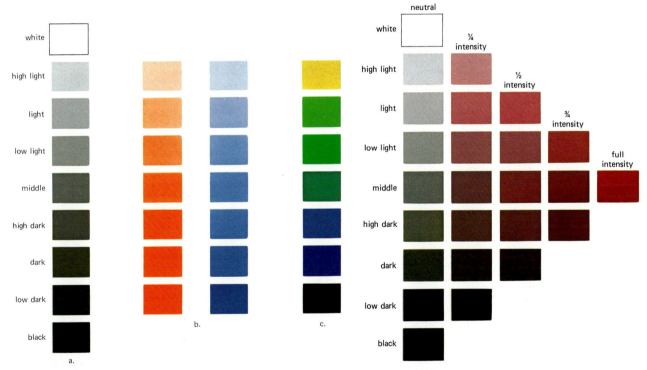

Plate 13. The value scale indicates shades of gray between pure white and absolute black (a). Hues in the color wheel can also be arranged in such a value scale, as with yellow-red and blue (b). At normal value, all the hues forming the color wheel can also be arranged in a vertical scale of lightness and darkness, with gradations from yellow to purple or violet (c).

Plate 14. The intensity or chroma scale shows the full range of brightness of which a hue is capable, from pure color at full intensity to the varied tones made possible by successive degrees of graying.

Plate 15. Home of Norman and Lisette Ackerberg, Malibu, California. View of living room. Designer: Richard Meier, 1987.

Plate 16. Carol Colburn. *After the Rain*, detail. Acrylic on canvas, 54 × 60″ (122 × 152 cm). Gallery 3, Phoenix, Arizona.

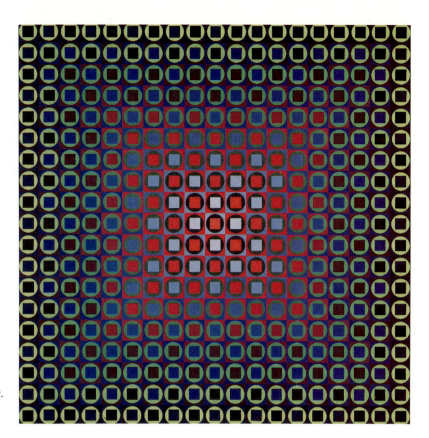

Plate 17. Victor Vasarely.
KEZD1-111. 1966.
33 × 33″ (84 × 84 cm).

Plate 18. Virginia A. Stroud.
Water's Edge. Offset print,
25½ × 17″ (64.8 × 43 cm).

YELLOW

YELLOW-
ORANGE

ORANGE

ORANGE-
RED

RED

RED-
VIOLET

PURPLE

BLUE —
PURPLE

BLUE

BLUE-
GREEN

GREEN

YELLOW —
GREEN

Plate 19. Complementary color pairs and the chromatic grays that result from their mixture. Artist: Frank R. Cheatham, Lubbock, Texas.

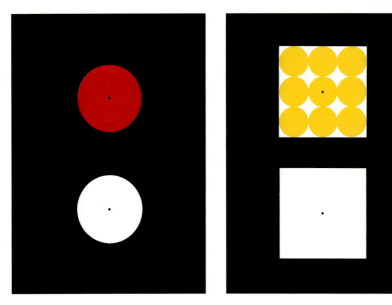

Plate 20. Experiment in *afterimage*. If you stare at the red circle for half a minute, then switch to the white one, you will see not white but blue-green, the complement of red.

Plate 21. Experiment in *reversed afterimage*. Stare at the yellow circles for half a minute, then switch to the white square below the circles. You will see not circles but the curved diamond shapes between the circles and squares, and they will be not white but yellow.

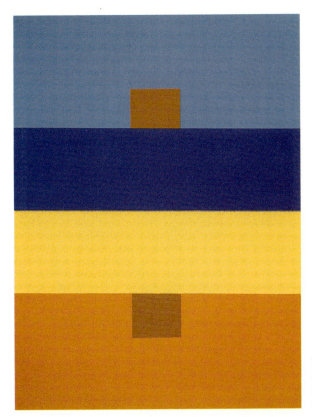

Plate 22. Josef Albers.
From *Interaction of Color,*
revised edition (1975) by
Josef Albers. Plate IV-1.

Plate 23. Camille Pissarro.
River—Early Morning.
Oil on canvas. The John G. Johnson
Collection of Philadelphia,
Philadelphia Museum of Art.

Plate 24. Rembrandt. *The Descent from the Cross.* 1651.
Oil on canvas, 4′8½″ × 3′7¼″ (1.43 × 1.11 m). National Gallery of Art,
Washington, D.C. (Widener Collection).

Analogous

Analogous colors, being next to each other on the color wheel, are obviously the most closely related of all hues, each having something of its neighbor in its composition. Simply reading the color names of any two analogous hues establishes this inherent compatibility. In designing a fabric or a room, one can be certain of a harmonious result when using analogous colors; however, there is also the possibility of monotony. Analogous colors, on the whole, will both be in the same range of warmth or coolness, and a room that is all cool—or all warm—can be less than comfortable to live in. The most effective analogous color harmonies often have an accent of a complementary color for balance, most generally a small area that acts as a stimulant in an otherwise bland composition. The painting in Plate 16, page 124, is an excellent example of an analogous color harmony, employing a varied range of rosy hues, exploiting the possibilities of deep tones for shadows and tints for expanses of sky, varying them with fluid lines as well as with an imaginative blending of variations on the two analogous hues. However, if the composition consisted only of the roses and purples, it would be not only harmonious but somber, even threatening. The flash of light blue in the sky leaps into the range of reds, which are the complements of the blues, but it retains a kinship by the fact that the blue is a violet blue with nothing of orange or yellow in it. Although it provides a striking balance to the reds and oranges, it maintains a part of them within itself, for it could only be mixed by the use of purple. This retention of kinship is a fundamental aspect of the harmony of the painting, yet the artist has handled it in such a way that it also provides one of the important principles of any composition, *emphasis* through contrast.

Complementary

Victor Vasarely has used two sets of complements in his painting in Plate 17 (p. 125), purple-blue and yellow, and yellow-red and blue. This is not an arbitrary mixture of complements, however; it is rather an experiment in the interaction of colors when placed in proximity. His squares are much like the circles we observed in the value scale on page 116, for they change drastically according to the hue and value of their neighbors; in fact , the longer we look at them the less sure we are of exactly what color any given square really is. Vasarely carried out extensive experimentation in color, exploring its architectonic (structural) qualities, its possibilities for three-dimensional illusion, and its interrelationships through gradations of tone. In this painting each unit influences its surroundings in such a way that the shapes become reflectors and vibrators, each one changing and moving as a result of the others. One senses that the artist must have worked in a state of both curiosity and excitement, for it is unlikely that such vibrancy could be the result of careful planning.

Split Complementary

In Plate 18 (p. 125), the artist has begun with blues and greens for landscape and jacket and then has balanced them by splitting the complements on both sides, gold and a tint of red-purple for flowers and the spot on the cheek, blending them together across the tints and shades of the green that unites them, both on the wheel and in the painting. This is a flexible and effective use of color harmony, extending the warm hues into tiny flecks in blouse and jacket that are echoed in flecks of white throughout, providing a sprightly pattern. The fundamental harmony can be named (split complement), but it is the artist's virtuosity that gives it character. Here, perhaps, we have the most important fact about color harmonies. The terminology is merely a means of identifying and categorizing what the artist knows instinctively.

Color Interaction

Color harmonies provide a key to the use of color, but the interactions between colors offer the key to mixing, combining, and creating with color. For the designer, perhaps the most important area of color interaction is found in the effects that complementary colors have upon each other.

Interaction of Complements

As we stated earlier, when two colors directly opposite each other on the color wheel are mixed in equal parts, the result is a neutral, usually a variation of gray. We stress this phenomenon because it is fundamental in the art of mixing color. The chart in Plate 19 (p. 126) tells us far more than the word does. Grays formed from the mixing of complements retain the color quality of both complements and can be varied infinitely by the variations of proportion in the mixture. Red and blue-green mixed equally produce gray, but if a fraction more red is added, the gray becomes warm, even rosy. If the green predominates, the gray will be a cool gray. This system applies to the mixture of beiges, which would have a bit of orange added to the complementary gray, and to an entire range of grays that would be different from one another because of the complements used. Plate 19 shows the subtle difference possible through the use of different complements. If lighter values are desired, yellow may be used; if greater depth is required, purple can be the answer. It is, of course, possible to lighten or darken with white or black, but one must remember that there will be a certain amount of chroma or color intensity lost with the use of white or black. This is not necessarily undesirable. Mixing color is a matter of experimentation and results vary with the chemical composition of the paint, with the light where the final result is displayed, and with the individual peculiarities of the human eye.

Simultaneous Contrast

The graying effect of mixing complements becomes even more tantalizing with the discovery that placing complements *next* to each other has exactly the opposite effect. *Complementary colors mixed together produce gray, but complementary colors placed next to each other become, not grayer, but more intense.* Josef Albers, one of many specialists who have made a career of studying color, has left us a series of experiments that make this phenomenon clear.

If you look at Plate 20, page 126, you will see two circles, one red and one white, each with a small black dot in the center. Fix your eyes on the dot in the center of the red circle and stare at it for half a minute. Moon or sickle shapes may appear around the periphery, but do not be distracted; continue staring. Now, when your eyes have become thoroughly used to the red circle, quickly switch them to the white one, focusing once more on the little black dot. If you have the usual reaction, you will see a circle that is not white but blue-green, the complement of red.

Albers reasoned that this reaction is due to the fact that the human eye is tuned to receive any one of the three primary colors of red, yellow, and blue (as perceived in light, rather than on the color wheel). Staring at red fatigues the nerve ends in the retina so that a sudden switch to white (which consists of red, yellow, and blue) will register only a mixture of yellow and blue, which in this case appears as blue-green, the complement of red. The complement thus seen is called the *afterimage*.

This theory of the tiring nerve ends in the retina would explain the increased intensity of adjacent complements. If circles of red and blue-green are placed side by side and the eye concentrates on the red until the nerve ends tire, the eye, when moved to the blue-green, will perceive only the blue and yellow mixed together. The blue-green will therefore be of maximum intensity.

Albers stated unequivocally that color is the most relative medium in the field of art. Not only does human perception of color differ widely, the scientific aspects are still very much in question. However, theories such as simultaneous contrast can give us clues as to how colors will react when used in design. Knowing that colors that are least related (complementaries) appear most brilliant when placed in close proximity can influence choices in many situations. Since every pair of complements contains both a warm and a cool hue, we can expect a warm hue generally to look warmer when it is placed next to a cool hue and the cool hue to look cooler, for every color tends to emphasize the complement in the color next to it. This is true in all the variations of value and intensity as well. A grayed blue will look cooler next to yellow-red than it will if placed next to purple, the cool quality being essential to its natural hue which will at the same time seem brighter. It is this simultaneous contrast of warm and cool that determines the most flattering colors in dress. The skin tones of a person with a pale bluish cast of complexion will take on a warmer cast in proximity to colors in the yellow-red range, whereas a florid complexion wearing blue-green will take on some of the qualities of the blue-green and thus will appear less rosy.

Such relationships stress the importance of seeing color as a part of a total composition. Many interior design problems have arisen from purchases of a single object that looks wonderful in the shop but changes character entirely when set in the room for which it was intended. Any combination of colors, from everyday clothing to a stage set for an opera should be considered in its totality and, if possible, under varying conditions of light, before final decisions are made.

The illusory quality of color is demonstrated by another experiment that Josef Albers termed *reversed afterimage*. Look at the yellow circles in Plate 21, page 126. Once again, fix your eyes upon the circles, staring fixedly for half a minute or so. Now shift focus suddenly to the white square below the circles. One might logically expect to see purple or blue circles (the complement), but this is not the case. One does not even see circles, but the curved diamond shapes resulting from the difference between the circles and the squares. These are not in the complement but are yellow. Albers characterized this as a double illusion and gave it the name *reversed afterimage* or *contrast reversal*.

Interaction of Analogous Colors

Since complementary colors produce a neutral when mixed in equal parts, we can conclude that colors farthest from each other on the color wheel lose the most reflective light when mixed. Conversely, colors adjacent to each other, analogous colors, will retain the highest degree of reflective light, or intensity, when combined. This is an important aspect of mixing color. For instance, an equal mixture of yellow and blue makes green. A mixture of yellow-green and blue-green also makes green. If the intensity of all original hues is equal, then the green made from yellow and blue will be duller than the green made from yellow-green and blue-green, which are closer to each other on the color wheel. The greater the distance between two colors on the color wheel, the more the intensity of their mixture will be lowered.

On the other hand, the closer colors are placed to one another, the more their differences increase. This applies not only to hues but to value and intensity as well.

Color Interaction and Tonality

Tonality is defined as the relationships of colors within a composition or design, and it obviously is closely related to the interrelationships that we have been considering. The limitless possibilities can be demonstrated by one more of Josef Albers' experiments, as shown in Plate 22 (p. 127). In this plate, Albers has placed two squares of neutral gold in two positions, one surrounded by two cool blues of different value, the other, a square of identical size and color surrounded by two warm colors, a yellow and an orange. The effects of the adjacent colors are dramatic: surrounded by blue, the square becomes lighter and more gold, whereas when flanked by yellow and yellow-orange, it becomes dark enough to be considered light brown. In Albers' own words: "Color deceives continually."

In order to be a successful designer, it is not necessary to be able to explain all these relationships scientifically. The goal is to develop the eye, to recognize the changes that take place, and to know how to bring about an effect that is necessary to the success of a design. The designer must be aware also that the human eye registers variously in different people, and the name of a hue means something different to everyone who hears it.

The Psychology of Color

Psychologists have long known that certain colors have the power to evoke specific emotional responses in the viewer, partially because of symbolic associations with warm and cool and all the reactions that this psychological temperature involves. Color stylists make a career of designing color harmonies for subways, factories, hospitals, airports, and other public buildings, and their services depend upon a thorough knowledge of the relationships of color to human reaction.

In general, warm colors stimulate and cool colors relax. Doctors' offices are usually painted in light blue or green, and restaurants and bars are more apt to be decorated in warm colors that will stimulate the appetite and thirst. Employers have found that employees suffer from chills when working in blue surroundings and that they produce at higher levels when stimulated by bright colors.

The famed Notre Dame football coach Knute Rockne had the locker rooms for his own team painted red and those of the visiting teams painted blue. When halftime came, the visitors instinctively relaxed in their soothing quarters, while the home team remained keyed up and ready for a winning second half. Similar psychology has been adopted in painting the stalls of racehorses, proving that color psychology is not limited to human reaction. Although cats and dogs are color-blind, insects react emphatically to color. Mosquitoes avoid orange but approach red, black, and blue. Beekeepers wear white to avoid being stung, for they have found that if they wear dark colors, they are besieged. The knowledge that flies dislike blue has helped the meat-packing industry.

Beyond these general, shared responses to color, each individual may react in a special way to particular colors. Each of us brings to the perception of visual stimuli a collection of experiences, associations, and memories that may be triggered by a given color. This could be the color of one's room as a child, or the color of the sky on a special well-remembered day. Color can evoke strong responses, pleasant or unpleasant, and even the viewer does not always understand the reason for the response.

Color and Space

The *local color* of an object is the color of its actual surface, as opposed to the color that it appears to be when placed in colored surroundings. Objects with warm local color appear to be closer to the viewer than cool objects do. An interior designer uses this fact in making a room seem larger by covering dominant pieces of furniture in soft light colors, particularly in the cooler ranges, and landscape painters interpret the same knowledge into cool distances with warm buildings or figures in the foreground. Such considerations apply not only to hue but also to value and intensity. The *tones*, grayed versions of any hue, are subtle and useful in all kinds of situations where modulation is desired.

Balance of Color

When we speak of color harmony, we must assume that the alternative is inharmonious or "clashing" color. Actually, any hue can be made to harmonize with any other hue or group of hues, simply by the use of the proper value or gradation. Two hues that seem incompatible when placed together at normal value can be blended into subtle harmony if one, or both, are grayed into pleasing tones, or one is made very dark and the other bright or light. We have seen how shapes interweave with space, and spaces with each other in order to create pattern. In the same way, colors must interweave and balance, in warmth and coolness, in subtlety and intensity, in lightness and darkness. A single stroke of contrast may be the difference between a mediocre design and a masterpiece, and a slight graying of tone may transform a crude work into a distinguished one.

Art historians can identify a painting as to period, and often even to painter, by the use of color. The Venetian painters of the Renaissance bathed their works in the golden glow that pervades the Venetian islands. The French Impressionists rebelled against the academic ways of painting by breaking color into its components and letting small brush strokes loaded with components shimmer across the canvas. In Plate 23 (p. 127) the water of the Seine is not painted blue or green, but is a vivid texture of short thick strokes in a combination of warm and cool tones. The trees are not green; they are masses of dabs of blue and yellow which, seen by the human eye, approximate green. The German Expressionists working before and after World War I deliberately tried to make their colors jar in order to express their horror at a world where such a war could take place. In the twentieth century painters have experimented in many ways and they continue to do so as the computer reveals new possibilities and innovative theories about color emerge.

Physicists can tell us about color composition, and psychologists can tell us something about how the human eye perceives it. Color stylists tell us how color may affect us physically and emotionally. It is the designer who synthesizes all these qualities and reveals perhaps the most important of the many aspects of color, its effect upon the human spirit.

Summary

Color has three properties, *hue, value,* and *chroma.* Hue is the color as it appears on the color wheel, value is the comparative lightness or darkness of a color, and chroma (or intensity) is the brilliance or purity of the color. The Munsell color theory is based on a color wheel with five key hues: *red, yellow, green, blue,* and *purple,* all at their normal or middle value. A *tint* is lighter than the normal value and a *shade* is darker than the normal value. Any two colors next to each other on the color wheel are *analogous.* Colors opposite each other on the color wheel are *complementary.* A *monochromatic* color harmony is based on one color. Neutrals are grayed colors or *tones. Achromatic neutrals* have no color properties, being mixed from black and white. Neutrals mixed from complementary colors are known as *chromatic neutrals.* A color harmony is a combining of colors into an aesthetically pleasing composition. *Tonality* is defined as the relationships between colors within a composition or design.

For Further Exploration

1. *Monochromatic harmony.* Using tempera paints and white drawing paper, paint twelve 3 × 4″ rectangles in as many variations as possible of a single hue. Make at least two of them neutrals,

mixing the hue with different amounts of its complement but keeping the tone as close as possible to gray or beige. Make two shades, one by using purple to darken the hue, one by using black. Make two tints, one by using yellow to lighten the hue, one by using white. Vary the other six rectangles as to chroma, using paint pure from the jar, then varying it with bits of its complement (to achieve tones) and with bits of the analogous hues on each side of it. Mount all the rectangles on a 12 × 18″ sheet of white paper, arranging them in gradations as much as possible and labeling each to show how you achieved it. Use this sheet as a guide in your subsequent work in color.

2. *Analogous harmony.* Paint 12 nonobjective shapes in two analogous colors, for example, blue and blue-green. Using the complements, mix as many variations as possible, lightening with yellow or white and darkening with purple or black. Paint a 9 × 12″ sheet of paper in one of the two colors as it came from the tube, then arrange the 12 shapes on it to form a composition, adjusting shapes and color gradations so there are accents as well as harmony. Paste in place.

3. *Complementary harmony.* Follow the instructions for #2, using two different analogous colors. In addition, paint a 4 × 6″ piece of paper in the complement of one of the colors. Cut it into a small interesting shape and place it in the composition for accent, possibly repeating it in a very small area (a line or a dot) elsewhere in the composition. Compare the results with those in #2.

PART 3

The Principles of Design

Rhythm

The elements of design are the materials of the designer; the principles establish the methods by which these materials are set in motion. Just as we discovered that shape and space flow in and out of one another, that mass is the three-dimensional aspect of shape, and that texture can be the result of line or color, so we will find that the principles inevitably work together. If we seem to isolate them, it is only for the sake of analysis and an understanding of their individual properties and potential for design.

The principles we will consider are *rhythm*, *variety*, *unity*, *balance*, *emphasis*, *proportion*, and *scale*. We begin with rhythm, the principle governing our heartbeats and our breathing, our days and our seasons, the constellations and the sea; in short, the underlying principle of the universe.

The Nature of Rhythm

The word *rhythm* derives from a Greek term meaning "to flow," and its essence did indeed flow throughout the entire universe of the ancients. Long before the Greeks, rhythm was considered the creative principle of the universe, not only in the manifestations of nature but in its regulated presence in human life: in waking and sleeping, in working and resting, in desire and fulfillment, in birth and death. In a world considered to be ruled over by vengeful and merciless gods, often wreaking havoc on human efforts, Greek philosophers and artists created a world of the mind in which catastrophe was excluded and a divine order ruled. This universe permeated Greek life with the rhythms of the ideal, whether in dance or drama, philosophy or science, poetry or architecture. The Greek *visual* arts are vivid examples of rhythm.

Varieties of Rhythm

Metric Rhythm

In music, meter provides an underlying structure through which rhythm flows smoothly. The structure, denoting a fixed time pattern, establishes the *beat*, or regular pulsation, often expressed by a drum or bass, that sets the pace to which we respond emotionally, sometimes

146

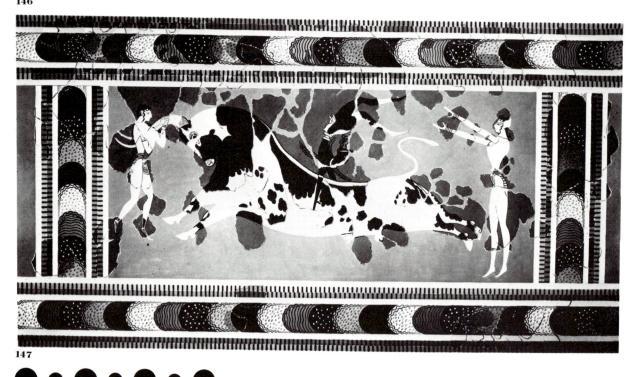

147

● ● ● ● ● ● ● ●
148

146. The regular rhythm of
a drumbeat can be shown visually
as a series of equally spaced dots.

147. *Bull Leaping,*
reconstruction of fresco in the
Palace of Minos, Knossos, Crete.
c. 1500 B.C. 34 × 63″ (86 × 160 cm).
The University Museum,
University of Pennsylvania,
Philadelphia.

148. Dots of varying size indicate
variations in rhythm, in this case
an alternating beat.

149. Tampan maju (bridal ornament)
from Sumatra, Lampon region.
Cotton and rattan backing with
beadwork, shells, and mirror pieces.
59 cm (23.2″) × 72 cm (28.3″).
Courtesy Anita Spertus and
Robert J. Holmgren, New York.

150. Emphasis followed by two
lesser beats illustrates visually
the familiar rhythm of the waltz.

dancing or swaying or tapping our feet. Visually, metric rhythm can
be expressed by the dots in Figure 146. The rhythm consists of regularly repeated pulsations, the kind of beat one sets with a tapping
pencil or hears in the drumbeat of a marching band. We see its aesthetic interpretation in the Cretan fresco in Figure 147. There are two
expressions of simple metric rhythm here in the borders surrounding
the bull and his attendants. The more obvious is in the large petal-like
shapes that overlap to form a continuous band across top and bottom,
linked by two vertical bands in the same design. Although the colors
do not alternate, the drumbeat of the shape is unmistakable. Variations in texture and color, some dotted and some striped, are inten-
tional devices for providing interest, disciplined by the regularity of
the smaller borders at both edges, their rigid dark lines spaced with
almost mechanical regularity. Together, these rhythmic borders
frame and contain the flowing rhythms of the figures in the main
panel.

The second series of dots in Figure 148 has an alternating
rhythm, one that must be tapped out with a pencil or spoken as drum-
beats for the impact of the accented beat to be evident. This rhythm is
eloquently worked into the Sumatran beaded tampan in Figure 149.
This textile is traditionally placed near the bride's seat at the wedding
ceremony and, worked in shells, beads, and pieces of mirror, this particular tampan is a highly prized example. The dominant beat is obvious, but the lesser beat, involving a traditional figure of horse and
rider, is related in shape and height but just sufficiently lighter and
smaller to provide the alternating rhythm.

149

In Figure 150 we see a third set of dots representing a rhythm we have all hummed, whistled, or danced to, the rhythm of the waltz. Our association of the waltz with the glittering aura of Vienna makes even more fascinating the fact that the same rhythm has been used visually in a print carved of sealskin, inked, and printed by an Eskimo artist of

150

151

the Canadian Arctic (Fig. 151). Parr has given us a marvelous visual parallel in this print of blue geese feeding. The strong beat is undeniable, and the smaller beats provide a double bonus of rhythm and humor.

Flowing Rhythm

Just as rhythm permeates every aspect of a musical composition, so rhythms bind together the visual work of art. The example in Figure 152 is only a portion of a screen presumed to have been destroyed during the German occupation of Paris during World War II. Long considered to be one of the great masterpieces of the ironworker's art, it was discovered in late 1986, blackened and discarded, in the basement of a house in South America. The sixty years of neglect served an aesthetic purpose, for cleaning brought out a mellow patina in its iron and electroplated brass, a metallic film resulting from oxidation. Reflecting the Art Deco period of the 1920s, the screen is based on plant forms translated into sweeping rhythms such as those visible in Figure 152. The manner in which the beat in music forms the structure for flowing rhythms is visually obvious here, for the repetitious floral medallions build a steady beat underlying rippling lines and flowing arcs.

The painting of the Tuscan countryside in Figure 153 is a succession of rhythmic curves that carry us gently back into the landscape, plowed fields, and roads and ridges of hills, all flowing back and forth across the canvas over the beat of the dark cypresses that accentuate the curves. The "beat" is not so much a metric repetition here as it is a series of accents that underscore the rolling hills.

151. Parr. *Blue Geese Feeding.* Print, 30 × 25″ (76.2 × 63.5 cm). West Baffin Eskimo Co-operative in Cape Dorset, Canada.

152. Edgar Brandt. *Oasis Screen* (detail), 1927. Iron with brass applied by electrolysis.

153. Sheppard Craige. *Towards Pienza #1.* 1985. Oil on canvas, 4′2″ × 2′10″ (1.27 × 0.86 m). Courtesy Katharina Rich Perlow Gallery, New York.

152

153

154

155

154. Victor B. Scheffer.
Surf at South Point,
Island of Hawaii. Photograph.

155. Amanda McKerrow in Fokine's
Les Sylphides.

156. Kay Sekimachi. *Hanging.*
Multilayer nylon multifilament
weave; length 40″ (1.02 m).

Swirling Rhythm

In speaking of the "beat" in rhythm, we have been noting one of the characteristics of a certain type of rhythm, in which a periodic pulsation establishes a basic pattern. In flowing rhythm this repetition is softened and modulated, as in the roar of the sea, which, while punctuated with the intermittent crash of breakers, maintains a continuous flowing and swirling movement (Fig. 154). The rhythms of the ballet are even more diversified, since the figures are repeated at less regularly spaced intervals, yet combine and flow into an essential rhythm of swirling and soaring, floating and dipping (Fig. 155).

The nylon hanging in Figure 156 swirls vertically, plunging downward. The manner in which the filaments thin out toward the bottom suggests that the swirling goes on indefinitely, beyond the limits of our vision, trailing off at last as a tune would trail off in our minds, leaving overtones and perhaps an echo. This type of rhythm does not have the precision and repetition of the rhythm based on a set meter, but emanates a more haunting quality, unmeasurable but compelling.

156

Climactic Rhythm

Some of the most dramatic rhythms in music are those that begin gently, growing in strength and intensity until they crash to a resounding climax. Wagner's operas have many examples of arias that lead the audience upward into ever greater suspense until the climactic release explodes upon the stage. Rock music is also replete with climactic rhythms, rising and crashing above a predominant beat.

Music has a distinct advantage over the visual arts in the matter of building to a climax, for the audience is in place and the conductor or singer can lead them through the stages of the composition gradually and with increasing emotional impact. It is seldom that the viewer of a painting, for example, studies the work for a length of time equivalent to that spent listening to a musical selection; therefore the painter must rely on spectacular devices if the painting is to carry a dramatic impact.

One of the most effective devices is the triangular composition. By its structural nature, the triangle is designed to begin with a slow heavy base and lift us ever higher to a peak or climax. Rembrandt has exploited it to the full in his painting in Plate 24, page 128. The triangle is based in shadowy, even mysterious, figures in the foreground, with light focused on the one to the far right, whose tragic mien underscores the highlighting of face, chest, and hand. From the face, a subtle trail of subdued highlights leads our eye to the full radiance of the triangle itself, bathed in golden color accented by the red of the central figure's shirt, which continues in the hand holding the body of Christ. Two shadowy ladders form the sides of the triangle, the one on the left reinforced by the outstretched arms which become a dominant diagonal, a line traditionally symbolizing action and violence. With the draperies filling the triangle into a solid golden mass, the climax still remains at the peak, the point toward which all the mysteries of light and shadow are rising, the spot at which the hand is being released from the cross, which is the symbol and reason for all that is taking place within the painting.

Rhythm, Time, and Motion

As we stated at the beginning, rhythm is a matter of meter, of time, a structure over which larger rhythms flow. Any work involved with rhythm, then, is necessarily an expression of time and, inevitably, also of motion. The visual expression of motion has fascinated many painters, most prominent of whom were the Italian Futurists, who worked around 1909. One of their goals was the expression of the dynamic energy and movement of mechanical processes. They devised ingenious ways of translating motion into their canvases, centering mainly on the use of multiple images of a figure that would make

157

157. *Ibbarola. PA–18.*
1959. Oil on canvas,
4′9½″ × 3′8⅞″ (1.46 × 1.14 m).
Solomon R. Guggenheim Museum,
New York.

158. Ictinus and Callicrates.
The Parthenon, Athens.
447–438 B.C.

it seem to move across the canvas, in much the way filmmakers at the time were discovering that successive images, slightly altered, would produce action on the movie screen. Contemporary painters have experimented with the concept of video frames and even comic-strip techniques to provide a feeling of motion, of arriving at a climax, sometimes combining these techniques with painting, sometimes with experimental photographic techniques.

In design, any rhythmic work implicitly involves both time and motion. The amount of time the *viewer* spends cannot be controlled by the designer, except in cases of industrial and architectural design, but the element of time is *expressed* in any rhythmic composition. In Figure 157 the beat is so dominant that one cannot escape it: five values make it throb throughout the canvas, echoing from the lightest through clearly articulated gradations to very dark. The distribution pulsates and the curvilinear shapes flow and swirl. Shapes drift together like amoebas to form other shapes, then move on, creating still further patterns. Where rhythm is present, there is inevitably a marking of time, whether a steady beat or a flow, and there is visual movement, for rhythm can never be static. A person who "feels" rhythm unconsciously moves with it, feeling it within, whether it originates in music or in a visual work.

Rhythm as a Unifying Force

We mentioned at the beginning of the chapter that ancient Greek architecture provides a vivid example of visual rhythm, and an analysis of one of the most famous examples will illustrate the statement.

In looking at the Parthenon (Fig. 158), we immediately see two manifestations of rhythm: the columns repeated around its perimeter and the grooved panels (triglyphs) recurring at intervals throughout the frieze above the columns. These two elements are enough to characterize the building as rhythmic, but the full ramifications are not visible at first glance. Built of blocks of Pentelic marble with no mortar, the Parthenon is an architectural expression of all the subtlety of thought and philosophy for which the Greeks have been respected through the centuries. In Greek temple design, flexible units known as modules were used to ensure a unified relationship of each part to the total building. These modules were not degrees of measurement but variable units, such as the diameter of a column, which would be different for different buildings. What appears to be a rectangular

158

building is actually a study in harmonious curves; it is said that there is not a straight line in the Parthenon. This is the result of *entasis,* a slight curving outward toward the center of each column to prevent the weight of the upper temple from seeming to make the columns buckle. It is also affected by horizontal subtleties: the placing of the columns is closer at the corners and the columns are thicker, because since they are seen against the sky they would otherwise seem to be slimmer than the others. Sculpture positioned above eye level slopes slightly outward toward the top to compensate for the position of the viewer on the ground. Unfortunately, most of the sculpture of the frieze and the pediments (triangular shapes) at each end suffered at the hands of time and battle and are now in the British Museum, where it is not possible to relate them to their role as rhythmic elements of the total composition. In place, the figures must have been enormously powerful, with rearing horses, swirling garments, and a festive crowd in procession around the entire temple.

The analysis of the Parthenon in relation to rhythm is of importance for several reasons, but perhaps the most vital is the way in which it underscores the fact that rhythm cannot be imposed upon a composition. It is not something that one applies, like color or texture. Rhythm *underlies* natural processes, and it should be a part of the artist in any creative work. All creative processes can set up rhythms, and all works can convey them. Some artists work to the accompaniment of music in order to translate the rhythmic sounds into their work. Others express a natural sense of rhythm without conscious effort, much as rhythm is expressed naturally by a dancer. In creating a visual design, an artist may lend a *physical* rhythm to the application of brush strokes, the impact of hammer on chisel, the thudding of the shuttle on the loom, or the humming of the potter's wheel. The rhythmic leg motion in working the pedals of a potter's wheel is vitally important to the smooth turning of the pot; in fact, the entire body is engaged in rhythmic motion when a potter or weaver is at work. On the other hand, the rhythms in painting or sculpture may be primarily visual, deliberately introduced into the work to provide flow and unity but introduced from the beginning, a part of the process throughout. Rhythm must be the guiding principle from which all other aspects of the work naturally evolve.

Summary

Rhythm is the underlying principle of the universe, manifesting itself not only in the tides and constellations but in the human heartbeat and other natural rhythms of human life. Rhythm can be categorized into four principal types: *metric rhythm,* based on a metered beat as in music; *flowing rhythm,* which undulates above the beat to sway and ebb like the flow of water; *swirling rhythm,* which eddies and surges in circular motion; and *climactic rhythm,* which grows in volume and intensity, leading to a resounding climax. Rhythm is composed of *meter,* which is measured time, and *motion,* which moves in many directions. The Parthenon is an architectural example in which rhythm and harmony reach their ultimate expression. Rhythm cannot, however, be *added* to any composition; it must be implicit in the process of creation and in the experience of the artist or designer during that process.

For Further Exploration

1. On a 12 × 18″ sheet of white paper, lay out an allover pattern demonstrating meter (refer to Figs. 147 and 157), but using a natural shape. Be aware of the necessity for a rhythmic beat but also of a flowing movement throughout the composition. Paint the shapes and spaces in tempera, making the color harmony a significant element in the rhythm by repeating colors at intervals and varying their values and intensity.

2. On a 12 × 18″ sheet of black paper, lay out geometric shapes in a metrical rhythm. Cover the entire sheet with shapes, varying them to as many as five basic shapes, then fit them together in a rhythmic design, making certain the finished work exhibits meter, flow, and movement. (Refer to Fig. 157.)

3. On a 12 × 18″ sheet of white drawing paper, paint with brush loaded with tempera your own impression of a specific piece of music—a rock performance, a ballet, a number in modern dance. Work without being conscious of the elements of rhythm but concentrating totally on the music, using a tape or recording as background if desired. When you have finished, analyze the result to see how well it expresses the elements of rhythm that we have studied: meter, flow, swirl, climax, motion, and time.

Emphasis

Emphasis is the clap of thunder, the peak of the mountain, the roar of the waterfall in the depths of the forest. It is the dominant beat in rhythm, the climax toward which a musical composition builds, the theme or character in a literary work that holds our attention and that we remember. The achievement of a goal, a moment of deep happiness, a visual experience that appears spectacular: these provide emphasis, being high points that illumine our everyday existence. Our individual lives are a series of climaxes that stand out in memory, sometimes unhappily but occasionally as the turning points of our lives.

In visual design, emphasis is the point toward which our eye turns immediately when we walk into a gallery, the aspect of a piece of sculpture that catches our attention, the dominant shape in a wall hanging. Emphasis is the aspect of a work that makes it seem important.

Emphasis by Location

Generations of art students were taught that a painting or drawing had to have a "center of interest," a focal point. The exact spot where this point should be was well-established: the human eye, looking at a rectangular canvas, so the theory went, naturally and inevitably moved at once to a point slightly to the left of center and just above it. This was the automatic center of attention and therefore the place where the most important figure should appear, or where the crucial action of the painting should take place. This was the spot for the most vibrant color, the most interesting shape.

Twentieth-century artists have dispensed with this revered theory along with many others, yet it is not difficult to find examples that echo it. We can safely assume that Pierre Clark was not concerned with that aspect of placement when he constructed his sculpture *Furious Duchess* (Fig. 159), yet our eye goes directly to that spot on the work where the banded piece is most noticeable and where the one circular form, actually painted red, serves as a link between the other components of the work. Their location may not be planned around the traditional center of attention, but it undoubtedly reinforces our concentration upon them.

Ed Paschke has used the same location in his work in Figure 160, in which the one blackened eye immediately draws our attention. Whatever we wish to make of the painting after the initial impact, the first moment is certainly one of focusing on the eye.

159. Pierre Clark.
Furious Duchess.
1986. Painted aluminum,
9′7″ × 11′2″ × 6″ (2.93 × 3.41 m).
Courtesy DiLaurenti Gallery.

160. Ed Paschke. *Chow Femme.*
1986. Oil on canvas,
5′8″ × 6′8″ (1.73 × 2.03 m).
Courtesy Phyllis Kind Gallery.

159

160

Emphasis Through Drama

Francisco Goya uses both location and drama to hold our eye in his painting in Figure 161. The white figure highlighted against the darkness would provide sufficient emphasis, but lines of all kinds converge upon him from every part of the painting. There are the rifles with fixed bayonets, the grim attention of the other figures in the group, the streak of light in the foreground leading our eye into the painting, the box of light in strong contrast to the braced knees of the executioners outlined against it, and in the foreground the prostrate bodies of those who have already fallen. The painting depicts the Spanish resisters overtaken by the armies of Napoleon, and all of the devices of the painter's skill form a rising crescendo leading to the figure garbed in white, arms outstretched in a crucifixion pose.

Goya was a Romanticist, for whom color and emotional quality were essential means of expression. Jacques Louis David was a Classicist, who favored clean-cut lines, dignity, and a formal handling of even the most emotional scene. His *Death of Socrates* (Fig. 162) is certainly as dramatic a subject as Goya's executions, yet his handling of it defines and illustrates the distinction between romanticism and classicism. There is certainly a point of emphasis, a focal point. It is not left

161. Francisco Goya. *Executions of the Third of May, 1808.* 1814–1815. Oil on canvas. 8'9" × 13'4" (2.67 × 4.05 m). Prado, Madrid.

162. Jacques Louis David. *The Death of Socrates.* 1787. Oil on canvas, 4'3" × 6'5¼" (1.3 × 1.96 m). Metropolitan Museum of Art, New York (Wolfe Fund, 1931). Catharine Lorillard Wolfe Collection.

161

162

of center; it does not need to be. The artist makes striking use of light and tonality to achieve both emphasis and drama. The body of Socrates is also rigidly vertical, whereas all nine of the men surrounding him lean toward him. The upraised finger is the highest point in the foreground, creating a focal point within a focal point. Furthermore, David has positioned Socrates alone almost at the center of the canvas, thereby employing *isolation*, one of the most certain devices for emphasis. A color reproduction of the painting would show that Socrates alone is dressed in white, whereas his followers are all garbed in subdued tones of red, blue, and orange. As the supreme touch of the classicist, David has used a formal, almost equally balanced structure for his composition, with the arched doorway and lighted distant figures balancing the weight of the heavier cluster of figures at the right. Goya's composition is balanced in a different way, using the heavy figures at the right, interspersed with light accents, to balance the high drama of the central figure. Goya directs us to his focal point with visual lines; David presents his dramatic climax in magnificent isolation.

Contemporary artists frequently employ shock value as their means of emphasis. Depictions of violence and degradation, mangled bodies and horror inevitably draw our attention. This is emphasis through content, drama that compels us to look.

Emphasis Through Light

Both Goya and David have employed light as a means toward emphasis in their works, but since both paintings focus on a highly dramatic subject, it will be helpful to examine the use of light in itself as a means of achieving emphasis.

163. Claude Lorrain.
Pastoral Landscape—The Roman Campagna. Oil on canvas,
40 × 52-½″ (101.6 × 133.35 cm).
The Metropolitan Museum of Art,
Bequest of Adele L. Lehman,
in memory of Arthur Lehman, 1965.

164. John Singer Sargent.
El Jaleo. 1882. Oil on canvas,
7′10½″ × 11′5″ (2.41 × 3.49 m).
The Isabella Stewart Gardner
Museum, Boston.

165. Walter Landor.
Design for registered trademark
for Cotton Incorporated.

163

164

Claude Lorrain's principal interest was in landscape, and the figures he places within that context in Figure 163 serve as accents to add human interest. We are not particularly concerned with what they are doing, even though one small group is highlighted to serve as a focal point. The prevailing interest of the canvas lies in the vast sweeps of sky and water with their bright reflected light, filtering among trees and slanting across meadows.

It is interesting that when John Singer Sargent chose an admittedly theatrical subject for a painting, he used almost the reverse technique (Fig. 164). Here the light is behind the guitarists lined up in the background, dark berets bent and casting shadows in contrast to the expanse of light washing over the wall. The dancer, far from being spotlighted, is placed in front of the only dark area on the wall, her own black hair only a few shades darker, and her blouse so dark that it blends with the figures directly behind her. Yet with a flash as fiery as the chords on the guitars, her white face and arms strike out in contrast to the rest of the painting, resounding into the billowing lightness of her skirt. She is the reason for the painting, and her slanting stance in opposition to her extended arm slashes across the canvas in a strong diagonal that leaves no doubt about the fact. She becomes a flash of lightning within the dull interior.

165

Emphasis Through Shape

There is no more certain way to establish emphasis than by one striking shape. Symbolic shapes are frequently used commercially to signify a product to the public. There can be no doubt of the emphasis in the logo in Figure 165. The billowy shape of a ball of cotton is underscored and completed by the dark indication of a husk. Allowing the cotton to flow down into the word itself is a harmonizing note that provides a balance and a sense of order necessary to a simple design whose primary purpose is to catch the eye. This type of design can be used as advertising, on company stationery and labels, on an entire line of products that are to be identified as having been made of cotton. Having a distinctive shape is the first step in providing an identifying mark, one that is immediately associated with the product through repeated exposure to the public eye. Wherever the logo is applied, it provides a focal note, a reminder, and a point of emphasis.

Emphasis Through Contrast

The further we progress in our consideration of the principles of design, the more obvious it becomes that they are inextricably interdependent. The relief panel in Figure 166, for example, could be used as an example of *rhythm*, with the predominant band of pebbles as the main beat echoed in the small windows and other textures. We could certainly discuss the work as an excellent use of *variety*. Both of these possibilities only reinforce the fact that the principle of *emphasis* is actively at work here, for the panel of pebbles inevitably catches our eye immediately, not only because of its location just left of center but because the round pebbles contrast effectively with the little rectangles that are used throughout the composition. This composition creates obvious *balance* by the placement of the three small circles at lower right and, of course, the predominant sun, all of which amplify the roundness of the stones. (We will discuss balance further in Chapter 10.) The immediate effect in looking at the panel, however, is the consciousness of emphasis created by the center panel, and its contrast to the textures of the rest of the work. Any marked contrast immediately establishes emphasis, simply because it demands to be noticed. This terra-cotta panel reminiscent of a terraced Greek village uses the pebbles as the cobblestone street, symbolically the point of emphasis within the village itself.

Any national flag is a point of emphasis, flown from a ship, over government buildings, or anywhere in the world where the nation represented establishes a point of recognition. Many flags are similar in design, often with three stripes of color symbolic to the people of the nation represented but not readily identifiable by people not familiar with the country. As part of the British Commonwealth, Canada for many years had the British Union Jack in the corner of its flag,

166

166. Athanase Papavgeris. Low-relief panel. Terra-cotta with polychrome glaze decoration, height 29″ (73.66 cm).

167. The national flag of Canada.

167

making it similar to other flags within the Commonwealth. When Canada became actively interested in establishing a distinctive Canadian identity, the Union Jack was replaced with an entirely new design, the maple leaf, long a symbol associated with Canada (Fig. 167). The red leaf with its distinctive shape stands forth against a white center panel in cheerful contrast, echoed in two end panels of the same red. The Canadian flag has a distinctive symbolism and an identity that is readily recognizable anywhere in the world.

Subdued Emphasis

If emphasis is to be considered purely in the context of a focal point, much of design would appear to exist without it. The statement is frequently made, for example, that allover designs, being intended primarily as background in wallpaper and fabric, do not have points of emphasis. Since this is an area of perception, there is room for personal viewpoints; however, the case could be made that any design has emphasis, no matter how subdued that emphasis may be, for any mark upon a solid surface becomes emphasis to some degree. The fabric design in Figure 168 consists of red squares and rectangles superimposed upon a dark green grid on a dark blue background. It is unquestionably an allover design; yet in looking at it even briefly, one cannot help noticing the rectangles breaking the line of squares, certainly rhythmic beats in a diagonal flow of pattern. Again, the diagonals themselves create emphasis that would make a strong pattern in hanging draperies.

Emphasis, then, has a wider connotation than a simple spot in a work upon which the viewer's eye will focus. There is a hierarchy of emphasis in many works, just as a drama will have its stars, featured players, and supporting cast. The stars have the most obvious roles, but frequently the emphasis will be upon a supporting part played in a manner that makes it memorable. In any case, it is the cast that makes

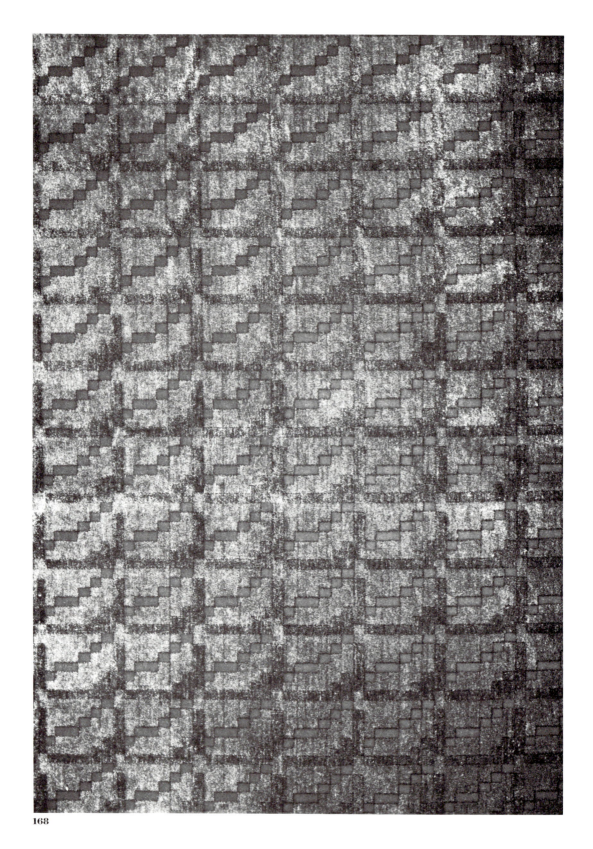

168

possible the star, and frequently in a visual design it is the supporting shapes or colors that cause one focal point to assume importance. Similarly, the human eye may see different shapes and lines in a work at different times so that the emphasis changes within a work according to the conditions under which it is viewed.

168. Marc Van Hoe. Fabric, *Ornament Collection*. Geometric step-patterned design in spun rayon and cotton velvet in red, green, and blue. Width 140 cm (55″). Mfr., Ter Molst, Belgium. N.D.

Summary

Emphasis in design is usually interpreted as a feature that predominates, allowing the rest of the design to work around it. Such emphasis can be achieved in many ways: by *location*, through *drama*, by *light*, by use of *shape*, and through *contrast*. Emphasis can also be achieved by the use of compositional *lines* directing the viewer to a crucial point, or by the *isolation* of a feature that the artist wants to emphasize. In the broader sense, emphasis may vary widely. Even subtle allover designs have their points of emphasis, often subdued but still contributing to the design quality.

For Further Exploration

1. With a linoleum block or stencil, create a motif for an allover design in which an element of emphasis dominates the block. This could be a design consisting primarily of small elements such as lines or circles with one large circle or square for emphasis. Cover a 12 × 18″ sheet of paper with the prints from the block or stencil, noting the effect of the repeated units of emphasis. Are they still showing emphasis, or do they become lost in the repetition? If the latter is the case, try printing another sheet, offsetting the blocks so that a different allover pattern results.

2. On a 12 × 18″ sheet of black construction paper, create a design of nonobjective shapes cut from colored construction paper. Make one shape the point of emphasis by (1) varying its shape from the others, (2) making it larger than any of the others, (3) making it a different color from any of the others, or (4) by making the other units direct the eye to the focal point by the way they are placed, leading to it or circling around it. (Refer to Fig. 159.)

3. On a 9 × 12″ sheet of white drawing paper, paint in tempera a stylized design based on still life: a bowl of fruit, a vase of flowers. Make one item the center of emphasis by one of the following methods: (1) make it larger and in a contrasting color, (2) give it an eye-catching visual texture, or (3) make it unusually interesting in shape.

CHAPTER 10

Balance

Like rhythm, balance is necessary for survival; in fact, it is balance that creates much of the rhythm in human life. Every intake of breath must be *balanced* by exhalation; periods of activity must be *balanced* by periods of rest. A particular type of balance enables human beings to walk erect in contrast to most other creatures on earth. Science and mathematics are founded on the principle of balance; in an algebraic equation the two sides must balance. In nature, we find balance everywhere: in the cycle of the seasons, the distribution of day and night—in short, all of the rhythms of nature involve some degree of balance.

Balance can be categorized in several ways. Of first importance is the distinction between *structural balance*, which involves the actual equilibrium of an object, and *visual balance*, which is concerned with perception and its psychological reactions. If structural balance is lacking, a building, a piece of sculpture, or a boulder will topple. If visual balance is missing, we will feel uneasy. Obviously, the two are closely related. Looking at an unbalanced structure of any kind is almost certain to arouse some degree of unease and tension in the viewer.

Structural Balance

Structural balance can be either *horizontal* or *vertical*. Balance of any kind is dependent upon an axis, a central pole of equilibrium around which the forces of an object or structure gravitate. A fundamental element in balance is *weight*, for it is only with equivalent amounts of weight or tension that balance is possible.

Horizontal Balance

Examples of horizontal balance in nature are limitless, including the soaring of an eagle with its enormous wingspread, the structural and visual balance of butterflies with their matching wings, the relaxed equilibrium of a well-fed leopard as it stretches itself for a nap in the branches of a tree. Probably one of the most fascinating examples of natural balance is the kangaroo, whose huge tapered tail coordinates with the action of its rear legs to propel it across great expanses of land in a perfectly balanced rhythmic motion (Fig. 169).

The principle of horizontal balance can best be illustrated by a diagram of a fulcrum and lever (Fig. 170) or, more familiarly, the seesaw of our childhood. When equal weights are placed on the lever

169. The kangaroo is a superb example of natural balance, with its huge tapered tail coordinating with the action of its rear legs to propel it rapidly across great expanses of land.

170. Diagram of horizontal symmetrical balance.

171. Thompson, Ventulett, Stainback & Associates. Regency Park. Cary, North Carolina.

169

170

at equal distances from the center, the lever balances in a level horizontal line. The minute the weight or distance is changed at one end, an adjustment must be made at the other. Most of us have memories of positioning different-sized children in order to make a seesaw balance and consequently swing smoothly up and down.

The building in Figure 171 gives us a pleasant sense of structural balance by its predominantly horizontal lines. In any building, of

171

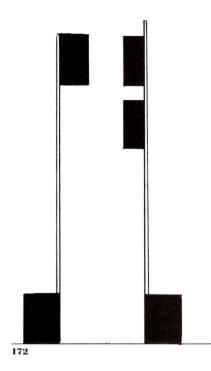

172

course, there must be vertical balance as well; a strong and sufficiently deep foundation is the first essential for a successful building, for it is this depth of foundation that holds the upper part of the structure secure. Still, in this case, we have no concern for security, for the alternating bands of glass and concrete are visually balanced and the structure appears solid and secure.

Vertical Balance

The importance of vertical balance in nature is obvious to every gardener, who knows that a tree or shrub must be planted deeply and securely if it is to survive. The giant trees of the forest are anchored by enormous root systems and when erosion or strong winds dislodge those roots, the tree topples.

The diagram in Figure 172 demonstrates the principle of vertical balance, in which the determining factor hinges upon the relationship of the height of the object to the weight at the bottom. Any weight distributed along the intervening distance must be adjusted to retain the balance.

We are all familiar with vertical balance in relation to masts of ships, flagpoles, and television antennas. The tall mast of a sailboat is balanced by the width of the beam or the weight of the keel. Flagpoles are firmly set in blocks of concrete. Television antennae, while not weighted heavily at the base by their own structure, are securely attached to roofs or buildings, thus appropriating the entire building as a huge counterweight that will allow the antenna to withstand storm and high wind.

In Figure 173 we see a tantalizing example of vertical balance. Nearly six feet high, this wooden pole has improbably tied itself in a knot that looks as though it should upset the balance entirely. In spite of realizing this probability, however, we are not unduly concerned because the artist has used the grain of the wood so skillfully that visual balance is assured. Not only does the grain of the laminations tie the knot, but it also seems to funnel it down to the base of the structure, where a particularly appropriate grain pattern sets the entire composition on a firmly established footing. Four areas of smooth grain provide careful balance to the flowing rhythms of the laminations, and the dark pegs are inserted at just the proper points to imply stability, including two that appear to anchor the structure to its base.

Visual Balance

We have made the distinction between structural balance, which concerns the actual physical stability of an object, and visual balance, which centers around our perceptual reactions. In visual balance we become more involved in the aesthetic quality of balance. The question is not so much whether the object will fall over as whether it gives the impression of being well proportioned and aesthetically pleasing. This question often relates to the matter of symmetry, an aspect of balance that we take for granted in human beings and therefore tend to transfer to our judgments of visual phenomena generally. Considered from this standpoint, there are two kinds of balance: *symmetrical* and *asymmetrical*.

173

Symmetrical Balance

In symmetrical balance, the *axis* is usually imaginary but its importance is fundamental. In two-dimensional works, for instance, the axis is an imaginary line drawn through the center of the composition either vertically or horizontally, dividing it into two identical halves. In the purest form of symmetry the halves would be mirror images of one another, as in Figure 174 if divided vertically. This identical symmetry is sometimes called *bilateral symmetry*. Most works of design, however, are not perfect mirror images. The painting in Figure 175 is more typical of what we consider as symmetrical balance. There is considerable variation between the two halves, yet the shapes and rhythms are so similar that we have the feeling that the work is actually symmetrical.

Possibly because of its predictability, symmetrical balance symbolizes stability and security, becoming an appropriate style for monumental buildings designed for formality and endurance. The symmetrical style of Greek and Roman temples is still found in ceremonial

172. Diagram of vertical balance.

173. H. C. Westermann. *The Big Change.* 1963. Laminated pine plywood, 4′8″ × 1′ × 1′ (1.42 × .305 × .305 m). Private collection, New York.

174. Designer, Peter Adam. 1984. Logo for GoTech, Inc. of Canada, Manufacturer of Styrofoam cups and plates. Design by Gottschalk + Ash International.

175. Philip Taaffe. *Yellow, Gray.* 1986. Silkscreen collage and acrylic on canvas, 7′ × 4′7¼″ (2.14 × 1.40 m). Courtesy Pat Hearn Gallery.

174

175

176

176. Schauspielhaus, Berlin, G.D.R.
Original architect: Karl Friedrich
Schinkel. Restoration of the exterior
under the auspices of the Institute
for Preservation. Architects: Eberhard
Gisske, Klaus Just, Manfred Prasser.
Location: The Platz der Akademie.
Photo courtesy of the Institute for
Preservation of Historic Monuments
of the G.D.R. From *Progressive
Architecture,* November 1986.

177. Edward Vason Jones, architect.
The Thomas Jefferson State Reception
Room. Department of State,
Washington, D.C.

178. Blown-glass model of
Trypanosphaera transformata,
a minute sea creature.
American Museum of Natural History,
New York.

179. Pier Luigi Nervi and
Anniballe Vitellozzi. Cupola
and dome, Palazzo dello Sport,
Rome. 1957.

177

buildings throughout the western world (Fig. 176). Similarly, the formality of symmetrical design is the favored style of interiors in buildings intended for use on state occasions (Fig. 177).

Radial Symmetry

When elements emanate from a central core, a sense of balance is established, just as a wheel will balance when laid flat upon an extending hub. This state of equilibrium is frequently known as *radial balance;* however, it can also be seen as a variation of symmetry inasmuch as the circular form can be halved at any point to produce two identical forms. Radial symmetry can be found abundantly in nature: one of the oldest of symbols is the circle with rays emanating from it to signify the sun god. Many flowers also have radiating petal configurations, as well as radiating seed structures, as in the case of dandelions and milkweed. Numerous forms of sea life develop in a radiating pattern (Fig. 178).

Radial symmetry is a basic form in architecture; the dome, an extension of the arch, is a classic structural classification. The sense of weight and movement inherent in radiating forms and in the symbolism of the dome arching toward the sky all contribute a unique character to a building, particularly when the interior of the dome is textured with mosaic, ribbing, or other pattern (Fig. 179).

As a two-dimensional expression, radial symmetry has distinct drawbacks. Even when placed on a round canvas, the sense of *radiating* that gives the dynamic quality to the form is impeded by the edge

178

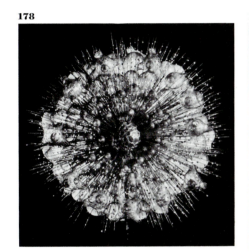

179

180

180. Jasper Johns.
Target with Four Faces. 1955.
Encaustic on newspaper over canvas,
26″ (66 cm) square, surmounted
by four tinted plaster faces
in wood box with hinged front,
overall dimensions with box open,
33⅝ × 26 × 3″ (85 × 66 × 8 cm).
Collection, The Museum of Modern Art,
New York (gift of Mr. and Mrs.
Robert C. Scull).

181. Diagram of asymmetrical
balance, showing two of many
possible ways in which to
distribute weight in order to
achieve balance.

182. Henri Cartier-Bresson.
Simiane la Rotonde. 1970.
Photograph.

of the canvas, which seems to send the radiation back toward the center, thus nullifying the original force. Jasper Johns, working with radial symmetry, arrived at the predictable shape of a target, not a vitally exciting subject for a painting in itself (Fig. 180). His originality in adding four plaster faces at the top moved the work into three dimensions and elicited considerable enthusiasm at the time it was introduced. The very interest that it aroused is perhaps an indication that the possibilities of two-dimensional radial symmetry are not to be taken for granted.

Asymmetrical Balance

We now return to the fulcrum and lever (or seesaw) as it applies to asymmetrical balance (sometimes known as *occult balance*). In Figure 170 we had a board with equal weights on each end, which caused it to pivot in a straight line, in perfect balance. In Figure 181, we perceive the adjustment that turns symmetrical balance into asymmetrical balance. The moment one of the weights is changed, an adjustment must be made; either the other weight must be changed to match it or other objects must be substituted and combined until an equal weight is established at each end of the board. In terms of the seesaw, the heavier child moves closer to the fulcrum and the lighter one moves back; if this does not bring the board or lever into balance, another small child is added and the necessary adjustments in position are made to bring the board to balance.

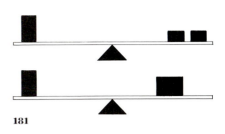

181

As can readily be seen, achieving asymmetrical balance is more complicated than working in simple symmetry, and it is infinitely more interesting. In two-dimensional works, the two halves will have equal *visual* weight but the shapes and colors will be disposed unevenly. In arriving at asymmetrical balance, the artist calls into play all the elements of design: texture may balance shape, values may balance one another, color may balance shape or size. The possibilities are infinite and challenging. As an example, let us analyze the photograph in Figure 182.

Perhaps the most remarkable thing about this photograph is not so much the superb balance as the fact that no one posed for it. No doubt dozens of people walked by without seeing anything unusual about the scene, but Henri Cartier-Bresson, with his artist's eye, immediately recognized the unique elements and recorded them. The

182

183

center of interest, of course, is the two small boys in the foreground, but they are balanced by the two little girls in their bookend pose *plus* the textural interest of the peeling wall at the left. Only a trained eye would have realized the necessity for the expanse of wall. The light patches balance the light panel at the right, pulling the composition together and complementing the figures of the girls. The arms of the man echo the triangular shape of the boys' legs, which are repeated in the letters on the disintegrating poster.

The balance in Figure 183 is deliberate, yet here again it is neither symmetrical nor static. The canvas is divided into two vertical panels but they are not of the same width, and the liveliness of the surface seems far more expressive of vibrating light than concerned with basic structure. Only careful analysis reveals the care with which details have been composed. Two strong curves lead our eye to the center of attention, the sailboat, and a series of opposing curves cuts across them, echoing the arc of the sail, the wiggles of the waves, and the arched windows and the balustrades of the buildings. Three light areas on the right balance the light form of the boat, and the strong verticals above it at left are reflected in the railing that provides a border at lower right. The thick black lines of the rigging on the sailboat appear in staccato accents on the white building at the top of the work, diminishing into dots that texture the embankment at extreme right. The balance here is both complex and subtle, composing the order that harmonizes a diversity of elements that could otherwise have become chaotic.

Balance is a vital factor wherever design is involved. We noted in Figure 171 the obvious balance of glass against concrete in the contemporary building design and can now understand the bands of glass being wider than the concrete, because the concrete is heavier visually. We can also see the importance of the vertical divisions between windows in balancing the strong horizontal lines of the total structure. Balance is crucial in interior design as well, in combining rough and smooth textures, using figurative visual textures with expanses of

184

solid-colored tactile ones, and in maintaining balance of scale between the size of the room and the furniture within it. The Japanese have long been masters of balance in landscape design, using vegetation sparingly for its texture against other natural patterns. Such attention to pattern can range from fine sand, painstakingly raked into designs, to large flat stones symbolizing stream beds and combined with mosses and wood for ultimate textural variety (Fig. 184).

We will be dealing a great deal more with balance as we pursue our explorations of design. To conclude this discussion, however, it is amusing to take note of a design that combines both symmetrical and asymmetrical balance. The storage unit in Figure 185 is solidly symmetrical when closed (as at the top) but when open it displays an exciting, almost improbable asymmetry. If symmetry tends to suggest repose, asymmetry is characteristically active and dynamic. In this example of design, one is able to fill the compartments however one will, and then with a quick movement transform the whole unit into instant and dignified order.

185

Summary

There are two kinds of balance: *structural* and *visual*. Structural balance concerns the physical equilibrium of a three-dimensional work, whereas visual balance concerns our perception of balance in a design. Balance of any kind is dependent upon a central axis around which the weight or tension must be equally distributed. Balance can be either *horizontal* or *vertical*. Visual balance includes *symmetrical balance*, in which two halves of a design are identical, and *asymmetrical balance*, in which the visual elements balance one another through interest and variety rather than total similarity. Symmetrical balance includes *radial symmetry*, in which the design is circular and appears to revolve around a *central point* or to radiate from it.

For Further Exploration

1. Fold a 9 × 12″ sheet of black construction paper in half horizontally and cut a design in it. You may find it helpful to refer back to Figure 96, imagining it folded in the center. When you have finished cutting, lay the design flat on a sheet of 12 × 18″ white paper and study the bilateral symmetry. Now begin snipping away parts of the design, first on one side and then on the other, adding bits of bright color or painting in areas of texture to balance shapes and spaces that are left. Work slowly and with careful consideration to the way in which each segment is balanced by another element in the design. When you have worked out a satisfactory balance, paste the cut pieces to coordinate with the painted or textured areas, forming a complete and balanced composition.

2. On a 9 × 12″ sheet of white paper, paint a cityscape in which the bottom half will be buildings of various heights and shapes and the top will be primarily sky. Working vertically, pull the composition into balance with varied textures—trees balanced by clouds, windows in buildings balanced by darker areas of sky or perhaps planes or birds flying. Pay special attention to *weight*, making certain that the buildings are balanced by enough interesting texture or variety of shape to prevent the picture's being heavy at the bottom.

3. Design a logo, using black drawing ink on white paper. Make it a personal logo using your own initials and perhaps a symbol of a special interest. Try making it symmetrical, then rearrange it (or try another design entirely) to make it asymmetrical. Discuss which of the two is more interesting and analyze the reasons.

CHAPTER ELEVEN

Proportion and Scale

Proportion and scale both have to do with size; otherwise, they are two distinctly different principles. It is important to understand the difference.

Proportion

Proportion is the principle that makes our world recognizable. Seeing familiar proportions of trees and buildings makes us know we are home. The proportion between visible sky and land can make the difference between a forest and a desert, and the proportion of water to land determines not only the character of our surroundings but the ways in which we travel and the kinds of recreation we pursue.

We recognize our friends by their proportions, identifying them from a distance before their faces are discernible. The proportion of leg to torso, of weight to height, of shoulder width to length of body—all these differ widely, creating individual human shapes. Proportions in our faces give us even more specific individuality. People sometimes undergo surgical procedures to alter the size of an individual feature, but it is not the *size* that is the primary concern. It is the relationship of a nose or mouth to the rest of the face that determines the overall appearance, the *proportions* of the features to each other. Most of us would feel quite different if an alteration were made in our proportions. Being three inches taller would make it possible to reach objects on high shelves, and being fifty pounds lighter would totally change one's attitude about clothes. Our proportions become an integral part of our life as well as of our appearance to the world.

Definition of Proportion

Proportion in design, as in people and landscape, is a matter of *relationship between parts*. Proportion is not *size* and it is not *scale*. For well over a century, the Venus de Milo was lauded in literature and song as the ideal of feminine beauty (Fig. 186). Originally the Greek goddess Aphrodite, the goddess of love, this particular version was unearthed on the island of Melos (or Milo) in 1820. Considered immediately to be the noblest of all the renditions of the goddess of love, she was known by the Roman name of Venus. Her actual measurements were far from what most women would choose, however. Gods and goddesses were consistently carved larger than life and the Venus de Milo

186. *Aphrodite of Melos.*
3rd–2nd centuries B.C.
6′8″ (2.03 m) high. The Louvre, Paris.

171

stands at 6′ 8″ high, with vital statistics correspondingly ample. She is at large *scale*, but that has nothing to do with her *proportions*. The fact that her waistline hovers around 45″ is simply one aspect of the balanced, harmonious, and aesthetically pleasing figure that has become famous as the ultimate in feminine beauty.

The Greek Concept

The Venus de Milo is only one expression of the classic Greek philosophy enshrining beauty and harmony in art and architecture and seeking the fundamental principles upon which nature and life in all its forms exists.

The Golden Mean

The belief in mathematics as a governing force in the universe is expressed in many Greek writings. Euclid is credited with stating the precept of the Golden Mean, a simple expression of the importance of *proportion* and *balance,* often stated as *moderation in all things.* As the key to living successfully, this simple statement holds as true today as it did in the time of the ancient Greeks. Whether we are speaking of eating, drinking, exercise, or rest, moderation and a balance among all the elements of our lives is the secret of keeping proportion, and consequently, physical, mental, and emotional health. Aristotle expressed this sense of balance by explaining that moderation is a median between two vices. For example, courage is a virtue. We think of its opposite, or balancing vice, as cowardice. Yet cowardice is only one end of the scale. At the other end is foolhardiness, which might be characterized as courage carried to an unreasonable extreme, thus placing it in the category of a vice. Courage, then, is the virtue or *mean* between the extremes of cowardice and foolhardiness. We can test this philosophy on any virtue we choose: generosity is the *mean* between stinginess and being a spendthrift, compassion is the *mean* between cruelty and indulgence.

The Artistic Application

Centuries of scholars have been intrigued by the manner in which the philosophy of the Golden Mean (sometimes called the Golden Section) was put into practical use by Greek painters, sculptors, and architects. By using a simple line as the mean between two other lines, they created a rectangle that became the basis for temple plans, for the composition of vases, and for the construction of sculpture. This is the way it works: at the bottom of Figure 187 are four lines, two of which (Line B) are the same. Line B is the mean between the other two lines, simply because it is longer than Line A in the same proportion that it is shorter than Line C. By using Line A as the width of the rectangle and combining Lines A and B to form the length of the rectangle, the Greeks created a unique and subtle shape within which they composed sculpture (Fig. 188), vases (Fig. 189), and many of the decorative elements of their architecture and painting. This shape has come to be termed the Mean and Extreme Rectangle, composed of three lines, of which one is the mean between the other two, the extremes.

187. The Golden Mean and Extreme Rectangle. The proportion of side *a* to side *b* is the same as the proportion of side *b* to side *a* plus side *b*. The smaller rectangle and the larger one are therefore in the same proportion. This rectangle is also known as the Golden Section.

188. Greek sculpture appears to have been composed within the proportions of the Golden Mean and Extreme Rectangle.

THE GOLDEN MEAN AND EXTREME RECTANGLE

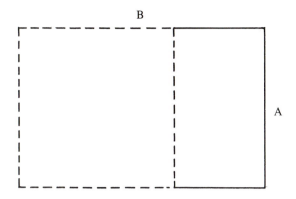

B

A

LINE A

bears the same relationship to

LINE B

that

LINE B

bears to

LINE A PLUS LINE B

187

188

189

189. The Golden Mean and Extreme Rectangle contain exactly the proportions of many Greek vases.

190. The logarithmic spiral is based on arcs of circles, which in turn are based on squares of graduating size.

191. Radiograph of the shell of a chambered nautilus.

192. Paul Caponigra. *Sunflower.* 1965. Photograph. Private collection.

193. Diagram of the seed structure of a sunflower.

The Spiral

The spiral is another form in which the Greeks saw the meaning of the universe. You will note that in the rectangle in Figure 187 a square is outlined in broken lines. This particular square, if repeated in orderly progression outward, as in Figure 190, forms the basis for the spiral. Circles circumscribed within each successive square flow into a curve that is exactly the same shape as the chambered nautilus (Fig. 191). Known as the *logarithmic spiral*, this progression governs the growth of much of nature, including snail shells, elephant tusks, rams' horns, and cats' claws—anything that grows in size by increasing on the outer edge so it does not change its shape. Thus the logarithmic spiral makes it possible for natural forms to grow to tremendous size without losing their fundamental *proportions*.

The Fibonacci Series

The Greek discoveries in the area of proportion lay obscured for twelve centuries until a medieval European scholar named Leonardo

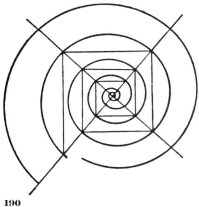

190

191

da Pisa made them the basis for many of his mathematical studies. Known as Fibonacci, he discovered, among other things, a series of numbers having a close relationship to the laws of natural growth. Like the elephant tusks and rams' horns, the series develops in a regular pattern, with each succeeding number being the sum of the previous two: $1 + 1 = 2, 1 + 2 = 3, 2 + 3 = 5, 3 + 5 = 8, 5 + 8 = 13, 8 + 13 = 21$, and so on indefinitely. Fibonacci, working with numerical values and mathematical relationships, found a precise and specific numerical relationship between this series of numbers and the Mean and Extreme Rectangle. Furthermore, Fibonacci and his followers discovered that the numbers in his series coincide exactly with the numbers of seeds in the various rows or layers in pine cones, artichokes, pineapples, and sunflowers (Fig. 192). Such growth patterns also follow the structure of the spiral (Fig. 193).

192

193

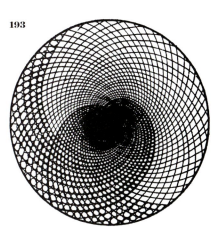

Dynamic Symmetry

At the beginning of the twentieth century, Jay Hambidge, a classical scholar at Yale, became interested in applying the Mean and Extreme Rectangle to the composition of paintings, dividing the space on the canvas according to its *proportions*, building the painting upon the framework thus established. He called the system Dynamic Symmetry, and the concept appealed to many artists, who saw it as a guarantee of pleasing proportions within a work, with a subsequent assurance of harmony and order. Thelma Winter executed several works in enamel

194

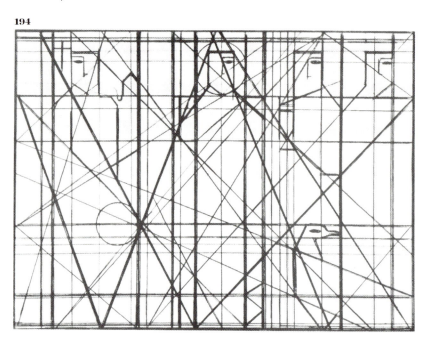

195

on metal using Dynamic Symmetry. In Figure 194 we see her schematic division of space according to geometric principles, establishing the primary horizontal, vertical, and diagonal lines upon which she ultimately composed her symbolic human figures (Fig. 195).

The Contemporary View

If our discussion of proportion seems to have centered on the ancient Greeks, it is because of the vital and enduring contributions they made, linking the concept of proportion to universal truths and to all fields of knowledge. Two thousand years later, the Greeks continue to represent an ideal of beauty that has never been surpassed, as we saw in Chapter 8 in our discussion of rhythm.

Twentieth-century artists, however, have felt a need to go beyond traditional means of expression, living and working as they do in a world totally different from anything that has gone before. The Industrial Revolution, two world wars, space and air travel, and the threat of the atomic bomb have made it necessary to find new and even startling means of communicating the artist's relationship to the universe. These means have assumed widely varied forms. René Magritte, a Belgian painter working early in the century, saw painting as both a way to knowledge and a means of moral liberation. His approach was to produce surprise effects by bringing together incongruous objects, creating new ones, and transforming those that were familiar. Among other things, he painted burning stones and wooden skies and hundreds of wonderfully imaginative images. Throughout his career he composed at intervals a series of studies based on the human torso, jarring the viewer with the realization that the painter could dictate at will the ways in which such basic realities were viewed. In Figure 196 his shock effect depends entirely upon his innovative use of proportion.

194. Thelma Winter. Schematic diagram using dynamic symmetry.

195. Thelma Winter. *Christ and the Apostles.* 1956. Enamel on steel, 5′ × 7′6″ (1.53 × 2.29 m). Bethany Evangelical Lutheran Church, Ashtabula, Ohio. (Executed in collaboration with Edward Winter.)

196. René Magritte. *La Folie des Grandeurs.* 1961. Oil on canvas. 39½ × 32″ (100 × 81 cm). (Private Collection, U.S.).

196

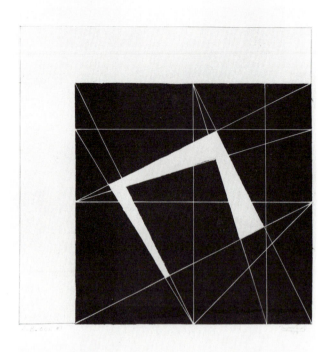

197

197. Jack Tworkov. *L. B. OOK #1.*
1979. Oil on Kindura paper,
14 × 11″ (35.6 × 27.9 cm).
Courtesy Nancy Hoffman Gallery.

198. Mark Innerst.
Reservoir Hill. 1986.
Oil and acrylic on board,
23¼ × 22¼″ (59 × 56.5 cm).
Courtesy Creative Artists
Agency, Los Angeles, California.

199. Romare Bearden.
Lamplite Evening.
1986. Collage,
11 × 11⅜″ (27.9 × 28.8 cm).
Private collection.
Courtesy Cordier & Ekstrom.

200. Rodrigo Moynihan.
Self-Portrait.
1986. Oil on canvas,
20 × 16″ (50.8 × 40.6 cm).
Courtesy The Robert Miller Gallery,
New York.

Later in the century, painting became abstract, avoiding any reference to recognizable objects. Many artists who worked in abstract style relied entirely upon proportion for structure and pattern. The painting in Figure 197 could be a study in dynamic symmetry. Its interest relies entirely upon the division of space and the light and dark lines and shapes that articulate it. It is a composition in which *proportion* is the predominant force.

Scale

Scale refers to *relative* size. On our state road map we see a legend telling us that 1 3/4″ is equal to 30 miles; on a United States road map this legend tells us that 1 3/4″ equals 200 miles. Both maps are the same size. The latter map covers more territory, so the territory has to be shown at a smaller scale. The roads between cities look shorter and the lakes and other features appear smaller.

One of the first decisions an artist or designer has to make about a work is the scale at which it will be rendered. Like the map, the canvas or paper remains constant; the extent of what will be shown upon it depends primarily on *scale*. If a vast landscape painting is envisioned, everything about it will be small in scale (Fig. 198). If the subject is a group of figures or the interior of a room, the scale will be larger (Fig. 199). If we plan a portrait, the scale may be close to life-size,

198

199

depending upon how much of the figure is to be shown (Fig. 200). In designing fabric or wallpaper, scale depends upon other considerations. Drapery and upholstery fabrics generally have larger-scale designs than fabrics for clothing, but the ultimate use of the fabric is a determining factor in choice of scale. Large rooms and wide expanses

200

of window can accommodate larger patterns than small areas can, and a modern interior may use bold splashes of color or shape whereas a "country-style" interior, seeking cosy intimacy, will be furnished in small allover prints.

Scale as Symbol

Large scale is logically associated with power, physically as well as symbolically. The lion's reputation as king of beasts presumably rests on his size and ferocity, and his association with power and dignity have carried over into heraldic imagery throughout Europe (Fig. 201). Artists in all ages have depicted the most important characters in a work as much larger than the rest, as in the stele (upright stone) commissioned by an Akkadian king 4000 years ago to celebrate his victory over invading armies (Fig. 202). The king stands at the top, dressed as a god and twice the size of his own men, towering over the fallen enemy. In Christian art Christ is the towering figure in any group. In anthropomorphic design throughout the world, gods, in human form or otherwise, are the largest figures in the composition.

201

202

203

Monumental Scale

Enormous scale in architecture usually has its origin in human traits, as the tangible and visible expression of a fear or aspiration.

Human Ego

Some of the largest structures ever built are the Egyptian funerary tombs and temples. Clustered in vast "funerary districts," these monuments were erected by a pharoah to house his mummified body after death, and were furnished with every possible convenience, sometimes including live slaves, to assure his afterlife as a comfortable continuation of his power on earth. The three great pyramids at Gizeh and numerous temples elsewhere (Fig. 203) were built with the primary purpose of self-glorification for an individual.

201. Lion passant guardant and Lion rampant, favorite symbols in British heraldry. Both designed by G. Scruby.

202. *Victory Stele of Naram-Sin.* c. 2300–2200 B.C. Stone, height 6′6″ (1.98 m). The Louvre, Paris.

203. *Funerary Temple of Hatshepsut,* Deir el-Bahari. 18th Dynasty, c. 1480 B.C. Canali Lodovico, Rome.

Devotion

Just as gods are depicted as larger than life in painting and sculpture, so the temples built for their worship traditionally dominate the landscape surrounding them. Only the most magnificent domes were worthy of the mosques of Islam, and the medieval cathedrals of western Europe soared almost beyond human vision with their vaulted ceilings and spires symbolizing a majestic God through use of space (Fig. 204).

One of the world's most beautiful monumental buildings is the result of devotion to a human being. Erected in the 17th century by Shah Jaha, the Moslem emperor of India, the Taj Mahal (Fig. 205) was designed as tribute to his wife who, having borne fourteen children, died at the age of thirty-nine. Designed in huge scale, its dome rising 210 feet high, it is built of solid white marble and intricately decorated with lacy carving and precious gems. Its sole purpose was to house the remains of the Shah and his wife, but its motivation was the expression of everlasting devotion.

Security

Huge scale is implicit in fortresses and castles, built to impress and intimidate as well as to defend. Krak des Chevaliers is one of a chain built to guard the route of the crusaders as they made their way to Jerusalem. Protected on three sides by precipices, it stands on a spur of black basalt rock in the Syrian desert. The human figures on the ramp to the left in Figure 206 provide a graphic measure of its impressive scale.

204

204. *Cathedral of Amiens,* France. 1220–1279. Interior length 438' (133.6 m), nave width 48'   (14.6 m), vaults 139' (42.4) high.

205. *Taj Mahal.* Agra, India. 1630–48. 186' × 186' × 187' (56.7 × 56.7 × 57.0 m) high.

205

Elegance

Castles were built to impress with their impregnability; palaces were built to impress in another way. Whether the habitation of a king, emperor, or archbishop, the castle is a symbol to the world of high station in society and of wealth. Many palaces are treasure houses of art, gathering in the best works in crystal, silver, and gold that could be commissioned or transported from all parts of the world. One of the most famous is Versailles, the fulfilled dream of Louis XIV of France, who engaged the best artists and architects of his time to plan not only the buildings but the extensive and elaborate gardens (Fig. 207).

206
207

Diminutive Scale

If huge scale bolsters the human ego, diminutive scale has a special appeal, a combination of childhood wistfulness and a protectiveness for things small. The model railroad holds a lifelong fascination for many people, offering endless opportunity to add details and landmarks to a world that is part mechanics and part fantasy. Model ships present a similar allure, particularly to someone who has spent part of a lifetime at sea. Dollhouses have been the delight of children for generations. Huge buildings represent a need to create something larger than life, but the world of miniatures makes the human being a giant in control of an entire landscape and of the lives of the toy people who inhabit it.

Scale as Perception

Sometimes our reaction to scale is a matter entirely of perception. Chinese artists characteristically express a veneration for nature by showing the human form as a minute entity amid the awesome beauty of a natural setting. In Stephen Lowe's painting in Figure 208, the figure is perceived as a tiny speck wrapped in the bleak tonality of a world in which he is totally alone. The dark bark of the pine tree looks enormous, even overwhelming. Scale here is the very essence of the

206. *Krak des Chevaliers.* Syria. Crusader castle. 12th–13th centuries.

207. Palace and Gardens of Versailles. 1662–1688. Gardens designed by André Le Nôtre.

208. Stephen Lowe. *The Hermit.* 1972. Chinese watercolor on rice paper, 23 × 37″ (58 × 94 cm). Private collection.

208

209

work, imparting the fundamental Chinese philosophy in a deeply emotional way. In the wood engraving in Figure 209, by contrast, Rockwell Kent has treated the human wanderer in the western manner. Here it is the man who is important, the conqueror of the mountains.

Most of us have delighted in the story of *Alice in Wonderland*, laughing at the antics of the Mad Hatter and the Cheshire Cat. The characters remain with us, but the real fascination lies in what happens to Alice when she takes the magic potion that makes her very large and then reduces her to normal size again. Her perceptions of her own size and the complications engendered by sudden changes in scale are a crucial part of the story (Fig. 210).

209. Rockwell Kent. *Voyaging.* 1924. Chiaroscuro wood engraving on maple in black, white, and olive green; 6″ (15 cm) square. National Gallery of Art. Washington, D.C.

210. John Tenniel. *Alice after Taking the Magic Potion,* illustration from *Alice's Adventures in Wonderland* by Lewis Carroll, written in 1865.

211. Scene from Act I of Richard Wagner's *Parsifal.* Produced by Wieland Wagner, Bayreuth Festival, Germany. 1968. Collection Bildarchiv Bayreuther Festspiele.

210

211

Scale for Emphasis

Large scale is inherently dramatic, and theatrical productions frequently make use of its potential for striking effects. It is particularly appropriate to opera, in which the tragedies of human lives are played out against the larger workings of fate. In Wieland Wagner's production of *Parsifal*, the setting, while simple, conveys a magnitude that dwarfs the human beings involved in the mystical plot (Fig. 211). The manipulation of lighting combines with the scale to convey solemnity and a sense of the supernatural in the quest for the Holy Grail.

Many painters do immense paintings to emphasize the message they wish to convey, which may be as simple as the fact that the world has become increasingly complex and inhuman. Commercial artists find scale equally useful in conveying a message. The composition in Figure 212 was created for an advertising campaign by a company that specializes in recycling industrial solvents. Although the Statue of

Clean up your act, America.

212. Photograph created by Dick Greene and Arnold Paley of Brand Advertising as a part of a campaign for Safety-Kleen, a company that specializes in recycling industrial waste products.

Liberty is depicted by a live model standing in a 55-gallon drum in the middle of a plastic-lined pool, the photographers manipulated the scene to produce the compelling picture of the statue gradually sinking beneath a New York harbor filling up with sludge. The message is difficult to ignore.

As principles of design, proportion and scale are both of primary importance. All the elements and principles of design interact and support one another, and we separate them only for purposes of study. Since both proportion and scale are related to size, it is easy to confuse them, but there is a very clear distinction to be made: proportion is a matter of size relationships *within* a given entity (whether an object or a work of art), whereas scale refers to the size of the entity as gauged against an *outside* measure, such as the human figure.

Summary

Proportion is a matter of relationships between parts. The Greeks expressed proportion in the Golden Mean (or Golden Section), by means of which they developed the Mean and Extreme Rectangle that is the basis for many of their works of art and architecture. The Greeks also saw universal importance in the form of the spiral, and their studies were revived in the late Middle Ages through the Fibonacci series of numbers relating the growth of natural forms to the Golden Mean. Dynamic Symmetry is a system based on these studies of proportion.

Scale refers to relative size as gauged against some constant, such as the human figure. Large scale has been used through the centuries to symbolize power, to express human ego, to embody devotion, to obtain security, and to impress the world with one's social importance. Diminutive scale appeals to people for different reasons, providing a tiny world over which a human being can exercise complete control. Scale is perceived in many ways, expressing the philosophy of the artist, attracting attention, and giving dramatic emphasis.

For Further Exploration

1. On a 12 × 18″ sheet of drawing paper, draw a rectangle that measures 10″ on one side and slightly above 6″ on the other. Bisect one corner of the rectangle and drop a diagonal to the far side, forming a square. Studying the diagram in Figure 193, draw five lines, vertical, horizontal, and diagonal, that will divide the spaces in an interesting manner. Paint the resulting shapes, being aware of balance and texture as well as value. Create a balanced abstract composition. The result will be an exercise in dynamic symmetry.

2. Follow the steps in Project #1 but after drawing the lines, develop a realistic painting within the framework—still life, landscape, or figures.

3. Choose a familiar object such as a flower, a piece of fruit, or a seed pod, and paint it at very large scale. Develop textures and shapes that you have not previously noticed at the regular scale, and make them an important part of the composition.

4. On a 12 × 18″ sheet of white drawing paper, compose a painting consisting of familiar objects drawn to such a large scale that none of them fits completely on the paper. Overlap several shapes, letting them all run off the paper, leaving only parts of each object. From this "blown-up" scale, compose a painting. You may find that it has become abstract but still retains some of the characteristics of the original subject. Experiment until you find a composition that pleases you, then paint it, using visual texture and variations of tone, in any of the color harmonies we have studied.

CHAPTER TWELVE

Variety and Unity

No element or principle of design stands alone. Even a single line on a sheet of white paper becomes not only *line* but a contrast in *value*, and it immediately creates *shape* in the *space* in which it operates. In every chapter on an element or principle we have necessarily been involved with interrelationships with other elements and principles. We are linking variety and unity together in one chapter because these two are particularly interdependent. Variety without restraint can become chaotic, but variety created with an underlying sense of unity becomes both interesting and harmonious. Conversely, excessive concern about unity in a work can lead to monotony and even boredom. The immediate means of relieving such a condition is by the introduction of variety. Thus, these two principles depend upon each other for the *balance* that is essential for any effective design.

Variety

If rhythm is the *underlying* principle of the universe, variety is certainly the principle that is most obvious. Variations in flowers, rocks, butterflies, animals, and seashells offer such enchantment that people travel the world in search of specimens for their collections. Near at hand, rocks, soil, broken sidewalks, and dirt roads all have their range of colors and textures from mineral deposits and vegetation, and there is variety in the shape and size of puddles, glinting from changing lights.

Contrast

The essence of variety is contrast: rough against smooth, light against dark, large against small. In Figure 213 the photographer used dramatic lighting to emphasize all of these. The result is a fascinating interplay of shapes and textures whose relationships seem to shift as we watch. The intense lights and darks flow throughout, unifying the rugged surface into a harmonious composition. This is an excellent example of choosing and combining natural elements to establish the principles of variety and unity working together.

An eloquent expression of both unity and variety through the use of a single material can be seen in the cast aluminum sphere in Figure 214. A simple metal sphere would be unified but it would not

213. Minor White.
Capitol Reef, Utah. 1962.
Photograph. Gelatin-silver print,
12⅛″ × 9¼″ (30.73 × 23.5 cm).
Courtesy Minor White Archive,
The Art Museum,
Princeton University, N.J.

214. Robert Bart. *Untitled.*
1965. Cast aluminum,
12¾ × 17¾ × 17½″ (32 × 45 × 44 cm).
Courtesy Leo Castelli Gallery,
New York.

213

214

be interesting; therefore, Robert Bart has covered the surface with a fretwork that radiates and expands with the curvature of the mass, the frets being small at the two poles and increasing in size toward the center. What arrests our attention, however, is the slicing open of the sphere, revealing perfectly smooth surfaces within. These now lie exposed and in startling contrast to the patterned exterior, though the use of rivets along the inside edges serves as a transition from the smoothness to the extreme roughness.

The same principles operate in quite another medium in Figure 215. This textile was woven and then decorated by the batik method, long an art among the people of Indonesia. This Javanese example is designed on the diagonal, a form considered to be of superior merit because, when worn, it is more interesting than designs on a horizontal or vertical axis. There are two unifying devices here: the allover consistency of the background pattern and the repetition of identical ovals over the entire surface. As always, the design quality lies in the variation. Every alternate oval is turned at right angles: this immediately varies the visual pace. Even more important, perhaps, is the fact that each oval is unique, with an individual design unlike that of any of the other ovals on the fabric. This is variety carried to a superlative degree, yet there is nothing chaotic about it, for the regularity of the ovals and their skillful placement guarantee a unified pattern. These careful design considerations have made this particular textile a superb example of the art of batik.

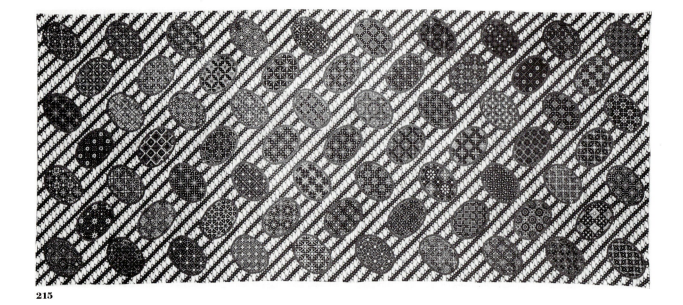

Originality

All art depends in some degree upon the quality that makes it unique, the original conception or use of materials arising from an individual artist's imaginative vision. In Figure 216 several professional designers have exercised their talents and imagination upon an age-old and utilitarian object, the chair. Each of the results is original in the extreme, even bordering on fantasy.

216

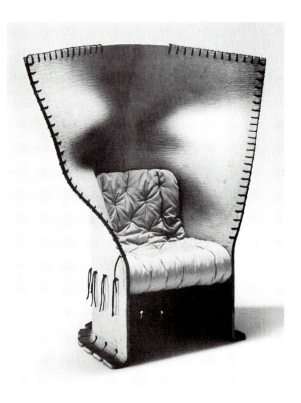

The chairs demonstrate the originality resulting from treating a specific object in individual ways. Originality is also demonstrated by the treatment of a specific *motif* as a theme, building a complete composition upon it, as a musical work is built upon a theme and variations. Such a work is the large tapestry in Figure 217, in which the entire composition consists of variations on the triangle. The triangular shape is older than the pyramids, but in the hands of Viennese weaver Maria Plachky it attains a dynamic contemporary quality, varying in size and shape, interpreted in different colors whose contrasting values sparkle even in a black-and-white reproduction. Just as the triangular shape thrusts to a sharp tip, the composition radiates outward in an orderly progression that imbues the surface with movement.

On the other side of the world, Dorothy Torivio of the Acoma Pueblo in New Mexico has used the diamond shape, this time curved with a counterpoint of petal shapes (Fig. 218). The form of her pot is in the tradition of the pueblo, which has existed since the year 1200. Her versatility, however, has leaped beyond the traditional forms of pueblo pottery decoration, combining ancient symbols in a new and original way entirely her own. The indented diamond signifies leaves as it has always done in pueblo design, the cross within it means the four directions, and the white dot in the center indicates snow. Yet the surface of the pot shimmers with movement, causing it to be compared to the "Op Art" of contemporary painters. The versatility of the potter has carried revered traditional forms into a new world, retaining ancient meaning in a new and original form.

215. *Kain panjang.* Java, Jogjakarta region. Batik, cotton; warp 8′ (2.45 m), weft 3′4″ (1.04 m). The Sylvia Bishop Collection. Palm Beach, Florida.

216. Left, Leslie Goodchild. *Easter.* Carved beech with lacquer finish. Middle, Jeffrey Maron. *Antelope Spiral.* At Art et Industrie, New York. Right, Gaetano Pesce. *Feltri.* Mfr., Cassina, S p A, Milan.

217. Maria Plachky. *Modulation Centrale.* Tapestry, 10′2″ × 10′2″ (3.09 × 3.09 m). Vienna.

218. Dorothy Torivio, Acoma Pueblo, New Mexico. Black and white plate and seed pot. Gallery 10 Inc. Scottsdale, Arizona.

217

218

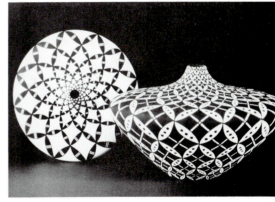

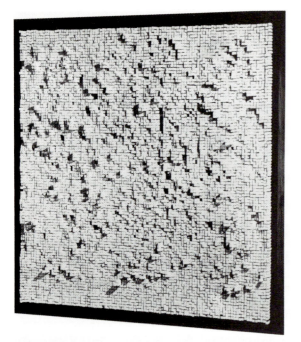

219   **220**

219. Vjenceslav Richter:
Relief Meter.
Movable aluminum elements,
39 × 39 × 7″ (100 × 100 × 18 cm).
Belgrade.

220. Louise Nevelson.
Sky Cathedral. 1958.
Wood construction painted black,
11′3½″ × 10¼″ × 1′6″
(3.44 × 3 × .46 m).
Collection, The Museum of
Modern Art, New York
(gift of Mr. and Mrs. Ben
Mildwoff).

221. Church of the Transfiguration,
Kizhi, USSR. 1714.

Variety Through Structure

We have been analyzing examples of variety achieved through shape
and texture, but in some cases it is the fundamental structure that is
responsible for variety. Such a case is the aluminum panel in Figure
219. Composed of aluminum cubes similar in size, this work could be
as monotonous as a flat wall mosaic executed in solid color. In this
case, however, the artist varied the heights of the units, arranging low
and high cubes in what appears to be a haphazard fashion but that
catches the light from whatever source, translating cubes and shadows
into a lively and ever-changing pattern. The shadows, combined with
the lines between the cubes, create an allover texture that makes a
square meter of aluminum into a varied and interesting design.

Sculptor Louise Nevelson made even more dramatic use of structure in her assemblages of "found objects"—bits of wood, wheels, old
newel posts, and other miscellaneous oddments that many people
would scarcely have noticed. Since they were all of wood, she sorted
them into similar sizes and shapes and enclosed them in boxlike
shelves, also of wood. Finally, she painted the entire composition the
same color. The result (Fig. 220) is a unified and dynamic composition, carefully composed of vertical and horizontal shapes, diagonals,
curves, and combinations. Furthermore, she retrieved articles discarded because they had outlived their usefulness, and gave them an
entirely new aesthetic purpose.

Architecture has appeared in many styles through the centuries,
from medieval castles to high-rise condominiums. The Russian
church in Figure 221 displays what may well be the extreme limits of
variety in a wooden structure. The series of onion domes reaching
upward, the curved niches behind them, and the molded serrated

221

shingles all represent ways in which wood can be formed and bent with careful skill. Behind this variety, however, lies an overriding unity, through the repetition of the dome shape throughout the structure, and the continuation of the textural richness on both domes and gable. Moreover, the series of crosses on the domes provides not only a symbolic harmony but a very real visual thread that harmonizes and unifies the diverse structural masses.

Unity

Few designs include every element and principle of design. Some works have no color. Others have only smooth texture. Some have a minimum of variety or rhythm. However, one principle is essential to any work of art or design: the principle of unity. No work can function aesthetically without the sense of unity that relates its parts and harmonizes its elements into a total composition.

Opposition and Transition

One of the surest means of achieving unity is by transition, a gradual blending of two opposing elements. Such elements, embodying the concept of *opposition,* set up a dynamic force that gives interest to a composition but that produces at the same time a tension that can make a work disquieting. For example, jarring colors next to one another or the juxtaposition of rough and smooth textures can be extremely effective, or they can be dissonant elements in a composition. When the latter is the case, unity can be achieved by using gradations of the colors that finally blend into one another or by repeating the varying textures at intervals throughout the work.

The design by M. C. Escher in Figure 222 is a superb example of unification through transition. It begins with thirteen fish and thirteen waterfowl, which, if not opposite in shape, are certainly dissimilar. The first step toward unification is the placement so that all 26 are headed in the same direction. With careful manipulation, the artist has worked out the two diverse shapes so that, with perceptive placement, the negative shapes between members of one species is similar to the positive shapes of the other; in other words, the spaces between

222

222. M. C. Escher.
Lucht en Water 1. (Sky and Water 1).
1938. Woodcut,
17⅜ × 17⅜″ (44 × 44 cm).
Haags Gemeentemuseum, The Hague.

the fowl are similar to the shapes of the fish, and the fish are held together by shapes resembling the fowl. A third unifying device is the diamond shape in which the figures are composed, a simple turning of the basic square that forms the total work. A fourth device is the border of lines that pulls the entire composition together, gradually blending almost imperceptibly from black on white at the top to white on black at the bottom.

Variety is also skillfully handled. The top goose and bottom fish are rendered realistically through a detailed depiction of surface texture. Working toward the center, each line of figures becomes increasingly abstract until realism disappears completely and both fish and fowl become intermingling shapes forming an abstract design. The reversal of background—black geese against a white ground and white fish against a black ground—is a means of achieving both unity and variety, since in each case the background flows into the figures in the opposing area. This is an eloquent example of the interaction of variety and unity. In this work it would be impossible to separate them.

Unity Through Color

Escher's transition into unity is a matter of shape and value; in Gauguin's painting in Plate 25 (p. 209), unity is achieved through color. The painting is divided into two sections quite opposite in nature. The bottom half appears to be primarily horizontal and almost entirely green except for the figures of the animals and swineherd. The horizontal stone wall cuts across the canvas, making the clean division between bottom and top. Above this line the landscape rolls and swells, the color becomes warm and varied, and the geometric forms of buildings provide sharp accents. The only transitional forms are the cow, with its head reaching into the upper section, the head of the man, and the steeple of the church, which bridges both halves. These form links between top and bottom, but they are not strong enough to provide unity. This is left to the triangular field of green lying against the hill in the center of the work, reflecting and amplifying a small green hillock in the same color at the swineherd's feet, a bright yellow-green that brings out the color in the grass and, in its yellow rim, repeats the color of the pigs.

Unity Through Value

Caravaggio, painting in 16th-century Italy, made dramatic use of *chiaroscuro* (light and dark) to give a strong emotional quality to his work. In the painting in Figure 223, a work recently discovered after centuries of obscurity, the contrasts are less theatrical than in many of his works, but there is a pronounced light at the right in opposition to the velvety dark of the shirt on the player at the left. The manner in which these two extremes are reconciled is obvious yet skillful transition. The dark and light are simply combined into stripes, first broad stripes widely spaced on a light ground near the highlight, then narrower stripes, equally dark and light in width, on the figure in the center. The motif is carried through the feather on this figure's cap, which leads our eye toward the darkest area, here broken by the face of the player on the left, which is much lighter than the faces of the

223

other two. Hands, faces, and the game board all play their roles in the transition, being placed strategically to play light against dark in satisfying balance.

Unity Through Line

Any textile has built-in unity because of the fibers that form the framework of the fabric, regardless of the woven design. This unity can be a matter of texture or of line, depending upon the character of the fibers. The quilt in Figure 224 has the same sort of advantage, simply because the artist used striped fabric throughout. No matter what he does with the fabric, and he does a great deal, the stripes provide *lines* that establish unity. However, the line is not limited to the stripes in this case but includes the undulating edges where pieces of different colors come together. We note four small points of emphasis, in which the lines (stripes) are translated into fragments tipped at angles to form tiny diamond shapes. These are placed within a bigger square that echoes other such squares that in turn combine to create large shadowy squares underlying the strong rhythms of the work. Not one stripe curves or bends, yet the surface of the quilt seems filled with flowing movement. This work shows the same intricate planning and interlocking that we saw in Escher's fish and fowl,

223. Caravaggio.
The Card Sharps. c. 1592–95.
3′2⅜″ × 4′5⅝″ (0.98 × 1.36 m).
Kimbell Art Museum,
Fort Worth, Texas.

224. Michael James.
The Concord Cotillion.
Cotton and silk quilt.
Courtesy of the artist.

225. Poster for National Air and Space Museum. Design by Miho. Earth Photos by NASA.
(©1976 Smithsonian Institution).

224

225

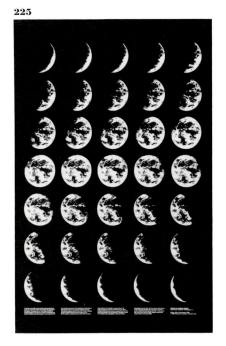

but there is no need for transition here. Unity is provided not from the blending of opposites but by the overriding linear character of the fabrics that compose it.

Unity Through Shape

The poster in Figure 225 is perhaps the ultimate example of unity through shape, since it is composed entirely of circles of the same size, representing the earth as seen from outer space. Thirty-five circles placed in close proximity on a black background would hardly escape having unity; the problem would be to avoid monotony. This has been done in a subtle and logical way. Since we are dealing with space, the earth is shown in different degrees of shadow so that each row differs considerably from the rows above and below it. In fact, only the center row shows complete circles; from that horizontal axis, the rows become increasingly shadowed, ending in slim crescents at both top and bottom. The gradual modification of the circular shape lends variety to the poster. It also involves the viewer in *closure,* as our perception completes the partial shapes to tell us they are all still circles. Inevitably, we sense a flow of action; our eye is guided throughout the composition, coming to fulfillment in the center row of complete earth forms.

Unity Through Repetition

It should now be obvious that any of the elements of design can be used as unifying devices: color, value, line, shape, space, or texture. The unifying aspect of an element lies in its repetition. This, of course, was eminently obvious in the poster above, yet any color or shape repeated at intervals throughout a work will unify it, pull it together, relating the various areas, even when the shape is not readily obvious.

Renoir's *Le Moulin de la Galette* (Fig. 226) employs this means of achieving unity but in a very subtle way. Our first impression of this composition is that the canvas seems filled with a *mass* that moves and changes constantly. Upon closer analysis, however, we find that the artist has carefully composed the crowd into a series of triangles. A dancing couple forms a natural triangle, and this motif has been expanded to include the predominant group of large figures in the foreground so the smaller shapes seem to radiate backward from it. In counterpoint to the triangles are the circular shapes of heads and hats, beginning large in the foreground and shrinking to dots in the background, then repeated with emphasis on the globes of the lighting fixtures overhead. These lights serve an additional function. They are light blue in color and thus repeat the light blue that is used throughout the composition, in the surface upon which the figures are danc-

226

ing, in a dress just left of center, and especially in the striped dress of the girl in the foreground.

The Illusion of Motion

Figure 227 is a page from a Book of Hours, a compendium of devotional texts used by the Roman Catholic Church, divided into eight parts representing the "hours" of the liturgical day as practiced in the monastic life. It was the custom for artists in the Middle Ages and later to create such books in calligraphic script and to illustrate (illuminate) them for members of reigning families. The Limbourg Brothers produced a unique version in which miniature paintings filled whole pages, including a complete set for the activities of each month, as they took place within the duke's realm. This example shows us February, in which, characteristically, all kinds of symbols are included: the village and familiar landscape, the calendar and signs of the Zodiac, and the peasants doing the chores of the season. With so much symbolism to be considered, the work could easily become a chart delivering a message, but it is unified into a lively composition by the subtle S-curve sweeping from lower left to the semicircular calendar at the top, a curve formed by depiction of the various activities taking place. These are distributed in such a way that they lead our eye

226. Auguste Renoir.
Le Moulin de la Galette.
1876. Oil on canvas,
4'3½" × 5'9" (1.31 × 1.75 m).
Louvre, Paris.

227. Limbourg Brothers.
February from the *Très Riches Heures of Jean, Duc de Berry.*

227

228

throughout the painting, following the movements of the figures. Thus, by the use of the elements and principles of design, the artist is able to control the viewer's reactions, directing the eye to what the artist wants us to see.

In contrast to the measured pace of the peasants is the motion of the painting in Figure 228. Here we sense several levels of action, similar to what we see in the layers of floating sea life in a tidal pool. We can look at this work for a very long time without seeing all the nuances of movement and depth represented. The dark forms become transparent in places, thus appearing to float over other forms, and the splashes of white are like bursts of foam. The title does not reveal the artist's reference, so we interpret the work according to our own experiences and associations. There is no question as to the unity of the work, however. The lights and darks are repeated in perfect balance, and the lines in both light and dark race throughout, providing a unified framework. Even as we look, these seem to move and change, and it is this sense of motion that is the primary unifying force.

Symbolic Unity

Harmony and unity are closely allied. Harmony of color provides unity, and other kinds of harmony lead to a symbolic unity that is less apparent. In the Chinese painting in Figure 229 we can distinguish unifying details—the craggy forms of vegetation that culminate in a mere suggestion at the top of the mountain, the triangle of the pagoda repeated in the tips of the hills, the horizontals of bridge and buildings opposing the stark verticals of waterfalls and rock. Yet the most com-

228. James Brooks.
Number 27, 1950.
Oil on canvas,
37 × 46″ (94 × 117 cm).
Collection of Whitney
Museum of American Art.
Purchase, with funds from
Mr. and Mrs. Roy R. Neuberger.

229. Attributed to
Li Ch'eng (Ying-ch'iu).
*Buddhist Temple amid Clearing
Mountain Peaks.* 10th century.
Ink and color on silk,
44 × 22″ (1.12 × .56 m).
The Nelson-Atkins Museum of Art,
Kansas City (Nelson Fund).

229

pelling sense of unity comes not from an inventory of details, but from the overall sense of the grandeur of nature. The painting is an expression of Tao, which seeks harmony in all things, conveying the mysterious unity that lies behind all the elements of nature. The harmonizing, and therefore unifying, force here is the philosophy of unity itself and the enveloping mist with which the artist has chosen to express it.

As we have seen, the elements and principles of visual design interweave and flow together, becoming interdependent components of the total composition. Not all of them will necessarily appear in one composition, but they form a body from which the designer can choose; they are the tools with which one works to create a successful design. We are now ready to explore the *physical* tools and materials of the designer and the ways in which they too affect the designer and the design.

Summary

Variety and unity are inevitably interdependent, relying upon each other for the balance between chaos (from excessive variety) and monotony (from extreme unity). Variety is the most obvious of the design principles in nature, where its essence is contrast. In works of art, variety results from the originality of the artist, who may achieve it in many ways, including the use of diverse elements in the structure of a work.

No work of art or design can function aesthetically without unity. Unity is often achieved by opposing forces brought into harmony by means of transition. Unity can also be achieved through color, value, line, shape, and repetition of any of the elements of design throughout a work. Unity is achieved as well by the illusion of motion in a composition, and symbolic unity can be attained by the overall spirit of a work, which imbues it with innate harmony.

For Further Exploration

1. Divide a $9 \times 12''$ sheet of white paper into twelve squares. Using tempera and a small brush or felt markers, *vary* each square as much as possible from the others, using dots, lines, cross-hatching, tiny floral or leaf motifs, and so on. Study the finished effect. How much is variety and how much is confusion? Much will depend on whether you have carried the same colors into various areas, or repeated shapes, or established directions. The object is to establish as much variety as possible.

2. Now cut out the squares in Project #1 and arrange them on a $12 \times 15''$ sheet of black paper. Trim them into different shapes, varying their sizes. Segregate them according to color and motif and experiment to see if dominant directions can be achieved by arranging the pieces in new ways. If you cannot achieve unity, paint new squares to provide it, either by repeating colors and textures or by echoing patterns that already exist. When you have a composition that is harmonious, paste the squares in place.

3. Using a compass and a ruler and a $12 \times 18''$ sheet of white paper, draw a row of $1''$ circles along one $12''$ edge of the paper, leaving a $1''$ border and approximately $\frac{1}{2}''$ between circles. On the opposite edge draw a row of $1''$ squares at the same distance from the edge and the same distance apart as the circles. Using ink or paint, combine these two opposing rows into a unified composition by means of transition. Possible methods would be to use similar allover patterns in a square and a circle, to use the same color on opposite sides of the paper, and to create new shapes between the two rows, shapes that are part square and part circle.

4. On a $12 \times 18''$ sheet of paper, paint three $1''$ stripes of one color along the $18''$ edge, approximately half an inch apart. Along the opposite edge paint three similar stripes in the complementary color. Unify the composition by repeating the two colors in different areas of the paper, combining them, superimposing them, and making use of texture and pattern.

PART 4
Design in Action

The Influence of Materials on Design

Different materials have different qualities—of appearance, of durability, of the manner in which they respond to manipulation. In our exploration of the ways in which designers work, it will be helpful to look at some of the materials available and at the qualities that make them respond to the hands of the artist. First, we will consider the *characteristics* that make materials workable.

Characteristics of Materials

Plasticity is the predominant trait of clay. It is also a quality of glass, although glass, to be plastic, must be in a hot molten state. This is true as well of the large body of contemporary design materials designated by the term *plastics*, a term arising from their extreme ease of shaping. Plasticity is a characteristic of artist's paints and is the quality that makes it possible to manipulate them with a brush or palette knife.

Malleability derives from the Latin word for mallet and refers primarily to manipulation through the use of various tools. The malleability of metals makes it possible for them to be hammered in addition to being melted down and cast or shaped by any number of industrial processes. The term can be applied to wood or to clay, but in general it refers to the capacity of metal to be extended or shaped under some degree of pressure. Gold, the most malleable of metals, can be hammered into gold leaf—sheets thinner than the finest tissue paper.

Related to malleability is the quality of *tensile strength*, by virtue of which a material resists breakage under pulling or bending forces. It is tensile strength that allows metal to span great distances without underlying support at the center, as in much contemporary architecture and especially in suspension bridges (Fig. 230). Still another related characteristic to be found specifically in metal is *ductility*, a quality that permits it to be drawn out in fine wires.

Flexibility refers to the capacity of a material to be bent, twisted, or turned without breaking. Most obvious among flexible materials for the artist's use are textiles, fabrics, and leather. Wood can be made flexible in several ways. It can be *laminated* by cutting it into thin sheets and gluing them together. It can be shaped into *bentwood* by application of steam. Many designers shape it into sculptural forms, using a combination of bending and carving (Fig. 231).

230

231. Golden Gate Bridge.
San Francisco.

231. David N. Ebner.
Sculptural writing chair. 1978.
Bubinga, 30 × 18 × 18″
(76.2 × 45.72 × 45.72 cm).
Collection of Mr. and Mrs.
Mohlmann.

232. Killoanig. *Carving of a Man.*
Spence Bay, North West Territory.
c. 1978. Soapstone, 12 × 7 × 5″
(30.48 × 17.78 × 12.7 cm).

233. Henry Moore.
Reclining Figure. 1945–46.
Elmwood, length 6′3″ (1.91 m).
Private Collection, U.S.

234. Grain patterns of wood.
Most wood is cut in one of
three ways, each presenting a
distinctive grain pattern.

231

The *rigidity* of a material can be exploited by the designer. The sculptor and carver work *against* a rigid mass, pitting human hands and strength against a substance that yields but does not bend. Metal, wood, and stone all provide such rigidity. The sculptor welds or rivets rigid metal or carves from resistant plastic, wood, or stone (Fig. 232). Many of the materials of architecture and furniture design are necessarily rigid, since they must support weight and provide permanent shape. Landscape designers use rigid materials in walls and fountains to accent the softness of plantings and splashing water.

Plate 25. Paul Gauguin. *The Swineherd, Brittany.* 1888. Oil on canvas,
29 × 36½″ (74 × 93 cm). Private collection, Los Angeles.

Plate 26. Erasmus Grasser.
A Morris Dancer. 1480.
Painted wood,
height c. 25″ (63 cm).
Munich Stadtmuseum, Germany.

Plate 27. Winslow Homer, U.S. 1836–1910.
Woodsman and Fallen Tree. 1891.
Watercolor on paper.
14 × 20″ (35.6 × 50.8 cm).
Museum of Fine Arts, Boston.
Bequest of William Sturgis Bigelow.

232

233

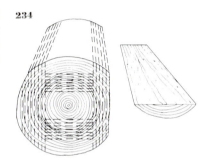

Solidity combines rigidity with mass. It is a quality that is found more often in sculpture than in the other arts, since the sculptor carves from a solid block, usually of wood or stone. Solidity makes possible the carving out of positive and negative masses to form a unified design (Fig. 233).

Materials as Components of Design

Wood

The growth pattern of trees determines the grain of the wood. In temperate zones, trees produce two rings of growth each year. The early or spring wood is lighter than the later or summer wood, so the rings alternate between light and dark to form a definite grain pattern. Grain is also affected by the branching characteristics of a tree. Knots form where a branch begins, so a tree with many branches, such as pine, will produce knotty lumber.

The method of sawing lumber has a great deal to do with the way in which the grain shows (Fig. 234). Even so, each type of tree presents its special grain pattern.

Wood is classified in two ways. *Hardwood* comes from deciduous trees, which generally have broad leaves that are shed annually. Hardwoods (maple, oak, walnut, mahogany, and the fruitwoods such as cherry and pear) are difficult to carve but take fine detail without splintering. They are widely used for furniture and have provided exquisite carved panels in castles and cathedrals.

Softwoods generally come from coniferous trees. The terms *hard* and *soft* refer to the cellular structure rather than to actual hardness, although the so-called softwoods are usually easier to work than hardwoods. The innate beauty of wood makes it possible simply to stain it, wax or oil it, and buff it to a soft *patina*, the term for a mellowing of surface quality.

234

Plain (flat) sawed
(cut tangent to annual rings)

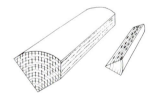

Quarter sawed
(showing figure)

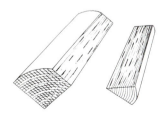

Rift sawed
(showing a pencil line grain)

The Influence of Materials on Design   **211**

Carved wooden figures are often *polychromed* (Plate 26, p. 210) to give a lively quality, and the rich grain of certain woods has led to a highly developed art of *inlay*. This may mean the inserting of small pieces of finely colored and grained wood into a wood background to form scrolls, arabesques, scenes, fruit, flowers, and so on in the art of *intarsia*, widely used in furniture in Italy in the 15th century and later. It may mean *parquetry*, in which flooring is inlaid with wood in geometric patterns (Fig. 235). Or it may mean *marquetry*, in which ivory and shell are combined with wood in decorative furniture design.

We have mentioned the use of laminated wood and bentwood (p. 207). Plywood is a form of laminated wood but with the layers alternating in grain at right angles to one another. There are three or five layers, usually, giving greater strength than could be found in a board of the same thickness. When the outer or visible layer is of finer wood than the others, this layer is known as *veneer*. Veneer, a thin layer of decorative wood used to enhance strong structures, is widely employed in furniture design.

As a design material, wood offers infinite variety in grain and texture, ease of workability, and an innate warmth and flow not to be found in any other material.

235

235. Parquet flooring in the waiting room of the new addition to the Frick Collection, New York. Harry Van Dyke, architect; John Barrington Bayley, designer. Courtesy The Frick Collection.

236. Rhyton. Persian, 5th century B.C. Gold, height c. 6¾″ (17 cm), diameter at mouth 5½″ (14 cm). Metropolitan Museum of Art, New York. (Fletcher Fund, 1954).

237. Chunghi Choo. *Decanter.* 1980. Silver plate on copper, 8 × 6 × 5″ (20.32 × 15.24 × 12.7 cm).

236

237

Metal

The value of metal to the designer lies in its potential for being formed. Because of its flexibility, metal can be hammered, stretched, and shaped in many ways. The diverse visual qualities of the various metals are also of tremendous value in design. *Gold,* considered the most precious of metals throughout recorded history, has long been shaped into many forms, both decorative and practical (Fig. 236). Both gold and *silver* are too soft to be worked in their pure state so they are *alloyed*—combined in a fluid state with another metal. Silver is usually alloyed with copper, whereas gold may be alloyed with both copper and silver.

Another way of combining metals is to *plate* a layer of metal on top of another metal, in much the same way as veneer is applied to wood. The flowing form of the decanter in Figure 237 has been given a rich gleaming surface by the use of silver plating.

Pewter, an alloy of tin with varying amounts of antimony, copper, and lead, has been used since the days of the Roman Empire and possibly before. Both pewter and silver frequently bear *hallmarks,* tiny stamped insignia that identify a work by maker and place of origin and that testify to the purity of the metal. These marks are indications of excellence and are invaluable guides for collectors of old pewter and silver.

Other alloys used by designers are *brass* and *bronze.* An alloy of copper and zinc, *brass* has a long history, especially in the Orient and the Middle East, where brass objects have been manufactured for centuries. Typically, these works are incised with elaborate designs, and they may be inlaid with enamel or other contrasting materials. Brass has a yellower color than copper and it takes a high polish. Among its uses are musical instruments, ceremonial pieces for churches, and decorative door hardware. *Bronze,* an alloy of copper and tin and various other metals, is darker, harder, and longer lasting than brass. Its

238

239

rich brownish-red color makes it popular for desk accessories, medals, and commemorative plaques. Most bells are cast from bronze, since its qualities include not only durability but the potential for a rich tone. In addition, bronze is the primary metal for cast sculptures, including the large statues that dominate parks and plazas around the world (Fig. 238).

Aluminum is noteworthy for being among the lightest and most plentiful of metals. It does not rust, and it can be treated in a variety of ways—chasing, etching, and hammering—to produce practical and relatively inexpensive bowls, trays, and kitchen utensils. It is also used by contemporary sculptors (Fig. 239).

Mexican designers have achieved a distinctive style in the use of *tin*, which they adapt to a full range of fanciful forms, frequently painting portions of them, stippling or piercing them by the use of pointed nails, or setting them with colorful stones. Sometimes backed by wood for solidity, Mexican tin finds shape in wastebaskets, lighting fixtures, Christmas decorations, and mirror and picture frames (Fig. 240).

Iron has a long history of both decorative and practical uses. Iron tools more than five thousand years old have been found in Egypt, and for centuries farmers all over the world used tools forged from iron. Medieval blacksmiths created architectural accessories whose beauty still embellishes old churches and castles (Fig. 241).

Steel, like iron, is a structural material of enormous importance in the contemporary cityscape. Basically an alloy of iron and carbon with

an admixture of other elements, steel is manufactured in thousands of different types and in different compositions to serve specific purposes. The alloy of stainless steel contains about 12 percent chromium and often a small percentage of nickel to prevent corrosion. Almost no home built today could be entirely without steel, for it appears in structural members, plumbing fixtures, sinks, countertops, appliances, and an infinite number of other places. Nor have the aesthetic aspects of steel been ignored, for it is frequently used in sleek, clean-lined furniture and has become a staple in practical, inexpensive kitchenware and table settings.

Effective design in metal depends on the designer's knowledge of the potential of the many metals available as well as a thorough grounding in the processes by which metal can be formed. We will discuss these processes in Chapter 16.

Stone

Our oldest known buildings and monuments were erected of stone. Among the earliest known designs are those carved on the stone tools and structures of primitive peoples. The Egyptian pyramids, built of limestone quarried from the cliffs along the Nile, and the Parthenon, erected from Pentelic marble from the mountains of Greece, have survived through the centuries to tell us of the customs, beliefs, and especially the artistry of ancient peoples. Most of the medieval cathedrals were built of granite or sandstone, the hard and enduring varieties of stone that nevertheless yielded to the hands of sculptors to produce amazingly intricate forms (Fig. 242). Buildings today make use of a variety of stone, from marble to "fieldstone," which gives a warmth to interiors when used in walls and fireplaces. Design in stone relates closely to the geographical area in which the artist works. The Eskimos of northern Canada carve in soapstone, which comes in a range of grays (Fig. 232) . The people in the Orient and Central and

238. Augustus Saint-Gaudens. *William Tecumseh Sherman*. 1903. Bronze. Over lifesize. Grand Army Plaza. New York.

239. Dorothy Gillespie. *Conjured Image of a Past Presence*. 1980. Enamel on aluminum, 8 × 5 × 5′ (2.44 × 1.52 × 1.52 m). Courtesy Birmingham Museum of Art (gift of Silvia Pizitz).

240. Mexican tin mirror and candleholder.

241. Doorhinge. German. 15th century. Wrought and incised iron. Length 19½″ (49.5 cm). Metropolitan Museum of Art, New York. (gift of Henry G. Marquand, 1887).

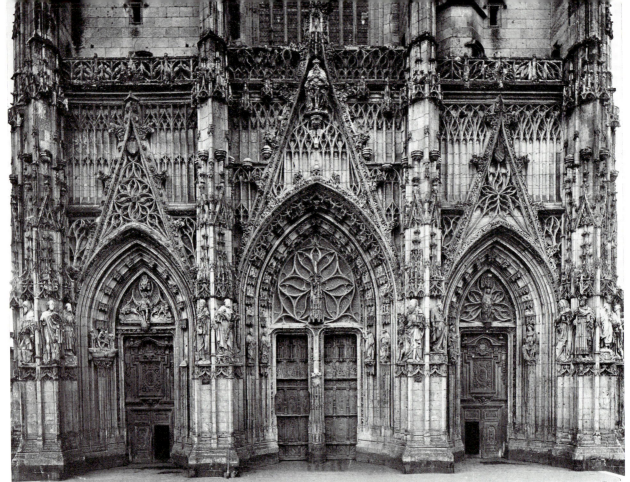

242

243

South America have created symbolic works in jade for many centuries. Being extremely hard, jade is not carved with chisels but is worked with blasts of wet sand or crushed stone, or with drills of carborundum. It comes in a gamut of greens and a creamy white with an elegant translucence (Fig. 243).

There are, in addition, the many precious stones used as jewelry and as symbols of wealth, royalty, or religious devotion. Semiprecious stones are used in jewelry by many contemporary designers.

Concrete

Concrete is a mixture of cement, sand, stone, and water. The cement is a carefully standardized product produced by manufacturers from alumina, silica, lime, iron oxide, and magnesia burned together in a kiln and finely pulverized. It is generally termed Portland cement, a name given to it in 1824 by an English cement maker, who saw a strong resemblance between hardened cement and the so-called Portland stone that was much used for building in England at that time. Ancient Egypt and Rome both used concrete for construction. Today concrete is cast in decorative building blocks and in panels such as we saw in Figure 140.

A stunning development in the use of concrete was made in the mid-20th century by Italian architect Pier Luigi Nervi with his inven-

216 *Design in Action*

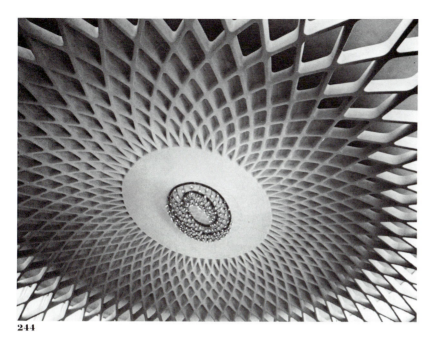

244

242. Façade of Saint Wulfran. Abbeville, France. Begun 1488.

243. *Regardant Feline with Bifid Tail.* Chinese, 6th–10th century A.D. Light grey-green jade with white and black markings; 3¼ × 4⅛″ (8.26 × 10.41 cm). Asian Art Museum of San Francisco (The Avery Brundage Collection).

244. Pier Luigi Nervi. Interior of dome. Baths at Chianciano. 1952.

tion of *ferrocement.* Ferrocement is composed of layers of steel mesh sprayed with cement mortar so that the total thickness of the material is only slightly greater than that of the mesh itself. The result is superior strength coupled with elasticity, a combination that stands great strains without cracking yet can be used in amazingly thin shells and intricate designs (Fig. 244).

Clay

Clay is composed of alumina, silica, and various other elements, frequently including materials that give it color. Geologically, there are two types: *residual clay*, which has remained in the place in which it was formed, and *sedimentary clay*, which has been carried by the action of water and wind to be deposited in new locations. Sedimentary clay picks up impurities as it moves, and it also breaks down in particle size. The impurities contribute color, and the finer particle size means the clay will be more plastic.

Rarely does one clay offer all the characteristics desirable for ceramic design. Most often clays are mixed to yield a clay *body,* and these can be classified into three basic types according to the temperature at which they are fired.

Earthenware fires in the lowest temperature range, at about 2000 degrees Fahrenheit. A rather coarse, porous ware, it is usually reddish in color and is never completely waterproof except when glazed. Unglazed earthenware pots are ideal for plants because the water can "sweat" through the walls. The Italian "terra-cotta" (baked earth) refers to this ware, which is also used for sculpture and red-clay tiles.

Stoneware fires in the middle range of temperatures. The clay is usually light gray or tan, is relatively durable, and has a warm, earthy quality that makes it a popular choice for decorative bowls and vases and for dinnerware.

The Influence of Materials on Design **217**

245

246

The highest-fired ware of all is *porcelain*, made from a very pure and usually white clay. In firing, porcelain becomes extremely hard and glossy; it can therefore be molded into thin and translucent forms such as the fine dinnerware treasured by generations of brides. Contemporary potters vary both the color and the forms of porcelain to express contemporary trends (Fig. 245). The term *china* refers to a white ware similar to porcelain but firing at a lower temperature, so called because in the 17th century such ware was brought to Europe from China.

Clay is the very substance of the earth and as such it has played a long and vital role in civilization. Every ancient culture developed ceramic techniques (Fig. 246).

Glass

Glass is among the most naturally beautiful of all materials. Simply molded, colorless, and unadorned, it provides a fascinating study in transparency, fluidity, and sparkle. We think of it as fragile, but many types are as hard and durable as steel.

245. James Makins.
Dinnerware and Goblets. 1984–85.
Porcelain, thrown.
Courtesy of the artist.

246. Jars. Crete. 1600–1500 B.C.
Buff-colored earthenware with red-and-black slip. Herakleion Museum, Crete.

247. Cut-crystal chandelier.
1969. 21″ (53 cm). Designed by Carl Fagerlund, Orrefors, Sweden.

Like clay, glass is based in the earth, although it is also formed on the moon by volcanic action and the bombardment of meteorites. Its chief ingredient is silica sand in its purest possible state. Most glass is manufactured, but *obsidian,* a shiny black substance created by volcanic action, is an example of glass that has formed naturally. As long ago as 27,000 B.C. primitive people carved it into flints, arrowheads, and simple tools.

Chemically, glass consists of silicon dioxide fused with metallic oxides; when cooled, this substance becomes a brittle solid. There are literally thousands of types of glass, but they fall generally into six broad categories.

Lead glass is the aristocrat of glasses. A complex of potassium-lead silicate, lead glass, often known as crystal, is the most important to the designer. Its high refraction makes it useful for lenses and prisms, and because of its brilliance when cut, it serves for fine table crystal, decorative cut glass, and reflective chandeliers (Fig. 247).

247

Windows, lighting fixtures, table glasses, bottles, and other common glass products are made from *soda-lime glass,* which is inexpensive and easy to form.

Borosilicate glass has the special property of being highly resistant to heat and temperature changes. It therefore goes into such hard-working products as cooking utensils, laboratory equipment, and aircraft windows.

Fused silica, 96 percent silica glass, and *alumino-silicate glass* are all remarkably tough materials that have been developed for scientific and industrial applications. They function in such demanding places as missile nose cones, laser-beam reflectors, and space-vehicle windows.

Various compounds are added to molten glass to improve its appearance. Iron oxides, often present as impurities, give glass an undesirable greenish or brownish cast, so decolorizers must be used. Coloring agents, on the other hand, give the jeweled tones that distinguish stained-glass mosaics as well as the various hues that can be seen in tableware.

Perhaps the most important element in glass design is space, since transparency provides an added dimension. When glass is backed with silver nitrate or other coating to form a mirror, this quality becomes almost infinite.

Fiber

Fibers are one of the ancient materials of design, having provided baskets, clothing, and even shelters since earliest times. Today, by definition, a fiber is a thread, or something capable of being spun into a thread, and is usually associated with *textiles,* which are *woven fabrics.* There are four principal fabrics most generally used: *silk, cotton, linen,* and *wool.*

The Chinese discovered the silkworm and developed the art of silkmaking from the cocoon of the silkworm, which is spun in one continuous thread. *Silk* is soft and fine and is frequently given body by weighting, shaking the fabric in a solution of sugar or metallic salts. Variations of silk include crepes, satins, pongee, and shantung, resulting from different weaving techniques or the use of a different variety of silkworm.

Cotton is the most valuable of the fibers, as each strand has a natural spiral twist that provides strength and resiliency.

The linum (flax) plant produces *linen*, which is a better conductor of heat than cotton and gives a sensation of coolness when worn.

There are many varieties of wool, which may come from sheep, alpaca, vicuña, and various goats, such as the Angora and the Kashmir, both of which produce long silky hair. Like human hair, wool is composed chiefly of keratin with a shaft that is somewhat twisted, causing the fibers to interlock closely during spinning and weaving and to adhere firmly when pounded or felted.

Synthetic Fibers About 1910 the Dupont company created rayon, intended as a substitute for silk, whose price was rising steadily. Although called "artificial silk," rayon actually has nothing in common with silk, since it is composed entirely of cellulose. For many years, however, "silk stockings" were actually knit of rayon. In 1935 Dupont produced *nylon*, the first of the synthetic fibers to be used widely in textile manufacture. It is only one of a large family of plastics based on coal, among which *polyester* is the most familiar, being widely used in combination with cotton to prevent wrinkling. *Ultrasuede*, the invention of a young Japanese designer, while not technically a fiber, is widely used for fabrics, combining the elegance of leather with a lighter body and washability. Many of the synthetics have been troublesome in clothing, causing allergic reactions; however, designers readily find other uses for them, many of them purely decorative. Fibers in themselves are an important medium of design (Fig. 248).

248. Karen Jenson Rutherford. *Indiana Wandering 111.* 1986. Linen, ink; 27 × 16″ (68.6 × 40.6 cm).

248

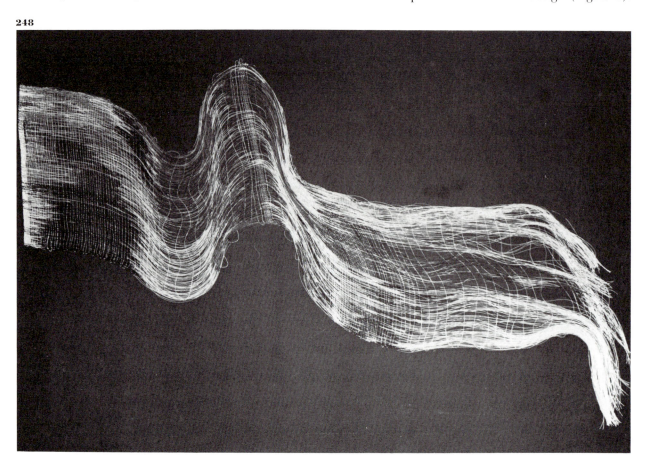

Plastics

The most contemporary of all design materials are the versatile substances we categorize as plastics. All plastics share a basic chemical trait: they are composed principally of carbon compounds in long molecular chains. Each type of plastic on the market today has been developed by polymer chemists to have a specific molecular structure, which in turn offers a definite combination of properties. The process of developing plastics began in the middle of the 19th century with the invention of celluloid to replace the ivory lost because elephant herds were being decimated. A hundred years later plastics became a major material in industrial design. There are two main divisions in the field of plastics.

Thermoplastic substances can be softened and resoftened indefinitely by the application of heat and pressure, provided there is not enough heat to cause decomposition. *Thermosetting* plastics, on the other hand, undergo a chemical change during the curing process; after that change takes place, the shape becomes set and cannot usefully be modified again when exposed to heat or pressure.

Since plastics now number in the hundreds, we will limit our discussion to those most useful to the artist and designer. These can be divided into "families."

Acrylics are thermoplastic materials with outstanding brilliance and transparency. Because they can be molded into large, unshatterable shapes and are readily carved, withstand weather and hard use, and accept a high polish, acrylics have become popular with sculptors and jewelers. Acrylic-based paints are among the most popular artists' media today.

Polyester is a thermoset plastic commonly used by designers for casting or embedding. Several different chemical types are available, but in fabric form, polyester can make a huge unbroken sheet. When reinforced with fiberglass, laminated polyester can be highly expressive and can be saturated with intense colors.

Epoxy, another thermoset plastic popular with designers, resembles polyester in many ways. It costs more but does not have the shrinkage factor associated with polyester castings, and it can be cast in the studio without elaborate equipment because it will cure at room temperature after the components have been mixed. When combined with metal powders, epoxy can yield a cold-cast metal similar in appearance to foundry-cast metal.

FRP, or fiberglass-reinforced plastic, is literally a plastic with which fiberglass has been combined for added strength. It appears in molded and laminated furniture, boat hulls, and automobile bodies. These plastics are weather-resistant and can be colored as desired. Artists use polyester-reinforced fiberglass as a sculpture medium because of the great freedom it provides in modeling. When applied to figural sculpture, this material can be amazingly lifelike (Fig. 249).

Melamines are exceptionally hard and durable plastics that have become a staple in countertops and casual dinnerware. Depending on their composition, these plastics can be transparent, translucent, or opaque, and they are available in many colors.

Polyethylenes may be flexible, semirigid, or rigid in form. A waxy surface identifies them in such products as squeeze bottles and freezer

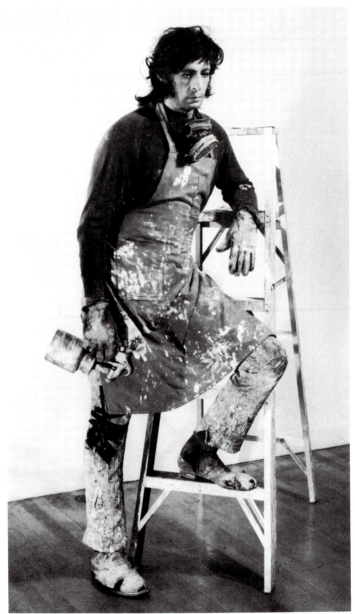

249

containers. Polyethylenes are resistant to breakage, weather, and extremes of temperature, and thus are practical for outdoor sculpture.

Vinyls are tough, lightweight plastics best known for their applications to fabrics, floors, and walls. Designs can be printed onto vinyl fabric, and the shiny "wet" look of vinyl appeals to many contemporary sculptors.

The variations of plastics number in the hundreds, with more developments being made, many with brand names identifying specific characteristics. Some are experimental, some have been proven highly toxic, and others, used extensively in interior design, have been looked upon with suspicion by doctors who treat the increasing allergies among Americans. Plastics tended to suffer from an early association with imitating traditional materials, as in the case of melamine dinnerware patterned after well-known pottery or china designs, or vinyl flooring imitating ceramic tile. Such uses, while practical, forced plastics into the role of "cheap imitation," from which they have effectively emerged into an independent status. We now recognize and appreciate the fact that machine fittings of plastic, in addition to not rusting or requiring lubrication, have more resilience than their metal counterparts, and clear plastic windows can be expected to withstand more strain and storm than glass. Contemporary designers have given plastics an identity entirely their own through the design of decorative accessories and hardware for architecture and interior design. In addition, plastics continue to fulfill their original purpose in reducing the depletion of the earth's natural materials.

Today the designer has access not only to new technological materials but to colors and textures from every part of the world. With such abundance and variety, possibilities for originality are literally boundless. In Chapter 16 we will discover some of the ways in which designers convert these materials into works of art.

Summary

Much of the effectiveness of any design depends upon the characteristics of the material used. Among the pertinent qualities of design materials are *plasticity, malleability, tensile strength, ductility, flexibility, rigidity,* and *solidity.* Various materials have different design possibilities. *Wood,* depending upon its grain for its species and the way in which it is cut, is found in carving, *parquetry* (inlaid flooring), *marquetry* (inlaid furniture design), in *laminated wood* and *bentwood* for furniture, and in *veneer,* in which a thin layer of fine wood is used over cheaper, stronger woods. *Metal* is important to the designer because of its potential for being formed. It may be plated with another metal, hammered, cast, and shaped in many ways. *Stone* is important in building and in carving. *Concrete* was used in ancient Egypt and has achieved a new form in *ferrocement,* steel mesh sprayed with cement mortar, which makes possible a lacy and graceful form. Clay may be residual or sedimentary, with various forms used by designers. Glass is noted for its transparency, fluidity, and sparkle. Various compounds are added to molten glass to give it color. Fiber is one of the most ancient of materials. Natural fibers are now supplemented by synthetics, which are used for fabrics or as a design medium in themselves. Plastics number in the hundreds but are divided into several families that add to the materials of the designer.

Forming Techniques

From earliest times people have molded clay or whittled wood to create objects of original design. These acts represent basic techniques for forming materials into designed objects. Such techniques are generally categorized in one of two ways: the *additive method* and the *subtractive method*.

Additive and Subtractive Techniques

In the *additive* method, material is built up or joined together to form a shape or mass. This is usually considered a sculptural technique, but it applies in many other areas as well. Anything that is welded, riveted, built with hammer and nails or screws, molded or formed in layers, erected with mortar, or otherwise built into a larger entity from smaller components can be considered to be created by the additive method.

The *subtractive* processes work in reverse, beginning with a large block or mass and cutting away certain parts to leave the desired effect. Subtractive processes include *carving*, *sawing*, and *turning*. Generally speaking, the subtractive method is more demanding than the additive one, for material cut away cannot readily be replaced. For this reason, sculptors and others make preliminary models of clay, which can be altered without permanent effect, perfected at small scale, and then used as a guide for the full-scale work.

Forming Techniques for Metal

In working with metal, the sculptor may rivet or weld. *Riveting* consists of cutting holes in two pieces of metal, inserting a metal bolt or pin, and then hammering the plain end down to form a second head. Often these heads form an integral part of the design (Fig. 250).

Welding is a technique for fusing metals based on the fact that acetylene and oxygen will produce a flame hot enough to fuse most varieties. Originally restricted to industrial uses, welding has become an effective method for contemporary sculptors. Most use bronze for fusion welding, in which an acetylene torch is applied to the metals to be joined as well as to a welding rod that melts and fuses with them; the resultant joining is of tremendous strength and durability. Im-

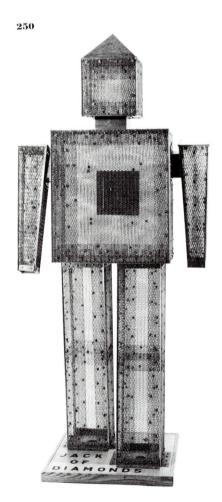

250

mense welded sculptures are indirectly an outgrowth of an industrial civilization, but they are even more the vision of the contemporary artist, who designs for settings surrounded by soaring buildings.

Several of the methods for converting metal into designed objects cannot be considered either additive or subtractive.

Hammering, one of the oldest methods, is still much used. Softer metals such as gold or tin can be hammered cold. *Raising* is a variation of hammering in which the metalworker strikes a flat sheet with hammers, working from the back and sometimes over a rounded form of wood or metal to create a bowl or saucer. *Beating down* reverses the process; the worker places the flat sheet over a recessed area and then hammers the metal into the depression.

Harder metals such as iron must be hot-hammered, or *forged.* A century ago the blacksmith and the ironmonger were as familiar as the corner grocer, serving the needs of an agricultural society by making and mending farm equipment as well as the harnesses and horseshoes that were a vital part of transportation. Today blacksmithing is experiencing a rebirth, both as a way of making tools, and as a medium of design (Fig. 251). In simplest terms, forging calls for a piece of metal to be heated in a furnace until it is red-hot (sometimes white-hot), then held on an anvil with tongs and pounded with hammers.

Spinning is the method by which round objects are formed on a revolving *lathe,* a process similar to turning wood. Flat sheets of soft metal are pressed over wooden forms that turn on the lathe to create the round shapes of pitchers, goblets, vases, and sometimes jewelry.

Methods for forming metal objects for mass production will be discussed under Industrial Design in Chapter 19.

250. H. C. Westermann, *Jack of Diamonds.* 1981. Galvanized wire lath and corner beading with brass bolts and washers, on a wooden base, 6′8″ × 3′3″ × 1′11″ (2.02 × .97 × .59 m). Collection Mr. and Mrs. Alan Press, Chicago.

251. L. Brent Kington. *Weathervane #27.* 1980. Forged mild steel, 47 × 14 × 51″ (1.19 × .36 × 1.3 m). Collection the artist.

251

252

Forming Techniques for Glass

Glass is one of the few materials that must nearly always be worked in a state too hot to handle. Furthermore, molten glass cools and hardens very quickly, so the forming must be done in a short time and with great skill. There are four basic methods for forming glass.

Pressing is the oldest technique, in which semifluid glass is taken from the melting pot and worked into shape with paddles or other tools. In large-scale production, machine-operated presses force the glass into molds that shape the outsides of objects, while plungers are inserted to smooth the insides. Pressed glass is used for tableware, bowls, and vases, often in molds patterned after designs used in colonial America.

One of the most dramatic of all forming techniques is the ancient art of *glassblowing*, believed to have been invented in the 1st century B.C. The blowpipe is a hollow metal rod about four feet long with a mouthpiece at one end. The glassblower dips up a small amount of molten material with the other end, rolls or presses it against a paddle or metal plate to form a rough cylinder, then blows into the mouthpiece, producing a bubble of glass (Fig. 252). During the blowing, the blower controls the form by twisting the pipe, rolling with a paddle, cutting, shaping with a caliper, or adding more molten glass. The process is exciting and dramatic.

Glassblowing can be done in molds; however, in the last two decades there has been a strong revival of freehand glassblowing. Wonderfully novel effects can emerge from the blowpipe in the hands of a designer. Frequently the blown form is cut and polished.

Rods and cylinders, glass fibers, and some panes of window glass are made by a process known as *drawing*. This method calls for the molten glass to be pulled from the furnace by some device that controls its shape, such as a core to form tubes or a long, narrow trough to

252. Bob Held and Marvin Lipofsky blowing glass at the World Crafts Council Conference, Toronto, 1974.

253. Maria Martinez of San Ildefonso Pueblo constructing a pot by the coil method. Courtesy Museum of New Mexico.

form sheets. Drawing can also be done by hand. Affixed between two blowpipes, a glob of hot glass is drawn as the blowers gradually move apart.

Rolling produces uniform sheets of glass, such as those needed for plate-glass windows or mirrors. Rolling is a factory technique, but some artists have explored its potential in sheet-glass constructions.

Like clay or plaster and many plastics, glass in a molten or liquid form can be poured into molds and allowed to harden. This process is known as casting, and we will discuss it in detail in Chapter 16, since it is one of the fundamental processes of sculpture.

Forming Techniques for Clay

Sculptors often use clay in the additive method, a process known as *modeling.* This process enables the artist to build up, tear down, change, and modify the work as it progresses. Clay, wax, and plaster can all be used in this way and are usually built on an *armature,* or framework of metal, cardboard, wood, or other fairly rigid material, which supports the work as a skeletal structure supports the human body. Sculptors often use this method for making models of works they will later cast in metal or carve in stone.

The potter can handle clay by one of two general methods: hand-building and throwing. Hand-building breaks down into several different methods, which include pinching, coiling, and slab construction.

Pinching requires no tools; it is a simple process of pressing the clay between the fingers to produce a form, and it has definite limitations as to shape and size.

In *coiling,* the potter begins with a flat slab for a base, then gradually builds walls by coiling ropes of clay upon one another (Fig. 253). In Figure 75, page 68, we saw a pot made by this method by Maria

253

254

255

256

Martinez and her grandson Popovi Da; here we see her in the process. The walls can be left to show the ridges of the coils, or they can be smoothed with a gourd rind or a simple metal tool (Fig. 254). This method is used by Native American potters exclusively, following the tradition of centuries. It is an immensely versatile technique, with no restrictions as to size and shape.

Slab construction consists of rolling out flat sheets of clay, cutting them to size, and joining the slabs (Fig. 255). Slabs are the obvious method for making ceramic boxes, but they are also effective in creating earthy forms that speak of the living essence of clay and its relationship to natural forces.

Throwing on the potter's wheel is the most efficient means of creating round symmetrical objects, such as bowls, plates, mugs, and vases. Potters' wheels may be powered by kicking (Fig. 256) or by motor. In either case, the potter works upon a flat disc that turns at varying speeds as the ball of clay centered upon it emerges into the desired form. This is a highly skilled technique requiring months—perhaps years—of practice to achieve complete control (Fig. 257). During the throwing process, various devices can be employed to provide texture, ranging from a comb or fork to the potter's fingertips. Wheel-thrown pieces display an absolute symmetry, the result of a rhythm that unites the artist and the material in a creative unit (Fig. 258).

In the process of drying, the pottery forms go through the *leather-hard* stage, when the clay is dry enough to be handled without marring but still moist enough to be malleable. At this point it may be stamped, carved, or decorated with small coiled embellishments, and generally

254. The final form of the pot is achieved through shaping with hands and smoothing with a simple tool such as a potsherd or a gourd rind. Courtesy Museum of New Mexico.

255. In the slab method, sides and base are formed separately and then joined by the use of a wooden tool.

256. Denton Vars side-treadle potter's wheel, designed by Bernard Leach. Hardwood frame, weighted flywheel, fiberglass pan; 13″ (33.02 cm) aluminum wheel head.

257. Throwing clay on the potter's wheel.

258. Roseline Delisle. *L'Ogive.* Porcelain, thrown. 15 × 4½″ (38.1 × 11.4 cm) diameter. Courtesy Dorothy Weiss Gallery, San Francisco.

257

258

trimmed and blended into a smooth finished design. It is now ready to be fired.

The thoroughly dry *greenware* is fired in a kiln, which may be built by the potter and heated by gas, electricity, wood, coal, or oil, using fire brick and other materials for its construction. The heat of the kiln is measured by pyrometric devices, usually a small cone placed inside the kiln in front of a peephole. When the proper heat for firing is reached, the cone bends and the kiln is turned off and allowed to cool for eight or more hours before it is opened. The greenware has now become *bisque*.

If a glaze is desired, a second firing takes place, after the bisque ware has been brushed, dipped, or sprayed with a liquid composed of glaze powder ground into water. The powder contains silica, alumina, and flux, plus metallic oxides to provide color. When the pot is placed in the kiln for the glaze firing, it is usually chalky white or gray, but during the firing the chemicals in the glaze fuse permanently with the clay of the pot, resulting in brilliant color or in visual texture.

Forming Techniques for Fibers

Fibers are usually used to create fabrics by means of two techniques, *interlacing* and *pressure*.

Chief among the interlacing techniques is *weaving*, an outgrowth of basketry in which reeds and grasses are interlaced by working them in and out to form a solid surface. Fibers must first be spun, twisting them together into a long unbroken strand or *yarn*, which can then be used in interlacing. Today spinning is being practiced by many weavers, who often raise their own sheep, card the wool, and follow the process to its conclusion in beautiful handwoven fabrics. Originally fibers came from natural sources, as we mentioned in Chapter 13; today, in addition to synthetic fibers, weavers frequently work into their textiles such materials as glass, weeds, twigs, and paper. In Figure 259 James Bassler has combined silk, linen, sisal, and plastic.

The process of weaving consists of the interlacing of two sets of yarns arranged at right angles to one another. The instrument for weaving is the loom, which has developed in varying degrees of complexity throughout the world (Fig. 260). The principle of weaving depends upon the lengthwise yarns (the *warp*) being held rigid and parallel while the crosswise yarns (known variously as the *weft, woof,* or *filling*) move back and forth in and out across the warp yarns, to create a *web*, or fabric.

Although modern looms appear complicated, all looms depend on the same simple principles. First, the warp must be kept under tension. Second, there must be some device to raise selective warp yarns, to create a *shed* for the weft to move through (Fig. 261). In plain weave the weft is supposed to move over one yarn and under the next evenly across the fabric, so the shed would be one-up-and-one-down throughout. Third, it is necessary to secure each weft yarn into position in the cloth, a task that is accomplished by a beating mechanism. This device has two parts: the *reed*, whose function is to keep the warp yarns perfectly aligned, and the *beater*, a framework that holds the reed (Fig. 262). After each passing of weft yarn through the reed, the beater is pulled against the web so that the reed places the new weft

259. James Bassler. *Skins*. 1985. Silk, linen, sisal, and plastic. Woven (painted warp/wedge weave technique). 4′ × 3′9″ × 2″ (1.22 × 1.14 × .05 m). Courtesy of the artist.

260. Hand-weaver at work on a simple loom.

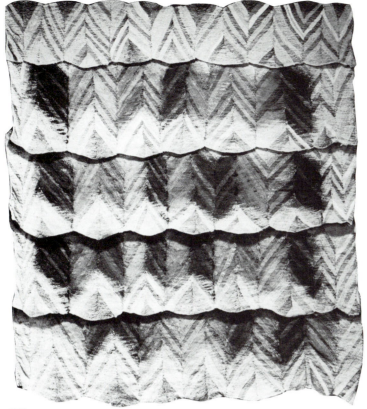

259

260

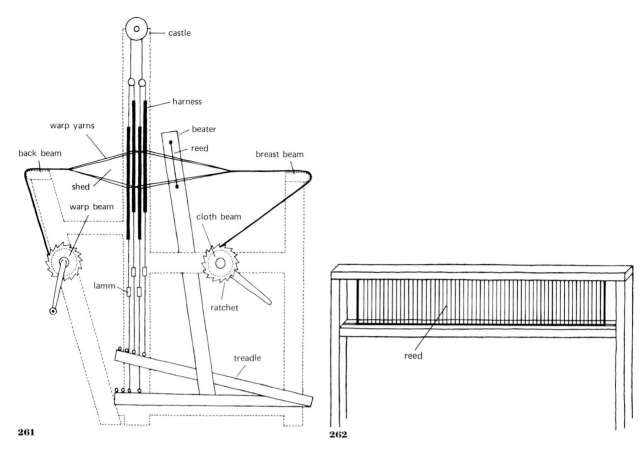

261. Diagram of a counterbalance loom, showing the basic parts common to all modern floor looms.

262. The beater of the loom showing a reed in position.

263. *The Unicorn in Captivity,* from *The Hunt of the Unicorn.* Franco-Flemish, c. 1500. Wool and silk with metal threads. 12′ × 8′3″ (3.66 × 2.51 m). Metropolitan Museum of Art, The Cloisters Collection, New York (gift of John D. Rockefeller, Jr., 1937).

securely against the previous one. Further refinements to the loom are convenient but not essential, making possible a variety of different weaving techniques.

Tapestry is a specialized form of weaving in which weft yarns are controlled by hand. Rarely does a single weft yarn move completely across the fabric. Instead, yarns of a particular color or texture appear and disappear on the surface of the web as the pattern demands. Tapestries have been created for centuries in many parts of the world. Perhaps the most famous is a series called *The Hunt of the Unicorn,* woven about 1500, probably in Flanders (Fig. 263). Contemporary weavers treat tapestry weaving in quite a different way, creating textures that are both actual and visual (Fig. 264).

The tapestry here makes use of *pile* weave, creating a depth resulting from stand-up yarn such as is seen in velvets, carpets, and terry cloth. Shag rugs are the result of an unusually long pile.

In *knotting* techniques, the yarns are not merely interlaced but are tied—together or to each other. Most knotting methods involve only a single set of yarns oriented in the same direction, rather than the crossing yarns of weaving. This is the method used in *macramé,* a technique employing combinations of knots, and originating in the fishing nets of early mariners.

Other methods of creating fabrics from yarns include *knitting* and *crocheting,* in which successive loops of yarn are pulled through one another to construct a fabric.

263

One of the oldest methods for making fabrics is by *pressure,* compressing or pounding fibrous materials. In the cold regions of the world early cultures developed *felting,* in which loose fibers are bonded together by a combination of heat, moisture, and pressure. In warmer climates, the bark of paper mulberry trees was pounded into a fabric that was brittle and brightly dyed; often dried leaves and flowers were pressed into it. This is the *tapa cloth* of the South Seas and other southern climates that we saw in Figure 121.

These, then, are the basic forming techniques for materials most frequently used by designers. In the world of contemporary design,

264

individuality is highly esteemed, and this often comes from improvisation on the traditional techniques, the use of new materials, and combinations of methods that formerly seemed unlikely. The material presented here could be only the beginning of personal experimentation in the search for an individual style.

Summary

Forming techniques fall into one of two general categories: *additive* and *subtractive*. The additive approach to sculpture includes riveting or welding in metal, and modeling in other materials. The additive method as used in clay includes *hand-building* and *throwing*. Hand-building consists of *pinching, coiling,* or using *slab construction. Throwing* is done on the potters' wheel. The subtractive method includes *carving, sawing,* and *turning* in wood, *hammering, raising, beating down, forging,* and *spinning* in metal. Glass is formed by *pressing, blowing, drawing, rolling,* and *casting. Casting* is also used for clay and plastics.

Fibers are used to create fabrics by means of two techniques: *interlacing* and *pressure*. Chief among the interlacing techniques is *weaving*. There are many variations on the weaving process, including *tapestry, pile,* and *knotting*. Fabrics are also created by *knitting* and *crocheting*, by *macramé*, and by *felting*, which is done with pressure.

264. Alice Parrott. *Tapestry.* Hand-dyed wool with rya and flossa knots, 2¾ × 4⅔′ (.84 × 1.40 m).

CHAPTER FIFTEEN

Structure and Decoration

From what we have learned in the last two chapters, we are aware that materials and forming techniques offer the designer almost limitless scope for originality. In a general way, however, these two factors determine both the structural and decorative design of any object.

Structural design refers to the way an object is formed and shaped. Decorative design usually implies some kind of surface embellishment. Our knowledge of forming techniques helps us realize that separating the two is impossible, for in many cases structure and decoration are intrinsically related.

Structure as Decoration

In a piece of weaving the structural design is the result of the choices made by the weaver in the matter of colors and sizes of fibers, but the decorative design emerges because of the way in which these elements are combined (Fig. 265). Today many weavers add color to their fibers with paint and ink, with the result that the color supplied by the fiber

265

265. Jack Lenor Larsen. *Labyrinth*. 1981. Upholstery fabric, jacquard "repp," worsted wool, Kelim group.

266

and the color applied with the brush are indistinguishable. A similar situation exists in the art of mosaic, in which small pieces of glass or ceramic (*tesserae*) are set in plaster or concrete and then washed over with *grout*, which fills the cracks between the tesserae. The excess grout is wiped off, and the remaining outlines give unity to the design (Fig. 266). However, sometimes the designer colors the grout to accommodate the colors of the tesserae, and this is no longer purely structural design but decoration.

In spite of these inevitable interrelationships, it is helpful to consider structural design and decorative design separately, simply because we react to them in different ways. Decoration can generally be seen with the eyes and felt with the fingers (except when done on a very large scale), but our reaction to structure is more *kinetic*, related to motion and our muscular responses. Even when we run our fingers over a pot, we are not feeling texture so much as the wholeness of the form, and when we walk around a piece of sculpture or through a building or landscape, we are surrounded, even dwarfed, and we react by expanding our senses to take in the design that surrounds us.

266. Miriam Sommerburg. *Menorah Triptych.* 1963. Mosaic, 30 × 29″ (76.2 × 73.7 cm). Collection the artist.

Perception of Structural Design

Our relationship to structural design is influenced by two factors: *scale* and *position*.

We experience the structure of a seashell by holding it in our hand, running our fingers over and around it. We can stay in one position and experience all aspects of the shell, since we can twist it and turn it to provide every possible viewpoint. Perceiving forms of larger scale is quite another experience. We may perceive the curves of rolling hills and valleys from a distance, but we experience them fully only as we wander through them, allowing them to unfold around us and to change form according to our position in space. Similarly, we perceive mountains jutting in jagged angles against the sky, but we experience their structure only by moving among them, permitting their plunging canyons and steep cliffs to enter our consciousness by becoming challenges that affect our lives at that moment. Again, the surface of a body of water with its waves and currents is an entirely different entity to the viewer standing on the shore and the person guiding a boat over it. To the latter, the waves, while beautiful, become the expression of a structure to be encountered and respected, with its depths and eddies carrying a possible threat.

Our reactions to human designs vary in the same way. We respond to the structure of a handmade mug as we handle it, cup it, and feel its form. The structure of fabric becomes more obvious when we run our hands over it, fingering the varying thickness of the fibers.

Larger structures involve more complex perception, entailing an awareness of *space* and *time*. The structural design of a building, a landscape, or a city can best be appreciated through the consciousness of the space created by the structure and the time we allow ourselves to feel its impact.

The Importance of Space and Time

We have discussed positive and negative space as aspects of two-dimensional design (p. 71). In Chapter 16 we will find that they are vital elements in any work of sculpture. The importance of space to architecture becomes clear if we conceive of space as being unlimited until the architect demarcates it by erecting walls. The quality of the designed space determines the success of the building, for it is within the negative space that the inhabitants live and move, the positive space of walls and ceilings being textured and colored only after the negative spaces have been established. One could even say that the delimitation of space *is* the structural design of a building, with the walls being merely the decorative design that defines and enhances it.

Anyone who would "feel" a building in all its possibilities must take time to sense the dimensions of its relationship to the human personality. It is this relationship that makes it possible for an individual to unite with a specific space in such a way that it becomes an integral part of existence. The space becomes "home," the most intimate of connections between space and the human spirit.

The *passing of time* plays an important part in design. Works in metal achieve a patina that changes the appearance of the surface, wood mellows and deepens in color, paintings change color, and industrial designs simply wear out and cease to function. In a house, personal spaces change to reflect growing families and developing personalities, becoming even more intimately a part of human history and all its associations, collections, and heirlooms.

Materials as Structural Design

Often the innate qualities of a material determine the character of a design. A comparison of two bridges provides a graphic example. The primary purpose of a bridge is to overcome an obstacle to travel, a deep ravine or a body of water. It must also be safe; therefore it must be made of materials that will withstand the stresses of its particular location. Some of the most picturesque bridges have been covered wooden structures crossing quiet meandering streams, but few of them remain after several decades of changing seasons and increasingly demanding traffic. The bridge in Figure 267 was built by the Romans as an aqueduct over two thousand years ago with the road

267

268

bridge added in 1747. It is built of stone and is heavy and durable like
the segments of Roman bridges and aqueducts still to be found all
over western Europe. The bridge in Figure 268 is the product of a
different time. It is made of reinforced concrete, which gives it a grace
and delicacy resulting not only from the ability of the material to span
the large distance but from the engineer's using slim vertical supports
at either end. Both structures fulfill their purpose admirably. Their
design speaks of two periods twenty centuries apart, and the difference in concept results at least partially from the emergence of steel as
a material for reinforcement.

The work in Figure 269 could only have been made of wood.
Conceivably it could have been *cast* in glass or metal or molded in
ceramic, but its character would have been entirely different. The

269

269. Eduardo Chillida.
Abesti Gogora 111. 1962–1964. Oak,
6'9⅝" × 11'4⅛" (2.07 × 3.46 m).
Art Institute of Chicago
(Grant J. Pick Purchase Fund).

270. Masakazu Kobayashi.
W³W to the Third Power. 1977.
Vinylon, 7'8" × 6'1" × 1'11"
(2.34 × 1.85 × .58 m).
Courtesy Allrich Gallery,
San Francisco.

271. Andries D. Copier.
Unique Piece C. B. 7.
Blue with green spot. 1958.
Free blown, 14¾" (37.47 cm).
Museum Boymans van Beuningen,
Rotterdam.

charm of the piece is in its blockiness, the grain and cracks of the wood, the marks of nails, and the sawed openings. The interlocking forms are intriguing because they are solid and bulky, yet they appear to interweave as fibers might do. The eye seeks the key to how the pieces work together and why the total sits just as it does. Here the material *is* the structure and the most important aspect of the design.

Tremendous variety is possible in the fiber arts, which include techniques ranging from lace making to tapestry weaving. Many contemporary artists combine fibers with other materials in works of fantasy such as the construction in Figure 270. Here again material and structure are inseparable. It is the particular substance of the vinylon fibers that makes possible the unusual looping of the structure, combining flexibility with sufficient body to hold a shape.

Every effective design exploits the material to some degree, making its intrinsic qualities a part of the design. The glass vase in Figure 271 goes further than this: it becomes the ultimate statement on the material in all its transparency, fluidity, and inherent beauty. The vase looks as though it had just swirled off the blowpipe, making the design as dependent upon the process as it is upon the material from which it is formed.

240 *Design in Action*

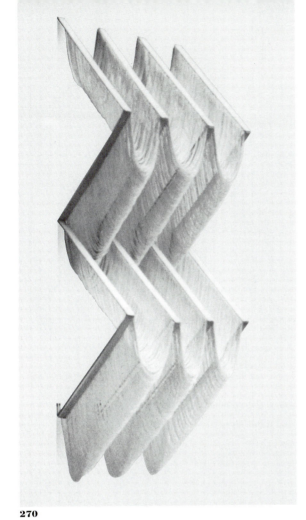

270

271

Decoration as Structure

Some decorative design, while ornamental in purpose, becomes equally structural in its ultimate function. The two needlepoint panels in Figure 272 were designed as part of a decorative frieze to facilitate the expansion process of a church in Colorado, where the new addition and the original structure needed a unifying element. Consisting of fourteen panels, the frieze covers an area approximately three by forty feet, in which designer Ann Jones has articulated the unfolding of biblical history in emblematic colors and meticulous symbolism, with every detail imbued with meaning. The designs were translated into *needlepoint* by members of the church congregation, a process in which colored yarns are worked through a stiff mesh backing, converting the decorative elements into a structural fabric. This was duly mounted on a gallery of the building, making the panels an integral part of the interior structure. The two panels shown depict the Old Testament story of the flood and the Chi Rho, the best known of the monograms of Christ.

Even more than needlepoint, *lace making* is a matter of a decorative concept that builds into a structure as its creation progresses. The

272

273

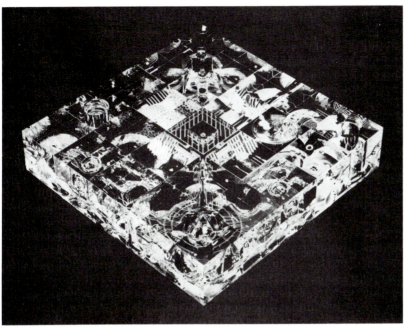

272. Ann Jones.
The Ark and *Chi Rho*. 1987.
Needlepoint 32 × 32" (81.3 × 81.3 cm).

273. Marian Powys. *Lace*. c. 1924.
9 × 6" (22.86 × 15.24 cm).

274. Eric Hilton. *Innerland*.
1987. Crystal.
Width and length 19⅜" (49.2 cm),
height 3⅞" (9.8 cm).
Engraved by Ladislav Havlik,
Lubomir Richter, Peter Schelling,
and Roger Selander. Courtesy
Corning Museum of Glass,
Corning, New York.

274

piece in Figure 273 obviously was envisioned by the designer before she began to work, and it was only as her vision unfolded in her hands that the lace itself evolved.

The work in Figure 274 will serve as a fitting example for the transition between structure and decoration. Conceived by a Scottish sculptor, this structural block of crystal has been engraved, cut, and sand-sculpted by four glassworkers to represent the artist's conception of the unity of life, the oneness of time and space. Within the crystal landscape, the viewer may wander in mind along countless paths in which refracted light breaks into all the colors of the rainbow or gleams or blazes with spheres representing cells of being, radiant patterns of energy, and mountains, which when scaled, reveal the inner eye. Here the decoration is not applied to a surface but is enclosed within the structure, emanating through it, revealing new images from every direction in which it is perceived. Such diverse elements could lead to a chaotic result, particularly when reflected and multiplied by the qualities of glass, but, conceived in the mind of a sculptor, they become unified into a coherent *composition*.

Composition

Composition is the term by which we indicate a unified work of art, whether it is musical, literary, or visual. A composition is the total of all the elements and principles of design as they affect a specific subject, concept, or expression. It is, in essence, the *structure* of a *two-dimensional* work, and as such must be considered before we can regard any discussion of structural design as complete.

275

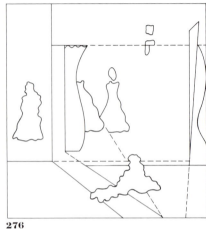

276

Perhaps the most direct way to understand composition is to analyze a two-dimensional work, a painting that has been accepted as a
successful composition for more than a century. In his painting *The
Daughters of Edward Darley Boit* (Fig. 275), John Singer Sargent started
with a rectangular canvas within which he subsequently placed certain
shapes representing recognizable things—four girls, a rug, architectural elements, and two large vases. Although the painting is a portrait
of the four girls, they are not placed in the center with the setting
subordinate to them. Instead, the room and its contents form a *composition* into which each figure fits with its own contribution to the continuity of the whole. The diagram in Figure 276 may give us some idea
as to how the artist planned the space. The point of emphasis is the
youngest daughter who, with her doll, forms the largest light shape in
the painting. She is near the apex of a triangle formed by the edge of
the rug and by the daughter leaning against the vase in the background. This strong angle is repeated softly in the light triangle in the
right background. The large vases repeat the forms and values of the
figures of the girls and echo the pattern of the carpet, which helped to
lead our eye to the focal point. In any composition, the artist leads our
eye where he or she wants it to go, and Sargent causes our glance to
flow throughout the painting by means of well-distributed lights.
These provide rhythm and balance and contribute as well to the texture. The composition is the result of the elements of design used in a

skillful way, following the principles of design, which are also the principles of composition.

One of the most useful ways to study composition in painting is to lay a sheet of tracing paper over a work and draw the salient lines, as we have done in Figure 276. In this way, recognizable objects are transformed into the shapes and spaces that compose a work. Design in painting, of course, includes color and value, which can also be indicated as shapes and forms. Value is of vital importance in the Sargent portrait, giving the contrast that, in the end, does indeed make it a study of the four girls.

Decorative Design

The way in which shapes and lines have been used to decorate human artifacts and the human environment is one of the most interesting studies in design. Entire volumes are devoted to the immense variety that has occurred in different periods and different parts of the world, based on the principal sources of all human design: *nature*, the *human figure*, *geometry*, and *abstract shapes*. One of the most compelling aspects of this area of design is the way in which decoration becomes symbolism.

Symbolism

The *dragon* has probably enjoyed the most varied representation of any animal form in history, appearing in various guises throughout the world. In early mythologies the dragon was associated with evil and destruction, particularly among nations infested with venomous reptiles. The ancient Greeks and Romans, however, believed that dragons had the ability to understand and to convey to people the secrets of the earth. Consequently, the dragon was seen as a benign and protective influence, yet because of its fearsome qualities it was adopted as a military emblem by the Romans. It flourished throughout British history on coats of arms and battle standards at the same time that it was an all-encompassing power to the people of the Orient. Okokura Kakuzo, a contemporary Japanese author, writes: "His claws are in the forks of the lightning, his scales begin to glisten in the bark of rain-swept pine trees. His voice is heard in the hurricane which, scattering withered leaves of the forest, quickens the new spring. The dragon reveals himself only to vanish."[4] Being fanciful in conception, the dragon lends himself to the most elaborate imaginative and decorative of visual interpretations (Fig. 277).

Equally decorative are the interpretations of animal forms in the totems of the Native Americans of British Columbia. The whale, the raven, and all the beasts of the northern forest are considered brothers to human beings, and they achieve a highly designed stylization at the hands of tribal artists. A headdress such as the one in Figure 278 becomes decorative design for the person who wears it. Similar figures are carved or painted on chests, door lintels, and small objects for tribal use.

Sometimes design motifs are used in a distinctive way to form a kind of pattern that is a new entity in itself. Such an entity is the

[4] Hugh Honour, "The Light from the East," *The Arts of China* (New York: American Heritage, 1969), 9–10.

277

278

arabesque, which was used extensively in Renaissance painting and carving to symbolize the natural beauties of the world in contrast to the somber concentration on the sins of the world in the Middle Ages. In Islamic art the arabesque is geometric and angular, whereas the Renaissance interpretation is curved and flowing (Fig. 279). Although

279

280

the name derives from Arabic design, it is more often applied to the curving style in which animal and human figures are included, an element forbidden by Islamic belief.

A different kind of *intertwining* is the distinctive decorative style developed in the monasteries of the British Isles from the seventh to eleventh centuries. This intricate straplike ornamentation was used extensively to enrich manuscripts. Painted in glowing colors touched with gold, these manuscripts have become unique treasures of decorative art (Fig. 280).

Decorative Processes

The processes for applying decorative design to different materials vary considerably. Although a few, such as etching, are used on many surfaces, the particular qualities of most materials make it simpler to discuss their decorative possibilities individually.

Metal

Although the natural appearance of metal, oxidized, highly polished, or mellowed by time, is a decorative asset, the most usual methods of

277. Chinese medallion with five-clawed dragon. 18th century. Embroidery with gold wrapped thread. Metropolitan Museum of Art (anonymous gift, 1944).

278. Tshimshian clan headdress, collected by C. F. Newcombe at Kitkatla, British Columbia, 1895–1901. Painted wood with seashell teeth and bear canines; height 17″ (43.18 cm). base diameter 12½″ (31.75 cm). Canadian Ethnology Service, Canadian Museum of Civilization.

279. Arabesque design. Front of a chest. French, Valley of the Loire. c. 1535. Musée des arts decoratifs. Paris.

280. Detail from *The Book of Kells*, Irish, late 8th century. Panel at end of genealogy of Christ according to St. Luke. Trinity College, Dublin.

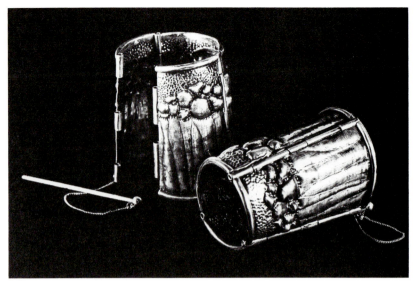

281

working metal surfaces are *chasing* and *repoussé* (Fig. 281). Both are accomplished with rounded tools held against the metal and struck with a hammer, so that a depression is formed. In chasing, the work is usually done from the face or outside, forming a *recessed* design on the finished piece. Repoussé, from the French verb meaning "to push back," is done from the back, and therefore the lines or images are *raised* on the surface.

Engraving and etching involve incising or cutting fine lines into the surface of the metal. In *engraving*, a sharp tool is used. In *etching*, the metal is covered with an acid-resistant substance such as wax and the design is cut through the wax onto the metal, exposing it. Acid is then applied and allowed to eat into the metal in the exposed areas. Sometimes incised lines are then filled with a black material called *nigellum* to create color contrast, with the result called *niello*.

Metal can be textured by *hammering* or *torch texturing*, in which a welder's torch is held against the surface until it melts and begins to flow.

Enameling is a process by which ground glass particles are applied to metal in either a dry or pastelike state, then fired until the particles melt, forming a smooth lustrous coating on the metal. Cloisonné (French for "partitioned") refers to a pattern delineated by tiny flat wires known as *cloisons*. These are affixed to a metal base and the enamel applied between them. Firing causes the enamels to fuse with both the cloisons and the base, which makes possible a tiny network of metal running through the areas of color, an art form well-known throughout the Orient and Middle East. Contemporary designers tend to simpler forms in which the metal plays the role of border and accent (Fig. 282).

Plique à jour enamel resembles stained glass, because the metal base material is removed after firing to leave only the cloisonné wires and the enamel, a shell of transparent or translucent color interspersed with the lines of the wires.

282

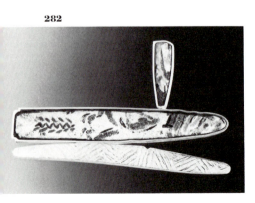

Champlevé is a process by which the portions of metal to be enameled are engraved or cut out. Enamel paste is then applied to the depressions and the piece fired.

Clay

Decorative design in ceramics usually means a glaze, although clay can be carved or embellished with small rolls of clay applied before the ware is fired.

Glazes can be mat or shiny, translucent, transparent, or opaque, brilliantly colored or subdued. Glazes fired in the low-temperature range tend to be brighter. Among the most important bright glazes are *majolica*, a style that originated in Italy, and the more ornate French version known as *faience*, which includes touches of gold. Both are usually fired on earthenware and have bright-colored designs on a subtle background of white or gray.

A number of special effects are possible with glazes, among them the *salt glaze* on the vase in Figure 283. This is produced by throwing salt into the kiln during the glaze firing. It was a favorite technique of early American potters, whose blue salt-glazed jugs are prized as collectors' items.

Crackle glazes result when the rate of expansion or contraction in the clay body of a piece is different from the rate in the glaze. *Raku* is a Japanese technique associated with Zen Buddhism in which glazes are low-fired and are used on bodies with a high proportion of grog (hard clay that has been ground into small particles) to give a soft earth-toned surface. Barbara Segal's *Shattered Sun* (Fig. 284) combines the effects of a crackle glaze with a raku technique. This piece also makes use of a *luster glaze,* which includes gold or silver for an even richer quality.

281. Anne Echelman Kantor. *Cuff bracelets.* 1975. Silver with repoussé and chased decoration.

282. Jamie Bennett. *Aiuola # 16.* Limoge and cloisonné.

283. Tom Turner. *Bottle vase.* 1976. Blue porcelain with salt glaze, height 8″ (20.32 cm). Private collection.

284. Barbara Segal. *Shattered Sun.* 1975. Raku-fired clay with amber luster and white crackle glaze, diameter 14″ (35.56 cm). Private collection.

283

284

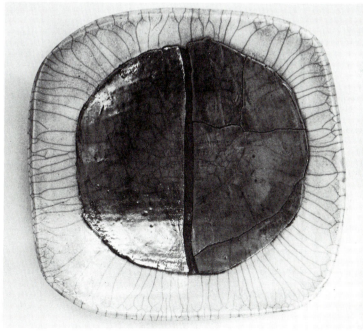

285

Glass

Etching on glass creates a frosted texture or gives a linear quality to a design. Glass is etched in the same manner as metal, using wax and acid.

Laid-on designs consist of separate shapes of glass applied to the body of the object. These can be different in color and sometimes are gilded for luxurious effects.

Heavy crystal may be ornamented by *cutting*. A characteristic feature of European castles and state drawing rooms in both Europe and the United States is the sparkling chandelier composed of small pieces of cut crystal. Early in the 20th century, "cut glass" became a favorite style of tableware, with goblets, fruit bowls, and pitchers incised in intricate designs. Today this role is being revived by glass factories in France and Ireland which emphasize the elegance of objects composed of surfaces dancing with reflected lights. Most cutting is done with rapidly turning diamond wheels.

Engraving is used for the finest crystal since it enhances the surface without detracting from the inherent qualities of brilliance and clarity. This, too, is done with wheels of diamond or copper.

Glassmaking reached a peak in Venice, where it is still carried on in workshops on the island of Murano, which has been a glassmaking center since 1292. One of the Venetian specialties is *millefiori* glass, in which narrow rods of colored glass are bundled together, partially fused, then sliced into discs for mounting in the body of glass as it is being fired. The discs appear in the finished piece as small rings of color, giving the effect of flowers floating within the glass (Fig. 285).

Stained glass has little to do with other types of glass since it is closer to painting in its final results. It is made by coloring glass with metal oxides, molding it into sheets, or blowing it into a bubble that is then split into sheets. When the sheets have hardened, they are cut into individual pieces and joined by being inserted into U-shaped strips of metal, usually lead, which can be bent to accommodate the design. The work is then mounted with supports of metal bars.

Mosaics are often made of *tesserae* of glass, although the early forms were designs laid in concrete with little colored stones. There are two methods of making mosaics, the *direct* and the *indirect*. In the

285. Millefiori glass bowl. Roman. 1st century B.C. Metropolitan Museum of Art, New York (gift of Henry J. Marquand, 1881).

286. Village scene panel from the Woman's Cooperative in Bogota, Columbia. 1978. Appliqué and embroidery on cotton; 3′10″ × 5′11½″ (1.17 × 1.82 m). The Liberty Textile Collection, courtesy Liberty Life Ins. Co.

direct method the tesserae are laid directly into wet mortar. In the indirect method, the work is done from a full-scale drawing or *cartoon* that is a representation of the design in reverse. The tesserae are placed on the paper with a special paste, and much of the mosaic composition is completed before the mortar is applied to the base on which it is to appear. When the mortar is ready, the paperbacked mosaic is set face down against it and pressed into the mortar. After the paper has dried, it is peeled off. Grout can then be added to fill the crevices.

Fabrics

Ornamentation of fabric can be covered under two broad categories: *fiber techniques* and *printing techniques*.

Fiber techniques include all the methods that call for a yarn or thread to be worked through a fabric, and it is generally designated as *stitchery*.

Embroidery is a specialized form of stitchery in which the individual stitches are highly decorative, formed in a variety of ways to express whatever pattern is intended.

Crewel requires using a twisted ropelike thread, and its technique is similar to that of embroidery.

Appliqué concentrates less on the stitches themselves than on what they hold together. Small pieces of material, usually fabric, are applied to a fabric background with tiny stitches that do not show as part of the finished design (Fig. 286). Sometimes embroidery stitches are used to outline or accentuate the design.

286

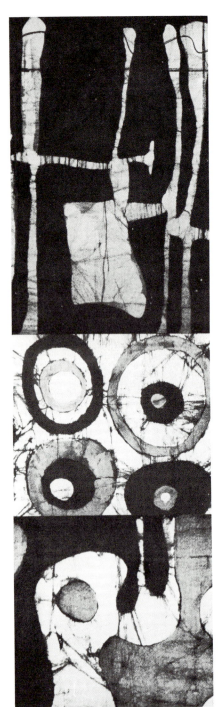

287

Printing techniques for fabrics include *silk screen* or *serigraphy*, essentially a stencil process in which ink or dye is pressed through a layer of fine silk mounted on a wooden frame with only the pattern exposed and the remainder of the screen blocked out. This technique is described more fully in Chapter 19.

Batik and *tie-dye* are both resist printing methods, which means some device prevents color from penetrating the fabric where it is not wanted, but the control is less specific than in the use of silk screen. In *batik*, nonprinting areas are coated with wax and then the fabric is dipped in dye. Only the unwaxed areas of the cloth will accept the dye and when the wax cracks during the dipping the color seeps through, giving the cloth a characteristic visual texture of fine lines (Fig. 287). When the dye has dried and set, the wax is melted off and reapplied in other portions of the fabric for the printing of the next color. In *tie-dye* the nonprinting sections of the fabric are twisted and tied tightly when the fabric is dipped. Re-tying makes possible the application of successive colors. This method is less precise and often gives a furry effect around the colored areas.

Finally, images and patterns can be *photoprinted* onto fabric using the techniques of photography. This is typical of the experimental techniques resulting from combining traditional methods, many of which lead to striking results. We have listed the basic structural and decorative processes that are the tools of the designer. It is the individual designer who determines their possibilities.

Summary

Structural design refers to the way in which an object is formed and shaped. Decorative design usually implies some kind of surface embellishment. Sometimes the structure *is* the decoration, as in weaving or mosaic. We perceive structure through space and time, depending on the scale of the work and our position in relationship to it. Materials determine the character of a work of art and frequently become its basic decoration. On the other hand, decorative design sometimes *becomes* the structure, as in needlepoint or lace making. *Composition* is the term for structural design in a two-dimensional work. *Decorative design* often uses symbolism. Decorative processes vary according to the material used.

Both structural and decorative design depend on the elements of design: *line, shape and mass, space, texture,* and *color;* and on the principles with which they are combined: *rhythm, variety, emphasis, balance, proportion, scale,* and *unity.*

287. Inge Dusi. Details of three batiks. Santiago.

PART 5

Design for Visual Communication

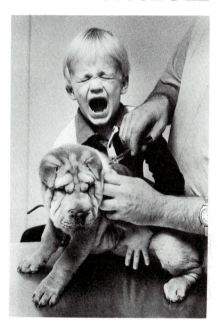

CHAPTER SIXTEEN

Painting and Sculpture

In our discussion of structure and decoration, we have been concerned with the actual *form* of a work and its *embellishment*. We now focus on another aspect of design and art, *communication*. A design may seek to communicate the virtues of a commercial product, as in advertising design, or it may communicate an interpretation of a literary work, as in book design or the performing arts (Chaps. 17 and 18). In this chapter we will explore two categories of art that usually attempt to communicate to the viewer some personal reaction to the world or to a specific experience.

Attributes of Painting and Sculpture

The three traditional attributes of painting and sculpture are *subject*, *form*, and *content*. The relative importance of the three varies from work to work. In contemporary works, there is frequently no subject, even in the mind of the artist, but rather a concentration on form and a content that may be a vague aesthetic reaction or a firm political commitment or any variation between. When all three attributes exist in a work, they are interlocked; it is difficult to isolate them for analysis, in the same way it is difficult to arrive at the quality of "green" by analyzing blue and yellow. For the sake of understanding, we will separate the three attributes for consideration, using one painting that obviously has all three.

Anna Kuerner is a detail of a larger work by Andrew Wyeth, but the traditional attributes are so eloquently expressed in it that it serves our purposes well (Fig. 288). Wyeth is an artist who has made one section of the world his own, painting the area around Chadd's Ford, Pennsylvania, and a summer home in Maine in depth and intricate detail. Anna is the wife of Wyeth's neighbor in Chadd's Ford, a German farmer. This is the *subject*. Even in the detail of the work, the *form* has a balanced structural design, with the geometric fretwork of the window and shelf providing a structured backdrop for the rounded forms of the figure and the soft folds of her apron. The form is not a matter of simple contrast, however. Beyond the window the curves are repeated in the pond and the rolling slope of Kuerner's Hill, one of Wyeth's favorite places to sit as he contemplated the landscape. Note how skillfully the curvilinear shapes are repeated in the nearby wallpaper, and again, how the two fenceposts echo the uprights of the window frame, elements moving forward and backward into space in a harmony simi-

288

lar to that of a repeated and modified theme in music. This movement and sense of space, playing against the primary content of the woman's character, are an important part of the *content*, which portrays in a simple straightforward manner her physically hard life, her personal determination, and even, above the downward corners of her dauntless mouth, the flicker of humor in her eyes. In the three attributes, the work communicates to us not only the personality of the subject but a great deal about the artist. We sense his admiration and love for the people of his area and we feel as well his appreciation for the landscape, with its dry grasses and still ponds.

We will see how these attributes operate in sculpture as well, but first let us consider the technical aspects of painting.

The Materials of Painting

The materials of painting center around pigments, powders ground into a binder. There are two basic categories of pigment: *organic* and *inorganic*. Organic pigments are derived from carbon; they tend to be light in weight and transparent, yet high in tinting strength. With the growth of organic chemistry, such pigments are being made synthetically in increasing amounts and wider ranges of color. Inorganic pigments are called natural mineral, or earth, colors, and are mined from the earth, deriving their color from oxides in the soil. They, too, are now being made synthetically.

In creating a painting, the painter must first have a *support*, something upon which to paint. This may be a wall, a wooden panel, a piece of masonite, a sheet of paper, or, most traditionally, a piece of canvas tightly tacked to a rigid frame, which provides a taut, drumlike,

288. Andrew Wyeth.
Anna Kuerner (detail). 1971.
Tempera on panel,
13½ × 19½″ (34.29 × 49.53 cm).
Private collection. Photograph
Courtesy Brandywine River Museum.

289. Jasper Johns.
Between the Clock and the Bed.
1981. Encaustic on canvas,
6′ × 10′6¼″ (1.83 × 3.21 m).
Collection, The Museum of Modern Art,
New York (given anonymously).

slightly resilient surface that responds to brushstrokes. Frequently a *ground* is applied to wood or canvas, first a coating of glue to seal the pores and then a coat of paint, usually white, to provide a smooth painting surface.

The artist applies paint with a brush or painting knife. These are available in a wide range of widths, lengths, and shapes. Painters characteristically accumulate an assortment of brushes to fill various needs.

Painting Media

The oldest known painting medium, and the most permanent, appears to be *encaustic*, a mixture of hot beeswax and pigment perfected by the ancient Greeks. The mixture is applied to a wood support with a brush or a metal instrument called a *cauterium*. As the wax cools, the cauterium is heated and successive layers are applied, making possible considerable plasticity and modeling. After centuries of neglect, encaustic is finding favor among contemporary artists for the possibilities it offers for unusual texture (Fig. 289).

Tempera generally has egg yolk as a binder, although animal and vegetable glues can also be used. It is most often applied to a ground of *gesso* (plaster or gypsum mixed with glue), built up on wood panels, but it can be worked on canvas. It has an opaque quality and is usually laid on in small brush strokes, building up layers that provide both luminosity and meticulous modeling. *Anna Kuerner* (Fig. 288) is painted in egg tempera.

289

290

291

290. Raphael.
Madonna of the Chair.
Florence, Galleria Palatina.
c. 1516

291. Vincent van Gogh.
Cypresses. 1889. Oil on canvas,
36¾″ × 29⅛″ (93.3 × 74.0 cm).
Metropolitan Museum of Art,
New York (Rogers Fund, 1949).

292. Adolph Gottlieb.
Incubus. 1947.
Gouache on paper,
25¼ × 17⅜″ (64 × 44 cm).
North Carolina Museum of Art,
Raleigh, North Carolina
(bequest of W. R. Valentiner).

Casein, with a binder of milk curd, is water soluble and can be applied to gesso panels, cardboard, paper, and other surfaces. It is opaque but, like tempera, is thinned with water.

Oil paint came into general use in the 15th century. The binder is linseed oil, which dries slowly, allowing time for precise manipulation. Oil paint can be applied in one thick layer (making it possible to cover changes in the work) or it can be built up in successive thin layers, or *glazes*, by using oil or turpentine to dilute the paint. This use of transparent glazes is responsible for much of the glow and meticulous modeling that we see in the work of 16th- and 17th-century masters. It has been said that Raphael used more than a dozen successive glazes in his paintings, allowing time between for each to dry thoroughly (Fig. 290). In contrast is the *impasto* technique, in which paint is applied with palette knife or heavily loaded brush in a layer so thick that the paint assumes a plastic quality of its own (Fig. 291. For closeup of texture see Fig. 132, p. 108).

Watercolor is bound by gum arabic. Many artists are devoted to watercolor for its sparkle and freshness and for the speed with which a work can be completed. In *transparent* watercolor the white paper is left to provide highlights (Pl. 27, p. 210). *Gouache* is an opaque version of watercolor containing a paste of zinc oxide. In gouache techniques, white paint is usually employed for highlights (Fig. 292).

Wall painting includes frescoes and murals. *Fresco,* as mentioned in Chapter 6, is the medium of many of the great wall paintings of the Renaissance. Pigment suspended in lime water is applied to wet plaster so that as the plaster dries the color becomes a part of the wall. *Murals* are usually executed in oil or acrylic on canvas that has been secured to the wall.

Acrylic polymer emulsion is the most widely used of the new synthetic media. It is favored for its durability and quick drying qualities, and since acrylics generally dissolve in water, it can be used in either watercolor or oil techniques. The use of glazes is particularly adapted to acrylics since they dry quickly, and because of their porous surface, successive glazes can be built up at once without danger of peeling. A thick paste of acrylic or polymer applied to a support can provide an adhesive surface for a collage, allowing the artist to press assorted materials into the medium to achieve unique effects (Fig. 293). Such effects generally come under the heading of *mixed media,* in which paint of several types may be combined, or one type may be used with any combination of materials, many of which may not usually be associated with painting.

292

293

Directions in Contemporary Painting

The 20th century has been a proving ground for much that is experimental in the arts, and a comprehensive treatment of its development in painting has filled books and provided material for entire college courses. It has been a time of *-isms*, movements away from traditional styles, sometimes identified by scoffing critics, sometimes by young rebels more involved in heated discussion than in actual work. Many *-isms* have flared briefly and disappeared; others, practiced by a group devoted to a certain doctrine and developing within its framework, have become currents influencing the development of contemporary painting.

Since our purpose is to explore the role of painting in the field of design, we will confine our discussion to the ways in which certain movements have provided a unique expression of the elements and principles of design.

Les Fauves

Centered around Matisse, this group of artists was given its name by a critic who found their broad vibrant strokes of color shocking, and wrote a review calling them Les Fauves (the wild beasts). Merging form and content into a vivid surface, they also upset traditional ways of depicting figures, objects, and perspective. (See again Fig. 81.)

Impressionism

Mentioned in Chapter 7, Impressionism was also revolutionary in its concept of color, breaking hues into their components and applying them as tiny brushstrokes or as dots (as in Pointillism), which the human eye perceived as color and light. Camille Pissarro and Georges Seurat were two of many who experimented with the effects of light on water, reflected light, and color as affected by the changing light throughout a day (see again Pl. 23, p. 127). The Impressionist use of implied space was another innovation, as discussed in Chapter 5.

Cubism

In reaction to Impressionism, the Cubists, working largely in neutral tones, stressed sharply outlined geometric shapes. Led by Pablo Picasso and Georges Braque, they were deeply influenced by Paul Cézanne, who felt that geometric masses—the cone, the sphere, and the cylinder—were the basis of both nature and painting. In Cubism, subject matter is barely recognizable, and the planes seem to slip and slide over one another in a kind of static rhythm (Fig. 294). Shape and space are of primary concern, with balance achieved through distribution of shapes and values.

294

295

295. Wassily Kandinsky.
Composition 8, No. 260.
1923. Oil on canvas,
4′7″ × 6′7″ (1.41 × 2.0 m).
Solomon R. Guggenheim Museum,
New York.

296. Franz Marc. *Kämpfende Formen.
(Forms in Combat).* 1914.
München, Staatgalerie Moderner
Kunst.

297. Joan Miró.
Carnival of Harlequin.
1924–1925. Oil on canvas,
26 × 36⅝″ (66.04 × 92.96 cm).
Albright-Knox Art Gallery,
Buffalo, N.Y. (Room of
Contemporary Art Fund, 1940).

Abstraction

Closely allied to Cubism, Abstraction emerged at about the same time, preceding World War I. In a period of restlessness and experimentation, both movements reduced subject to the point of departure for innovations in line, space, shape, and texture. The guiding force in Abstraction was Russian-born Wassily Kandinsky, one of the most significant figures in the history of painting (Fig. 295). Although he insisted that words could not get at the true meaning of his work, Kandinsky summed up the essence of Abstraction: "The observer must learn to look at the picture as a graphic representation of a *mood* and not as a representation of objects."[5]

German Expressionism

Like Kandinsky, the German Expressionists emphasized painting mood rather than objects and they worked at depicting the inner nature of things, employing a highly personal imagery that often evolved into grotesqueness. During this chaotic period under the cloud of war, there was much distortion of form in painting and an expression of inner turmoil and rebellion. There was also vibrant color and a striking sense of design. A work such as Franz Marc's painting in Figure 296 exemplifies design quality at its best, with great swirling rhythms and a spectacular balance of light and dark.

[5] Bernard S. Myers, *The German Expressionists* (New York: Praeger, 1917), 214.

296

Surrealism

With the popularization of the teachings of Sigmund Freud, many artists in the late 1920s gravitated to the realm of dreams and the unconscious, and subject reappeared as a dominant element in painting, though often in fantastic form. Symbolism became crucial, and the term "Surrealism" was coined to identify a nonrational intuitive manner of working, recreating chance relationships and strange combinations of symbols as they often occur in dreams (Fig. 297). Here the predominant design qualities are rhythmic movement and a strong linear quality, along with variety of shapes and an overall texture. At other times, familiar objects are represented in a crisp vacuum, with neither texture nor pattern.

297

298

Abstract Expressionism

The trend begun by Kandinsky reached full fruition in the nonobjectivity of the Abstract Expressionists. While Abstraction concerns the essence of a recognizable object, sometimes discarding all reference to the object itself, *nonobjective* painting disregards any reference to an object at all, beginning with forms, lines, and rhythms whose reference to recognizable forms is purely coincidental. As a movement, Abstract Expressionism was the ultimate in nonobjective painting, with dynamic rhythms and jabbing colors and shapes. The term *action painting* characterizes its radical departure from previous modes, and its enormous canvases and vitality began a trend for gigantic works, making it one of the first American developments in art to attract worldwide attention (Fig. 298).

Op Art

We have observed the work of Vasily Vasarely (Pl. 17, p. 125), in which the science of optics was the predominant force, leading to experiments with color, shape, line, and the resultant sense of movement and rhythmic quality. There is no subject, but there is strong form involved in the exploratory nature of these works. Often there is striking visual texture as well.

298. Jackson Pollock. *Number 17.* c. 1951. Duco on canvas, 4′9⅞″ × 4′10⅝″ (1.47 × 1.49 m). Collection Mr. and Mrs. S. I. Newhouse, Jr. New York.

299. Barnett Newman. *Twelfth Station* (from *Fourteen Stations of the Cross*). 1965. Acrylic polymer, 6′6″ × 5′ (19.8 × 1.53 m). Collection Annalee Newman.

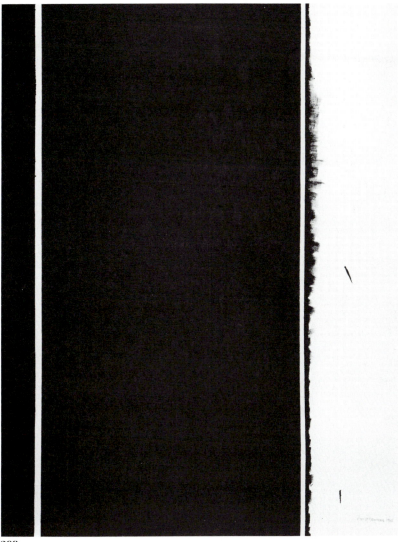

299

Minimal Art

Op Art moved into Minimal Art by logical progression. Once subject had disappeared, it was logical to experiment in another way, by arriving at a work of art by the least possible means. This meant resorting to color and shape, no more. Sometimes even shape was not evident, as in Color Field painting, which simply covered a canvas with solid color, sometimes with a line or two of contrasting color (Fig. 299).

Current Trends in Painting

The invention of the camera had turned painters from realistic representations, making it seem useless to attempt in paint what the camera could accomplish in a fiftieth of a second. In the 1960s, however,

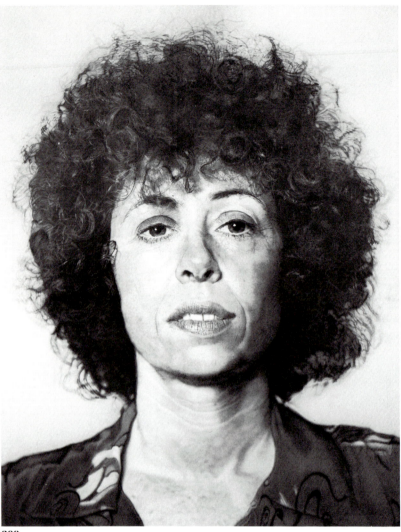

300

300. Chuck Close. *Linda*.
1975–76. Acrylic on canvas,
9 × 7′ (2.74 × 2.13 m).
Courtesy the artist.

301. Harry Hoursaros.
Pythian Maidens. 1981.
Oil and acrylic on canvas,
4′6″ × 4′6″ (1.37 × 1.37 m).
Private collection.

painters began to use the camera as an ally. The reasoning was that photographic images, movies, television, and magazines are as important a part of our reality as actual phenomena; therefore the artist paints as the camera views the world. Chuck Close makes it clear that he is painting from photographs and that the results are not what the human eye sees. His portraits show every hair and wrinkle (Fig. 300). This is known as *Photorealism*.

Movements in contemporary art usually arise in New York, where they are given publicity by museum directors and the media and by wealthy collectors eager to be associated with anything new. Sometimes a trend will last a few years and vanish. Some trends, like abstraction, resurface at intervals or persist in the work of artists who feel strongly that abstraction is the only appropriate style of expression in a technological and impersonal society. Some trends have strong political associations, decrying the ills of modern society. One of the most articulate of recent trends has been grouped under the term *Post-modernism*. Moving away from the depiction of the human face and figure, Post-modernists expressed a revived interest in emotional quality and human values, stressing the *conceptual*, in which values and perceptions spring from the human mind rather than from outer reality. In this context, one segment of the group concentrated on ornamentation, creating works vividly, even garishly, colored, borrowing images from Oriental rugs, Chinese porcelains, and Islamic decor (Fig. 301).

Post-modernism has been replaced in the limelight of movements by the *Simulationists*, who exhibit work they feel expresses a soulless society in the context of a capitalistic system. The relationship of their work to design is more evident than its role as communication, since it is individualistic and subjective, often darkly pessimistic. Some such works are more sculpture than painting; others are a combination of both (Fig. 302).

Perhaps one can best appreciate the work of contemporary painters by realizing that they have been preceded by centuries of masters whose work has tapped every conceivable resource of richness and skill. If they sometimes seem dedicated to shock and sensationalism, it may be that the only motivation left to them is, as one critic expressed it, to attract attention.

301

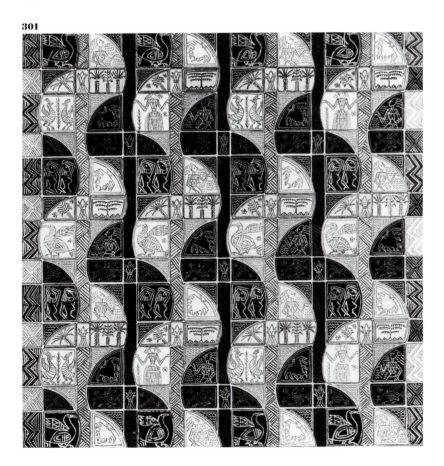

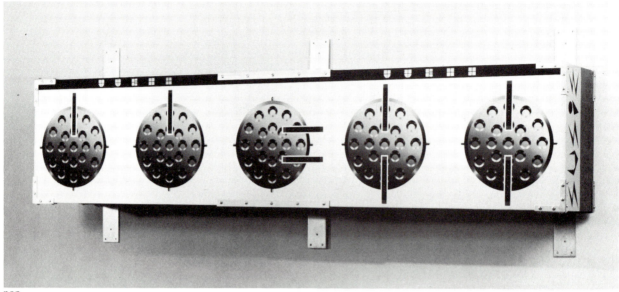

302

Sculpture

Traditionally, painting and sculpture have been considered as two distinctly different forms of expression. We viewed paintings as they hung on walls, and we looked at sculpture by walking around it, examining it from every angle. Contemporary work erases much of the distinction: paintings are frequently three-dimensional, and sculpture is often brightly painted. Both are sometimes combined in entities known as *constructions* or *environments*. Figure 302 is typical of much contemporary design in that it defies traditional labels. Since the lines have become blurred, we are considering painting and sculpture together, seeing their similarities: huge scale, impersonalization, technological methods of creation. At the same time, we will note their traditional differences.

Categories of Sculpture

The traditional tools of the sculptor included an assortment of chisels, mallets, and gouges used in the subtractive technique, to carve wood or stone. Today, however, there is no limit to the tools of the sculptor. Many artists make models and sketches and take them to an iron foundry or a factory to have the pieces cut and the final work fabricated. Even so, the two traditional categories of sculpture still apply. *Freestanding* sculpture stands free of any attachment to a background; it is the kind of work that can be viewed from all angles, that people walk through or even play on. *Relief* sculpture, on the other hand, consists of forms carved or modeled from a panel that not only forms the background but is an important part of the work. The depth of the raised composition varies, from *bas-relief* (low relief) to *haut-relief* (high relief), which usually stands half or more as high from the background as the natural circumference of the figures would be if standing free.

302. Ashley Bickerton. UUEHH. 1986. Saatchi Collection. London.

303. Lorenzo Ghiberti. *Gates of Paradise*. East doors of the Baptistry, Florence. 1425–1452. Gilt bronze, height 18′6″ (5.64 m).

303

One of the great masterpieces of bronze relief sculpture is seen in Figure 303. After a rigorous competition during the Renaissance, this important project was finally awarded to Lorenzo Ghiberti, who used several levels of relief to imply both action and distance. The *subject* was to be the Old Testament, with numerous incidents represented within each panel, which measured only 31¼ inches (79 centimeters) square. Included in some of the panels were more than a hundred figures, as well as ships, architecture, and details of landscape. Such a formidable subject could only be depicted by consummate skill, and Ghiberti accomplished the feat in a *form* that continues to astound viewers, who travel from all parts of the world to see it in the heart of Florence. Figures in the foreground are in haut-relief verging on roundness, whereas the background slopes gently to relief so low that it gives the effect of aerial perspective. Viewing the two doors as a total design, we are impressed by the overall balance—of arched architectural details, grouped figures, vertical lines, and deep shadows. The composition is bordered by a band of human figures interspersed with plant and animal forms completing the overall effect of opulence tempered with dignity. In *form*, the work fulfilled the requirements of the ecclesiastical authorities who established the competition, but the content encompasses a great deal more. These are the doors to the baptistry, which is a separate building from the cathedral, sitting across the street but serving as a vital part of it. Their content is the expression of all that the cathedral stands for, a fitting expression of its highest celebrations and ceremonies. In its elegance of style, it also expresses its own time, a period in history in which the Church was associated with luxury, opulence, and the finest work of highly esteemed artists.

Casting Methods

Ghiberti's doors were cast in bronze after being modeled in wax, a medium that made possible the wealth of intricate detail. For works of metal and clay, hollow casting is preferred, since this results in a thin lightweight layer of material, minimizing the danger of cracking. Hollow casting necessitates a mold composed of at least two sections—one for the outer surface and one for the inside. The classic method for hollow casting metal, especially bronze, is the *cire-perdue*, or lost wax, technique.

In cire perdue casting, the sculptor builds a model of wax around a core of some nonmelting material, such as clay. Next, an outer mold, usually of clay, is applied to the wax model, conforming to it in every detail. To make the cast, the wax is melted out and replaced with molten metal. Several identical sculptures can be produced from the same mold. Furthermore, the sculptor is not confined to the compact form required for materials that could break easily, but is free to make extensions into space as the design requires.

Another popular casting method depends on molds made of damp sand, which is solid enough to hold a shape but will release the cast material after it has hardened. Bronze, plaster, plastics, and concrete are the materials often cast by this technique, and the surface texture resulting from adhering sand particles can be left or smoothed. Panels for exteriors of buildings are often *sand-cast* by pouring liquid concrete into flat molds of sand modeled in reverse.

Sculpture and Space

One of the most famous of all works of sculpture is primarily a work of nature. Less than five inches tall, the Venus of Willendorf was unearthed in Central Europe, obviously a natural stone form that was perceived as a fertility symbol and embellished with primitive tools to emphasize its significance (Fig. 304). Seymour Lipton's work (Fig. 305), created 30,000 years later, has some of the same textural quality and the sense of curving forms, but there is a fundamental difference: in the Venus, space flows *around* the bulbous masses, whereas in Lipton's *Sanctuary* the space enters into the work in a modified spiral that

304. Venus of Willendorf. c. 30,000–25,000 B.C. Stone, height 4⅜″ (11.18 cm). Natural History Museum, Vienna.

305. Seymour Lipton. *Sanctuary*. Nickel-silver over steel, height 29¼″ (74.3 cm). Collection, The Museum of Modern Art, New York (Blanchette Rockefeller Fund).

304
304   305

becomes an interaction of positive and negative space. This interaction was important in the sculpture of ancient Greece and of the Renaissance, but it became one of the earmarks of the Baroque style of the 17th century. In painting and architecture the Baroque was an opulent and impressive decorative style characterized by pastel coloring embellished with gilt and heavily garnished with swirling cupids, garlands, and elaborate motifs from nature. In sculpture it also swirled and flowed, as in the *David* by Bernini in Figure 306. Bernini was said to use space like a plastic material to be molded, his figures surrounded by the fluid forms of space, which enveloped them in a theatrical interplay of stone and light.

Contemporary sculpture has an even more crucial relationship with space. Much of it is fabricated in a factory from the sculptor's drawings, designed to be placed in city parks or plazas where enormous scale is necessary if it is not to be dwarfed into ignominity. Huge scale in turn demands open spaces to surround it, to act in and around it, and generally to place it in context to its surroundings. George Sugarman's *Kite Castle* in Plate 28, page 291, rests in New York's Dag Hammerskjöld Plaza, where it creates a lively relationship with the cityscape. Its forms and spaces interact with the buildings that surround it, the space of the plaza, the pedestrians who move around and through it, even the backdrop of passing vehicles. The viewer can observe it from an infinite number of angles, both on the ground and through the windows of adjacent buildings—and over periods of extended time. Each different viewpoint changes the configuration of solids and spaces.

306

306. Gian Lorenzo Bernini. *David*.
1623. Marble. Galleria Borghese,
Rome.

307. Gargoyles on the face of
Washington Cathedral,
Mount St. Alban. Washington, D.C.

308. Steve Keister. *USO #66*. 1980.
Formica and acrylic on plywood,
$30 \times 13 \times 30''$
($76.2 \times 33.02 \times 76.2$ cm).
Blum Helman Gallery.

Sculpture and Light

In drawing or painting, shape is translated into mass by means of shading or tonality. In sculpture, this transformation takes place as a result of light.

As we noted in Chapter 6, the Greeks made a fine art of moldings because they could depend on the bright Greek sun to carve them into sparkling accents of light and shadow. The play of light dramatically articulates the forms on the Washington Cathedral in Figure 307. Not only the moldings and arches but the gargoyles depend on light for their form. Observe the difference in the two gargoyles: one, drenched in light, is *outlined* by shadow; the other one, placed so shadow engulfs its underside, is outlined in light.

When sculpture is installed indoors, the source of light is more static and therefore must assume maximum effect. Some contemporary artists install moving lights as part of their work, providing the kind of dynamics that comes from changing sunlight. Others, like Steve Keister, engage light as the major element of the work itself (Fig. 308).

307

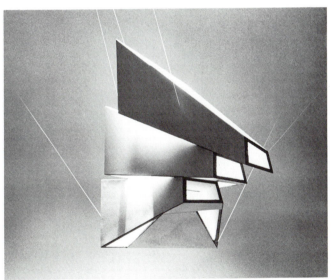

308

Directions in Sculpture

Twentieth-century sculptors have experienced the same release from traditional forms as painters have, and some of the movements that we discussed in painting have counterparts in sculpture. Cubist sculptures, as we see in Boccioni's work in Figure 309, show the same interest in sliding planes and geometric forms. There were also movements

309

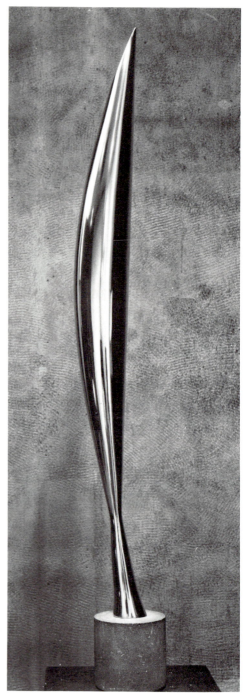

310

indigenous to sculpture, such as *Constructivism*, which emerged after World War I and which was described as an attempt to release earth-bound masses from the pull of gravity. *Abstraction* was as strong and revolutionary a force in sculpture as in painting. Brancusi's *Bird in Space* (Fig. 310) created a sensation when it appeared in 1919.

Contemporary Trends

Sculpture has exhibited many of the same characteristics as Postmodern painting—mythological and symbolic images and an emotional quality. When the human figure is depicted it has none of the idealism of past eras but is shown with merciless fidelity in all its mediocrity (Fig. 311). Duane Hanson's sunbather is a kind of three-dimensional Photorealism, but it is also related to Pop Art, a brief outburst in the sixties of banal images typical of American life—walls of Campbell's soup cans, huge hamburgers and hot dogs, and immense blowups of comic-strip characters.

The purpose of art for centuries was to create an orderly ideal world from which to escape harsh reality. Today artists take pride in *facing* reality. If they depict what *could* be, it is not in terms of the ideal but rather at the opposite pole, showing the full range of possible horror and violence. Still, each year shows new efforts to come to terms with contemporary life, and some present-day sculptors are bursting forth in organic forms, eccentric shapes, and a new look at nature. Steve Wood states his view by saying: "I'm looking for wonderment, to deny habit, to push back the envelope of reality just a bit—and the ultimate source is nature"[6] (Fig. 312).

[6]Steven Henry Madoff, "Sculpture Unbound," *ARTNews*, November 1986, 103.

309. Umberto/Boccioni.
Unique Forms of Continuity in Space.
1913. Bronze (cast in 1931);
43⅞ × 34⅞ × 15¾"
(111.3 × 88.4 × 39.9 cm).
Collection, The Museum of Modern Art,
New York (Lillie P. Bliss Bequest).

310. Constantin Brancusi.
Bird in Space.
(1928?) Bronze (unique cast);
height 4'6" (1.37 m).
Collection, The Museum of Modern Art,
New York (anonymous gift).

311. Duane Hanson.
Woman at Beach on Lounge Chair,
or *Sunbather.* 1971. Polyester and
fiberglass, polychromed; lifesize.
Wadsworth Atheneum.

311

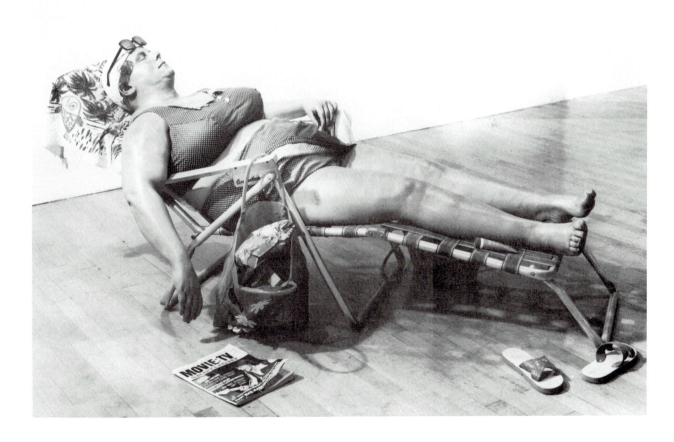

312

Sculpture and painting have converged in many ways. Both have burst beyond the traditional materials shown in Figures 288 and 304. Painters use buckets of paint and house painters' brushes to cover immense areas of canvas. Sculptors make use of metal foundries and factories to fabricate their works. Both seek new frontiers of expression and both, as always, rely on the elements and principles of design. With all the currents of passing trends, fads, and individual experimentation, these elements and principles remain the eternal truths that are the essence of any effective work, and the basis for visual communication.

Summary

Painting is based on pigments ground into a binder and applied to a support. Painting media include encaustic, tempera, casein, oil, watercolor, gouache, and acrylic. Painting has undergone many movements in the twentieth century, including *Impressionism, Cubism, Abstraction, German Expressionism, Surrealism, Abstract Expressionism, Op Art, Minimal Art, Photorealism, Post-modernism,* and *Simulationism.*

Sculpture has traditionally been classified as *freestanding* or *relief,* which includes *bas-relief* and *haut-relief.* There are many processes and materials used to create sculpture. Space is an important aspect of sculpture, as is light. Sculpture has gone through many of the same trends as painting. Contemporary works in both areas are characterized by huge size, technological methods and materials, and a search for new horizons of expression.

312. Steve Wood.
Particle in Peril. 1983.
Materials: wood, epoxy,
canvas, pigment.
Courtesy the artist.

Graphic Design and the Computer

In its broadest sense, the term *graphic* refers to anything written, drawn, or engraved, so graphic design could technically include any of the visual arts, especially those that involve a two-dimensional surface. However, there is a more specific area generally associated with graphic design, and that includes all work intended for *reproduction*.

Such reproduction could mean one or a hundred copies, as in printmaking, or mass reproduction for the media, as in advertising art. It could also refer to the rapidly growing field of computer design, which extends from desktop book publishing to designing the format introducing television programs. We will discuss each of these areas separately, starting with the category most closely associated with the work of the individual designer, printmaking.

Printmaking

A print is a work of art created by an indirect transfer method. Rather than making an image directly on a ground, the artist works on a "master" surface with the image usually in reverse. From this master, many impressions can be made on paper (Fig. 313). The principle is identical to that of the common rubber stamp.

313

313. A print being pulled.

314

Because it is general practice to strike a number of impressions from a single master, prints are often referred to as *multiples*. The artist creates an image on a plate, stone, screen, or other surface, then supervises the printing or undertakes it personally. The number of impressions, known as the *edition,* possible from a single original will vary with the material. A linoleum cut yields relatively few prints before the soft material begins to wear and the quality of the impressions diminishes. A steel-faced metal plate, on the other hand, is capable of striking many thousands of fine-quality prints. As a rule, prints are numbered as they come from the press, with the earlier impressions being the finest and therefore the most desirable. The artist will hand-sign each print that meets with his or her approval.

Prints begin with a drawing and incorporate the same compositional principles as paintings. Line, shape, texture, or value may be the predominant element, according to the printing technique used. Some have obvious decorative qualities (Fig. 314), while others are filled with emotional impact (Fig. 315).

Prints as works of art should not be confused with reproductions, which are copies of work done in some other medium, usually painting. While good-quality reproductions may be suitable for educational purposes, they can in no sense be considered works of art, since the artist had nothing to do with them. A print, on the other hand, is an original that may exist in several versions. It resembles, in a sense, a bronze sculpture for which there may be a number of castings from the mold. Sometimes the printmaker alters the image between impressions, so each print is slightly different from the others.

315

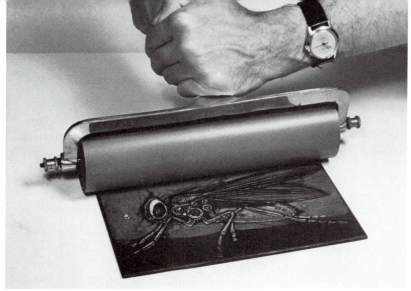

316

Printmaking Processes

Most printmaking processes can be placed in one of four categories: *relief, intaglio, lithography,* and *serigraphy.* However, today there are many variations, with considerable overlapping.

Relief

Relief describes any process in which the image to be printed is *raised* from the background on the printing surface and takes the ink directly (Fig. 316). The inked image is then transferred to the paper by pressure. The oldest printmaking processes are the relief methods. In their most typical form relief prints preserve the qualities of the material from which they are made, although images are sometimes built up on a plate rather than being cut from it. Such works are called *collagraphs.*

The most usual materials for the relief method are *wood, linoleum,* and *plastic.* Wood can be handled in one of two ways. A *woodcut* is made from a block of even-grained wood, on which the image is drawn and the parts *not* to be printed are cut away with knives or gouges. The block is then inked and the image transferred to paper by pressing or rubbing. Because they are cut primarily *with* the grain, woodcuts have a hand-hewn look that emphasizes the feeling of the wood itself (Fig. 317). A *wood engraving* is cut from the *end grain* of the wood, using a fine steel tool called a *burin,* which allows for finer lines and greater detail than is usual in a woodcut (Fig. 318). The process is still relief because the lines show as white against the dark background that is inked and printed (Figs. 319 and 320). Lucite is sometimes used instead of wood, making for smoother cutting.

Linocuts are made from linoleum blocks, usually made by gluing thick linoleum to plywood. Here again, the cutting is made easy by the material, which offers no resistant grain to cut against. Color prints are often made from linoleum, using a separate block for each color and cutting away all else. The blocks must be carefully lined up when

317

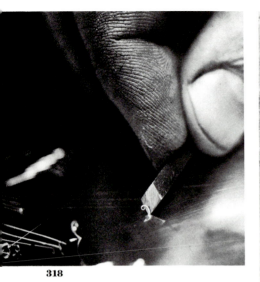

318

319

320

318. Burin in use, showing the curl of metal that is sometimes left on the plate, softening the effect of the finished print.

319. Thomas Bewick. Bison. Engraved wood-block. Los Angeles County Museum of Art (anonymous donor).

320. Thomas Bewick. *Bison*. 1800–1814. Wood engraving, 2 × 2¾″ (5.08 × 6.99 cm). Los Angeles County Museum of Art (anonymous donor).

321. Martin Schongauer. *St. Michael*. c. 1480–1491. Engraving, 6⅜ × 4½″ (16.19 × 11.43 cm). Courtesy of the Trustees of the British Museum.

printing, a process known as *registering*. This technique is also used in woodcuts, a Japanese practice that greatly influenced the Impressionist painters in their use of space.

Intaglio

The term *intaglio* derives from the Italian word *intagliare*, meaning "to incise." It describes a printing process that is just the opposite of relief, in that the parts to be printed are etched *into* the plate and are lower than the surface. Ink is retained in the incised areas and the plate wiped clean. Intaglio hand processes include *metal engraving, drypoint, etching, aquatint,* and *mezzotint.*

Metal engravings are executed with sharp tools (burins or gravers) on sheets of copper, zinc, or steel. The v-shaped burin is pushed into the surface of the metal plate, gouging out the image, after which ink is rubbed into the grooves. After the plate has been wiped clean, it is placed face up on the bed of a press with dampened paper laid on the face of the plate, covered by a felt blanket. Pressure is applied with the heavy roller of the press, which forces the paper into the grooves, tranferring the ink to the paper. Metal engravings have a linear quality much like pen-and-ink drawings (Fig. 321).

Before the invention of the camera, engravings were widely used as book illustrations as well as a means of reproducing paintings. Copper engraving is still employed for seals on documents, postage stamps, paper money, and fine stationery.

Drypoint differs from engraving only in the preparation of the plate. Drypoints generally are executed on copper plates with needle-like instruments that have steel or diamond points. The resulting lines differ from those made by a burin in that they are the result of the tool being *drawn across* the plate instead of being pushed into it. In the process, a tiny curl or *burr* of metal is raised along the edges of the lines. When the plate is inked, this burr retains the ink, so that the printed image has a velvety appearance recalling the darker accents of a fine pencil drawing (Fig. 322).

321

322

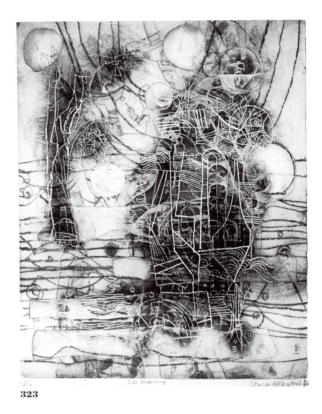

323

322. Egon Schiele.
Portrait of Franz Hauer.
1914. Drypoint,
5⅛ × 4¼″ (13.02 × 10.8 cm).

323. Shoici Hasegawa.
Les Oiseaux.
Lithograph, 29 × 22″
(74 × 56 cm).
Editions Vision Nouvelle,
Paris.

324. Mary Cassatt.
In the Omnibus. 1891.
Color aquatint with drypoint
and soft ground,
14⁵⁄₁₆ × 10½″ (36.35 × 26.67 cm).
Cleveland Museum of Art
(bequest of Charles T. Brooks).

325. Chuck Close. *Keith.*
1972. Mezzotint,
4′4″ × 3′6″ (1.32 × 1.07 m).
Courtesy Parasol Press, New York.

The term *etching* originates in the German word *essen*, meaning "to eat," and the printmaking process is the same as that described in Chapter 17 for decorating metal. The plate is coated with wax, the design is scratched through the wax with a blunt needle, and the plate is immersed in acid, which eats into the exposed lines, etching them permanently. Finally, the plate is inked and printed in the same manner as an engraved plate (Fig. 323). Etchings are generally characterized by a softer line than engravings.

Aquatint differs from the other processes in that a subtle tone is created on the plate itself. All linear elements are first etched on the plate and then the plate is covered with a powdered resinous substance. After the particles have covered the plate evenly, the plate is heated so that the resin will melt and adhere to the metal surface. The plate is then submerged in acid, which will bite the particles of metal not covered by the resin, resulting in a fine-textured tone. This tone becomes the light areas of the background. For darker tones, the plate is submerged at intervals, with the light areas blocked out with acid-resistant varnish, until a full range of tonal values is achieved. The resulting print will have a soft quality unlike that of any other printmaking process (Fig. 324).

Another variation on the etching technique is *mezzotint*, which is characterized by a velvety tone. Here the artist first works over the entire plate with a *rocker*, a tool with many sharp cutting teeth, to dig up the surface and produce an allover covering of burrs. If the plate were printed at this stage, the burrs would create a uniform black tone. To build intermediate tones, the artist partially removes the

324

325

burrs with a scraper, removing them entirely where highlights are needed. Mezzotint prints usually have a dark, rich, brooding quality (Fig. 325).

Lithography

Lithography is known as a *planographic* process because it employs a flat surface with neither raised areas nor depressions. The process depends on the mutual antipathy of grease and water. The artist draws on a stone with a grease pencil or with a brush dipped in a greasy paintlike substance. Next, the stone is treated with a solution of gum arabic to which a small amount of nitric acid has been added. Finally the stone is moistened with water, then inked with a roller. The areas treated with gum arabic accept the water and the greasy image areas accept the oil-based ink, so that only the parts drawn retain the ink for printing. The artist places damp paper on the stone and applies pressure, transferring the image to paper. The invention of lithography is credited to the German Alois Senefelder, who used a special limestone in his native Bavaria for drawing images, resulting in

326

a velvety texture unique to printmaking (Fig. 326). Bavarian limestone remains the classic ground, although in recent years lithographers have used zinc plates.

Serigraphy

Serigraphy, or *screen printing*, is a stencil technique as mentioned in connection with decorating fabrics in Chapter 17. The term "serigraphy" means "writing on silk," and silk is the traditional material for stretching on the wooden frame used for this process, although nylon and other materials are also sometimes employed. The artist blocks out the areas that are not to be printed, using a special preparation, then forces ink or dye through the mesh of the screen onto the paper. Color printing is relatively easy, requiring a separate screen for each color, and allowing for bright multiple color prints suitable for posters as well as for so-called art prints (Pl. 29, p. 292).

Mechanical Reproduction

Each of the printmaking processes described has its counterpart in commercial photomechanical reproduction, which is the means of printing books, magazines, newspapers, posters, and so forth. The corresponding planographic process in printmaking is *offset lithography,* or simply *offset.* The text and illustrations for this book were offset printed.

326. Pierre Auguste Renoir.
Portrait of Louis Valtat.
c. 1904. Original lithograph.
9′10″ × 7′10″ (2.98 m × 2.38 m).
Collection Jack Rutberg Fine Arts,
Los Angeles.

327. Page from the
Lindisfarne Gospels.
Late 7th century, British Library,
London (reproduced by permission).

Photolithography is a commercial technique used by many artists for its experimental possibilities. Stone, zinc, or aluminum is given a light-sensitive coating, then an image is created on film or acetate and projected onto the plate, after which it is exposed to light. The coating in the light-exposed areas hardens and accepts ink, while the coating in the unexposed areas washes away. The surface is desensitized in these areas with a special preparation, then the plate is inked and printed like any other lithograph.

Photoserigraphy is responsible for an entirely new type of lithographic print. The screen is coated with an emulsion by drawing a squeegee (roller) over it, then a film positive is secured to the glass on a light table and the screen placed over it. After a two- to five-minute exposure to light, the screen shows a pale latent image. The screen is now washed down with water, erasing the unexposed parts of the image and leaving the other areas hardened as a resist coating. The screen is then printed in the usual fashion. As in photolithography, the detail possible is practically unlimited.

Monoprint

The *monoprint* or *monotype* is made by painting on a flat surface of metal or glass with either paint or ink. The printing paper is pressed onto the colored surface and then peeled off, resulting in a print that cannot be repeated exactly. The effect is slightly different than could have been achieved by painting directly on the paper.

Book Design

A beautiful book holds a unique place among the world's treasures. In addition to its literary content, it can be a work of art in itself, a combination of fine papers, well-designed type, illustrations, beautiful binding, and a cover that has its own aesthetic appeal.

Books have a history almost as old as civilization, beginning with hieroglyphics and threading its way through papyrus and parchment scrolls to the codex, the binding of flat sheets of parchment together in the early Christian era. Calligraphy is found on scrolls throughout the world and illuminations were used to decorate them, particularly in the Orient and the Christian monasteries (Fig. 327). The modern book emerged largely because of the development of printing technology and photography.

Ideally, a book should be an entity in which format, text, and illustrations are sensitively coordinated to form a unified whole. Often the graphic designer has little control over text and illustrations, however, so the task becomes one of interpretation, finding the most effective means of presenting the book's contents. This is largely a matter of text design, layout, paper, and cover (Fig. 328).

There are many considerations in text design. The designer must choose a typeface and its size, a display typeface for such things as chapter titles and headings, perhaps a decorative numeral or initial letter. The size and shape of the page, the margins, and the space between various elements must be determined. If the book has illus-

327

328

trations, these and their captions must be integrated into the total design. All of these elements work together to create *unity*.

Typefaces have developed considerably since Gutenberg invented movable type in the 15th century, and today the range of possible faces is extraordinary (Fig. 329). Standard book design makes use of only a dozen or so. This text is printed in a typeface called "New Baskerville" with some of the principal headings in "Modern."

Closely related to the choice of typeface is the matter of *layout*. Design of the title page is crucial in introducing the reader to the book, but the design of every page is important and should be laid out in abstract block form. The arrangements of text and illustrations must be *balanced*, and the type must be grouped for *value*, which will depend on its size and the density of placement, as well as the distance

329

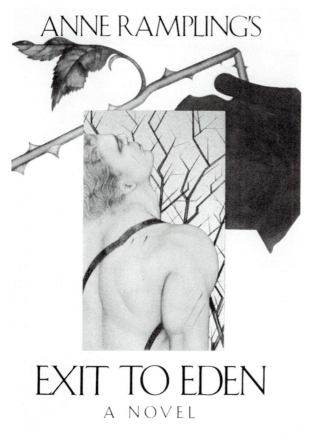

ANNE RAMPLING'S

EXIT TO EDEN

A NOVEL

We love to have a
heart-to-heart talk!

330   331

between lines and paragraphs. Emphasis will be supplied by illustrations and headings and sometimes by a decorative line embellishment in a border or at the end of a section. All of this should be seen as a satisfactory abstract design before it is translated into type and illustrations.

In the competitive setting of a bookshop, the cover design of a book could make the difference between the customer's picking it up or passing it by. In interpreting the book's content, the designer may choose a literal or symbolic representation of the contents (Fig. 330), an abstract design that alludes to the contents, or a striking combination of type alone, with no imagery.

A special category of books are those designed for children, which usually feature colorful and fanciful illustrations (Fig. 331). Since the book is aimed at novice readers or those who do not read at all, the designer must strive for immediate visual impact to engage the young audience. All design elements are therefore planned around the illustrations.

Magazines and Periodicals

Magazine design includes the same elements as book design but with a different emphasis. For one thing, the magazine designer usually has

328. *The Enveloping Herbs.* 1984. Direct mailer for *Champion International.* Art Director and Designer: Peter Good. Illustrators: Peter Good, Janet Cummings Good. From Graphis Annual 1985/86. Zurich.

329. Thousands of different typefaces are available today. Illustrated here are: Baskerville, Prisma capitals, Swinger Shadow, Andrich Minerva italic, LSC Manhattan, and Helvetica.

330. Book cover for *Exit to Eden* by Anne Rampling. Designer, Mel Odom.

331. Gyo Fujikawa. *We love to have a heart-to-heart talk!* 1978. Watercolor. 7½ × 8″ (19.05 × 20.32 cm).

332

333

much more control over the choice of illustrations and may be able to commission a photographer or illustrator for a particular article. Magazine design tends to be more casual, more flamboyant, and more colorful. The designer can follow styles and fads closely without fear of obsolescence, because the magazine, unlike the book, will probably be thrown away in a few weeks. The exception is the group of slick, sophisticated magazines catering to home design or fashion. Highly priced, these are designed for information and reference, with elegant photography and articles of lasting relevance.

On the whole, however, a magazine is meant to be read in odd moments and in spurts—in the dentist's office, under the hair dryer, while waiting for the car to be repaired. Thus, the layout will be designed in such a way that the eye is caught and moved along from place to place. Except in the case of scholarly magazines, which are generally kept for reference, the visual design should be such that one can scan the contents without even reading the text (Fig. 332).

As with a book, the cover of a magazine should be compelling. People usually decide quickly about the magazine they buy—while rushing for a train or checking out at a supermarket. Unless they are dedicated to a certain periodical on a regular basis, the appearance of the cover may well be the reason for the choice (Fig. 333).

Advertising

Advertising art has existed since 3000 B.C., when the Sumerians employed pictures to advertise their wares. Advertising as an industry is a natural outgrowth of the Industrial Revolution, when mass produc-

1889

1900

1921

1939

1964

1969

334

332. Magazine illustration for *Body Language,* by Marilyn Mercer. McCall's Magazine. Designer: Carveth Kramer.

333. Magazine cover for *Nebelspalter.* 1984. Designer, Barth. Gouache, 11¾ × 8⅔", (30 × 22 cm).

334. Logo for the Bell System, as it has appeared successively since 1889.

335. Brochure cover design for Gene London's Children's Broadcasts on CBS. Designers: Lou Dorfsman and Ira Teichberg. Artist; John Alcorn. For CBS Television Stations Division.

tion made goods so plentiful that it was necessary to seek buyers for them. The earliest known advertising agency opened its doors in England in 1812, and within a century and a half the advertising industry has grown into a giant multi-million-dollar business.

335

Until well into the 20th century, foodstuffs and other goods were marketed in barrels, tubs, or sacks with no indication of the source of supply. The *trademark* was developed as a kind of reward for products of excellent quality and a means by which the buyer could be assured of purchasing goods of similar quality in the future. Actually, the trademark became a stepping-stone for manufacturers developing their own businesses, for it quickly established their identities and provided them with an opportunity to extend their reputations. Styles in trademarks change through the years, yet the identity remains constant (Fig. 334).

Most advertisements consist of two elements: the words, or *copy,* and the *illustration.* The role of the graphic designer is to arouse sufficient interest to cause the reader to stop and read the copy. An effective ad is addressed to specific people, to fill specific needs or interests, or to help achieve specific goals. The ad in Figure 335, telling of a series of educational programs on television, is directed to parents.

There are two general types of advertising: direct and indirect. *Direct* advertising is used when the seller expects immediate returns. Department stores, supermarkets, and other retail outlets take this approach, especially when they have special sales. *Indirect* advertising is effective for building a reputation and establishing the desirability of a product or service, with an emphasis on future as well as immediate results. *Institutional* advertising is one form of the indirect approach, having as its aim the creation of goodwill for a particular firm.

336

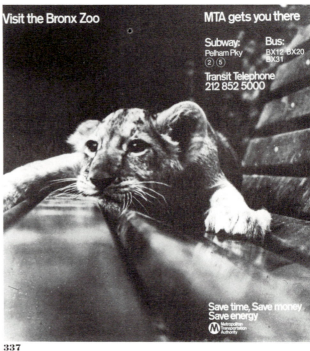

337

336. Ivan Chermayeff
(Chermayeff & Geismar Associates).
Crime and Punishment, poster for
Masterpiece Theatre. 1981.
Ink and chalk on paper,
22 × 26″ (55.8 × 91.4 cm).
Mobil Oil Corporation Collection.

337. Poster for New York's
Metropolitan Transportation
Authority. New York Metropolitan
Authority; Howard York &
Associates; and Michael Bosniak,
MTA.

One of the most effective forms in this category is the sponsorship of an artistic endeavor, such as drama, art, or music (Fig. 336).

In designing an ad, the first decision must be the type of consumer to be approached. In *factual* advertising, aimed at the no-nonsense individual, visual design focuses on a realistic representation of the product, which can be done in several ways. The product can be pictured alone, in a decorative setting, in actual use, or in combination with the results it is supposed to yield. This type of consumer would probably be most interested in practical hard-working products, such as washing machines or lawnmowers. The *imaginative* approach may feature something totally unrelated to the product, with the ad serving as an attention-getting device to introduce the product's name (Fig. 337).

Designing an advertisement is a matter of ideas, and producing an effective idea can be rigorous in the highly competitive market of today. Television commercials have the potential of reaching eleven million homes in the United States during an average minute of evening programming. All the association and symbolism used in magazine advertising are readily available to television, with the bonuses of dramatization, action, music, and characterization. Besides being fa-

Plate 28. George Sugarman. *Kite Castle*. 1973–1974.
Painted steel, height 18′ (5.5 m). Hammarskjöld Plaza, New York.
Courtesy Zabriskie Gallery, New York.

Plate 29. Audrey Flack. *Royal Flush*. 1977.
46½ × 64½″ (118 × 163.8 cm). Screenprint on masonite,
edition of 60. Louis K. Meisel Gallery, New York.

Plate 30. Dr. Alan Norton. *Fractal Domain of Attraction*.
July 1982. Computer Graphic Raster Image reproduced on 35 mm
Ektachrome slide, 4 dimensions. Collection IBM Research.

miliar with the principles of graphic design, the television designer must have a knowledge of film techniques. A well-conceived commercial may be more entertaining than the programs it supports.

Designing an advertisement is also a matter of the principles of design. Type and illustrations must be in proportion to one another, and colors and shapes should be arranged for a sense of total balance. Variety in type size and style as well as in visual textures adds to the overall effect. Unity is, of course, of the utmost importance in focusing the viewer's attention on the primary object, the product advertised.

Package Design

Self-service shopping makes package design as important as advertising, for the appeal of the wrappings may be the deciding factor in the consumer's choice of product. The best way to begin a package design is to gather together the packages of similar products and analyze them for similarities, weaknesses, and good qualities to be surpassed. A unique color combination or a totally new concept can make a product stand out in a display.

A particularly effective treatment for packaging is to create a "corporate image" (Fig. 338). This means supplying a visual impression that carries through every aspect of a company's business, with integrated designs for packaging, stationery, shipping materials, labels, advertising, brochures, warranties, and even the design of the corporate headquarters. The designer who assumes such an assignment can know that the entire consumer market—perhaps millions of people—will learn to associate the company with that particular design.

The elements and principles of design operate in every aspect of graphic design, with particular stress on attracting attention through variety and emphasis. It is interesting that the same basis that has served artists for centuries in creating works for us to enjoy at our

338. Corporate identity and packaging program designed for Tom's Natural Soap by A. R. Williams & Associates, South Lynnfield, Mass. The total design concept includes shipping cartons and letterhead (designer: Rod Williams); a poster (designers: Rod Williams, Frederick Pickel, and John Evans); and packaging (designers: Rod Williams, Fred Ribeck, Fred Pickel, and John Evans.)

338

leisure has become a dynamic force in the highly competitive world of 20th-century commerce.

The Computer

The most potent symbol of the 20th-century competitive world is the computer. In the space of twenty years, methods of transacting business have been revolutionized, and computer design and sales has boomed into a leading industry in its own right, worldwide. The public has quickly incorporated computer jargon into the vernacular, and we accept computerized letters, bank statements, and sales brochures as a matter of course. We have become accustomed to having any mishap in our commercial dealings blamed on the computer, thus wiping out the factor of personal blame, and we have resigned ourselves to the knowledge that computers in dozens of places probably have "profiles" of us, spelling out our personal tastes, whether in clothing, cars, or personal effects, as well as our financial status, whether we own our homes, and what political causes we support. Mail-order businesses serve hundreds of thousands of customers on the basis of such profiles, and when we telephone an order they can give us our own names and addresses simply by being told our post office zip code: it is all right there on the computer.

Computer Graphics

Such a wealth of information is not simply for storing but for the promulgation of business, and this means *communication*. For a long time after the development of the first electronic computer, computer output was primarily a matter of adding, subtracting, multiplying, and dividing; the advantage was that these operations were carried out at tremendous speed. Today some computers can perform hundreds of millions of calculations per second, a speed that led to the use of graphics in order to expand the usefulness of such lightning calculations. Since the computer "thinks" only with numbers, in the form of electronic impulses, plotting devices have been designed to translate the impulses into pictures. A pair of numbers can represent two coordinates of a point on a two-dimensional sheet of paper, and four numbers (two pairs) can define a line segment. Nothing even resembling a picture ever exists inside a computer, but computer programs can be written enabling the computer to produce numbers that make the plotter draw pictures.

There are several types of computer graphic devices. Pen plotters draw lines on regular paper; since many pen plotters have several different-colored pens, colorful plots are possible. Large flat-bed pen plotters produce large, accurate architectural and engineering drawings. High-speed ink-jet plotters project images by squirting an electronically controlled stream of ink at the paper. Precise laser plotters very rapidly draw sharply defined lines.

Borrowing from the television screen, the cathode-ray tube (CRT) draws an image on the screen with an electron beam that excites the phosphors of the tube face. The drawing can be *static*, resulting in interesting but random drawing, or it can be *dynamic*, working from a *data base* that supplies information telling whether certain design concepts all work. Automobiles and airplanes are designed in this fashion. If the designer adds an element to the design that will throw the total design off balance or prove unsafe, the computer immediately says so. The designer may work with color graphics on the screen, showing the projected design from all angles, or he or she may print it out on paper in various views, for purposes of demonstration or dispersal to staff or prospective customers.

The design of fonts (huge assortments of typefaces in numerous sizes) makes possible *desk-top publishing,* the most effective way of programming blocks or columns of print. This includes *digitizing* an image, inserting a photograph and letting the computer reproduce it, in amazingly accurate similarity. The use of graphics, as in drawings, charts, and diagrams, adds to the effectiveness of this system, which may turn out newsletters, interoffice memos, or letters to customers. The addition of graphics to business reports gives instant clarity to the necessary information (Fig. 339). Computers will produce the graphs and charts, add decorative borders if desired, and wrap the text around the graphic material.

The human designer determines such capabilities at the time the machine is being designed, and the knowledge of design must be combined with a thorough understanding of computer construction and operation.

339

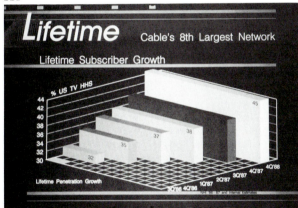

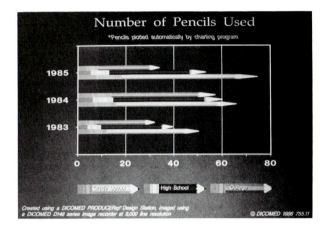

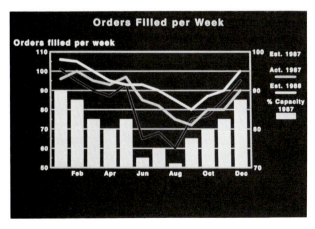

339. Top left: Created using a Crosfield Dicomed IMAGINATOR™ Design Console and imaged on a D148 Series Color Image Recorder. © 1987 Slidecrafters Inc. Dicomed Corporation, Minneapolis. Top right: Created on a Crosfield Dicomed PRODUCER$_{xp}$™ Design Station and imaged on a D148 Series Color Image Recorder. © Crosfield Dicomed Inc., 1986. Dicomed Corporation, Minneapolis. Bottom left: Lotus Graphwriter II. Lotus Development Corp., Cambridge, Massachusetts.

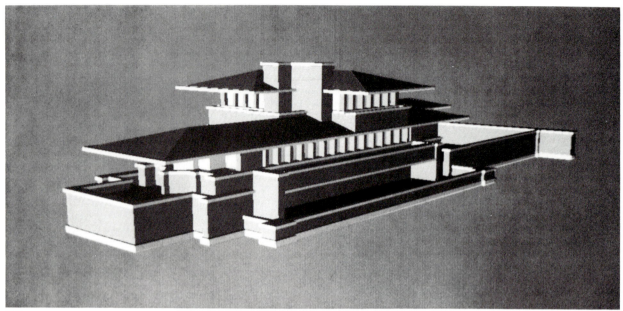

340

The Computer and the Designer

Originally *speed* was the primary advantage of the computer, and this was extended into many areas. By trying designs on the computer, for instance, the weaver, potter, sculptor, and even the painter or graphic artist can eliminate hours of experimentation with sometimes messy materials. The weaver uses a computer to explore the various combinations of color and weave structure as elements of design, letting the machine generate all the possible color permutations of a given pattern and thus eliminating hours of working with graph paper or the loom. Whatever the field of design, the computer does the job quickly and cleanly.

Not only will the computer produce *architectural drawings*, it can project *three-dimensional images* of finished buildings, allowing the prospective builder or buyer the simulated experience of approaching the structure from various angles. Using color, this can be extended to a series of projections that will give the sense of walking through the building as well (Fig. 340).

Ship designers have made effective use of the computer for years. Computer graphics were responsible for the structural grid model of the *Eagle* at Newport Beach, California (Fig. 341), and computers continually monitor the performance of experimental yacht designs as a model is pulled through tank-generated rough and calm seas. When the yacht *Australia II* took the America's Cup away from the United States for the first time in 132 years of yacht racing, the triumph was preceded by four months of computerized research and testing in Holland. When the United States regained the cup two years later, it was after thorough and extensive use of every computer technique available. Thus the computer has become a partner in many areas of design, a partner that not only speeds up the design process but does so with vision, efficiency, and success.

340. Computer-generated image of Frank Lloyd Wright's Robie House, displayed on a 1000 × 1000 raster display. The geometry was modeled using an input routine designed by Wayne Robertz, the modeling was performed by Dan Ambrosi. Cornell University, Ithaca, New York, Program of Computer Graphics, Dr. Donald P. Greenberg, Director.

341. Structural grid for model of yacht *Eagle*. The simulated yacht structure is exposed to stresses to check stability; if there are weak panels, they can be identified and corrected early on.

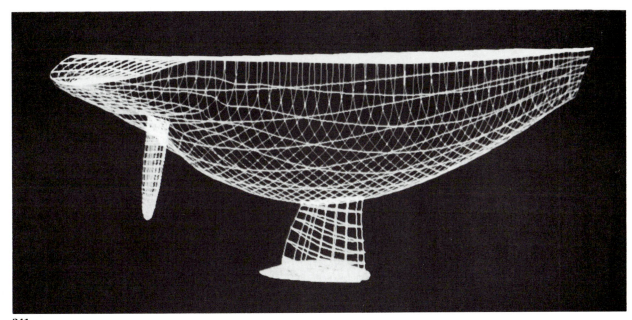

341

The Computer and Art

The artist emerges in every stage of civilization, leaving records available to succeeding generations that would be possible in no other way. It is only natural that the discovery of the potential of the computer for colorful images would provide sufficient inspiration to open up an entire new field. An image on the computer consists of thousands of tiny dots, in the manner of the Pointillist painters of the Impressionist period. A straight line running from the top of the picture on a computer to the bottom is, in fact, composed of about a thousand individual dots, far too many to be discernible as such, but clearly visible as a line. The principle is similar to that of the halftone in printing, in which original copy is photographed through a screen that breaks the picture up into little dots for purposes of newspaper reproduction. Looking closely at the newspaper photograph, we can see the dots, but glancing through the paper casually, we are not aware of them.

Early in 1982 an exhibition was organized at Lehigh University in Pennsylvania at which 22 major artists exhibited works produced by computer techniques. Although the works were admittedly experimental, indications were that the artists were taking computer art seriously. Now artists have mastered many of the techniques of painting, including the depiction of perspective. Figure 342 not only shows the walls of a room but also performs the difficult feat of decreasing the distances between lines as they recede toward a vanishing point.

Other aspects of traditional painting have been simulated by computer techniques, including shading, landscape images, fantastic forms based on nature, and forms that look like something lifted from a moonscape (Pl. 30, p. 292). The artists are not merely playing with the computer; they are working from mathematical analyses and formulas to discover what certain combinations will produce.

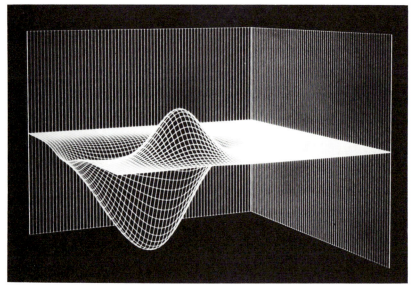

342

Early in the 1980s the computer made its way into the realm of film with a production entitled *Tron,* in which 286 of the 350 backgrounds were drawn by computer. For 15 of the film's 105 minutes, everything on the screen—settings, vehicles, and even a character— was the work of high-speed data-processing equipment. Other computerized designs have become familiar introductions to television programs, such as the "NBC Nightly News" (Fig. 343).

Artists have used tools since the cave drawings were made with sticks of charcoal, and we noted that contemporary painters and

343

sculptors have broken away from the traditional equipment of their art as well as from traditional imagery and expression. The emergence of the computer as an artistic medium is becoming increasingly respected. Certainly it was born of contemporary technology, and future periods of civilization may well see it as the most typical expression of 20th-century life. Once a miracle available only to millionaires, computers are becoming both more sophisticated and less expensive. Innumerable software companies are emerging that can open up whole new areas to the owner of a home computer as well as to designers of our most advanced equipment. The computer also has the advantage of durability, which many artworks do not have. With the data base on file neither time nor weather can cause destruction of the art produced by the machine. In any case, the computer has already secured its place in the field of graphic design, with each of the continuing developments in the field adding to its potential for communication.

342. *Floating Mountains.* A program called PICTURA plotted this picture in perspective with hidden lines removed. Drawn on an Information International, Inc. FR80 and recorded on 35-mm color film. Calculation done on a CDC 7600 computer. (©1980 Melvin L. Prueitt)

343. Computer-generated imagery. The opening of the NBC Nightly News.

Summary

Graphic design refers to all work intended for reproduction. Printmaking techniques fall into four categories: *relief, intaglio, lithography,* and *serigraphy.* Commercial versions of graphic reproduction include *offset lithography, photolithography,* and *photoserigraphy.* A *monoprint* cannot be exactly duplicated.

Book design involves format, illustrations, and text as well as paper, cover, and binding. *Magazine design* has a more casual orientation than book design, since it is not meant for permanent possession.

Advertising design consists of *copy* and *illustration.* There are two kinds of advertising: *direct* and *indirect. Institutional advertising* is a facet of indirect advertising. Design for advertising may be *factual* or *imaginative* in approach. *Package design* is a kind of advertising, since the appearance of the product can be crucial in attracting customers.

The *computer* is the most potent tool of 20th-century communication. *Computer graphics* is an important field of design, adding clarity to information stored and presented by the computer. The computer helps the designer in other fields by making it possible to project work in advance rather than having to experiment. Computer art is no longer a novelty but is being taken seriously as an art form.

CHAPTER EIGHTEEN

Photography and the Performing Arts

Photography began as a science, developed into a fine art, and since the advent of television has taken a starring role in communication. As communication, it can be an instant and graphic means of transmitting information or it can be an eloquent form of design. In any of its roles it is, first of all, a collaboration between an individual and some highly sensitive mechanical equipment, the most important of which is the camera.

The Camera

In simplest form, the camera is a light-tight box with an opening at one end to admit light and a receptive ground at the other to take the image. The diagram in Figure 344 shows the essential features of all cameras. Light enters the camera through the *aperture.* The amount of light entering can be controlled by the *diaphragm,* which regulates the size of the aperture, and by the *shutter,* which determines the amount of time during which light may enter. A *lens* gathers and refracts the light, throwing it onto the light-sensitive field at the back of the camera, the film.

344.

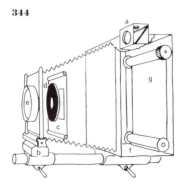
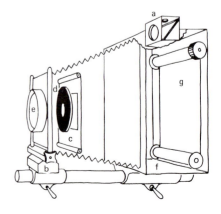

344. The essential parts of a camera: *a* viewfinder; *b* focusing system; *c* shutter; *d* aperture with diaphragm; *e* lens; *f* light-tight box; *g* film.

345. Enrico Ferorelli. *The Alps.*

Differences in cameras result mainly from the quality of their lenses and from the distance between the lens and the film (*the focal length*). The most sophisticated equipment is that which allows the photographer maximum control in distance, shutter speed, and diaphragm openings. Special lenses permit photographs of very broad vistas (*wide-angle* lenses), of subjects that are either very far away (*telephoto* lenses) or very close to the camera.

After a photograph has been exposed, the film is removed from the camera, developed, and, except for transparencies, printed on special paper. It is in these steps that recent developments have given the photographer unprecedented latitude for creativity.

Attributes of a Photograph

Like paintings and prints, photographs have the attributes of *subject*, *form*, and *content*. Historically, subject was the photograph's reason for being, since it was presumed to capture things, places, and people with more accuracy than any painting or drawing. We know now that this is not necessarily true. Variations in setting and use of different lenses can cause distortion, and a photograph quickly snapped can catch a person in an uncharacteristic gesture or expression. As an art form, photography is more concerned with capturing essence or mood, in other words, *content*.

Contemporary photographers also find challenge in new *forms* made possible by the manipulation of light and angle. A photograph can become a total abstraction, dissolving into interesting design (Fig. 345). It can become an abstraction in another way, by making a

345

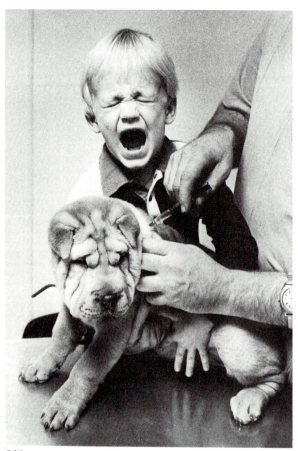

346

347

346. Four-year-old Cory J. Scholar reacts to his puppy's distemper shot (Chinese Shar-Pei puppy). Photo by Janet Kelly © Reading Eagle/Times.

347. Art Kane. *Greeting.* For Eastern Airlines.

348. John L. Huszar. *Double Portrait, Georgia O'Keeffe and Ansel Adams.* 1980. Taken during the filming of a documentary on Adams.

general statement of content far beyond the contours of a specific model. A photograph of a child, for example, may be a portrait of a particular child, but it may also be a symbol of childhood, a commentary on impishness or innocence, a contrast in light and shadow, a study of form, or possibly all of these things at once. It may sometimes be even more (Fig. 346).

The entire field of news photography whirls around *people* and what happens to them, and volumes have been filled with the results, some of them historic documents, some masterpieces of character study, some epics of dramatic action. For the designer with camera in hand, the human form and face offer every possible combination of elements and principles. The beauty of human relationships can be captured in a photograph more poignantly than in the most eloquent words (Fig. 347).

The Photograph as Symbol

Sometimes character studies reach far beyond the obvious expression of human life into symbols of an era. In Figure 348 we see two people

348

who have had long creative careers: Ansel Adams, an eminent photographer of nature and landscape, and Georgia O'Keeffe, the painter, whose husband, Alfred Stieglitz, is credited with establishing photography as an artistic medium. No photographic study could be more eloquent than this portrait of two friends, each with a lifetime of artistic experience depicted in a face, each a leading figure in the artistic world of their time. Even with such content, however, the photographer took care to compose an excellent design. O'Keeffe's dark coat is repeated in Adams' glasses and the shadows in his shirt, while his own light clothing is balanced by her hair and hands. A background whose middle value plays through the shadows in the faces gives unity to the extremes of light and dark.

The photograph in Figure 349 was one of a collection of photographs taken throughout the seasons for a publication on the city of Boston. By use of special lenses and an imaginative angle, the photographer has created an effective design from the old street lamps, the gabled buildings with their details from another era, and the striking thrust of the skyscraper reaching unencumbered toward the sky. In the contrasts of textures and form, he has also symbolized a new century, a modern voice soaring above the outdated arches and crenelations of the past.

349

The Photograph as Document

News photography was one of the first forms for the medium, adding graphic urgency to the stories in the daily newspaper. In such a role, the photographer was in the thick of the action and inevitably made many records that became historic documents of a community, and sometimes of worldwide events. The photograph in Figure 350 placed

350

351

Sam Shere in the ranks of chroniclers of history, a producer of documentary evidence.

Every day in communities throughout the world, the photographer performs a similar, if less dramatic, function. Figure 351 is typical of the work of newspaper photographers who make a career of being in the right place at a crucial moment. Such photographs not only transmit immediate awareness of current events but also become a part of the history of the community.

Commercial Photography

Photography for commercial purposes surrounds us—on book jackets and record albums, in magazines, posters, and on billboards. This does not touch on commercials on television, an entire field in which photography is the medium for *translating* ideas for promoting commercial products. Certainly photography is the single most important element in the advertising of travel and airline industries (Fig. 352).

Photography has a less commercial function in the sale of books, where it is considered primarily a means of *clarifying* material, yet its impact on the potential buyer cannot be underrated. For generations, textbooks were dull affairs consisting of printed words and diagrams. Then someone conceived the idea of making the text come to life with photographs. History books printed color photographs of battle sites and monuments, geographical shots of nations, even including reproductions of works of art representative of a given period. In this way, the student became aware that history was more than an assortment of

349. Robert Llewellyn. *Boston.* Designer: Donald G. Paulhus, for Foremost Publishers, Inc.

350. Sam Shere. *Explosion of the Hindenburg.* Lakehurst, N.J. 1937.

351. Ron Tarver. *The Fireman.* 1981.

352

dates and battles, that it included people and their creative efforts as well. In books on science, theories and experiments are now punctuated with attractive pertinent photographs, and even books on math and languages find ways to illustrate their subject matter. Needless to say, a book on the visual arts would be totally ineffectual without illustrations. We offer this book as an example of the importance of photographic accompaniment.

The Photograph as Design

The difference between a photographic record and a photographic work of art lies in the affinity that grows between the photographer and the subject, be the subject a person or a place. Sometimes a photographer produces a body of exceptional work about one special place in the world simply because there is a *resonance* there, a vital force that awakens memories, dreams, associations, and the full force of artistic creativity. This quality stimulates the photographer to see the textures, rhythms, emphasis, shapes, and balance that are combined in the final photograph.

The effects of light go far beyond the exposure of the film, and every photographer with consciousness of design finds light a valuable

352. Bert Glynn. *New Zealand.* For Pan American Airways. 1971. Poster design: Ivan Chermayeff and William Sontag.

353. David Cavagnaro. *Dry Grass Seed Stalks Against the Rising Sun.* San Geronimo Valley, Calif.

354. Paul Caponigro. *Canyon de Chelly, Arizona.* 1970.

353

354

ally. Light delineates tactile textures and produces visual texture, accenting, highlighting, and silhouetting as the artist desires. David Cavagnaro and his wife Maggie discovered, during three years of studying the California grasslands, an entire world of miracles of light and shadow—sparkle of dew, sunlight on spiderweb, and tree branches silhouetted against the mist. Dry grass seed stalks photographed against a rising sun become a striking design (Fig. 353).

Light was an influential partner in the creation of the photograph in Figure 354. This is a subject that has been photographed thousands of times. It required the eye of a designer to see the possibilities of dark shadow over brilliant stone, of clumps of dark piñon against horizontally striated cliffs. The focus is on the habitations built by human beings, but the eye is led to them dramatically by the ascending and descending dark shapes. Nature is monumental and enduring, and the works of human hands are small and transitory: this is the content of the work, eloquently expressed by the eye and hand of an artist who understood the power of light.

A different use of light produced effective emphasis in Figure 355. Here a portion of the California Palace of the Legion of Honor is bathed in fog. A bronze cast of Rodin's statue *The Thinker* sits brooding as though on the brink of the world, an arch leading to nothingness just beyond him. We view him between two giant col-

355

umns in shadow with the uneasy feeling that if we step through into the court and its tentative light we, too, may be led to the brink.

Special Effects

Many photographers use photography as a field of experiment, making their equipment work for them in various ways. The sense of movement is implicit in many news photographs, but the feeling of intense speed in Figure 356 was not captured with a high-speed lens setting. Instead, the model was motionless but the camera was rotated on a tripod during the exposure. The old adage that the camera never lies has been moved by new techniques into the realm of legend.

Even more compelling evidence can be seen in the photograph of New York in Figure 357. This image was recorded by a Zoomar camera, which registers a complete 360-degree view in one exposure. The approaches to the Brooklyn Bridge in this image swoop and bend like dancers moving to an unheard tune. The unique combination of size, shape, and image that characterizes the *form* of the work also provides the fantasy of its *content*.

355. Philip L. Molten. *California Palace of the Legion of Honor, San Francisco.* 1960.

356. Yale Joel. *Illusion of Speed.* 1965. Photograph taken with panning camera.

357. *The Brooklyn Bridge.* Photograph taken with the Zoomar 360 Panoramic camera.

356

357

Special Techniques

Special effects are produced by the use of photographic equipment in unusual ways; special techniques are ways in which contemporary artists combine photographic processes with other forms of art. Many artists combine photographic images with paintings in a kind of collage; others use them on Styrofoam figures to take photography into the realm of three dimensions. One of the most individual styles is one in which J. Seeley combines the photographic image with the materials and processes of photo silk screening. For the image in Figure 358 a single model was double-exposed on conventional film in two positions on a large sheet of black backdrop paper. The camera was

358

mounted on a boom above the model as she posed on her side. The negative was then enlarged onto a large sheet of graphic arts film to accentuate the contrast of the striped costume and as a practical preparation for the final printing of the image in white ink on black art paper. The combination of special photographic and printmaking techniques gives Seeley's prints a unique quality.

Television

With television, the camera brings great music, drama, and current happenings into one's own home. Since the invention of video, laser beams or electronic devices transmit images from the television set to tapes or discs that can be seen at the viewer's convenience in full color on the television screen. A video recorder can even capture material from one television channel while the viewer watches a different one.

Both film and video have long moved beyond the area of dramatic production. The educational potential was recognized early and has been developed, particularly by public television stations, which present a wide range of documentary films in all fields of knowledge. Nature films in particular show the camera in one of its most rewarding roles, allowing the viewer to watch the habits and movements of wildlife in beautiful natural settings, providing through the telephoto lens and the infinite patience of the photographer an experience that would otherwise be unavailable to most viewers. News broadcasts are taken for granted as viewers cease to marvel at the miracle that unites people all over the world in shock, anguish, or rejoicing as they witness within hours events taking place thousands of miles away, or even view them simultaneously.

358. J. Seeley.
Skywire Twins with Chair.
1979. Photo screen print.

359. Sleigh scene from
The Nutcracker as staged at
Lincoln Center, New York. © 1987
by Martha Swope.

The Performing Arts

Probably the highest artistry in television is achieved in cultural productions, works of art in themselves, transmitted to the home screen through the skill of the photographer. The viewer of such productions is the recipient of the results of months of work by professional designers.

Set Design

There are two requirements for an effective set. First, it must be *expressive of the production*—its spirit, mood, historical period, locale, social stratum, and season. Second, it must be *practical* enough to meet the needs of the action. Doors must be wide enough to permit passage of players in costume, banisters must be strong enough to be leapt over or slid down, balconies must support whatever action takes place upon them. Special effects may have to include making a person fly through the air as in *Peter Pan*, a swan glide across the stage as in *Lohengrin*, or a sleigh glide upward as in *The Nutcracker* (Fig. 359). In addition, the set must lend itself to rapid construction, be easy to shift and store, and stand up under continued use.

The elements and principles of design come into play with the first decisions of the director and designer. If the play is formal, the

359

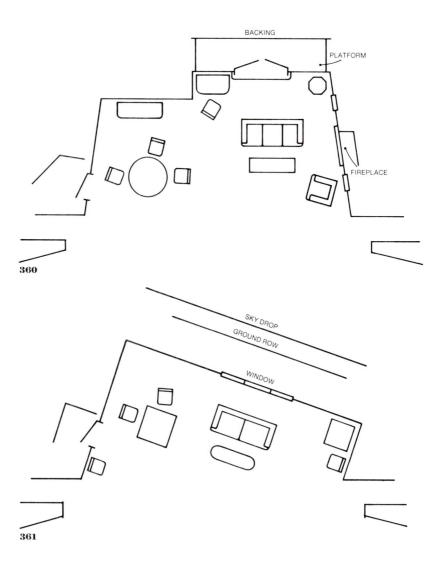

360. Diagram of a stage set on a parallel axis.

361. Diagram of a raked stage set.

362. *Macbeth* by William Shakespeare. Produced by Yellow Springs Area Theatre, Ohio, directed by Paul Treichler.

363. David Fielding's staging of Wagner's *Rienzi* at the London Colosseum, September 1983.

set will be *conventional,* that is, on an axis parallel to the footlights (Fig. 360). Such a layout would be most appropriate to classical Greek drama, Shaw, Ibsen, and O'Neill, for example. A *raked* set (with its axis on an angle to the footlights) offers the informality suitable to modern comedy, fantasy, and domestic drama; it also limits the space for action (Fig. 361).

Once orientation is established, the *architecture* must be designed. Some of the most effective settings are the simplest, relying upon symbolism for impact. The setting in Figure 362 is for Macbeth, and all the brooding masses and mysterious recesses of a medieval castle are implied with one simple pointed arch.

As in the other arts, theater has become increasingly innovative during the 20th century. Shakespeare is played in modern dress, opera is sung in English instead of in the Italian or German in which it was written. David Fielding, working at the London Colosseum, has single-handedly revolutionized the staging of musical drama. Among

362

363

his most startling effects is his staging of Wagner's much-neglected opera *Rienzi*, side-stepping its setting in the 15th century to place it in the Rome of Mussolini's time, complete with an aerial bombardment of Fascist propaganda (Fig. 363).

Design with Lighting

Nowhere does light play a more important role than in theatrical design. With no verbal clues at all, lighting can create an atmosphere that sets us in a particular time, place, and culture. In the outdoor setting of a Shakespearean festival, light can shift through shrubbery and across lawns to create rooms in English castles or scenes on battlefields with no actual stage set at all.

In *general illumination*, lighting makes it possible for the audience to see the entire stage. In *specific illumination*, light molds and models to control audience reaction. Seasons, weather, and localities all require special approaches, from the harsh light of the tropics to the hazy light of London fog.

As with music, light can manipulate an audience so subtly that viewers are not consciously aware of it. A flood of warm rosy light raises the spirits, implying gaiety, whereas a dimly lit set may suggest the sinister and the supernatural. A sudden flood of light predicts a moment of triumph. Shadows set the mood for violence.

364

Contemporary Trends

Innovation in the performing arts has brought ever more original approaches, as in David Fielding's staging of classical opera or theater, or in the ballet presentation of Beethoven's Ninth Symphony (Fig. 364).

The Los Angeles Festival of 1987 saw the opening of an eleven-hour saga based on the *Mahabharata*, the national epic of India, at 100,000 stanzas, the longest poem in the world. The dramatic production is the result of twelve years of work on the part of director Peter Brooks and encompasses, through a maze of plots and subplots, spectacle and poetry, wisdom and sensuality, the gigantic simplicity that underlies the world. The contemporary relevance of the work is one reason Brooks gives for his gigantic undertaking (Fig. 365). Another reason is the virtually limitless potential for the use of design. Costumes are rich in *color* and *texture* and action flows with *rhythm* and *emphasis*. The dramatic impact depends in large degree on the ways in which *proportion* and *scale* are used, and *variety* is the very essence of the production.

Sensationalism of quite another sort characterized the *Floating Opera* presented in Seattle in September 1987. With the cast performing on a barge bright with *color* and *texture*, the opera sang its way through the waterways of Seattle as crowds gathered along the banks. All dramatic productions have *line;* the line of a figure against a contrasting background, the lines of furnishings in an interior set or of

364. Maurice Béjart's Ballet of the 20th Century in a production of *Beethoven's Ninth Symphony*.

365. Scene from *Mahabharata*. © 1987. Martha Swope.

314   *Design for Visual Communication*

365

architecture when the action is out-of-doors. In this case, the production moved in a smooth line throughout the city, leaving its audience in its wake. The climax came when two helicopters dropped two artificial islands into the waters of Puget Sound, and members of the cast, carrying flaming torches as points of brilliant *color* and *emphasis*, swam to the islands for the finale.

Such productions are only one example of theatrical performances brought into hundreds of thousands of homes through television. Many productions of operas, concerts, or drama are performed and taped specifically for television viewing, and others are photographed as they take place on the great stages of the world. People who could never reach a theater and others with a long career in cultural affairs watch the leading musicians of the world perform at their best, in artistically conceived settings, of which the details can be appreciated through closeup shots. The bonus of intermission interviews with performing artists and conductors, with casual background shots and telling closeups, brings the world of concert and theater into a personal relationship with the viewer. Portrait shots of members of the audience give a sense of sharing in the general response, while panoramic views of the setting bring the glamour into the living room.

Analyzing the broadcast of a symphony concert could become a dissertation on design. The closeups of hands performing on the various instruments, the character studies of individual performers, the textural shots of the total orchestra superimposed over the dramatic focal point of the individual conductor—all of these provide a mon-

366.

tage of the elements and principles of design. Complementing the artistic qualities of the music are the visual rhythms of violin bows moving in unison; the balance and proportion of long-range shots and closeups of starring singers (Fig. 366); character shots of the conductor's face, expressing the full gamut of emotions the music evokes; the contrasting values of light faces against dark clothing and the rich shapes and gleaming wood or brass of instruments; and the space swirling with sound around the performers in the immense hall. Here is artistry at its finest, displayed in consummate musical skill and, less obvious but equally important to a viewing audience, in the sensitivity of a staff of skilled photographers, technicians, and designers.

Summary

Photography is a collaboration between an individual and equipment, most important of which is the camera. An effective photograph has three attributes: *subject, form,* and *content.* A photograph can be a *symbol* evoking entire worlds by its content. It can be a *document,* fixing on film the great or tragic events of the world. It performs commercial functions in advertising, in cover designs, and in illustrating informational books. Photography as design depends largely on light in order to emphasize the elements of design inherent in the subject. Special *effects* can be achieved by unusual use of equipment; special *techniques* are created by artists using the photographic medium in combination with other media. The affinity between the camera and the theater began with the motion picture. Design in the performing arts is a matter of set design, lighting, interpretation, and symbolism. Contemporary trends seek ways to attract an audience away from television, using sensational effects. Meanwhile, television brings the great performances of the world into the home, providing intimate and informational sidelights that have never before been possible for the average viewer.

366. José Carreras as Don Alvaro in Metropolitan Opera Company production of *La Forza del Destino,* opera by G. Verdi. Met production September 1983. Carreras is singing the recitative from Act III, "La vita è inferno all' infelice."

PART 6

Design for
Environment

CHAPTER NINETEEN
Fashion and Industrial Design

Our personal world is the sum of all the circumstances and conditions that influence our life and development. It is our special domain, the vantage point from which we interpret ourselves, and from which we gather strength to make our contribution to society and to the world. In relation to our environment we are all designers, as we exercise the choices that make us and our society what we are.

In considering design for our personal world, we will begin at the center and work outward into the larger environment. In this centric interpretation the center is ourselves, the character and personality we reveal to those around us. Since the first impression we make is primarily visual, our interest will be focused on how we look and thus, to a large degree, on what we wear.

Fashion Design

The Role of Clothing

Our clothes afford us protection, adornment, and an image of who we are. The psychological aspects of dress have always included a feeling for adornment, arising from the days before actual clothing was worn but the body was elaborately painted and tattooed with magic symbols. Archaeologists assure us that such decoration arose from a desire for power against one's enemies. As long as one's body was ornamented, one was elevated above the mediocrity of simple nudity.

The association of ornamentation with protection persisted into the Middle Ages, when suits of armor, in which the wearer would usually be totally hidden from sight, were elaborately etched with familial symbols and other decoration in keeping with the social and military rank of the wearer (Fig. 367).

Apparel as a status symbol is, of course, all around us. Uniforms are a symbol of power when on policemen or admirals in the navy and a sign of conformity when worn as a symbol of a school. They carry a connotation of authority based on knowledge and wisdom when worn by judges, church dignitaries, or faculty members in a university. And they speak of wealth and social status when made from luxurious materials and identified with the name of a high fashion designer.

367. Suit of armor of George Clifford, third Earl of Cumberland. Metropolitan Museum of Art.

The Fashion Industry

Apparel is a $65 billion industry, the sixth-largest manufacturing employer in the United States, made up mostly of small operations with fewer than a hundred employees, centered on New York's Seventh Avenue. Although it seems fairly certain that human beings have worn clothing in some form for at least seven thousand years, it has been only in the past two centuries that people have been able to buy ready-made clothing. Before that time, clothing either had to be made in the home or ordered specially from a tailor or dressmaker.

Most apparel designers are motivated by a keen interest in the human body as a medium of expression. They work with the interaction between fabric and movement, and with the coordination of lines of garments with the lines of the human form. The clothing designer uses the body as a painter uses canvas, arranging lines, shapes, spaces, colors, textures, and patterns to achieve a satisfying design. Most fashion designers also have a sensual attraction to materials, creating garments that will exploit the qualities of fine fabrics.

368

368. Hyacinthe Rigaud. *Louis XIV*. 1701. Oil on canvas, 9'1/2" × 6'5/8" (2.75 × 1.84 m). Louvre, Paris.

369. Karl Lagerfeld design sketches for the House of Couture Chanel, Paris. Courtesy *New York Times Magazine*.

369

Haute Couture

From the 17th century, when all of Europe was dazzled by the brilliance of the French court (Fig. 368), Paris has been the center of *haute couture,* or high fashion. It was in Paris that aspiring fashion designers served apprenticeships in the salons, and the semiannual showings of new collections exerted influence all over the Western world. While the garments shown were usually one of a kind, copies flourished in New York shops, providing the buyer with the prestige of wearing a garment associated with the name of a famous designer but at a lower price. Gradually the influence spread to Spain, Italy, and the United States, each of which added outstanding designers to the list of haute couture.

Although the brilliant era of Parisian dominance has passed, fashion design continues to be a leading industry. Coco Chanel, whose Paris establishment was legendary, is still a name of importance in spite of the designer's death in 1971. Perfumes and associated products are sold under her name, and a new generation of designers such as Karl Lagerfeld continue the name and the tradition (Fig. 369).

In the United States the design scene includes influences from other parts of the world in designers such as Oscar de la Renta, born in Santo Domingo of Spanish parents, but working in the United

370

371

States since 1963. Today he designs influential garments for American trendsetters, including the dress worn by Nancy Reagan when she served as hostess to Raisa Gorbachev in Washington (Fig. 370).

Among other prominent American designers, Donna Karan provides stunning suits and other costumes in her annual showings (Fig. 371) and Geoffrey Beene works without fanfare for a large socially prominent clientele (Fig. 372).

A new wave of design talent has recently emerged in Milan, not only in industrial design but in fashion. The Missoni bubble dress (Fig. 373) is typical of the flair and imagination with which the new Italian designers deal with fashion. Designs for men have become a part of the fashion scene as well (Fig. 374).

The field of fashion has a long tradition behind it, and it will continue to be a moving force in contemporary life as long as designers exert flair and imagination to lift people from the mundane considerations of everyday living into a world of glorious fantasy. Today many of the designers are wealthier than the clients for whom they design, a tribute to the power of creative imagination when applied to personal prestige.

People who are considered trendsetters in fashion delight in showing off sensational new examples of the designer's art and are willing to pay thousands of dollars for a single gown to prove it. *Fash-*

370. Mrs. Nancy Reagan and Mrs. Raisa Gorbachev during a tour of the White House, 12/9/87. Mrs. Reagan is wearing an Oscar de la Renta dress.

371. Double-breasted stretch twill jacket and skirt with cashmere bodysuit. Donna Karan, New York.

372

373

374

372. Geoffrey Beene working with a model at his workroom. *The New York Times*/Fred R. Conrad.

373. Silk jersey bubble skirt with matching top and contrasting print capelet jacket, worn over a tulle petticoat. Missoni, Milan.

374. Stonewashed indigo cotton denim short dungaree jacket; whitewashed cotton chambray dungaree workshirt; blue and white stripe cotton seersucker trousers. Polo Ralph Lauren Corporation, New York.

375. Sketches for Little Red Riding Hood and Jack (Jack & the Beanstalk) from *Into the Woods,* 1987 musical by Stephen Sondheim and James Levine. Costume designer: Ann Hould-Ward.

376. Joseph Kosmo. ZPS Mark 3 (Zero Prebreathe Suit, Third Configuration). Johnson Space Center, Houston, Texas.

ion is a *sociological and cultural phenomenon* dating back to the seventeenth century and beyond.

Style, on the other hand, is the expression of an individual personality, and it remains constant in spite of variations in color and garment. A woman may dress consistently in soft ruffly clothing: this is her style. A young man may seem always to be wearing a black leather jacket and jeans: this is his style. People who pursue executive careers choose the style typical of top executives; in this way they *look* the part they hope eventually to fill, influencing their superiors to see them as successes even when they are starting their career. This is a *psychological phenomenon*, a symbolic means of projecting what we are or hope to be.

Costume Design

If individual style is symbolic of personality, theatrical costume symbolizes character, period, and even the philosophy of the playwright. Stage sets, even when totally bare, often need only one character in costume to convey to the audience the period and social level in which a play will take place.

The elements and principles of design are equally important in fashion design and in costume design. Free and rhythmic movement is imperative and the costumes must accentuate the lines of the body, either flattering them or caricaturing them depending on the character portrayed. Costume design has special considerations, however. Action is "blocked" to create balance and order on the stage, and the costume designer works with color, line, and texture to establish relationships among the players and to create a total composition of players and set design. The star must be garbed to hold attention and to express the character being portrayed (Fig. 375). The designer must

375

be thoroughly familiar with the script and have a wide practical awareness of sources for materials and props. Furthermore, the costume must be in harmony with the set. A character in a flowered dress will not be effective sitting on a flowered sofa. The costume designer also works with lighting technicians, knowing that comedies are usually played under pink or amber lights, while mysteries are generally shrouded in blues and greens.

Space Apparel

The prospect of a station in space has necessitated a special category of design that could be considered either apparel or industrial design and perhaps most logically, both. The extremely crucial and specific needs embodied in space suits are less a matter of appearance than of sustaining life under demanding conditions never before encountered by human beings. The most important factor is pressure, which must be maintained at a level consistent with the pressure inside the spacecraft yet that will allow for adjustments and assure the flexibility essential for space walks on a station where daily maintenance chores will be performed. Without the proper pressure in the suit, the drastic changes encountered would cause instant death to its wearer. Obviously, the design of space suits is a long, careful scientific process. The ZPS Mark 3 (meaning Zero Prebreathe Suit, third configuration) shown in Figure 376 is one of two current designs being refined and tested for official use by the United States space program.

Industrial Design

If the space suit is apparel, the techniques involved in designing it are closely allied to industrial design, in the necessity to meet strict standards and rigid practical requirements. It differs from most industrial design in the fact that it is intended for a small group of highly specialized people, and therefore the economics of mass production and marketing are not a factor in its design. The conveniences in our homes, the equipment in our offices, and our means of rapid transportation are all results of the vast field of industrial design, in which products are created for mass production that becomes fundamental to our world (Fig. 377).

Industrial design differs from other fields of design in several ways. In corporate industrial design, the designer works as a member of a team, and major decisions concerning economics and marketing are made before a project ever reaches the designer. An individual designer rarely receives credit in such a situation. In addition, the industrial designer is restricted by the machinery available. To be economically feasible, a product must be designed to accommodate existing equipment or to require retooling only within practical economic limits. A third difference is in the gap between the designer and those who buy the finished product. A profile of consumer needs may be projected, but once the product is on the market the designer can learn whether it is satisfactory only by indirect means—by looking at sales charts, for example, or by seeing the product being used by customers. Furthermore, the general public is far more critical of industrial design than of works of art. The person who will stand before a

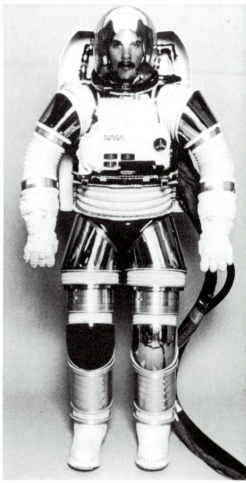

376

377

painting apologizing for the lack of background to appreciate it will not hesitate to express disdain or outrage over the faults of a washing machine or power saw.

Categories of Industrial Design

Products designed for mass production easily number in the millions. All, however, fall into one of four broad categories.

Consumer products are the objects that people use in their homes and recreational activities. They include electrical and other appliances, plumbing fixtures, lighting equipment, garden implements, radios and television sets, stereo components, luggage, furniture, sports gear (Fig. 378), toys, and children's vehicles.

Commerical and service equipment encompasses the fixtures for stores and offices, gas stations, restaurants, barber and beauty shops, and similar enterprises. The items range from desks to scales to typewriters, data processing equipment, computers, and even lighting equipment (Fig. 379).

Durable goods are such things as heavy equipment and machine tools, agricultural machinery and equipment, industrial furnaces, and power generators.

Transportation design embraces all modes of transportation, from airliners to sailboats and yachts. Included in this category is automotive design (Fig. 380).

377. Bench saw. American Machine and Tool Co.

378. Super Swallowtail (SST). Designed by Chris Price, Chris Wills, and Bob Wills for Wills Wing, Inc.

379. Ernesto Gismondi. Wall Lamp, *Stria*. 1986. Polyester reinforced with fibreglass, with white painted metal. 150 W. opalin lamp. H 38 cm (15″), W 36 cm (14″). By Artemide, Italy.

380. Jaguar XJ-S. 1988

378
380

379

381

The Industrial Designer

Industrial designers may not receive personal credit for their designs, but they can expect many of them to touch the lives of millions of people. For example, the designer of a telephone could within reason expect that virtually every person in the United States would at some point pick up that telephone and talk into it, perhaps several times a day. The person who designs a bicycle or a toothbrush might see that design exported around the world to serve literally billions of people. Raymond Loewy, who founded a design studio in 1927, was the first designer after the onset of the Industrial Revolution to speak out in America about the necessity of some aesthetic control over mass production. Born in France and originally an illustrator, Loewy had been exposed to the efforts of designers in England and Germany to infuse technology with aesthetics, and he personally transformed the face of America with such designs as the Frigidaire, a streamlined engine for the Pennsylvania Railroad, the Farmall tractor for International Harvester, Studebaker cars, and, perhaps most ubiquitous of all, the Coca-Cola bottle (Fig. 381).

Design and Manufacture

The techniques used in industrial production are so sophisticated and so varied that it is almost impossible to generalize about them. Because of the great expenditure of money involved, the problem-solving process is detailed and extensive. Research into the potential market includes exploring who might use the product, why they would want it, how much they would be willing to pay, what competitive products already exist, and what original features could be added to make the new product superior. The analysis of the problem includes all aspects of materials, color, structure, production, cost, and marketing. Decisions about what type of customer will be interested can influence the material and the ultimate price and marketing procedures, with more expensive products being advertised in expensive magazines, for example.

When the general characteristics of the product have been established, the designer begins with sketches, proceeds through several models in clay or other working material, and finally develops a *prototype* of the finished product.

The techniques used in production fall into several broad categories. *Casting* in molds is one of the most common techniques used. *Extrusion* calls for a molten material to be forced through shaped openings, after which it hardens upon cooling. *Stamping* is a fully automatic process in which material, usually metal, is cut, shaped, and combined into the desired form. *Lamination* and *fabrication* in industrial terms usually apply to plastics.

Contemporary Trends in Industrial Design

In recent years, a new attitude toward industrial design has promoted a flourishing sense of competitiveness among the designers of many nations. In Britain, France, and other countries, design is being promoted deliberately as part of government policy, and international competitions in Milan and elsewhere not only attract innovation but result in personal recognition for winning designers.

One reason for this new approach is that much new work has a simple directness that does not require huge factories and massive investments in tooling and craftsmanship. Designers in Paris and Barcelona, for example, are working with simple metal-bending machinery. Technological advances have made it possible to substitute miniature microprocessor circuits for mechanical moving parts, thus removing many of the concerns with function that formerly dictated the shape and form of various products. Designers who have for years put everything from radios to washing machines in the same forms, described by one designer as a barrage of square white boxes, are now able to miniaturize radios, stereo equipment, computers, and many other familiar appliances (Fig. 382). For those appliances that require larger size, the concentration is on the symbolic and expressive aspects of design, substituting pastel colors for brushed aluminum and replacing aggressive textured knobs and a profusion of dials with simplified, more tactile controls. In short, appliances are coming of age; their function now taken for granted, they are about to become decorative assets to our homes in the same way our furnishings are. As one small aspect of industrial design, they have become essential parts of our personal environment.

381. Alexander Samuelson.
Coca-Cola bottle.
The Coca-Cola Co., Atlanta.

382. Copy-Jack 40.
Mfr. Plus U.S.A. Corporation.
Closter, New Jersey.

382

Summary

Clothing is the most intimate part of our environment, providing protection and comfort as well as projecting our personal image. The fashion industry is the sixth largest employer in the United States, and haute couture is now important in this country as well, after long being centered in Paris. Fashion flows in cycles, but style is the characteristic image of an individual.

Costume design uses the elements and principles of design in much the same way that fashion design does, but it must also accommodate the stage set, the script, and the lighting of the production for which it is designed.

Industrial design differs from other fields of design in several ways, primarily the manner in which the products are manufactured and the fact that designers work as teams. Industrial design falls into four categories: *consumer products, commercial and service equipment, durable goods,* and *transportation.*

CHAPTER TWENTY

Furniture and Interiors

Interior design is concerned with creating spaces for human activity. Whether planning enormous areas for sporting events, conventions or cultural affairs, or an intimate apartment, the interior designer composes environment. Interior design encompasses *interior decoration*, which is the arrangement of furnishings to satisfy specific tastes, and progresses into the articulation of space, the structure molding it, and the experiences, character, and personality of the people who move within it.

The Manipulation of Space

The architect molds space by enclosing it, but the interior designer must manipulate space that is already defined by walls, and often by doors, windows, and other architectural features. The designer begins with documents—statements of purpose, of existing features, of requirements of the client, of preferences in colors, styles, and materials, and of furniture—and translates the three-dimensional space to be designed into a two-dimensional drawing. In Figure 383 we see a floor plan for a living-dining area in a New York City brownstone house.

383. Floor plan showing furniture arrangement for New York City brownstone house remodeled by Joseph Aronson for his family.

383

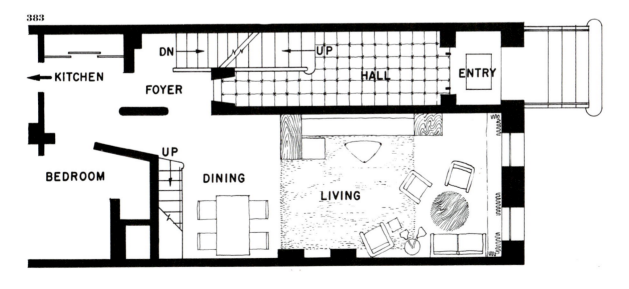

KITCHEN · DN · UP · HALL · ENTRY · FOYER · BEDROOM · UP · DINING · LIVING

0   2   5   10

384

Such a house, attached on each side to similar houses, and facing directly onto the sidewalk, offers one of the least flexible of interior spaces. Here the space has been skillfully designed, first by diagramming the area to scale, then by analyzing the activities that would take place within it, and, finally, by arranging the furniture, also drawn to scale, within each section of the area. The result is a compact design that effectively serves the needs of its occupants (Fig. 384).

There are various ways to manipulate space, and even to extend it. In Figure 385 we see space extended by use of glass, both as wall and in the ceiling. What appears to be a narrow passageway becomes a walkway through a flood of light streaming down from above and pouring in from the courtyard, where plants seem to grow into the passageway from outside. By the further use of glass on the far side of the courtyard, the sense of space seems almost infinite.

The extension of space by use of *line* is eloquently expressed in the home in Figure 386. Although the ceiling is structurally high, the height has been given added importance and drama by the use of "clustered" supports in the center of the room and a strongly linear design in the room divider at one end, a design that echoes the sup-

384. Interior view of Joseph Aronson brownstone house in New York City.

385. A house in Belvedere, California, shows integration of landscape, architecture, and interior spaces. Designers: Callister, Payne & Bischoff.

386. Vertical lines seem to heighten room. Edmondson House. Forrest City, Arkansas.

385

386

387

ports as well as providing a panel of texture that identifies with the fireside benches, and even with the three candles in the dining alcove. In a design in which space and shape are implicit, the element of line has become the dominant and most articulate factor.

Long, narrow rooms can be broken by room dividers such as bookshelves, a decorative screen, plants, or a partial wall of stone (Fig. 387). Each segment of the area thus acquires new dimensions, and the original unseemly proportions disappear. A square room, or one excessively large, can be made more intimate simply by furniture groupings, small units arranged for conversation, eating, watching television, or listening to music. The walls of a room are simply the beginning of interior design; the end result depends largely on the furniture and its treatment in relation to the existing architectural structure. Its color and form can be the keynote of a room; a valued piece of antique furniture can be the focal point around which the room is designed.

Furniture

The chair is more than three thousand years old and the table even older. What has happened to furniture design in the intervening centuries tells a colorful and human story of people, their ambitions, their

387. Silverstone residence near Taxco, Mexico. A partial wall of rough-hewn stone dramatically modifies a long, narrow space while echoing its mountainous site. Architects: Anshen and Allen.

388. Regency fauteuil (armchair) with Aubusson tapestry. c. 1735. Private collection.
Courtesy Didier Aaron Ltd., London.

388

wealth, and the ways in which they chose to live. Among the most elaborate designs were those created for royalty. The chair in Figure 388, although relatively simple in form, is ornately carved and upholstered in the finest tapestry. It is a product of the Regency period, in which the Duc d'Orleans acted as regent for Louis XV.

The English Cabinetmakers

The 18th century in England saw a phenomenon not equaled before or since. During the same century in which the French furniture shown above was being created, four major influences changed the face of English furniture, each in a distinctive way, using what had been done before and elsewhere, but putting a mark upon it that made it uniquely English. Before this time no individual cabinetmaker had been given credit for his work; after the end of the century this situation again prevailed. Meanwhile, English cabinetmaking experienced a blossoming that transformed English homes and many of those in the United States, where its influence is still felt in reproductions of 18th-century furniture.

Thomas Chippendale Chippendale did not initiate new styles; he commandeered existing styles and made them his own by subtracting the heaviness of the Georgian and Dutch influences prevalent at the

389

390

389. Chippendale mahogany
claw-and-ball foot tea table.
New York, c 1760–1770.
Height 27¼″ (69.2 cm),
length 34½″ (87.6 cm),
depth 21″ (53.3 cm).
Israelsack, Inc.,
New York.

390. Chippendale chair.
c. 1750. Mahogany
38⅝ × 23 × 13⅝″ (98 × 58 × 35 cm).
Metropolitan Museum of Art,
New York (gift of
Judge Irwin Untermyer, 1951)

391. Decorative details
characteristic of the Adam Style.

time. While preserving the excellent qualities of the current style, he
gave it *grace and lightness.* As can be seen in his table in Figure 389, he
was capable of elaborate carving, with the acanthus leaves and claw-
and-ball feet, yet the form is not overpowered by the ornamentation.
It retains its integrity as a classic form that has been embellished.
Rather than ostentation, there is dignity and elegance.

Chippendale is credited with substituting *mahogany* for the darker
walnut of the time, and so with introducing lighter color as well as
more graceful lines. He was a carver without peer, and his use of his
favorite *Chinese* and *Gothic* motifs became familiar earmarks of his
work. His chairs often display the flowing lines of ribands in their
backs (Fig. 390). He was also responsible for the ladder-back chair.

The Adam Brothers The years between 1763 and 1793 are known as
the Golden Age of London, primarily because of the work of Robert
Adam and his brothers William, John, and James. Robert and James
were both in turn made royal architects to King George III, and in the
process they revolutionized the appearance of London. Designing an
entire area of London known as Adelphi, they also built numerous
town and country houses, specializing in their interiors, for which they
frequently designed all the furniture, stucco ceilings, niches, and
moldings. A Scotsman by birth, Robert Adam traveled to Dalmatia,
making extensive drawings of the private palace of the Emperor Dio-
cletian, an experience that influenced his entire career. The Adam
name in furniture is particularly associated with motifs from wreaths,
the honeysuckle plant, fans, and elements from ancient vases
(Fig. 391). Their furniture dropped the curvilinear lines of Chippen-

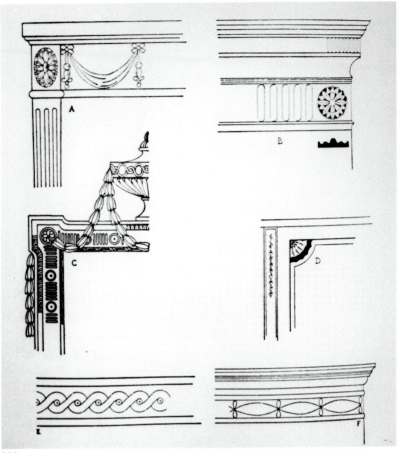

391

dale in favor of straight structural lines—slim legs with spade feet or straight and rounded with fluting.

George Hepplewhite Hepplewhite's work constituted a style rather than a career. His shop was the source of many works of fine furniture but like many of his contemporaries, he borrowed from the Adam brothers and others, resulting in a style of his own that was widely copied. For that reason, historians tend to speak of work being in the Hepplewhite style rather than claiming that it actually came from his hands. In any case, the style was one of grace and lightness, devoted to mahogany and to the use of lighter ornamental woods for inlay and cabinet work (Fig. 392).

Thomas Sheraton Sheraton's primary influence was through his books. He was disparaging of his contemporaries in the field, yet he had a wide influence through his writings and drawings. He championed severity and simplicity of line, avoiding graceful curves and highly recommending inlay instead of polychromed or painted furniture, which he considered perishable (Fig. 393).

392
393

392. Early Hepplewhite period centre writing table, c 1775. Mahogany, height 2′7½″ (.8 m), length 4′11½″ (1.52 m), depth 2′7½″ (.8 m). Norman Adams, Ltd., London.

393. Sheraton inlaid mahogany dwarf secretaire-bookcase. England, c 1800. Height 5′8″ (1.72 m), length 3′2″ (.96 m), depth 1′4″ (.41 m). Hyde Park, New York

394. Frank Lloyd Wright. The Lloyd Lewis House, Libertyville, Ill. 1940.

Contemporary Furniture Design

Furniture is exactly what the term states: a means of furnishing a space with necessary provisions for human use. Great castles brought forth ornate furniture to coordinate with their elaborate wall and ceiling frescoes and intricate plaster decorations. The masterpieces of 18th-century England adorned and complemented high-ceilinged rooms in country houses and London townhouses. This interaction was one of the strong points of the Adam success; the sensitive coordination of the total environment—outer architecture, interiors, and furnishings, all designed to create a unity.

The first 20th-century architect to design furnishings for his houses was Frank Lloyd Wright. His greatest contribution to the field of architecture was the so-called prairie houses, which seemed to grow from their surroundings and become a part of the landscape rather than something imposed upon it. Interiors were open: rooms flowed into one another and the outdoors seemed to enter and mingle with the interior. Wright expressed horror at the mere idea of people moving into his creations bringing the impedimenta of years and imposing it on the purity of his creation. He therefore insisted that all furniture be of his own design. As a result, much of the storage space and other furniture was built in. Tables and seating arrangements were designed for a specific place in the total design, and many of them were fixed in place permanently (Fig. 394). In some of his houses, Wright also designed all the tableware and linens.

394

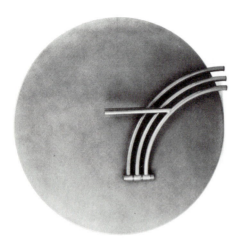

395

396

Wright's houses and his furnishings have a timeless quality that does not become outdated. He is credited with popularizing built-in furniture, which has since been a standard feature of American homes, both for convenience and for its space-saving potential. Today, however, because of the increasing mobility of the population, furniture is being designed to be lighter, more adaptable, and more easily moved from place to place. Sofas can be made into beds, tables have multiple uses, and chairs can be stacked to save space.

Recent furniture design competitions have resulted in infinite variety—whimsical, fantastic, even outlandish creations. However, two characteristics prevail: the works are lightweight and they are portable. The table in Figures 395 and 396 can easily be folded for storage, but when it is in use, the structure is rounded to give the piece a rhythm and unity that are a decorative accent to the space in which they function.

The Elements and Principles of Interior Design

In no area of design are the elements and principles more obvious or more dynamic than in the design of interiors; in fact, it is doubtful if there is a paragraph in this chapter that does not in some way mention or imply their importance. We have noted the manipulation of *space* by use of *line*, and our entire discussion of furniture has been centered on the element of *shape* as it relates to *mass* and space. There remain the elements of color and texture to be given further treatment, either of which can transform the character of a room.

Color

We learned certain psychological connotations of color in Chapter 7, such as that warm bright colors tend to stimulate and cool colors

395. Philippe Starck. Folding Table, *Tippy Jackson*. Three-legged bent-steel with turned sheet-steel top, varnished in dark metal gray. H 71 cm (28″) D 120 cm (47¼″) Manufacturer, Aleph, Italy.

396. Philippe Starck. *Tippy Jackson* in standing position.

397. A concrete wall can provide tremendous textural interest when combined with stones of various sizes. Designer: Emile Norman.

(blues and greens) are soothing. Warm colors also seem to make a room smaller, whereas cool colors appear to move the walls farther apart. Although these assumptions are generally true, in interior design they should not be taken as the final word. Response to color is one of the most personal of aesthetic responses, and any effort to design for specific people must, first of all, consider their individual color preferences.

Texture

Like color, texture is a personal matter, a choice that is not always entirely conscious. In the 1930s, *modern* design introduced a new era, streamlining rooms in a sleek style that swept away the clutter of the past, the kind of interior in which many people had been reared. Barely a decade later, the sterility of such rooms began to bother their inhabitants; they seemed cold and impersonal. Frank Lloyd Wright had begun building houses with the materials from the sites where they would remain—massive fieldstone, brick from local quarries, rough-hewn wood from nearby forests. The effect was warm and inviting and closely related to the earth. A new generation of designers began to link their designs with a feeling for ecology and natural fibers and textures, and interior design acquired a new dimension.

In Figure 397 a concrete wall, necessary as a safeguard behind an open fireplace, has been given tremendous textural interest through the use of stones, varied in size and color and given emphasis by the interaction of bands of plain concrete, or concrete textured by inserting stones and then removing them. The result is a wall that dominates the room, becoming a work of art as well as a structural element.

397

In Figure 398 texture has been added in several ways, lending *variety* to the texture itself. In the background is a portion of a wall built of heavy stones, a strong textural element in its own right. In front of it is a linear panel, contrasting vertical lines with the horizontal lines of the wood panel adjoining it. To break the plain surface of the panel, a tub of bamboo has been placed before it, its feathery foliage almost filling the area. The hanging vine on the wall responds.

Balance and Rhythm

In the examples above, the balance is obvious. Stone-textured bands are balanced by plain concrete to form a design rather than a textured wall of stone. Wood panels are balanced by growing plants. Such balance is inherent in any well-designed room. Furniture must be balanced by areas of space, allowing for the *rhythms* of movement. Balance and rhythm are both served by repetition of elements within the room, colors in rows of books repeated in cushions or rugs, the color of curtains or draperies picking up a color in upholstery, even the

398. Growing bamboo becomes the point of emphasis in this study of interior textures. Architect: Mark Mills. © Morley Baer.

399. Dramatic accent relates the fireplace to the scale of the furnishings in a small living room. Architect: Aaron Green.

selection of flowers for an arrangement on the coffee table that will coordinate with colors in fabrics or carpet.

Proportion and Scale

Scale in a home is dictated by the size of the people who live there. Visitors to French palaces are amazed at the small size and delicacy of the furniture, graphic proof that the human race has increased in scale. Tall people require not only long beds but high counters and cabinets, as well as a feeling of space adequate to give a sense of ease. Furniture must be scaled to room size, of course, but the first consideration must be the people who will use it. Large people need sturdy furniture. Small people also require consideration. Cabinets that are always a few inches out of reach can be an eternal frustration, and a soaring ceiling can seem overwhelming, particularly if it involves high windows that will need attention.

We noted in Figure 386 a device for making a wall seem higher; in Figure 399 we see a relatively small living room in which an overpowering fireplace wall has been brought into scale. The architect has used two devices for this purpose: first, the heavy dark ceiling beam forms a strong demarcation between wall and ceiling, both because of its dark color and by its being on the diagonal, which cuts firmly across the horizontal lines of the brick and the opposing lines of the ceiling decking. Second, the bank of light concrete directly over the fireplace opening is exactly level with the tops of the furniture, thus bringing the fireplace into direct proportional relationship with the furnishings and, at the same time, providing emphasis on the focal point of the room.

399

Public Interiors

The approach to the design of public interiors is only slightly different from that applied to the design of homes. Public spaces are less personal, obviously, but designers are approaching them in ways that minimize the institutional quality so long associated with them. Courtrooms, dentists' offices, hospitals, museums, corporate offices, and luxury liners all have their own distinctive flavor, some exciting and attractive by association, others ominous for the same reason. To improve the latter, decorators are using color and texture to advantage; nubby fabrics, growing plants, and original art all contribute to a feeling of intimacy. Other devices are soft music, indirect lighting, and interesting artifacts. The more homelike an environment is, the more reassuring it will appear.

Reception areas of commercial and industrial buildings often provide the visitor with a first impression that may have lasting associations. Frequently the interior is designed by the architect, who envisions lighting and furnishings as a part of his or her original conception. The reception area in Figure 400 is imposing and spacious, designed to symbolize the stature of the company whose offices it houses. The architect has brought it down to human scale, however,

400

400. Paul Rudolph, Reception area of Burroughs, Wellcome & Co., building. North Carolina. Designed in concrete-aggregate and glass. 1974–1975.

by the use of interlocking concrete forms overhead, some of them textured in aggregate to give interest and to relate them to the low walls surrounding the carpeted passageway. The sloping outside walls and windows become a part of the juxtaposed patterns of the concrete, and the inner walls, sloping in the opposite direction, provide balance, at the same time minimizing the vast entrance area. Plants are placed in oversized tubs, cylindrical in form to soften the dynamic geometry of the structure. At the end of this impressive entrance, the visitor encounters a flight of low steps, definitely human in scale, leading to a human-sized desk, designed in the same forms as the ceiling. However preoccupied, a person entering this building must experience a feeling of respect.

Time, Motion, and Light

Any building, to be appreciated, must be experienced night and day and through the range of seasons. *Time* is required to notice vistas from windows or views down hallways, to linger over groupings of plants, or to contemplate a wall of prints or paintings. In a building such as the one shown in Figure 400, many visits would be required to appreciate all the details; however, a person could look in any direction and confront an attractive aspect. There are homes in which this is also possible.

Full appreciation of a structure, whether home or public building, results from *motion*, the ability to experience the spaces, contemplate the walls and what hangs on them, and to explore out-of-the-way corners or hallways. In public buildings, provision must be made for handling clients or patients, a way in which they enter and perhaps a different route by which they depart; in any case, sufficient room so there is no congestion or confusion in the traffic flow. Traffic patterns in a house control the rhythms of daily life, making it possible for family members to move about their various projects without interfering with one another. They allow dinner guests smooth passage from fireside to dining table and make it possible for occupants to hurry to a door or telephone without hitting a corner of a table or bumping into a chair. Traffic patterns are easier to arrange in large areas, of course, but they are less a matter of unlimited space than of careful planning.

Light as an artistic medium has unique qualities. We can neither touch nor feel it, yet it has the ability to transform a familiar environment into a place of mystery and magic. Adequate sunlight in a house is the result of good weather and wise orientation, but dramatic lighting at night is the result of effective design. Taking our cue from theatrical lighting, we can recess fixtures behind beams and soffits, causing a work of art or furniture grouping to be spotlighted. We can wash a wall with light from hidden fluorescent tubing or create a focal point with a striking lighting fixture (Fig. 401). Since light changes colors, the use of lamplight can transform walls and fabrics. Designers at Brunschwig and Fils, one of the most respected fabric design firms, make their fabrics in varying colors, taking into account the differences in light in various parts of the country. Light also changes textures, creating deep shadows that emphasize their roughness or highlight their smoothness.

401

Contemporary Trends in Interior Design

Since the 1970s, interior design has undergone profound changes, in tune with the changes in social attitudes. There are two major types of housing today: the expensive city apartment that is home to aspiring young executives, and the home that has moved away from the city, seeking the peace and simplicity of earlier days. Some people who work in the city choose to spend time commuting for the privilege of feeling in tune with the peace of country life. Others, dwelling in city apartments or townhouses, glory in the urban scene: the movement and excitement, the challenges and opportunities for professional and cultural growth. The apartment in Figure 402 has been designed for city living, providing the sparkle of city lights from all the windows yet encompassing the interior in soft lighting from soffits and ceiling, allowing the kind of relaxation that detaches one from the turmoil and becomes a viewing platform overlooking the life beyond. Although the materials and shapes are sophisticated and contemporary, curves predominate, eliminating harshness. Particularly striking in this photograph is the manner in which the colors of the night world of the city are reflected in panels within the apartment.

The recent changes in attitude toward interior design stem from two principal factors: the enthusiasm for country living results from an increased interest in ecology and the value of the earth's resources combined with nostalgia for the past. The sophistication of city living reflects a desire to have a home that is individual rather than a type existing in thousands of variations. People today are more widely traveled, having roamed the world in their college years, and subsequently they are more knowledgeable about the arts. They see their home as a base for expressing these experiences, a special spot that, in a chaotic

401. A large wooden grill provides scale and character to the lighting in this dining room, faceting the light to make the furnishings sparkle. Architect: Alden Dow.

402. Apartment ("Untitled 2"). Chicago. Architects: Krueck & Olsen. Project architect: Keith Lasko.

402

world, can provide peace and sustenance and an enriching quality to their lives.

Summary

Interior design is concerned with the manipulation of space. Furniture is an important factor in any interior. The 18th-century English cabinetmakers are considered a high point in furniture design. Contemporary furniture is lighter, more flexible, and more whimsical than in previous periods. The elements and principles of design are more obvious and more dynamic in interior design than in any other field. Public interiors use many of the same principles as the interiors of homes. Time, motion, and light are important factors in any successful interior design. Contemporary trends are toward expensive city apartments or, more frequently, toward country living and the nostalgia of furnishing homes in country style.

Architecture and the Environment

Architecture is a blend of art, creativity, and function. Increasingly, the architect works with other designers—teams of fellow architects, interior designers, landscape architects, and engineers—and with the public to arrive at the most functional and aesthetic solution to a design project. In some ways architectural design, the design of the buildings in which we live and carry out the many activities of human existence, is the most dominant and influential aspect of our environment. To the city dweller, architecture *is* environment (Fig. 403).

Structural Design in Architecture

Although new methods and materials have expanded contemporary architectural processes far beyond those used in past centuries, any understanding of architectural design should be based on familiarity

403

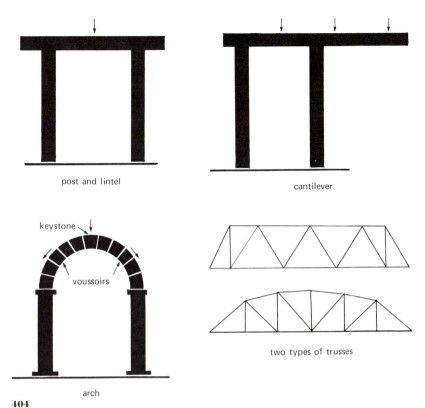

post and lintel

cantilever

keystone

voussoirs

two types of trusses

arch

404

403. New York City skyline.

404. The four traditional structural systems: post-and-lintel, arch, cantilever, and truss.

405. St. Peter's Basilica, Rome. Dome designed by Michelangelo. 1547. Dome 140' (42.7 m) in diameter.

with the four traditional structural classifications: *post-and-lintel, arch, cantilever,* and *truss* (Fig. 404).

The Parthenon (Fig. 158) stands as the classic example of *post-and-lintel* construction. In this system two verticals are erected, and the intervening space is bridged by a beam, or lintel. This arrangement creates angular space within two walls and a flat roof (or any variation of the peaked roof) above the horizontal beams.

The development of the *arch* provided architects with a new concept: curved and circular space. First used by the Mesopotamians, the arch became a truly revolutionary element in the hands of the Romans. They repeated it in *arcades,* placed arches at right angles to one another to form *vaults,* and rotated the arch on its central axis to create the *dome,* thus providing succeeding centuries of architects all over the world with the tool for some of their most imposing landmarks (Fig. 405).

The *cantilever* system came into prominence with the development of reinforced concrete—concrete poured over steel rods or mesh to give it support and stability. Having immense tensile strength, steel beams can span greater distances than either stone or wood. When this strength is combined with the strength of concrete under compression, a new and versatile material evolves. Beams imbedded in slabs of concrete and welded or riveted into place can support tremendous weights, even when extended into space. This extension provides a new concept of open space—an approach in which space is articulated rather than enclosed.

405

406

One of the best-known cantilever constructions was designed by Frank Lloyd Wright for the Edgar Kaufmann family in Pennsylvania, the house known as "Falling Water" (Fig. 406). Built on pylons or piers, anchored in a foundation of natural stone, the house has cantilevers of tawny-colored concrete projecting dramatically over the waterfall. The cantilevers, which also serve as terraces, have no support at one end. They form layers of solid structure counterbalanced by open space. Glass walls carry the feeling of space indoors, and contrast in texture with the stone of the chimney and the surrounding forest.

Trusses are employed when it is necessary to span longer distances than can be bridged by post-and-lintel construction. The truss consists of a rigid framework of bars, beams, or other material that is so strong that it cannot be pushed out of shape. Trusses have long been used for steel bridges as well as for large pavilions and aircraft fuselages.

The materials and technology of the 20th century have added immeasurably to the vocabulary of structural design in architecture. Quite apart from new materials is the *geodesic dome* patented by R. Buckminster Fuller in the 1940s. Just as a flat sheet of paper can be made into a dome by crumpling its surface into a series of small planes, an architectural dome can be created by the arrangement of small triangles combined with tetrahedron (Fig. 407). This system makes it possible to cover much larger areas with a dome than had been possible with traditional construction. The triangular modules can be made of lightweight metal and the resultant structure covered with suitable material, such as plastic, cloth, or wood. An added advantage of the geodesic dome is its energy efficiency. Any domed ceiling reduces the volume of air at the ceiling, but the pockets of faceted surface hold warmth as well.

406. Frank Lloyd Wright. Kaufmann House (*Falling Water*). Bear Run, Pa. 1936. Cantilevered concrete balconies and rough walls of local stone.

407. Bernard Judge's design for an experimental house of aluminum rods and plastic skin. Hollywood, California. Based on the geodesic dome principle developed by R. Buckminster Fuller. 45′ (13.7 m) in diameter. 1958.

407

Another revolutionary concept in architectural design is modular construction, which depends upon prefabricated modules or units shipped intact to the building site, where they are attached to one another to form a building. The major advantage of this system is cost saving, since units mass-produced at a factory are much less expensive than on-site construction, and time spent in building is held to a minimum.

Attributes of Architectural Design

In a sense, the attributes of *subject, form,* and *content* chart the progress of an architect's work on any given project. As an example, let us consider the Fribourg State Bank in Switzerland. *Subject* is stated in a set of specifications:

Site: Flat triangular site, approximately 165,000 sq. ft. at the apex of a city block adjacent to the railroad station piazza.

Program: Banking hall and offices, rental office space, restaurant, dance hall and underground parking. Three floors are underground, seven floors above, plus a penthouse level, more than 2 million cu. ft. altogether.[7]

Form becomes the architect's solution to the requirements stated in the "specs." Here architect Mario Botta has used reinforced-concrete bearing walls and columns as his structural components, the vocabulary with which he expresses his aesthetic convictions concerning what is needed.

[7] Nory Miller, "Transfigurer of Geometry," *Progressive Architecture*, July 1982, 57.

408

The first obvious need is a matter of urban *infill* or *retrofill*, that is, a blending of the new building with the established architecture that will surround it. This is such a fundamental problem in city planning today that a term has been coined to describe it; a new building must be *contextual*, in context with the existing cityscape.

In Figure 408 we see Botta's solution to the situation in Fribourg. Two wings unite the new building with the adjacent houses along each of the two avenues that form the triangular site, achieving a harmonious blending of the *façade* (the front surface) with its surroundings. This is accomplished by means of a convex curving that maintains the corner yet is raised at the street level to allow for the passage of traffic. Barely discernible in the photograph is the reverse or concave curving at attic level (behind the metal railing) which echoes the shape of the piazza below. Even immediately after the bank had been completed, it became an unobtrusive part of its environment.

The interior of the bank is another matter, for here is achieved an undeniable sense of grandeur expressing all that a bank should be without restraint from neighborhood traditions. Materials are not revolutionary—they are the green and gray marble and fine woods used for centuries, combined with the ordinary materials of basic construction. They are used in geometric *shapes* and varied *colors* and *textures*, distributed throughout the building in a balanced and rhythmic way. This is a bank of dignity and opulence, one that inspires immediate confidence. In this we find *content*, the manner in which the enclosed space meets the social goals for which it was intended.

Content in architecture cannot be accurately assessed until the building has been in use for some time. One of the most urgent social problems of the 20th century is overcrowded housing, particularly in city slum areas. Many solutions have been suggested, and structures

408. Mario Botta. Façade of Fribourg State Bank, Fribourg, Switzerland. Completed 1982.

409. Pruitt-Igoe housing project being blown up. Minoru Yamasaki, Pruitt-Igoe Housing. St. Louis. 1952–1955.

409

built accordingly, only to prove miserable failures. The outstanding example is the Pruitt-Igoe housing project built in St. Louis in 1952–55, a high-rise complex with all the proper formulas—separate pedestrian and vehicular traffic areas, play space, laundries and centers for gossiping, all in a clean, healthful environment. The *form* appeared the ideal solution to overcrowding and disease, and it was assumed by the planners that good health and improved behavior would inevitably follow. Instead, the crime rate rose astronomically, exceeding that in all other housing developments. In 1972, after the buildings had been continually vandalized, several of the slab blocks were blown up (Fig. 409). Architectural analysts attributed the failure of the project to the anonymity of the building, with its identical living cubicles, long corridors, and lack of controlled semiprivate space. Hygienic impersonality wiped out the human element, the last vestige of quality remaining to life in crowded surroundings. The *subject* was admirable and the *form* theoretically sound, but the *content* was a total failure.

Elements and Principles in Architectural Design

Mass is indigenous to architecture, serving practical as well as symbolic purposes. This is only one instance of the ways in which the elements and principles of design operate on a grand scale in architectural design. *Line* and *shape* tell us much about a community, frequently giving the community its character.

Approaching a city dominated by the vertical lines and elongated rectangles of skyscrapers, we expect density of population, heavy traffic, a wide variety of commercial enterprises, and some degree of in-

410

dustrial activity. New England villages nestling among billowing trees punctuated by the white spire of a church steeple speak for the traditional character of the people who live there and the security of long-accepted values. The massive colonial-style mansions of the South, with their impressive vertical columns, serve a purpose similar to the great country houses of England, impressing the viewer with the importance of land, money, and prestige. A house that blends into its surroundings states clearly that the builder and owner appreciate the beauty of the setting. The lines of the house in Figure 410 are horizontal and low to the ground to echo the lines of sea and dunes. Windows compose the wall facing the sea, and the natural finish of the wood weathers to the tones of sand and driftwood. Beach grasses growing wild against the walls settle the structure into the natural vegetation. *Line* here is used as a continuation of landscape, and *color* becomes a part of the landscape itself.

Color also has symbolic architectural associations. We react quite differently to the ideas of neat white farmhouses, red barns, brownstone houses, red brick Georgian houses in Philadelphia or Washington, D.C., and the earth tones of adobe buildings in New Mexico, so characteristic of people living close to the earth (Fig. 411). The grayness of cities has long been a cliché until recent years, when designers began seeing the cheerful possibilities of coordinating blocks by color. Cities in Florida, California, England, and Italy now sport entire blocks in lavenders, reds, pinks, greens, and blues, with color coding relating buildings within a complex, making identification possible.

With the increasing use of glass and concrete in city buildings, texture became a major concern of many architects. The problem is alleviated in various ways: concrete building blocks are now cast in a wide range of patterns, and glass blocks and decorative tiles provide the kind of accent known for centuries to cities in Spain and South

410. Naff (John M., Jr.) house, Pajaro Dunes, California. Designed by William Turnbull of Turnbull Associates. MLTW, San Francisco. Built in 1969. © Morley Baer.

411. Church at Trampas, New Mexico. Adobe. 17th century.

411

America. Panels in bas-relief are cast in concrete and erected on the façades of buildings, and some buildings in the heart of the city have mosaic designs that lend color and pattern to the entry area. We have shown examples of architecture throughout our chapters on the elements and principles of design; a glance back through them will serve as a confirmation of the dynamic way in which design and architecture interact.

Development of Contemporary Architecture

In the broadest terms, artistic expression has been categorized traditionally in one of two ways: *classical* or *romantic.* We compared examples in painting in Chapter 18: the clear, clean outlines of David's *Death of Socrates,* with its symmetrical balance and intellectual approach, and the romantic, darkly emotional quality of Goya's *Executions of the Third of May, 1808,* with its asymmetrical balance and swirling color. Classicism dates from the so-called Golden Age of Greece (480–400 B.C.) and the architecture of the period displays many of the qualities we noted in David's painting.

Classical architecture is based on three orders—the Doric, Ionic, and Corinthian—that determined the proportions as well as the amount and character of ornamentation (Fig. 412). The classic style has reappeared periodically throughout the history of architecture, taking various guises to suit the period and circumstances. Its dignity has given it an imposing role in human experience, taking form in banks and law courts, triumphal arches and opera houses throughout the Western world. Thomas Jefferson was an avid classicist, designing his home and the University of Virginia in the classic style and exerting a compelling influence when the French engineer Pierre l'Enfant

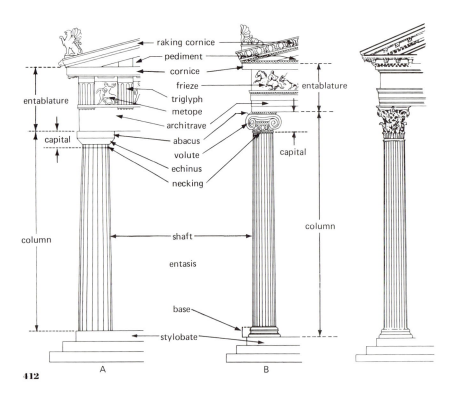

raking cornice
pediment
cornice
frieze
triglyph
metope
architrave
abacus
volute
echinus
necking
entablature
capital
column
shaft
entasis
base
stylobate
entablature
capital
column

412

A   B

was commissioned to lay out the design for Washington, D.C. Jefferson felt that a new republic, based on the highest ideals, could only be suitably expressed in classical architecture.

The *romantic* style of architecture was born of the so-called Gothic novels of the late 18th century, in which the action took place among ruins of mysterious and fantastic character, redolent of melancholy and mysticism. The essence of romanticism has always been the Palace of Neuschwanstein (Fig. 413). This was built high in the Bavarian Alps by King Ludwig II, a devoted patron of Wagner and yet presumed to be mad; he put the finishing touch on his creation by dying mysteriously with his doctor in the lake behind the castle. Wealthy Englishmen found the romantic style irresistible: country homes all over England boast towers and turrets and labyrinthine corridors. The trend flourished in novels as well as in architecture and leaped the Atlantic to appear in "gingerbread houses" in the United States, sometimes in the most unlikely places, such as remote mining towns (Fig. 414).

The reference to "Gothic" novels was not entirely arbitrary. The Gothic style of architecture, born in the 12th century and flourishing for several centuries in Europe, was the ultimate architectural expression of the Middle Ages and one of the supreme structural achievements of all time. Embodying the sociological and political ambience of the medieval European world, it also served as inspiration and comfort to thousands of ordinary people. The turrets, towers, and other details borrowed by the 18th-century romantics had their origin in the authentic Gothic style.

Twentieth-century architecture has its roots securely in the 18th century, with the development of processes for manufacturing iron

412. Comparison of Doric and Ionic orders, which, with the more elaborate Corinthian (right) formed the basic design of Greek architecture of the Classic Period.

413. King Ludwig II of Bavaria. Palace of Neuschwanstein. 1869.

414. S. and J. C. Newson. William Carson Residence, Eureka, California (now the Ingomar Club). 1884.

413

414

and steel for construction. Adaptation to the Industrial Revolution was difficult and gradual in many areas, and from the mid-18th century until the middle of the 19th century, architecture underwent a series of revival styles, accepting the advantages of the new materials but clinging to the imagery of the past. Older skyscrapers in New York today bear Greek temples at their tops, and some have gargoyles, originally designed as rainspouts on Gothic cathedrals but serving no practical purpose in their present context.

It was the great Chicago fire of 1871 that opened the way for a new style that would be distinctly American. Architects from the East came to rebuild the city, among them Henry Hobson Richardson, who had expressed his devotion to the Romanesque style in buildings ranging from the prototype railroad station to Trinity Church in Boston. Richardson designed the Marshall Field department store in Chicago, a link between the old and the new. In doing so, he laid the groundwork for Louis Sullivan, a brilliant young architect who cre-

415

ated the Wainwright Building in St. Louis, generally cited as the first American skyscraper (Fig. 415).

Sullivan designed buildings as an expression of the new materials of which they were constructed, stripping off the Greek columns and Gothic turrets previously considered to be important elements of architectural design, but adding inventive new ornamentation. His influence was carried forward by his protégé, Frank Lloyd Wright, who shared Sullivan's belief that architecture should be organic and alive. Meanwhile, at the Bauhaus in Germany, students of Walter Gropius were designing buildings of stark glass and steel. As these influences grew and mingled, an "International Style" emerged, marked by the acceptance of structural materials as part of the visual design. Walls were recognized as simply barriers to climate, and if maximum sun-

415. Louis Sullivan.
Wainwright Building. St. Louis.
1890–1981.

416. Walter Gropius.
Bauhaus, 1925–1926.
Dessau, Germany.
View from northwest.
Photograph courtesy
The Museum of Modern Art,
New York.

416

light was desired there was no reason not to build them entirely of glass (Fig. 416). In this style, basic steel and glass boxes opened the interior visually but kept interior spaces in traditional rectangular configurations. It was Wright who decried boxlike rooms and opened houses into flowing spaces, in which one room merged with another and interior and exterior became interrelated parts of the same composition. The contributions of his designs are still prevalent: window walls, open spaces, indigenous materials, and structures that seem a part of the ground upon which they stand.

Contemporary Trends

It is the nature of creative people to be innovative and to seek a means of expressing the moment in which they live. Young architects of the sixties rebelled against the style they termed "modernism," returning to simpler forms on the one hand and to complicated nostalgia on the other. The results fell into one of two categories: *vernacular* architecture and *Post-modernism*.

Vernacular Architecture

To most people, the term "architecture" means city buildings designed by experts, yet on a worldwide scale this description fits only 5 percent of all buildings. The rest are built by individuals for their own use, often without drawn plans or written specifications, expressing their own tastes and needs, and with no pretensions to aesthetic design. This is vernacular or "anonymous" architecture, the folk music of architectural design, carrying its own integrity and validity.

417

In its directness and lack of self-consciousness, vernacular architecture becomes a basic expression of a culture, of the dreams and values of a people. It is usually done with the site and climate in mind, working with nature rather than imposing upon it. It respects the work of other people and *their* houses, blending with the total environment. In its simplest form it was usually built by the owner, but later, building tradesmen took part, providing specialized skills.

Examples of vernacular architecture could begin with the first shelter of tree branches and continue to the present day. The adobe church in Figure 411 is vernacular architecture that has been built in the United States for three centuries. Adobe is built from the mud upon which it stands, patted with straw into bricks and dried in the sun, then plastered with the same mud after the building has been constructed. Similarly time-honored is the tradition of building storage barns in Switzerland from the wood and stone of the surrounding mountainsides, sometimes adding living quarters onto the barn for its natural warmth. Such buildings are frequently decorated with symbolic scenes and inscriptions that are part of the intimate family iconography (Fig. 417).

Post-modern Architecture

Post-modernism is not indicative of a style so much as of turning away from what has gone before. The rationale is that the modern style, evolving from the International Style, interpreted function as structural capability, so that houses, filling stations, and office buildings became very much alike. To counteract this anonymity, the Post-modernists began with revivals of past styles. A pure revival never satisfies a later period, however, so many styles and influences were combined, in a *radical eclecticism*. Eclecticism, the blending of many influences, can result in a watering down of previous styles. The term

417. Grain storage barn in the hamlet of Holleren in the Emmental-Berne area of Switzerland.

418. Christopher Owen's design for a house in New York's suburbs is a contemporary version of the International Style of architecture. 1975.

419. Michael Graves. Schulman House. Princeton, N.J. 1976–78.

radical was used to imply that this group would not imitate but would integrate the meanings and associations of diverse historical elements, set in modern form. The keynote of Post-modern architecture is "coding," the use of architectural symbols on two levels, by which traditional metaphorical meaning is assigned to contemporary elements. Houses traditionally looked like faces, with windows as eyes and the door as mouth. The International Style denied this animistic expression with expanses of glass or concrete and disguised entryways (Fig. 418). The Post-modernist sought not only to return to symmetry but to emphasize a recognizable physiognomy. The house in Figure 419 seems almost to wear a benign expression. To the contemporary coding of clean lines is added an assortment of elements that can be interpreted symbolically according to the associations of the viewer: columns set at heights and distances to emphasize the door, the shape of an Assyrian ziggurat (or temple), a smokestack, and the use of moldings to accentuate windows and to outline the roof against the sky.

Post-modern architecture was enthusiastically embraced by many architects who saw it as a means of using traditional architectural symbols in unorthodox ways, combining their classical training with imagination and even whimsy. In scarcely a decade, however, the move-

418

419

ment was being regarded as a kind of aberration whose principal value lay in causing architects to analyze and re-evaluate their work. Although it stated goals, they were fundamentally negative, rejecting the immediate past with no clear vision of the future. Its primary trait was a revival of the images of a distant past which, out of context, relinquished much of their original significance and became anachronistic at best and in many cases farcical. Finally, its only claim to originality, the cornerstone of any new style, was the way in which it combined old elements, an enterprise with distinct aesthetic limitations.

The Revival of Modernism

Modern architecture and design were born from the era of new technology and they remain closely related to it. The designers associated with its beginnings are found throughout this book: Le Corbusier, whose chapel at Ronchamp is shown in Figure 129, Josef Albers in his experiments with color in Chapter 7, Frank Lloyd Wright and his clean geometric forms and open spaces (Fig. 394), and numerous painters who shared the vision and philosophy of the builders. The world changes: designs for airports must be totally rethought because of terrorism and deregulation; cities are struggling to balance decentralization with renovation of centrally located slum areas; and the computer is taking over many design chores simply by digesting the "specs" and producing the logical solution to their requirements. The modern style of the future will not be the same as that of the past, but it will be in tune with technology and a fast-moving world if it is to be truly expressive of its time.

The Environment

The Environment and the City

The Finnish architect Alvar Aalto made the ultimate statement of architecture's relationship to the environment: "Architecture is not a science. . . . It is still the great process of synthesis. . . . Its task is one of bringing the world of material into harmony with human life."[8]

It was several generations after the discovery of the structural potential of steel before builders and city planners began to realize the truth of this statement. Harmony means balance, and cities everywhere were becoming overburdened with concrete, glass, and steel. New York City, situated on an island only 36 miles long, 25 miles at its widest, and with an underlying geological formation of metamorphic rock that would support towering skyscrapers, became the symbol to the world of the soaring city skyline. Parks and squares had been left throughout the island for the use of people, but the overpowering impression was one of throbbing, teeming activity encased in structural materials. The green areas often harbored people who were out of work or indigent and thus were not oases where most people would choose to linger. When Rockefeller Center was built in mid-Manhattan in 1932–35, a stunning new note was struck. A monumental complex of buildings, the construction included in its center a pond that

420. View of Rockefeller Plaza.

[8] Walter McQuade, "Aalto's Concern," *Connoisseur*, June 1987, 129.

420

becomes an ice-skating rink in winter, sculpture, a fountain, and a strip of landscaped gardens where blooming plants are changed with the seasons. Restaurants and benches make it possible for people to enjoy a few minutes of beauty during a busy day (Fig. 420).

Four decades later, cities all over the world are seeking the kind of balance epitomized by Rockefeller Plaza, erecting splashing fountains near the entrances to thirty-story buildings, reserving small geometric shapes among parking areas where trees and flowers are planted. Tree-lined streets are no longer the nostalgic memory of the small town but a reality in large cities where trees are planted in tubs along the borders of sidewalks, lending blossoms in spring, color in autumn, and often decorations of tiny white lights for the holidays. These are touches known for centuries in Europe, where life was more leisurely and buildings only gradually grew tall. Now, with our technological marvels around us, the United States has established a solution in the formation of planning commissions for city growth.

Rehabilitation

The complexities of city life make it doubtful that any architectural project alone will solve all urban difficulties. Underlying aesthetic and sociological efforts is the problem of finance. Most cities have an abundance of office space and a shortage of low-rent housing. The reason is obvious. While office space can be rented for big money, low-rent housing is not only financially unrewarding but may carry a burden of sociological problems and degeneration.

As the life of any city moves uptown from its beginnings, an area of dilapidation remains in the wake of the move, often near a railroad station or along a river that has become a city dump. Many cities are focusing on such sections and transforming them into quaint attractions.

The need to eliminate urban blight caused concerned citizens of Denver to renovate Larimer Square, long known as the "skid row" of

421

Denver. Oldtime façades were retained, while arcades and walkways encouraged artists and shopkeepers to establish galleries (Fig. 421). Ethnic restaurants attracted customers seeking an unusual experience. Such renovations have blossomed throughout North America— Old Town in Chicago, Ghirardelli Square in San Francisco, and Gastown in Vancouver, B.C., among others.

In some cities the problem is one of preservation of the city itself. Decentralization has drawn shoppers to suburban shopping centers in overwhelming numbers, deserting downtown and causing revered department stores to close their original establishments. In many cases an entire new city center has been created, with landscaped malls closed to automobiles, often with free transit to various stores. The decaying area in Baltimore is served by the Inner Harbor Program, which was established to renew 240 acres surrounding the harbor basin where the city originated. Planned in several stages, the thirty-year program includes major office buildings, apartments, and luxury hotels, with low pavilion structures housing restaurants, shops, theaters, and other visitor attractions. Some older buildings are being retained for flavor, and structures in nearby neighborhoods are being restored to enhance the historic Baltimore image, many of them being sold for a dollar to people who promise to invest their own effort in the restoration (Fig. 422).

422

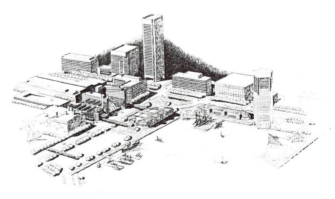

Environmental Design

The return of the human element is a major trend in contemporary environmental design, but perhaps even more important is the consciousness of the necessity to preserve the environment for future generations. Computers make environmental assessments, projecting population growth, densities, and relationships between the natural environment and that shaped by human beings. Such assessments are used in making national decisions that are politically enforceable, socially acceptable, and economically feasible. Yet when government threatens to wipe out beautiful wilderness areas to develop sources of energy, it is people who make the outcry that reverses the decisions. It is people who support the expenditure of more than twenty million dollars annually to clean up the streams and rivers of the world. It is people who demonstrate and rebel against environmental damage caused by industry, many of them with results that reach far into future generations.

Landscape Design

Contemporary landscape architects are also moving toward a personalization of the landscape. The formal gardens of Europe have been world famous for centuries, with their magnificent fountains, waterways, and sculpture accentuating the formal plantings, which included the *parterre,* or designed flower bed (Fig. 423). Public gardens on a less grandiose scale can be found throughout the world, but perhaps the gardens that reach us most intimately are small plantings

421. Larimer Square in Denver is graced by intersecting arcaded walkways and attractive shop fronts.

422. View and drawing of Harborplace in Baltimore.

423. Blenheim Park, Oxford, England. 18th Century. Garden renovated in 1920s with landscapist Achille Duchene.

423

424

425

that we design and construct ourselves, enjoying the progress of plants throughout a season, delighting in the surprises that each new year brings (Fig. 424).

Changing the landscape is an organic pursuit; that is, one does not plant certain trees and flowers and assume that the work is complete and will remain that way, as in the completion of a pot or a piece of weaving. The proper approach is to lay out the area to be planted, to scale, on a sheet of paper. Possible plants and shrubs are then explored with careful notations as to heights to be expected when they mature. *Color* and *texture* are indigenous to any garden, and they should be considered from the standpoint of foliage at various seasons as well as in the matter of flowers and blossoms. *Shape* and *mass* often have to be projected; one of the pitfalls of landscape design is planting for the actual size of a plant rather than for its growth in the years ahead. The element of *space* can therefore be more important than the gardener realizes at any given time. Shape and space also enter into the position of plantings in regard to height; small plants at the back of a border can be totally lost in the exuberance of midsummer.

There are natural rhythms in any garden, but the most enjoyable plantings are reached by paths or trails, leading the visitor along a winding walk, perhaps with a bush or tree at a bend to hide what is just beyond. This gives the rhythm of the walkway a point of emphasis, even surprise. Other points of emphasis can be created with stones constructed so a pump recycles water to be a continual waterfall (Fig. 425). The sound of the water is relaxing, but any garden plays an even more vital role in the environment, since plants give off oxygen that is much needed in crowded cities and traffic areas. In company with water, plantings can do much to control climate.

Landscape is one of the most important areas of design. It requires a sound knowledge of botany, soil chemistry, and bacteriology, as well as a feeling for plants and a knowledge of climate and growing conditions. Perhaps even more, it requires a firm grasp of the elements and principles that will enable such knowledge to create an aesthetic result, one to be enjoyed by a private gardener or by thousands of people who pass through parkways daily.

Design for the Future

Never has the future held more fantastic possibilities, both exciting and depressing. As we look ahead, we are bombarded with problems: overpopulation, air and water pollution, crowding in cities, and denuding of the natural landscape through over-logging, over-planting, or over-development for energy sources. We feel at times that we are outgrowing the earth and destroying its resources.

It is natural for designers to project possible solutions, and such solutions are as varied as the problems. Plans have been drawn for satellite cities to be situated in "rural rings" around existing metropolises, a plan not too different from the situation that presently exists in some areas. There are also plans for cellular cities or towns in which a number of community units are placed around a central or urban core. Floating cities have been designed to solve the problem of decreasing availability of land, and we hear much of space cities, both orbiting communities and fixed extraterrestrial towns.

Never before have the world and its problems seemed so complex. We must be concerned not only with the condition of the earth but with the tons of "junk" known to be orbiting through space as a result of our space explorations. Many of the problems seem overwhelming, far beyond the range of one individual. We can perhaps find encouragement in the realization that all of the problems do not have to be solved at once, nor immediately. We can even take whimsical comfort in a look at the object in Figure 426. We have here a simple piece of wire that someone somewhere once bent into a useful shape. As a result it is a *design* that is used all over the world in various materials and colors and sizes, an item that many large corporations and isolated individuals consider a necessity.

Thus, once more, we come to the essence of design: one person, a spark of ingenuity, and a contribution is made to the world. Through many small contributions, large-scale results occur, and by making daily choices about the quality of life, by seeing the principles of design in operation, by making knowledgeable selections, and by creating in our own special way, we can hope to preserve a world in which there is an opportunity for each of us and for each of those who will inherit the world from us.

Summary

Architecture is a blending of art, creativity, and function. There are four traditional structural classifications: *post-and-lintel, arch, cantilever,* and *truss.* The geodesic dome and modular construction are contemporary additions. The attributes of architectural design are *subject, form,* and *content.* Contemporary architecture has developed from the Industrial Revolution and the use of steel and glass for construction. Recent contemporary trends are vernacular architecture and Postmodern architecture. Modernism is now being revived as the most appropriate style for the world of today.

426

424. Circular segments of clay pipe held tightly in painted wood frames create an airy screen for privacy. *House and Garden Guide.* © 1968 by the Conde Nast Publications, Inc., New York.

425. A pond and waterfall can be built in a small area, providing beauty of sight and sound.

426. One of the simplest possible designs from the standpoint of manufacture and material, the paper clip has become a necessity worldwide in all kinds of homes and business establishments.

Glossary

Abstract expressionism   A painting style of the late 1940s in which nonobjective forms were used to express emotional content. Also called *Action painting* because of the large canvases which necessitated violent physical action by the artist.

Abstraction   Originating with a recognizable form but simplified or distorted into a new entity, as a mountain might be abstracted into a triangular form.

Achromatic   Lacking the quality of color, as in black and white or any neutrals mixed with them.

Acrylic   A plastic substance used as a binder in paints, technically known as acrylic polymer emulsion. Also used as a medium for sculpture.

Actual space   Space involved in three-dimensional design such as pottery, sculpture, architecture, and so on, in which the space forms an integral element of the design.

Additive   Descriptive of a structural method in which form is created by building up materials, as by modeling or welding. Compare *subtractive*.

Aesthetic   From Greek *aisthetikos*, pertaining to sensory perception and usually associated with the contemplation of *beauty*. The viewer of a work of art is expected to experience an aesthetic reaction.

After-image   The tendency of the human eye to see a hue after looking for several minutes at its complementary hue.

Alloy   A substance composed of two or more metals or of a metal and a nonmetal intimately united, usually by fusing together and dissolving in each other when molten.

Analogous colors   Colors adjacent to each other on the color wheel; for instance, blue and purple-blue are analogous colors.

Appliqué   A technique for decorating fabric in which various shapes, colors, and types of material are stitched onto a background to create a design.

Aquatint   A printmaking process in which a porous ground of resin is applied to a plate, after which the plate is dipped by stages into an acid bath to create a range of tonal values.

Arabesque   A style of ornament that employs flowers, fruit, and sometimes human or animal figures to produce an intricate pattern of interlaced lines.

Arcade   A series of arches supported by piers or columns to form an open passageway.

Arch   A structural device, generally any opening spanned by a curved top supported by two uprights. The true Roman arch consists of wedge-shaped blocks converging on a keystone at the center of the opening.

Armature   A framework of metal, cardboard, wood, or other rigid material used as a basis for forming objects of soft materials, such as clay, plaster, or wax.

Atmospheric perspective   A means of portraying three-dimensional objects on a two-dimensional surface by lightening, graying, and blurring forms in the distance.

Bas-relief   A form of sculpture that is carved from, or attached to, its background. Meaning "low relief," it indicates a depth of carving less than half the natural circumference of the object carved.

Batik   A form of resist dyeing in which nonprinting areas are blocked out with wax, which cracks in the dyeing process causing a background of linear texture.

Beating down   A method of working metal in which a sheet is hammered over a recessed area to form bowls or other objects.

Bentwood   Wood that is bent rather than cut into shape, using steam to shape it.

Bilateral symmetry   Symmetrical balance in which a central axis cutting through the design would produce two identical mirror images.

Binder   The substance into which pigments are ground to produce paint, which will then adhere to a *support*.

Bisque   The term for pottery objects that have been fired but have no glaze.

Brass An alloy of copper and zinc.

Bronze An alloy of copper and tin and various other metals.

Burin A sharp tool used in engraving processes.

Calligraphy Beautiful or elegant handwriting such as is found in medieval manuscripts and on Oriental scrolls.

Cantilever A structural member, as in architecture, in which one end is firmly imbedded in an upright so that the other end can extend into space unsupported.

Casein A painting medium using milk curd as a binder.

Casting The process by which liquid or plastic material is shaped by pouring it into a mold and allowing it to harden.

Cauterium A metal tool used in manipulating *encaustic*.

Champlevé A style of enamel decoration in which the enamel is applied and fired in cells depressed or incised into a metal background.

Chasing A method of ornamenting metal by use of hammer and other tools without a cutting edge, applied to the front side of the work.

Chiaroscuro From the Italian meaning "light-dark" and referring to the use in two-dimensional works of dark and light modeling to achieve a three-dimensional effect. Often used for emotional or dramatic effect.

China A white clay ware similar to porcelain but firing at a lower temperature, so called because similar ware was brought to Europe in the 17th century from China.

Chroma The degree of brilliance or purity of a color. See also *intensity* and *saturation*.

Chromatic Possessing the quality of color, as in neutrals mixed from complementary colors rather than from black and white.

Chromatic neutrals Grays or tans mixed from complementary colors rather than from black and white.

Cire-perdue A method of casting sculpture in which molds are built around a wax figure exactly duplicating the work to be cast. When the mold is heated, the wax inside melts, leaving a thin shell into which the molten metal can be poured for final casting.

Classical style Originating from the Greek architectural style of the 5th century B.C. and generally applied to any art or architecture based on logical principles and clean uncluttered lines.

Cloisonné A style of enamel decoration in which the enamel is applied to cells formed by tiny brass wires on a metal (or other) background.

Closure The process by which we unify our perceptions to achieve a specific or total shape, as in seeing several curved lines we tend to perceive a circle.

Coiling A method of building clay objects by forming rolls of clay which are built upon one another while in the plastic state.

Collage Any composition into which paper, bits of cloth, and other materials have been pasted, usually in addition to the use of paint. From the French "to paste."

Color field painting A style of painting popular in the 1960s and 1970s in which a canvas was covered with a single color with perhaps a contrasting accent, meant to evoke an emotional response through the color alone.

Complementary Colors opposite each other on the color wheel; for example, yellow and purple-blue are complementary.

Composition The structural design of a two-dimensional work, consisting of the organization of the elements of design according to the principles of design.

Conceptual imagery Imagery derived from imagination, emotion, dreams, or other internal sources.

Concrete A mixture of cement, sand, stone, and water.

Content The message an artist or designer hopes to convey in a work, as in expressing a personal reaction or the importance of a social issue.

Contextualism Architecture designed to blend in with its surroundings, particularly in established city areas.

Crewel Embroidery in which a fabric is decorated with stitches done in slackly twisted yarns.

Crystal A high-quality colorless lead glass or quartz, used for fine tableware, chandeliers, and other glass objects of superior quality.

Cubism An art movement of the early 20th century in which objects were interpreted in geometric planes, neutral tones, and the breaking of objects into facets.

Diffraction The process by which a wave of light, after passing the edge of an opaque or solid object, spreads out instead of following in a straight line.

Dome An architectural structure generally in the shape of a hemisphere or inverted cup, theoretically the result of rotating an arch on its axis.

Drawing (1) A work depending primarily on lines and shading to depict the subject matter. (2) A method of making glass to form sheets.

Drypoint A method of *intaglio printmaking* in which a metal plate is needled with a sharp point that raises a burr, or curl of metal, which takes the ink, giving the drypoint a distinctive velvety quality.

Ductility The capacity for being drawn out or hammered thin, as in thin sheets of metal or metal wire.

Earthenware A rather coarse clay ware, firing at about 2000 degrees F., usually red in color and porous.

Eclecticism The blending of many influences and styles in one work.

Embroidery The technique of decorating fabric with colored threads worked in a variety of stitches.

Emphasis The principle of design that stresses one feature as being the center around which the rest of the design coordinates.

Enameling A style of decoration in which a coating of ground glass particles in various colors is applied to metal or other material and then fired until the coating melts, forming a lustrous surface.

Encaustic A painting medium consisting of pigment worked with hot beeswax.

Engraving To incise an impression on metal, glass, or other hard material, usually done with sharp tools in a linear style.

Etching To incise on glass, metal, or other hard material by coating with wax and then cutting through the wax with a sharp tool, applying acid to eat through the material where the wax has been cut away.

Extrusion A process in industrial design in which material is forced through shaped openings, after which it hardens upon cooling.

Façade Any face of a building (usually the front) that is given special architectural treatment.

Faience Earthenware colored with opaque colored glazes, often with metallic touches.

Ferrocement A form of cement composed of layers of steel mesh sprayed with cement mortar.

Fiber A thread, or something capable of being spun into a thread.

Figure-ground ambiguity In two-dimensional design, the relationship that exists between the principal image and the background shapes. The term "ambiguity" implies that both are of equal importance.

Flexibility Characterized by a readiness to adapt to new, changing, or different requirements, as wood that bends without breaking.

Focal length The distance between the lens and the film in a camera.

Font An assortment of typefaces used in computer graphics.

Foreshortening A method of depicting objects on a two-dimensional surface so that they appear to lie flat and/or recede into the distance. For instance, a foreshortened circular plate becomes an ellipse.

Forging A method of working metal by heating it in a furnace until it is red-hot (or white-hot) and then holding it on an anvil and pounding it into shape with hammers.

Form The actual shape and structure of an object. Also, the essence of a work of art, its medium or mode of expression. The substance of something, as "solid or liquid form."

Freestanding sculpture Work free of any attachment to a background.

Fresco A medium of wall painting in which pigment suspended in lime water is applied directly to wet plaster, becoming a part of the wall when the plaster sets.

Futurists A group of Italian artists and writers, originating around 1909 and interested in the expression of the dynamic energy and movement of mechanical processes.

Geodesic dome An architectural structure first devised by R. Buckminster Fuller, in which a dome is constructed of small modules based on the triangle.

Gesso A mixture of plaster or gypsum mixed with glue, used to build up wood panels or canvas as a ground for painting, usually in *tempera*.

Gestalt The principle that maintains that the human eye sees objects in their entirety before perceiving their individual parts. From the German word for "form," it is based in psychological theory.

Glaze A mixture of metal oxides applied to the surface of ceramic ware and then fired, providing waterproofing as well as decorative effect. Also a transparent application of paint, in which successive layers provide luminosity to a painting.

Graphic Referring to anything written, drawn, or engraved; more specifically any such work intended for reproduction.

Greenware The term for clay objects that are thoroughly dry but have not been fired.

Ground A substance applied to a painting or drawing surface as preparation for paint or ink. Also the substance used as preparation on a printmaking plate.

Grout A thin mortar used to fill the spaces between the pieces in a mosaic.

Hallmark An official mark stamped on an article to attest to its origin, purity, or genuineness, used especially in England on objects of gold, silver, and pewter.

Hardwood The wood from a tree that has the seeds contained in a closed ovary as opposed to being coniferous. Examples are usually deciduous, such as maple, walnut, and the fruitwoods. So called regardless of whether the wood is actually hard or soft.

Haute couture High fashion, the area of fashion design presided over by well-known designers who cater to the wealthy or prominent members of society.

Haut-relief A form of sculpture that is carved from, or attached to, its background. Meaning "high relief," it indicates depth of carving equal to more than half the natural circumference of the object carved.

Hue The quality that distinguishes a color from all other colors in the color wheel. The name of a color.

Ideographic Writing that actually represents the object it describes, as in Oriental calligraphy and early Egyptian hieroglyphics.

Illusionistic space Space indicated or implied on a two-dimensional surface through devices, such as perspective, employed by the artist for that purpose.

Imagery The representations or symbols used by the visual artist, often arising in the imagination. One speaks of an artist's fantastic imagery or pastoral imagery, denoting the general character of the work.

Impasto Paint applied to a support very thickly, usually with a palette knife, for the purpose of providing texture and a feeling of plasticity to the paint.

Implied space Space beyond the physical boundaries of a work of art but involved in the composition through devices employed by the artist. Such devices include cutting off a crucial shape by allowing it to extend beyond the boundary or implying that a figure within the composition is concentrating on something beyond what we can see.

Impressionism An art movement of the late 19th and early 20th centuries, in which painters broke hues into their components in an effort to capture the effects of light on color.

Infill See *retrofill*.

Inlay A technique by which small pieces of wood or stone, in varying grains and colors, are set into a contrasting surface (wood or stone) to form a pattern.

Intaglio Any printmaking technique in which the lines to be printed are recessed below the surface of the plate. Any depressed image caused by carving, cutting, or incising.

Intarsia A decorative use of wood, in which scrolls, arabesques, architectural scenes, fruit, flowers, etc., are reproduced by inlaying small pieces of wood in a background of wood.

Intensity The degree of brilliance or purity of a color. See also *chroma* and *saturation*.

Interlacing The term used for creating fabrics by weaving and similar methods, such as knitting and crocheting.

International Style A style in architecture originating early in the 20th century from several sources and featuring glass walls, steel structural elements, and lack of ornamentation.

Kinetic Related to the motion of bodies and the energy associated with it.

Laminated (1) Composed of layers of firmly united material, in which, in the case of wood, the grain all lies parallel. (2) Made by bonding or impregnating superimposed layers of paper, wood, plastic, etc., with resin and compressing under heat.

Leather-hard The stage at which clay is dry enough to hold its shape but still contains enough moisture to make carving or other decorative processes possible.

Linear perspective A system originating during the Italian Renaissance for depicting three-dimensional distance on a two-dimensional plane. Two principles are involved: (1) parallel lines appear to converge at a vanishing point on the horizon; and (2) forms diminish in size as they are perceived at a distance from the viewer.

Lithography A *planographic* or flat-surface printmaking technique, in which the large areas are neither recessed or raised. Compare *relief* and *intaglio*. Printing depends upon the mutual antipathy of grease and water.

Macramé A fiber construction technique in which form is achieved by knotting strands into varied patterns.

Majolica Earthenware covered with an opaque tin glaze and then decorated with colorful designs in other glazes before firing.

Malleability The capacity for being extended or shaped by beating with a hammer or by the pressure of rollers, as in forming metal into new shapes.

Marquetry Decorative work in which small pieces of material (such as wood, shell, or ivory) are inlaid to form elaborate patterns in a wood veneer that is then applied to furniture.

Medium The area in which an artist works, as in oil painting or printmaking, including the materials used but not limited by them. Also, a basis for mixing paint, usually a combination of oil and varnish.

Meter In music and in visual art, the underlying structure through which rhythm flows.

Mezzotint An *intaglio* printmaking process in which the plate is initially roughened with a tool called a rocker, then gradually smoothed for intermediate values, working from dark to light.

Millefiori Ornamental glass formed by cutting across sections of fused bundles of glass rods of various colors and sizes.

Minimal art An art movement of the mid-20th century in which the artist used a minimum of form, color, and shape, often resulting in canvases covered in a single color, which was known as Color Field painting.

Mixed media The term for any work that employs more than one medium, for instance, oil paint, ink, and charcoal.

Modern architecture A style with clean lines and geometric forms, using materials as obvious parts of the design, as in the modern skyscraper.

Monochromatic A color harmony based on a single hue, including all its variations of value and intensity. Also a work executed entirely in black and white.

Monoprint A print made by painting on glass or other flat surface with paint or ink, then pressing printing paper onto the image. Also called *monotype*.

Mosaic A surface decoration made by inlaying small pieces of various colored material to form pictures or patterns.

Motif A designed unit that is repeated to form an allover design.

Mural A wall painting usually done on canvas that is mounted on the wall.

Needlepoint Embroidery done on canvas, usually in simple stitches across counted threads.

Negative shape or space The shapes or space surrounding a positive image within a given area. When a shape is drawn, the negative shape or space is what surrounds it.

Neutral Having no hue. Colors such as grays, beige, black, and white, mixed either from black and white or from complementary colors.

Niello The art of decorating metal with incised designs filled with a black enamel-like alloy known as nigellum.

Nonobjective Refers to works that have no relationship to recognizable objects but are meant to be appreciated for their line and shapes, and perhaps color, alone. Synonymous with *nonrepresentational*. See *abstract*.

Normal value The degree of lightness or darkness in which a hue appears upon the color wheel, usually assumed to be in the middle of the value scale.

Obsidian A kind of shiny black glass formed by volcanic action.

Occult balance A term sometimes applied to asymmetrical balance.

Op Art The popular term for optical art, a movement in the sixties in which painters based their work on experimentation with the science of optics.

Originality The quality of having been created without recognizable reference to other works.

Overlapping The placing of one shape or form within a composition so it partially obscures another form, thus providing the illusion of shallow space within a two-dimensional area.

Parquetry A technique of inlaying floors with varied pieces of wood, usually cut to form an allover geometric pattern.

Parterre A garden in which the paths and beds are arranged to form a pattern, usually geometric.

Patina (1) A surface appearance of something grown beautiful with age or use. (2) A usually green film formed on copper and bronze by long exposure or by treating with acids, and valued aesthetically for its color and antique appearance.

Perceptual imagery Imagery derived from experience or perception of the natural world.

Perspective A system of representing three-dimensional space on a two-dimensional surface. See *linear perspective, atmospheric perspective*.

Pewter An alloy of tin, with varying amounts of lead, copper, and antimony. In early America, used as a substitute for silver in household furnishings because of its lower cost.

Photorealism A painting movement of the mid-20th century in which artists painted from photographs or depicted objects and people as they felt the camera would show them, complete with every minute detail.

Pictorial space The space involved in a two-dimensional surface, in which any indication of depth is illusory and is provided by devices of the artist.

Pinching The simplest method of forming objects from clay, consisting of forming an object by molding the clay with the fingers.

Plastic (1) Capable of being formed or molded, as clay. (2) Any synthetic polymer substance that can be molded or formed, such as polyester or acrylic.

Plasticity The capacity for being altered or molded, as in the case of clay.

Plate (1) A smooth, flat piece of metal which is etched or engraved with a design for printing purposes. (2) To cover with an adherent layer chemically, mechanically, or electrically, as silver is plated on copper to form *silver plate*.

Plique à jour A style of enameling in which usually transparent enamels are fused into the openings of a metal filigree to produce an effect suggestive of stained glass.

Polychromed Made with, or decorated in, several colors, especially carved wood that has been painted to bring out the form.

Pop Art An art style of the sixties in which banal images of everyday life were painted either in quantity or in huge size to express the mediocrity of everyday life.

Porcelain A pure white, hard ceramic ware that fires at very high temperatures, used especially for fine tableware, figurines, vases, and sculpture.

Positive shape or space The shape created within a given space and the space that it occupies, as opposed to the surrounding shapes and space, known as negative.

Post-and-lintel An architectural system in which a horizontal beam (lintel) is supported by two upright posts.

Post-modernism An art movement of the 1970s and 1980s in which artists revived an interest in human values and emotional content. In architecture, it involved a revival of traditional elements in new and novel combinations.

Pressing A method of forming glass objects by pouring the molten glass into molds and then pressing it against the sides of the mold with paddles or other tools.

Primary color A *hue* that theoretically cannot be created from a mixture of other hues, but from which all other hues of the spectrum are created. In light, the primary hues are red, blue, and green; in pigment they are usually considered to be red, yellow, and blue.

Radial symmetry A type of balance in which elements radiate from a central point, producing a circular shape or form.

Raising A method of hammering metal to form bowls and other objects, working from the back over a wooden form.

Refraction The process by which a wave of light, when passed through a prism, bends instead of pursuing a straight line.

Relief Anything that projects from a background, as in relief sculpture. Any printmaking process that depends upon a raised image for inking. See *woodcut, wood engraving.*

Repoussé A method of decorating metal by hammering with blunt tools from the reverse side.

Representational Consisting of images depicted in a realistic manner.

Residual clay Clay that has remained in the place in which it was formed.

Retrofill The designing of new buildings in a city, or the adding onto old ones, so that new construction blends with the older buildings.

Rigidity The quality of being stiff and unyielding, as in stone.

Riveting A method of joining metal by drilling holes and inserting a metal bolt or pin.

Romantic style A style of art and architecture generally thought to be based on the Gothic novels of the 19th century, in which the work is characterized by intense colors, turbulent emotions, and complex dramatic compositions.

Sandcasting A method of casting metal or concrete relief sculpture by pouring the material to be cast into molds of wet sand.

Saturation The degree of purity and brilliance in a color. See also *chroma* and *intensity.*

Secondary color Colors mixed by combining two primary colors, as green is mixed by combining yellow and blue.

Sedimentary clay Clay that has been carried by the action of wind and water to be deposited in new locations, as along river banks.

Serigraphy A printmaking process in which the image is transferred by forcing ink through a fine mesh in which the areas not meant to print have been blocked.

Shade Any degree of darkness in a hue that is below its normal (or middle) value.

Simulationism A movement of the 1980s in which artists seek to express a soulless society in a capitalistic world, using a wide variety of assemblages and objects, most of them technological in implication.

Simultaneous contrast The phenomenon by which

complementary colors appear to be brighter and more intense when placed side by side.

Slab construction A means of forming clay into geometric objects by rolling clay into flat sheets and cutting slabs from it, then joining the slabs into the desired form.

Slip Clay in a semiliquid state, used for casting or for forming in presses.

Softwood The wood of a coniferous tree such as fir or pine, so called regardless of whether the wood is actually hard or soft.

Solidity Having a uniformly close and coherent texture, as in a mass that is rigid, such as stone.

Spinning (1) The forming of fibers into yarns so they can be woven or otherwise used to create fabrics. (2) The method by which round metal objects are formed on a revolving lathe.

Split complement The two hues on either side of a complementary color on the color wheel. For example, on the Munsell wheel, purple-blue is the complement of yellow; therefore purple and blue become the split complements of yellow.

Steel An alloy of iron and carbon with an admixture of other elements.

Stitchery Any fabric-decorating technique in which the thread stitches predominate on the surface and carry the major design.

Stoneware A type of clay ware, usually light gray or tan, with a warm earthy quality and firing in the middle range of temperatures.

Structural balance The physical equilibrium of a work.

Stylized A term describing works based on natural forms but simplified, and perhaps abstracted, for design purposes.

Subtractive Descriptive of a structural method in which form is created by carving or cutting away. Compare *additive.*

Support The surface upon which a two-dimensional work is created, such as canvas, wood, or paper.

Symbol An image that represents something else because of accepted association, as in the case of national flags symbolizing the country they represent.

Tactile Capable of being experienced through the sense of touch, as the smoothness of satin or the roughness of tree bark.

Tactile texture The surface quality of a substance as it is felt by the fingers.

Tapestry A type of weaving in which the *weft* yarn carries the design and appears on the surface only in certain areas, not being carried across the warp as in usual weaving processes.

Tempera A painting medium using egg yolk as a binder.

Tensile strength The greatest longitudinal stress a substance can bear without falling apart, as the strength of wire or cable when stretched over long distances.

Tertiary color Colors mixed by combining one primary color and one secondary color. For example, yellow and blue produce the secondary color green, and yellow and green produce the tertiary color yellow-green.

Tesserae Small pieces of glass, tile, stone, or other material used to form a *mosaic*.

Textile A woven fabric.

Throwing The term for forming clay objects on the potter's wheel. Objects so formed are characteristically symmetrical and round.

Tie-dye A form of dyeing in which the fabric is twisted and tied in various sections so the dye does not reach the tied portions.

Tiering The process of portraying images on a two-dimensional surface in tiers or layers, as a means of indicating distance. The upper tier represents the most distant part of the scene while the lowest tier is equivalent to the foreground. Also known as *layering*.

Tint Any degree of lightness in a hue that is above its normal (or middle) value.

Tonality The relationships of colors within a composition or design.

Tone Any hue that has been grayed, either by the addition of its complement or by the use of black or white.

Triglyph A grooved panel alternating with sculptured metopes in a frieze of a Greek temple.

Truss A structural form in architecture consisting of rigid bars or beams arranged in a series of triangles joined at their apexes, especially used in bridge design.

Value The lightness or darkness of a color; its relative lightness or darkness in relation to a scale ranging from white to black.

Vanishing point In linear perspective, the imaginary point at which parallel lines appear to converge.

Vault An arched roof, usually of stone or concrete, created by two intersecting arches.

Veneer The thin layer of fine wood that is placed over a coarser stronger wood to give a piece of furniture or other object the appearance of superior quality.

Vernacular architecture Architecture built by the owners for their own use without pretense of professional design.

Vignette A representation in which the center of interest is sharply focused but the image fades out at the perimeter.

Visual balance Our perception of balance as it appears in a design.

Visual texture The visual surface characteristics of a substance without reference to its tactile quality; in other words, the quality of pattern on a smooth surface.

Warp In weaving, the lengthwise yarns held stationary on the loom and parallel to the finished edge of the fabric.

Weft In weaving, the crosswise yarns that intersect the warp to create a fabric.

Weighting A process of giving body to silk by dipping the fabric in a solution of sugar or metallic salts.

Welding A method of fusing metals by use of electricity or of acetylene and oxygen.

Woodcut A relief printmaking process in which the image is raised from the background by carving away the rest of the block. Carving is generally done with the grain of the block.

Wood engraving A relief printmaking technique in which the image is cut into the end grain of a wood block, resulting in a print of white lines.

BIBLIOGRAPHY

CHAPTERS 1–2 *Design as Universal Reality*

Albers, Anni. *On Designing*. Middletown, Conn.: Wesleyan University Press, 1971.

Arnheim, Rudolf. *Art and Visual Perception: A Psychology of the Creative Eye . . . the New Version*. Berkeley: University of California Press, 1974.

Blocker, H. Gene. *Philosophy of Art*. New York: Scribner's, 1979.

Cheatham, Frank R., Jane Hart Cheatham, and Sheryl Haler Owens. *Design Concepts and Applications*. Englewood Cliffs, N.J.: Prentice-Hall, 1987.

Collier, Graham. *Form, Space, and Vision*. 3d ed. Englewood Cliffs, N.J.: Prentice-Hall, 1972.

d'Arbeloff, Natalie. *Designing with Natural Forms*. New York: Watson-Guptill, 1973.

Ehrenzweig, Anton. *The Hidden Order of Art*. Berkeley: University of California Press, 1976.

Evans, Helen M., and Carla D. Dumesnil. *Man the Designer*, 2d ed. New York: Macmillan, 1982.

Faulkner, Ray, and Edwin Ziegfeld. *Art Today: An Introduction to the Visual Arts*. 5th ed. New York: Holt, Rinehart and Winston, 1974.

Fromme, Babbette Brandt. *Curators' Choice: An Introduction to the Art Museums of the U. S.* 4 vols. New York: Crown, 1981.

Gregory, R. I. *The Intelligent Eye*. New York: McGraw-Hill, 1970.

Grillo, Paul. *Form, Function, and Design*. New York: Dover, 1975.

Hall, Julie. *Tradition and Change: The New American Craftsman*. New York: Dutton, 1977.

Itten, Johannes. *Design and Form*. 2d rev. ed. New York: Van Nostrand Reinhold, 1975.

Knobler, Nathan. *The Visual Dialogue*. 3d ed. New York: Holt, Rinehart and Winston, 1980.

Lauer, David A. *Design Basics*. New York: Holt, Rinehart and Winston, 1979.

Nelson, George. *Problems of Design*. Whitney Library of Design, 1974.

———. *How to See: A Guide to Reaching our Manmade Environments*. Boston: Little, Brown, 1979.

Nordness, Lee. *Object U. S. A.* New York: Viking, 1970.

Ocvirk, Otto G., Robert O. Bone, Robert E. Stinson, and Philip R. Wigg. *Art Fundamentals: Theory and Practice*. 4th ed. Dubuque, Iowa: Wm. C. Brown, 1981.

Pearce, Peter. *Structure in Nature Is a Strategy for Design*. Cambridge, Mass.: MIT Press, 1978.

Pile, John F. *Design: Purpose, Form and Meaning*. New York: Norton, 1979.

Rader, Melvin, and Bertram Jessup. *Art and Human Values*. Englewood Cliffs, N.J.: Prentice-Hall, 1976.

Richardson, John Adkins, Floyd W. Coleman, and Michael J. Smith. *Basic Design: Systems, Elements, Applications*. Englewood Cliffs, N.J.: Prentice-Hall, 1984.

Westbrook, Adele, and Ann Yarowski, eds. *Design in America: The Cranbrook Vision, 1925–1950*. New York: Abrams, 1983.

Zelanski, Paul, and Mary Pat Fischer. *Design Principles and Problems*. New York: Holt, Rinehart and Winston, 1984.

CHAPTERS 3–7 *Elements of Design*

Albers, Josef. *Interaction of Color*. New Haven: Yale University Press, 1975.

Birren, Faber. *Color and Human Response*. New York: Van Nostrand Reinhold, 1978.

Ellinger, R. *Color, Structure, and Design*. New York: Van Nostrand Reinhold, 1980.

Ernst, Bruno. *The Magic Mirror of M. C. Escher*. New York: Ballantine, 1976.

Itten, Johannes. *The Art of Color*. New York: Van Nostrand Reinhold, 1974.

Libby, William Charles. *Color and the Structural Sense*. Englewood Cliffs, N.J.: Prentice-Hall, 1974.

Woods, Michael. *Perspective in Art*. Cincinnati: North Light, 1984.

CHAPTERS 8–12 *Principles of Design*

Bloomer, Carolyn M. *Principles of Visual Perception*. New York: Van Nostrand Reinhold, 1976.

Stix, Hugh, and Marguerite Stix. *The Shell: Five Hundred Years of Inspired Design*. New York: Ballantine, 1972.

Strache, Wolf. *Forms and Patterns in Nature*. New York: Pantheon, 1973.

Vasarely, Victor. *Notes Brutes*. Venice: Alfieri, 1970.

Wong, Wucius. *Principles of Three-Dimensional Design*. New York: Van Nostrand Reinhold, 1977.

CHAPTERS 13–15 *Design in Action*

Almeida, Oscar. *Metalworking*. New York: Drake, 1971.

Atil, Esin, *Ceramics from the World of*

Islam. Baltimore: Garamond/Pridemark Press, 1973.

Barry, John. *American Indian Pottery*. Florence, Ala.: Books Americana, Inc., 1981.

Bath, Virginia. *Needlework in America*. New York: Viking, 1979.

Beagle Peter. *American Denim*. New York: Abrams, 1975.

Berenson, Paulus. *Finding One's Way with Clay*. New York: Simon and Schuster, 1972.

Bernstein, Jack. *Stained Glass Craft*. New York: Macmillan, 1973.

Birren, Faber. *The Textile Colorist*. New York: Van Nostrand Reinhold, 1980.

Bishop, Robert, and Elizabeth Safanda. *A Gallery of Amish Quilts*. New York: E. P. Dutton, 1976.

Bress, Helen. *The Weaving Book*. New York: Charles Scribner, 1981.

Brodatz, Philip. *Wood and Wood Grains: A Photographic Album for Artists and Designers*. New York: Dover, 1972.

Brown, Rachel. *The Weaving, Spinning and Dyeing Book*. New York: Alfred A. Knopf, 1978.

Bunting, Ethel-Jane W. *Shindi Tombs and Textiles: The Persistence of Pattern*. Albuquerque: The Maxwell Museum of Anthropology and the University of New Mexico Press, 1980.

Bunzel, Ruth. *The Pueblo Potter*. New York: Dover, 1972.

Carron, Shirley. *Modern Pewter: Design and Technique*. New York: Van Nostrand Reinhold, 1973.

Clarke, Carl D. *Metal Casting of Sculpture and Ornament*. Butler, Md.: Standard Arts, 1980.

Constantine, Albert. *Know Your Woods*. New York: Scribner, 1972.

Constantine, Mildred, and Jack Lenor Larsen. *Beyond Craft: The Art Fabric*. New York: Van Nostrand Reinhold, 1972.

De Jonge, C. H. *Delft Ceramics*. New York: Praeger, 1970.

D'Harcourt, Raoul. *Textiles of Ancient Peru and Their Techniques*. Seattle: University of Washington Press, 1974.

Elson, Vivkie G. *Dowries from Kutch*. Los Angeles: Museum of Cultural History, 1979.

Espejel, Carlos. *Mexican Folk Ceramics*. Barcelona: Editorial Blume, 1975.

Evans, Joan. *Pattern: A Study of Ornament in Western Europe*. 2 vols. New York: Da Capo, 1976.

Forgione, Joseph, and Sterling McIlhany. *Wood Inlay*. New York: Van Nostrand Reinhold, 1973.

Forms in Metal: 275 Years of Metalsmithing in America. New York: American Crafts Council, 1975.

Gardner, Paul V., and James S. Plant. *Steuben: Seventy Years of American Glassblowing*. New York: Praeger, 1975.

Gittinger, Mattiebelle. *Splendid Symbols: Textiles and Tradition in Indonesia*. Washington, D.C.: The Textile Museum.

Gostelow, Mary. *A World of Embroidery*. New York: Charles Scribner, 1975.

Held, Shirley. *Weaving: A Handbook of the Fiber Arts*. 2d ed. New York: Holt, Rinehart and Winston, 1976.

James, George Wharton. *Indian Basketry*. New York: Dover, 1972.

Kahlenberg, Mary Hunt, and Anthony Berlant. *The Navajo Blanket*. Los Angeles: Praeger/Los Angeles County Museum of Art, 1972.

Krevitsky, Nik. *Batik, Art and Craft*. New York: Van Nostrand Reinhold, 1973.

Leach, Bernard. *A Potter's Work*. Pub. Jupiter England, New York: State Mutual Book, 1981.

Ley, Sandra. *Russian and Other Slavic Embroidery Designs*. New York: Charles Scribner, 1976.

Medley, Margaret. *The Chinese Potter*. New York: Charles Scribner, 1976.

Metal: A Bibliography. New York: American Crafts Council, 1977.

Metcalf, Robert, and Gertrude Metcalf. *Making Stained Glass*. New York: McGraw-Hill, 1972.

Miserez-Schira, Georges. *The Art of Painting on Porcelain*. Radnor, Pa.: Chilton, 1974.

Morton, Philip. *Contemporary Jewelry*. 2d ed. New York: Holt, Rinehart and Winston, 1976.

Nelson, Glenn C. *Ceramics: A Potter's Handbook*. 5th ed. New York: Holt, Rinehart and Winston, 1984.

Newman, Jay, and Lee Newman. *Plastics for the Craftsman*. New York: Crown, 1973.

Newman, Thelma. *Plastics as Design Form*. Philadelphia: Chilton, 1972.

Paak, Carl E. *The Decorative Touch*. Englewood Cliffs, N.J.: Prentice-Hall, 1981.

Patterns. Catalogue of 1982 American Craft Museum exhibition.

Petrakis, Joan. *The Needle Arts of Greece*. New York: Charles Scribner, 1977.

Pfannschmidt, Ernest Erik. *Twentieth Century Lace*. New York: Charles Scribner, 1975.

Picton, John, and John Mack. *African Textiles*. London: British Museum Publications, 1979.

Ramazanoglu, Gulseren. *Turkish Embroidery*. New York: Van Nostrand Reinhold, 1976.

Rees, David. *Creative Plastics*. New York: Viking, 1973.

Rhodes, Daniel. *Clay and Glazes for the Potter*. rev. ed. Philadelphia: Chilton, 1973.

Rowe, Ann Pollard. *A Century of Change in Guatemalan Textiles*. New York: Center for Inter-American Relations, 1981.

Sculpture in Fiber. New York: American Craft Council, 1972.

Shafer, Thomas. *Pottery Decoration*. New York: Watson-Guptill, 1976.

Silvercraft. Elmsford, N.Y.: British Book Center, 1977.

Smith, Paul J., and Edward Lucie-Smith. *American Craft Today*. New York: American Craft Museum/Weidenfeld and Nicolson, 1986.

Southwork, Susan, and Michael Southwork. *Ornamental Ironwork*. Boston: David Godine, 1978.

Thomson, F. P. *Tapestry: Mirror of History*. London: David and Charles, 1980.

Thorpe, Azalea S., and Jack Lenor Larsen. *Elements of Weaving*. Garden City, N.Y.: Doubleday, 1978.

Tiffany. Intro. by Victor Arwas. New York: Rizzoli, 1979.

Waller, Irene. *Textile Sculptures*. London: Studio Vista, 1977.

Wasserman, Tamara E., and Jonathon Hill. *Bolivian Indian Textiles: Traditional Designs and Costumes*. New York: Dover, 1981.

Westphal, Katherine. *Dragons and Other Creatures: Chinese Embroidery*. Berkeley, Calif.: Lancaster-Miller, 1979.

Willcox, Donald. *New Design in Wood*. New York: Van Nostrand Reinhold, 1970.

Young Americans: Metal. New York: American Craft Council, 1979.

CHAPTERS 16–18 Design and Visual Communication

Adams, Ansel. *Ansel Adams: Images 1923–1974*. Greenwich, Conn.: New York Graphic Society, 1974.

Ambasz, Emilio, ed. *The International Design Yearbook 3*. New York: Abbeville, 1987.

Artist's Proof: The Annual of Prints and Printmaking. New York: Pratt Graphics Center and Barre Publishers. Annually.

Birren, Faber. *History of Color in Painting: With New Principles in Color Expression*. New York: Van Nostrand Reinhold, 1980.

Bittner, Herbert. *Kaethe Kollwitz, Drawings*. New York: Thomas Yoseloff, 1970.

Blunden, Maria, and Godfrey Blunden. *Impressionists and Impressionism*. New York: Rizzoli, 1980.

Caponigro, Paul. *Paul Caponigro*. Millerton, N.Y.: Aperture, 1972.

Cavagnaro, David. *This Living Earth*. Palo Alto, Calif.: American West Publishing Co., 1972.

Chaet, Bernard. *An Artist's Notebook: Techniques and Materials*. New York: Holt, Rinehart and Winston, 1979.

Clarke, Beverly. *Graphic Design in Educational Television*. New York: Watson-Guptill, 1974.

Cooper, Helen A. *Winslow Homer Watercolors*. New Haven: Yale University Press, 1986.

Croy, Peter. *Graphic Design and Reproduction Techniques*. rev. ed. New York: Focal Press, 1972.

Defining Modern Art: Selected Writings of Alfred H. Barr, Jr. ed. Irving Sandler and Amy Newman. New York: Abrams, 1986.

Dixon, Dwight R., and Paul B. Dixon. *Photography: Experiments and Projects*. New York: Macmillan, 1976.

Douglass, Ralph. *Calligraphic Lettering*. 3d ed. New York: Watson-Guptill, 1975.

Ehncke, R. H. *Graphic Trade Symbols by German Designers*. Magnolia, Mass.: Peter Smith, n.d.

Eichenberg, Fritz. *The Art of the Print*. New York: Abrams, 1976.

Eisenstaedt, Alfred. *Witness to Nature*. New York: Viking, 1971.

Escher, M. C. *The Graphic Works of M. C. Escher*. New York: Ballantine, 1971.

Gardner's Art Through the Ages. 7th ed. rev. by Horst de la Croix and Richard G. Tansey. New York: Harcourt Brace Jovanovich, 1980.

Caunt, William. *The Impressionists*. New York: Weathervane Books, 1975.

Graphis Annual 85/86. Ed. Walter Herdeg. Zurich: Graphis Press, 1985.

Guzelimian, Vahe. *Becoming a MacArtist*. Greensboro, N. C.: Compute! Publications, Inc., 1985.

Haas, Ernst. *The Creation*. New York: Penguin, 1978.

Hall, Jim. *Mighty Minutes: An Illustrated History of Television's Best Commercials*. New York: Harmony, 1984.

Herbert, Barry. *German Expressionism*. London: Jupiter England, 1981. New York: State Mutual Book.

Irving, Donald J. *Sculpture: Material and Process*. New York: Van Nostrand Reinhold, 1970.

Janson, H. W. *History of Art*. 2d ed. Englewood Cliffs, N.J.: Prentice-Hall, 1977.

Johnson, Stewart J. *The Modern American Poster*. New York: Museum of Modern Art, 1983.

Jones, Dewitt. *Visions of Wilderness*. Portland, Oreg.: Graphic Arts Center Publishing Co., 1980.

Kelly, J. J. *The Sculptural Idea*. Minneapolis: Burgess, 1970.

Kowal, Dennis, Jr., and Dona Z. Meilach. *Sculpture Casting*. New York: Crown, 1972.

Lam, C. M., ed. *Calligrapher's Handbook*. New York: Taplinger, 1976.

Legg, Alicia, ed. *Sculpture of Matisse*. New York: Museum of Modern Art, 1972.

Life Library of Photography. New York: Time-Life Books, 1970–1971.

Lynes, Russell. *The Lively Audience: A Social History of the Visual and Performing Arts in America, 1890–1950*. New York: Harper & Row, 1986.

McCarter, William, and Rita Gilbert. *Living with Art*. New York: Alfred A. Knopf, 1985.

McQuillan, Melissa. *Impressionist Portraits*. Boston: New York Graphic Society Books/Little Brown, 1986.

Mayer, Ralph. *The Artist's Handbook of Materials and Techniques*. New York: Viking, 1982.

Mayor, A. Hyatt. *Prints and People*. New York: The Metropolitan Museum of Art, 1971.

Mendelowitz, Daniel M. *A History of American Art*. 2d ed. New York: Holt, Rinehart and Winston, 1973.

Moore, Henry. *Sculpture and Drawings (1964–73)*. New York: Wittenborn, 1977.

Muller, Joseph-Emile. *Fauvism*. Trans. S. E. Jones. New York: Praeger, 1967.

Murphy, Seamus. *Stone Mad: A Sculptor's Life and Craft*. Boston: Routledge and Kegan, 1976.

Peterdi, Gabor. *Printmaking*. New York: Macmillan, 1971.

Phillips, Dave. *Graphic and Optical Art Mazes*. New York: Dover, 1976.

Prueitt, Melvin. *Art and the Computer*. New York: McGraw-Hill, 1984.

Richter, Gisela M., ed. *Sculpture and Sculptors of the Greeks*. 4th ed. rev. and enl. New Haven: Yale University Press, 1971.

Roth, Laszlo. *Package Design*. Englewood Cliffs, N.J.: Prentice-Hall, 1981.

Roukes, Nicholas. *Sculpture in Plastics*. New York: Watson-Guptill, 1978.

Russell, Stella Pandell. *Art in the World*. New York: Holt, Rinehart and Winston, 1975.

Saff, Donald, and Deli Sacilotto. *Printmaking: History and Process*. New York: Holt, Rinehart and Winston, 1978.

———. *Screenprinting: History and Process*. New York: Holt, Rinehart and Winston, 1979.

Sandler, Irving. *The Triumph of American Painting: A History of Abstract Expressionism*. New York: Harper & Row, 1970.

Stella, Frank. *Working Space*. Charles Eliot Norton lectures delivered at Harvard, 1983–84. Cambridge: Harvard University Press, 1987.

Stone, Anna. *Sculpture: New Ideas and Techniques*. Levittown, N.Y.: Transatlantic, 1977.

Swedlund, Charles. *Photography*. 2d ed. New York: Holt, Rinehart and Winston, 1981.

Varney, Vivian. *Photographer as Designer*. Worcester, Mass.: Davis, 1977.

Wittkower, Rudolf. *Sculpture: Processes and Principles*. New York: Harper & Row, 1977.

Wood, Jack C. *Sculpture in Wood*. New York: Da Capo, 1977.

CHAPTERS 19–21 *Design for Environment*

Ambasz, Emilio, ed. *Italy: The New Domestic Landscape*. New York: The Museum of Modern Art, 1972.

Bacon, Edmund N. *Design of Cities*. New York: Penguin, 1976.

Ball, Victoria Kloss. *Opportunities in Interior Design*. Skokie, Ill,: National Textbook, 1977.

Bennett, Corwin. *Spaces for People: Human Factors in Design*. Englewood Cliffs, N.J.: Prentice-Hall, 1977.

Bloomer, Kent C., and Charles W. Moore. *Body, Memory and Architecture*. New Haven: Yale University Press, 1977.

Boericke, Art, and Barry Shapiro. *Handmade Houses: A Guide to the Woodbutcher's Art*. San Francisco: Scrimshaw, 1973.

Bring, Mitchell, and Josse Wayembergh. *Japanese Gardens: Design and Meaning*. New York: McGraw-Hill, 1982.

Carrington, Noel. *Industrial Design in Britain*. Winchester, Mass.: Allen and Unwin, 1976.

Charlish, Anne, ed. *The History of Furniture*. New York: Crown, 1982.

Diekelmann, John, and Robert Schuster. *Natural Landscaping*. New York: McGraw-Hill, 1982.

Drexler, Arthur. *Design Collection: Selected Objects*. New York: Museum of Modern Art, 1970.

Eckbo, Garrett. *Home Landscape: The Art of Home Landscaping*. rev. and enl. ed. New York: McGraw-Hill, 1982.

Faulkner, Ray, and Sarah Faulkner. *Inside Today's Home*. New York: Holt, Rinehart and Winston, 1974.

Faulkner, Sarah. *Planning a Home*. New York: Holt, Rinehart and Winston, 1979.

Floethe, Louise L. *Houses Around the World*. New York: Charles Scribner, 1973.

Giedion, Siegfried. *Architecture and the Phenomena of Transition: The Three Space Conceptions in Architecture*. Cambridge, Mass.: Harvard University Press, 1971.

Gombrich, E. H. *The Sense of Order*. Oxford: Phaidon, 1979.

Greenwood, Kathryn M., and Mary F. Murphy. *Fashion Innovation and Marketing*. New York: Macmillan, 1978.

Gruen, Victor, and Larry Smith. *Centers for Urban Environment*. New York: Van Nostrand Reinhold, 1973.

Hamburger, Estelle. *Fashion Business: It's All Yours*. New York: Harper & Row, 1976.

Harling, Robert, ed. *Dictionary of Design and Decoration*. New York: Viking, 1973.

Hatje, Gerd, and Peter Kaspar. *1601 Decorating Ideas for Modern Living*. New York: Abrams, 1974.

Hitchcock, Henry Russell. *In the Nature of Materials: The Buildings of Frank Lloyd Wright, 1887–1941*. New York: Da Capo, 1975.

Hoyt, Charles King. *More Places for People*. New York: McGraw-Hill, 1982.

Jencks, Charles. *The Language of Post-Modern Architecture*. 3d rev. ed. New York: Rizzoli, 1981.

Johnson, Timothy E. *Solar Architecture: The Direct Gain Approach*. New York: McGraw-Hill, 1982.

Kepes, Gyorgy, ed. *Arts of the Environment*. New York: Braziller, 1972.

Kohler, Carl. *History of Costume*. Magnolis, Mass.: Peter Smith, n. d.

Kurtz, Stephen A. *Wasteland: Building the American Dream*. New York: Praeger, 1973.

Larsen, Jack L., and Jeanne Weeks. *Fabrics for Interiors*. New York: Van Nostrand Reinhold, 1975.

Loewy, Raymond. *Industrial Design*. New York: Overlook Press, 1980.

Lynch, Kevin, *Managing the Sense of a Region*. Cambridge, Mass.: MIT Press, 1976.

Magnani, Franco, ed. *Living Spaces: 150 Design Ideas from Around the World*. New York: Whitney Library of Design, 1978.

Mathisen, Marilyn. *Apparel and Accessories*. New York: McGraw-Hill, 1979.

Mehrabian, Albert. *Public Places and Private Spaces: The Psychology of Work, Play, and Living Environments*. New York: Basic Books, 1976.

Moholy-Nagy, Sibyl. *Native Genius in Anonymous Architecture in North America*. New York: Schocken, 1976.

Mumford, Lewis. *Culture of Cities*. New York: Harcourt Brace Jovanovich, 1970.

Norberg-Schulz, Christian. *Meaning in Western Architecture*. New York: Praeger, 1975.

Parker, W. Oren, and Harvey K. Smith. *Scene Design and Stage Lighting*. 4th ed. New York: Holt, Rinehart and Winston, 1979.

Pecktal, Lynn. *Designing and Painting for the Theatre*. New York: Holt, Rinehart and Winston, 1975.

Peltz, Leslie Ruth. *Fashion, Color, Line, and Design*. Indianapolis: Bobbs-Merrill, 1971.

Philip, Peter. *Furniture of the World*. New York: Mayflower, 1978.

Phillips, Derek. *Planning Your Lighting*. New York: Quick Fox, 1978.

Risebero, Bill. *Modern Architecture and Design: An Alternative History*. Cambridge: MIT Press, 1983.

Russell, Douglas. *Stage Costume Design: Theory, Technique, and Style*. New York: Appleton-Century-Crofts, 1973.

Salomon, Rosalie K. *Fashion Design for Moderns*. New York: Fairchild, 1976.

Scully, Vincent J. *Modern Architecture: The Architecture of Democracy*. New York: Braziller, 1982.

Sproles, George B. *Fashion: Consumer Behavior Toward Dress*. Minneapolis: Burgess, 1979.

Stern, Robert A. M. *New Directions in American Architecture*. New York: Braziller, 1977.

Stoddard, Alexandra. *Style for Living*. Garden City: Doubleday, 1974.

Zakos, Spiros. *Lifespace and Designs for Today's Living*. New York: Macmillan, 1977.

Photographic Credits

Color Plates:

Plate 15: © 1986 Wolfgang Hoyt/ESTO. Plate 17: The Vasarely Center, New York. Plate 19: Frank R. Cheatham, Lubbock, Texas. Plate 22: Josef Albers Foundation, Orange, Connecticut. Plate 30: *Fractal Image* by Alan Norton, IBM Research.

Chapter 1   1: AMNH. 2: Grant M. Haist/National Audubon Society, PR. 4: A/AR. 6: G.W. Einstein Co., Inc., New York. 8: Joshua Schreier, New York. 9: Hoffritz International/Hammond/Keehn, Inc., New York. 10: M. 13: Stefano di Satella of Italy. 15: © 1988 M.C. Escher/Cordon Art, Baarn, Holland. 18: A.F. Kersting, London. 20: ETS. J.E. Bulloz, Paris. 22: A/AR.

Chapter 2   27: AMNH. 28: Professor Howard E. Bigelow, Dept. of Botany, University of Massachusetts, Amherst, Massachusetts. 36: Phillips, New York. 39: AMNH. 42: Contourpedic Corporation. 43: Wide World Photos, New York. 44: Jill Poyourow, Eastsound, Washington.

Chapter 3   46: Black Star, New York. 47: Am. Honda Motor Co., Inc., Gardena, California. 53: Walt Quade, Eastsound, Washington. From *Chinese Written Characters: Their Wit and Wisdom* by Rose Quong, Cobble Hill Press 1968, New York.

Chapter 4   68: George Jennings, Jr. 71: Carolina Biological Supply Co., Burlington, North Carolina. 72: British Tourist Authority, New York. 75: Courtesy Gallery 10, Scottsdale, Arizona. 76: Jan Lukas/PR. 78: Tung Yah Asian Arts, La Jolla, California. 80: Robert E. Mates, New York. 83: Gremillion & Co., Houston. 84: A/AR. 85: Ministry of Tourism, British Columbia. 86: Helmsley Spear, Inc., New York. 88: Nat Norman/PR. 91 Top: AMNH. 92 Bottom: Lee Boltin/AMNH. 94: Dick Busher, Seattle, Washington. 97: PR.

Chapter 5   99: Harry Murphy & Friends, Mill Valley, California. 104: David K. Specter, New York. 105: A/AR. 106: A/AR. 111: John Kleinhans. 112: Magnum Photos, New York. 113: Julius Shulman, Los Angeles. 114: AMNH.

Chapter 6   117: Esther Saks Gallery, Chicago. 119: Sigeo Anzai, Tokyo. 124: D. James Dee. 125: A/AR. 127: A/AR. 128: A/AR. 129: From *The New Churches of Europe* by G.E. Kidder Smith, New York. 130: Norman McGrath, New York. 131: Norman McGrath, New York. 132: Eliot Erwitt/Magnum Photos, New York. 134: James D. Toms, Eureka, California. 141: RS.

Chapter 7   145: Photofest, New York.

Chapter 8   152: Brain Lea Tart, Los Angeles. 155: John F. Mahoney, New York. 156: RS. 157: Robert E. Mates and Mary Donlon, New York. 158: Alison Frantz, Princeton, New Jersey.

Chapter 10   171: Jimmy Williams Photography, Cary, North Carolina. 178: AMNH. 179: A/AR. 182: Magnum Photos.

Chapter 11   188: A/AR (both). 189: A/AR (both). 191: Eastman Kodak Co., Rochester, New York. 199: Eeva-Inkeri, New York. 201: From *The Art of Heraldry* by Arthur Fox-Davis, Arno Press, New York, 1976. 203: H. 205: Government of India Press Information, New York. 206: A.F. Kersting, London. 207: French Embassy Press & Info. Division, New York.

Chapter 12   216A: Cy Gross Photography, New York. 216B: Cy Gross Photography, New York. 216C: Bella & Ruggeri, Milan, Italy. 217: AMNH. 218: Gallery 10, Scottsdale, Arizona. 219: RS. 221: Anne Odom, New York. 222: © 1988 M.C. Escher/Cordon Art, Baarn, Holland.

Chapter 13   230: Amnest Picture Agency, San Francisco, California. 233: © 1982 Sotheby's Inc. 238: Edmund V. Gillon, Jr., New York. 242: H. Roger Violett, Paris. 248: Joe Irwin, Jr. 244: A/AR.

Chapter 14   252: Marc Slivka, New York. 253: Wyatt Davis. 254: Tyler Dingee. 260: FAO Photo by Woodbridge Williams Photo Unit, FAO, Rome. 264: RS.

Chapter 15   272: Jill Poyourow, Eastsound, Washington. 277: Blake Praytor, San Francisco. 281: The Board of Trinity College, Dublin. 287: RS.

Chapter 16   290: A/AR. 303: A/AR. 306: A/AR.

Chapter 17   313: From *Collograph Printmaking* by Donald Stoltenberg. Davis Publications, Inc., Worcester, 1975. 316: From *Collograph Printmaking* by Donald Stoltenberg. Davis Publications, Inc., Worcester, 1975. 323: Vision Nouvelle, Paris. 331: Illustration by Gyo Fuji Kawa. Reprinted by permission of Grosset & Dunlap from *My Favorite Thing* by Gyo Fuji Kawa, Copyright © 1978 by Zokeisha Publications, Ltd. 338: Williams & Associates, South Lynnfield, Massachusetts. 341: Reprinted from *Popular Science* with permission © 1987 Times Mirror Maga-

Index

abstract, masses, 78; shapes, 68, Fig. 76; 69
Abstract Expressionism, 264, Fig. 298
abstraction, 10; in painting, 262, Fig. 295; in sculpture, 274, Fig. 310
achromatic, 118
Ackerberg home, Malibu, California, 120, Pl. 15 (p. 124)
acrylic polymer emulsion, 259–260, Fig. 293
Adam Brothers, 336–337, Fig. 391
additive principle of color, 116, Pl. 8 (p. 122)
additive techniques, 224
advertising, 288–293; copy, 289
aesthetics, 4–5
afterimage, 131–132, Pl. 20 (p. 126); reversed, 131–132, Pl. 21 (p. 126)
Ahir skirt, 109, Fig. 135; detail, 109, Fig. 106
Albers, Josef, 130–132, Pl. 20 (p. 126); Pl. 21 (p. 126); Pl. 22 (p. 127)
Aldridge, Peter, *Arcus*, 77, Fig. 92
Alice in Wonderland, 186, Fig. 210
alloys, 213–215
aluminum, 214, Fig. 239
Amiens Cathedral, 182, Fig. 204
analogous colors, 119–121, 132
Antti Nurmesniemi, slim-line push-button telephone, 35, Fig. 37
Anuszkiewicz, Richard, *Blue to Red Portal*, 68, Pl. 5 (p. 56)
Aphrodite of Melos, 171, Fig. 186
appliqué, 251, Fig. 286
aquatint, 282–283, Fig. 324
arabesque, 246, Fig. 279

arch, 349, Fig. 404
architecture, and the environment, 348–367; attributes of, 351–353; contemporary trends, 359–362; development of contemporary, 355–359; elements and principles, 353–355; modernism in, 362; Post-modern, 359–362, Figs. 418 and 419; skyscraper, 357–359; structural design in, 348–351; vernacular, 359–360, Fig. 417
armor, suit of, 319, Fig. 367
Aronson house, New York City, 331–332, Figs. 383 and 384
art, 4–5; and craft, 30; and design, 6; purpose of, 5
Art Deco, 142–143, Fig. 152
Artist with Ladder, Duane Hansen, 221–222, Fig. 249
Asada, Shuji, *Form-B*, 111, Fig. 138

balance, 156, 160–170, 172, 190; asymmetrical, 162, 166–169, 167, Figs. 181 and 182; 168, Fig. 183; horizontal, 160–162; 160, Fig. 170; 161, Fig. 171; in interior design, 342–343; occult, 166, structural, 160–162; symmetrical, 162–164; 163, Figs. 174 and 175; 164, Figs. 176 and 177; vertical, 162, Figs. 172 and 173; visual, 160, 162
Bart, Robert, *Untitled*, 190–191, Fig. 214
bas-relief, 268–270; 269, Fig. 303
Bassler, James, *Skins*, 230–231, Fig. 259
Bates, Wayne L., *Complex Cut Geometric*, 58–59, Fig. 62

batik, 104–105, Fig. 126; 192, Fig. 215; 252, Fig. 287
Bauhaus, 36
Bayeux Tapestry, 86–87; *Harold Swearing Oath*, 87, Fig. 101
Bearden, Romare, *Lamplite Evening*, 179, Fig. 199
beat, in rhythm, 139–142; 140, Figs. 146, 147, and 148; 141, Figs. 149 and 150
Beene, Geoffrey, 322–323, Fig. 372
Beethoven, *Missa Solemnis*, 49–50, Fig. 51; *Ninth Symphony* performed by Ballet of the 20th Century, 314, Fig. 364
Béjart, Maurice, Ballet of the 20th Century in *Beethoven's Ninth Symphony*, 314, Fig. 364
Bell System logo, 289, Fig. 334
bench saw, 325, Fig. 377
Bennett, Jamie, *Brooches from Deer Run Series*, 248, Fig. 282
bentwood, 207–208, Fig. 31
Berhang, Mattie, *Costello Ferry*, 103–104, Fig. 124
Bernini, Gian Lorenzo, *David*, 271–272, Fig. 306
Bewick, Thomas, *Bison*, 279–280, Figs. 319 and 320
Bickerton, Ashley, *UUEHH*, 267–268, Fig. 302
biomorphic, shapes, 72
black stem wheat rust, microscopic study, 65–66, Fig. 71
Blenheim Park Oxford, England, 365, Fig. 423
Blickensderfer Electric typewriter, 23, Fig. 23
Body Language, magazine illustration, 287–288, Fig. 332

Boehm, Michael, glasses, 58–59, Fig. 61

book design, 285–287; children's 287, Fig. 331; covers, 287, Fig. 330; layout, 286; type, 286–287

Book of Kells, The, detail, 247, Fig. 280

Botta, Mario, Fribourg State Bank, 351–352, Fig. 408

Brancusi, Constantin, *Bird in Space*, 274, Fig. 310

Brandt, Edgar, *Oasis Screen*, 142; detail, 142, Fig. 152

Braque, Georges, *Water Pitcher and Violin*, 261, Fig. 294

brass, 213

Breuer, Marcel, armchair, 36, Fig. 38

bronze, 213–214, Fig. 238

Brooke, James, *Ainlee*, 202, Fig. 228

Brooklyn Bridge, photograph, 308–309, Fig. 357

Buchwald, Howard, *Masquerade*, 7, Fig. 7

Bull Leaping, fresco from Palace of Minos, Crete, 140, Fig. 147

burin, 279–280, Fig. 318

cabinetmakers, English, 335–338

calligraphy, 50–51, Fig. 52; 285, Fig. 327

camera, 300–301, Fig. 344

Campbell, Patricia, *Constructed Light Wall II*, 32–33, Fig. 35

Canada, national flag, 156–157, Fig. 167

cantilever, 349–350; 349, Fig. 404; 350, Fig. 406

Capitol Reef, Utah, photograph by Minor White, 190–191, Fig. 213

Caponigra, Paul, *Sunflower*, 175, Fig. 192; *Canyon de Chelly*, Arizona, 307, Fig. 354

Caravaggio, *The Card Sharps*, 197–198, Fig. 223

Carcassone, 16; view of, 17, Fig. 18.

Carreras, José, 316, Fig. 366

Carson residence, Eureka, California, 356–357, Fig. 414

Cartier-Bresson, Henri, *Simiane la Rotonde*, 167, Fig. 182

casein, 258

Cassatt, Mary, *In the Omnibus*, 282–283, Fig. 324

casting, cire perdue, 270; in manufacturing, 328; methods in sculpture, 270; sandcasting, 270

cauterium, 257

Cavagnaro, David, *Dew-Covered Dry Grasses*, 27, Fig. 29; *Dry Grass Seed Stalks Against the Rising Sun*, 306–307, Fig. 353; *Orb Weaver Spider Web*, 25, Fig. 25; *Valley Oak*, 45, Fig. 45

Centennial Square, Victoria, B. C., 74, Fig. 85

Cesar, *The Yellow Buick*, 100–101, Fig. 118

Challenger space shuttle, 96–97, Fig. 115

chambered nautilus, 175, Fig. 191

Champion Paper Co., direct mailer, 285–286, Fig. 328

Chan, Tak Kwong, *The Horse—Away He Goes*, 64–65, Fig. 70

Chanel, Coco, 321

Chermayeff, Ivan, poster for *Crime and Punishment* on Masterpiece Theatre, 290, Fig. 336

Chianciano, Baths of, dome, 216–217, Fig. 244

Chihuly, Dale, *Cobalt Green Macchia*, 78–79, Fig. 94

Children's Broadcasts, CBS, brochure cover design, 289, Fig. 335

Chillida, Eduardo, *Abesti Gogoro III*, 239–240, Fig. 269

Chinese, ideography, 50, Fig. 52; jade, 215–216, Fig. 243; medallion, 245–246, Fig. 277

Chippendale, Thomas, 335–336, Figs. 389 and 390

Christ and the Apostles, enamel mural by Thelma Winter, 176, Figs. 194 and 195

chroma, 117–119, Pl. 14 (p. 123)

Chunghi Choo, *Decanter*, 213, Fig. 237

Church of the Transfiguration, Kizhi, USSR, 194–195, Fig. 221

circle, 74

cire perdue, 270

classicism, 152

clay, 217–218; decorative design in, 249, Figs. 283 and 284; forming techniques, 227–230; residual, 217; sedimentary, 217

Clerk, Pierre, *Furious Duchess*, 150, Fig. 159

clitocybe sudorifica, 27, Fig. 28

cloisonné, 248, Fig. 282

Close, Chuck, *Linda*, 266, Fig. 300; *Keith*, 282–283, Fig. 325

closure, 11–12, Figs. 11, 12, and 13

clothing, role of, 319

Coca-Cola bottle, 328, Fig. 381

Colburn, Carol, *After the Rain*, detail, 129; Pl. 16 (p. 124)

collage, 108

collagraph, 279, Fig. 316

color, 114–135; additive, 116–117, Pl. 8 (p. 122); and light, 114–115; and space, 133; balance of, 133–134, Pl. 23 (p. 127); complementary, 120–130; harmonies, 120–130; in interior design, 340–341; in landscape design, 366; interaction, 130–134; local, 133; primary, 116–117; properties, 117–119; psychology, 132–133; relationships, 119–120; secondary, 116–117; subtractive, 116–117, Pl. 9 (p. 122); tertiary, 117; theory, 117–134

complementary colors, 120–130, Pl. 19 (p. 126)

composition, 54, 243–245; 244, Figs. 275 and 276

computer, and art, 297–299; 298, Fig. 342; Pl. 30 (p. 292); and the designer, 296–297, Figs. 340 and 341; and graphics, 294–295; 295, Figs. 339a, b, and c; portable, 38, Fig. 41

computer graphics, 294–295, Figs. 339a, b, and c

concept, 30–31

concrete, 216–217

cone, 76, Fig. 89

constructions, 108

contemporary, concepts of space, 96–97; trends, architectural design, 359–362; industrial design, 328–329; interior design, 346–347; painting, 260–267; performing arts, 314–316; sculpture, 271, 275–276

content, in architecture, 351–353; in painting, 255–256; in photography, 301–302, Figs. 346 and 347; 308

Contourpedic Custom Wheelchair, 39–40, Fig. 42

contrast, 190–192; 193, Figs. 213 and 214; 192, Fig. 215

Copier, Andries D., *Unique Piece C. B. 7*, 240–241, Fig. 271

Copy-Jack hand copy machine, 329, Fig. 382

Corinthian capital, 105–106, Fig. 127

Cornelius, Philip, *Covered Jar*, 102, Fig. 120

costume design, 324–325, Fig. 375

craftsmanship, 28–30

Craige, Sheppard, *Towards Pienza #1*, 142–143, Fig. 153

Creation of the World, The, mosaic in St. Mark's Cathedral, Venice, 20–21, Fig. 22

Cretan jars, 218, Fig. 246

crown gall, microscopic view, 27, Fig. 30

crystals, in nature, 77, Fig. 91

cube, 74–75, Fig. 86

Cubism, in painting, 261, Fig. 294; in sculpture, 273–274, Fig. 309

Currier, Anne, *Teapot with Two Cups,* 31, Fig. 34

cylinder, 76–77, Fig. 90

David, Jacques Louis, *Death of Socrates,* 152–153, Fig. 162

decision making, 31–32

decoration, and structure, 235–252; as structure, 241–243; 242, Figs. 272a and 272b, Fig. 273; 243, Fig. 274

decorative design, 245–247, Figs. 277 and 278

decorative processes, 247–252

De Hooch, Pieter, *Interior with Card Players,* 93, Fig. 110

De Juan, Renaldo, *Gate #6,* 48–49, Fig. 49

de la Renta, Oscar, 321–322, Fig. 370

Delisle, Roseline, *L'Ogive,* 228–229, Fig. 258

della Francesca, Piero, and Luciano Laurana, *View of an Ideal City,* 91, Fig. 106; perspective diagram, 91, Fig. 107

de Rivera, José, Brussels Construction, 52–53, Fig. 55

design, advertising, 288–289; and art, 6; and manufacture, 328; as universal reality, 3–42; decorative, 245–247; elements, 8; essence of, 3–24; fashion, 319–325; for environment, 317–367; for the future, 367; for visual communication, 253–316; furniture, 334–340; graphic, 277–294; industrial, 325–330; interior, 340–347; layout, 286; magazine and periodical, 287–288; nature of, 4; package, 110, Fig. 137; 293–294, Fig. 338; principles, 8, 137; process, 25–42; stage, 311–316; through selection, 8; type, 286; visual, 16–24; with lighting, 313

dome, 349; geodesic, 350–351, Fig. 407

double rainbow, 115, Pl. 7 (p. 121)

Dresser, Christopher, silver-plated teapot, 32–33, Fig. 36

drypoint, 281–282, Fig. 322

Dubuffet, Jean, *Radieux Météore,* 28, Fig. 31

ductility, 207

Dufy, Raoul, *Sailboat at Sainte-Adresse,* 168, Fig. 183

Dusi, Inge, *Detail of Three Batiks,* 252, Fig. 287

Eagle, yacht design, 296–297, Fig. 341

Ebner, David N., *Sculptural Writing Chair,* 207–208, Fig. 231

Echelman, Anne, *Cuff Bracelets,* 247–248, Fig. 281

Edmondson house, Forrest City, Arkansas, 332–333, Fig. 386

Ehrlich, Bill, minimal living room, 107, Fig. 130

electromagnetic field, 114–115, Fig. 142

emphasis, 121, 150–159; by location, 150; subdued, 157–159; through contrast, 155–157; through drama, 152–153; through light, 153–155; through shape, 155

enameling, 248, Fig. 282

encaustic, 257, Fig. 289

entasis, 148

environmental design, 365–367; and the city, 362–363, Fig. 420; landscape, 365–366, Figs. 423, 424, and 425; rehabilitation, 363–364, Figs. 421 and 422

Equipo 57, *PA-18,* 146, Fig. 157

Escher, M. C., *Concave and Convex,* 13–14, Fig. 15; *Lucht en Water I,* 196–197, Fig. 222

etching, 282, Fig. 323; on metal, 248

evaluation, 39–42

Exit to Eden, cover design, 287, Fig. 330

Expressionists, German, 134

extrusion, 328

fabrics, decorative techniques, 251–252, Figs. 286 and 287

Fagerlund, Carl, cut-crystal chandelier, 219, Fig. 247

fashion, 322–324; design, 319–325; industry, 320–324

Ferorelli, Enrico, *The Alps,* 301, Fig. 345

ferrocement, 216–217, Fig. 244

fibers, 219–220; forming techniques, 230–234; natural, 219–220; synthetic, 220

Fibonacci Series, 174–175, Figs. 192 and 193

Fielding, David, stage set for Wagner's *Rienzi,* 312–313, Fig. 363

figure-ground ambiguity, 71–72, Fig. 82

Flack, Audrey, *Royal Flush,* 284, Pl. 29 (p. 292)

flexibility, 207

Floating Mountains, computer plotted picture, 297–298, Fig. 342

Foley, Stephen A. *Spinning Wheel,* 37, Fig. 40

forging, 225

form, 18–23; in architecture, 351–353; in painting, 255; in photography, 301–302, Fig. 345, 308; in sculpture, 269–270

Frankenthaler, Helen, *Nature Abhors a Vacuum,* 291, Pl. 2 (p. 22)

fresco, 104, Fig. 125; 259

Friedrich, Caspar David, *The Evening Star,* 54–57, Fig. 59

Fujikawa, Gyo, book illustration, 287, Fig. 331

fulfillment of purpose, 23

function, integrity of, 37–39

furniture, 334; contemporary design, 339–340, Figs. 395 and 396; eighteenth century, 335–338

Futurists, Italian, 145–146

Gad-dam Stilt Tree House, the Philippines, 36–37, Fig. 39

gargoyles, Washington Cathedral, 272–273, Fig. 307

Gauguin, Paul, *The Swineherd, Brittany,* 197, Pl. 25 (p. 209)

Geese of Medum, Egyptian, 86–87, Fig. 100

geometric, shapes, 66–68, Figs. 72, 73, and 74

German doorhinge, 214–215, Fig. 241

German Expressionism, 262–263, Fig. 296

gesso, 257

gestalt, 11

Ghiberti, Lorenzo, *Gates of Paradise,* 269–270, Fig. 303

Gillespie, Dorothy, *Conjured Image of a Past Presence,* 214, Fig. 239

Giotto, *Annunciation to Anna*, 90–91, Fig. 105

Gismondi, Ernesto, *Stria* wall lamp, 326–327, Fig. 379

glass, 218–219; decorative techniques, 250–251; forming techniques, 226–227; millefiori, 250, Fig. 285; varieties, 219

glassblowing, 226, Fig. 252

Glynn, Bert, *New Zealand*, 305–306, Fig. 352

gold, 213, Fig. 236

Golden Gate Bridge, 207–208, Fig. 230

Golden Mean, 172–174, Figs. 187, 188, and 189a and b

Go Tech, Inc. 163, 174

Gottlieb, Adolph, *Incubus*, 258–259, Fig. 292

gouache, 258–259, Fig. 292

Goya, Francisco, *Executions of the Third of May, 1808*, 152, Fig. 161

grain storage barn, Switzerland, 360, Fig. 417

graphic, 277; design, 277–294

Grasser, Erasmus, *A Morris Dancer*, 212, Pl. 26 (p. 210)

Graves, Michael, Schulman house, 361, Fig. 419

gray scale, 116; 118, Fig. 144

Greek orders, 355–356, Fig. 412; proportion, 171–174, Figs. 187, 188, and 189; 177; sculpture, 172, Fig. 188; symmetry, 163; temple design, 106, Fig. 128; 147–148, Fig. 158, 172; use of light, 105–106, Fig. 127, 272; vases, 172, 174, Fig. 189; visual arts, 139, 147, 172–174

Gropius, Walter, Bauhaus, 358–359, Fig. 416

ground, for painting, 256

grout, 236

Gruenebaum, Thomas, *Soho Wall Series #9*, 108, Fig. 133

Haas, Ernst, *Rainbow Rock*, 115, Pl. 7 (p. 121); *Wave-washed Coral*, 62, Fig. 66

haliotis fulgens, 26, Fig. 27

Hallman, Ted, acrylic screen, 28, Fig. 32

hallmarks, 213

Hamilton-Merritt, Jane, *Norway Street*, 111, Fig. 139

Hanson, Duane, *Artist with Ladder*, 221–222, Fig. 249; *Woman at Beach on Lounge Chair*, 275, Fig. 311

Harborplace, Baltimore, 364, Fig. 422

hardwood, 211

Hardy, Hugh, New York City living room, 107, Fig. 131

Harijan patchwork quilt, 67, Fig. 74

Hasegawa, S., *Les Oiseaux*, 282, Fig. 323

hatching, 52; cross-hatching, 52

Hatshepsut, funerary temple, 181, Fig. 203

haute couture, 321–324

haut-relief, 268–270, Fig. 303

Hepplewhite, George, 337–338, Fig. 392

heraldry, British, 180, Fig. 201

Hernandez, Augustin, Hernandez house, Mexico City, 95–96, Figs. 113 and 114

Hilton, Eric, *Innerland*, 243, Fig. 274

Hlava, Pavel, *Satellite*, 74–75, Fig. 87

Hokusai, *A Sake Bout*, 47, Fig. 48

Homer, Winslow, *Woodsman and Fallen Tree*, 258–259, Pl. 27 (p. 210)

Honda Hurricane, 46–47, Fig. 47

hue, 117–118

Huszar, John L., *Double Portrait, Georgia O'Keeffe and Ansel Adams*, 302–303, Fig. 348

IBM Quietwriter 8 typewriter, 23, Fig. 24

ideographic writing, 50

imagery, 13–16; conceptual, 13–15, Figs. 16 and 17; dual, 13–14, Fig. 15; perceptual, 13; visual, 13

impasto, 107–108

Impressionism, French, 134, Pl. 23 (p. 261)

industrial design, 325–330; categories, 326–327; manufacturing techniques, 328

inspiration, 26–28

intaglio, 280–283

intarsia, 212

integrity, 35–39; of form, 36–37; of function, 37–39; of materials, 35

intensity, 119

interior design, 331–347; contemporary trends, 346–347; elements, 340–341; principles, 342–343; public, 344–345

intertwining, 247, Fig. 280

iron, 214–215, Fig. 241

Isola, Maija, *Medusa*, 63–64, Fig. 69

Ives, Herbert E., color wheel, 117, Pl. 10 (p. 122)

Jack and the Beanstalk, costume design from *Into the Woods*, 324–325, Fig. 375b

Jaguar XJ-S, 326–327, Fig. 380

James, Michael, *The Concord Cotillion*, 198–199, Fig. 224

Japanese, garden, 169, Fig. 184; stencil on silk, 63–64, Fig. 68

Jewel in the Crown, The, 118, Fig. 145

Joel, Yale, *Illusion of Speed*, 308–309, Fig. 356

Johns, Jasper, *Between the Clock and the Bed*, 257, Fig. 289; *Cups 4 Picasso*, 71, Fig. 82; *Target with Four Faces*, 166, Fig. 180

Jones, Ann, *Chi Rho and The Flood*, 241–242, Figs. 272a and 272b

Kain Panjang, batik, 192, Fig. 215

Kandinsky, Wassily, *Composition 8, No. 260*, 262, Fig. 295; *Kleine Welten*, 70, Fig. 80

Kane, Art, *Greeting*, 302, Fig. 347

Karan, Donna, 322, Fig. 371

Keister, Steve, *USO #66*, 272–273, Fig. 308

Kelly, Janet, photo, 302, Fig. 346

Kent, Rockwell, *Voyaging*, 186, Fig. 209

Killoanig, *Carving of a Man*, 208–211, Fig. 232

Kingston, L. Brent, *Weathervane #27*, 225, Fig. 251

Kirchner, Ernst Ludwig, *Head of Ludwig Schames*, 279, Fig. 317

Klee, Paul, *Angstaubruch III*, 62–63, Fig. 67

Klimt, Gustav, *Standing Woman Looking to the Right*, 54, Fig. 57

knives, selection of, 8–9, Fig. 9

Kobayashi, Masakazu, W^3W to the Third Power, 240–241, Fig. 270

Kokoschka, Oskar, *Montana Landschaft*, 23, Pl. 1 (p. 21)

Kollwitz, Kaethe, *The Prisoners*, 278, Fig. 315

Ko Noda, package designs, 110–111, Fig. 137

Kosmos, Joseph, *ZPS Mark 3*, 325, Fig. 276

Koursaros, Harry, *Pythian Maidens*, 267, Fig. 301

Krak des Chevaliers, 182, 184, Fig. 206

Lagerfeld, Karl, sketches for House of Chanel, Paris, 321, Figs. 369a and 369b

Lamb, Russell Dixon, *Rising Wave,* 79–80, Fig. 95

laminated wood, 207

Landor, Walter, logo for Cotton, Inc., 155, Fig. 165

landscape design, 365–366, Figs. 423, 424, and 425; elements, 366

La Noue, Terence, *Sepik,* 259–260, Fig. 293

Larimer Square, Denver, 363–364, Fig. 421

Larsen, Jack Lenor, *Labyrinth,* 235, Fig. 265

Lauren, Ralph, 322, Fig. 374

layering, 88, Figs. 102 and 103

layout design, 286

Le Corbusier, *Notre Dame du Haut,* 106–107, Fig. 129

Les Fauves, 260–261

Levy, Ellen K. *January 28, 1986,* 96–97, Fig. 115

Li Ch'Eng, *Buddhist Temple Amid Clearing Mountain Peaks,* 202–203, Fig. 229

light, 59; and pigment, 116–117; and space, 91–93, Figs. 108, 109, and 110; diffraction, 116; in stage design, 313; refraction, 116

Limbourg Brothers, *Très Riches Heures de Jean, Duc de Berry,* 201–202, Fig. 227

Lindgren, Charlotte, *Mooring,* 50–51, Fig. 53

line, 45–60, 190; as direction and emphasis, 54–58, Figs. 58, 59, and 60; as form, 52–54, Figs. 55 and 56; as modeling, 52, Fig. 54; as pattern and texture, 58–60, Figs. 61, 62, 63, and 64; quality of, 47–49, Figs. 48 and 49; symbolic, 49–51, Figs. 51, 52, and 53; to extend space, 332–334

linocut, 279–280

Lipton, Seymour, *Sanctuary,* 270–271, Fig. 305

lithography, 283–284, Fig. 326

Llewellyn, Robert, *Boston,* 304–305, Fig. 349

loom, 230–232, Figs. 260, 261, and 262

Lorrain, Claude, *Pastoral Landscape: The Roman Campagna,* 154–155, Fig. 163

Lovejoy, Tim, *The Thirumalai Naick Palace, India,* 12–13, Fig. 14

Low, Frank and Robert Burridge, Contourpedic Custom Wheelchair, 39–40, Fig. 42

Lowe, Stephen, *The Hermit,* 185, Fig. 208

Macbeth, stage design, 312–313, Fig. 362

magazine design, 287–288, Fig. 333

Magician's Pyramid, Uxmal, Yucatan, 76, Fig. 88

Magritte, René, *La Folie des Grandeurs,* 177, Fig. 196

Mahabharata, stage design, 314–315, Fig. 365

Makepeace, John, *FSIAD FRSA,* 169, Fig. 285

Makins, James, Beverage Service, 7. Fig. 8; Dinnerware and Goblets, 218, Fig. 245

malleability, 207

Marin, John, *Lower Manhattan,* 54, Fig. 58; *Woolworth Building,* 14–16, Fig. 16

marquetry, 212

Martinez, Maria, and Popovi Da, San Ildefonso polychrome jar, 68, Fig. 75; working in coil method, 227–228, Figs. 253 and 254

mass, 72–80; abstract, 78, Fig. 93; and movement, 79, Fig. 95; geometric, 74–77, Figs. 86–92; natural, 72–74, Figs. 84 and 85; nonobjective, 78–79, Fig. 94

materials, as components of design, 211–223; as structural design, 238–240, Figs. 267–271; characteristics of, 207–211; expression of, 18; influence on design, 207–223

Matisse, Henri, *Heads of Jeannette,* 78, Fig. 93; *The Parakeet and the Mermaid,* 82–83, Fig. 97; *The Swimming Pool,* 3 panels, 70–71, Fig. 81

Maulbronn Abbey, Würtemberg, chapter house, 1–11, Fig. 10

McKerrow, Amanda, *Les Sylphides,* p. 144, Fig. 155

mechanical printmaking processes, 284–285

media, and materials, 28–29, Pl. 2 (p. 22); 29, Fig. 33

metal, 213–215; forming techniques, 224–226

metal engraving, 281, Fig. 321

Metropolitan Opera House, staircase and foyer, 95, Fig. 112

Mexican tin mirror and candleholder, 214–215, Fig. 240

mezzotint, 282–283, Fig. 325

Michelangelo, *David,* 73, Fig. 84; Sistine Chapel, *Lunette of Eleazar and Nathan,* 104, Fig. 125

millefiori glass, 250, Fig. 285

minimal art, 265, Fig. 299

Minos, Palace of, *Bull Leaping,* fresco, 140, Fig. 147

Miró, Joan, *Carnival of Harlequin,* 263, Fig. 297

Missoni, 322–323, Fig. 373

mixed media, 259

modules, 77

Molten, Philip L., *California Palace of the Legion of Honor,* San Francisco, 307–308, Fig. 355

Mondrian, Piet, *Composition with Red, Yellow, and Blue,* 16–17, Fig. 19

monochromatic colors, 120

monoprint, 285

Moore, Charles, *Death Valley,* 46, Fig. 46

Moore, Henry, *Reclining Figure,* 211, Fig. 233

Moore, Violet, baskets, 108, Fig. 134

Moraine Lake, Alberta, 3–4, Fig. 2

mosaics, 236, Fig. 266; 250–251

motif, 99

motion, illusion of, 201–202; in interior design, 345; rhythm through, 145–147; space and time, 94–96, Figs. 112 and 113

Moynihan, Rodrigo, *Self-Portrait,* 179, Fig. 200

Mungituk, *Man Carried to the Moon,* 278, Fig. 314

Munsell, Albert, color tree, 117–118, Pl. 12 (p. 123); color wheel, 117, Pl. 11 (p. 122)

murals, 259

Murphy, Harry, catalogue cover design, 83–85, Fig. 99

Muzahib, Mahmud, *Bahram Gur in the Turquoise Palace on Wednesday,* 88, Fig. 103

Naff house, Pajaro Dunes, California, 354, Fig. 410

Naram-Sin, victory stele, 180, Fig. 202

NASA museum poster, 199, Fig. 225

natural, shapes, 63–66, Figs. 68–71

Nauja of Rankin Inlet, painting, 88–89, Fig. 102

Navajo rug, 103, Fig. 123
NBC Nightly News, computer-generated imagery, 298, Fig. 343
Nebelspalter, magazine cover design, 288, Fig. 333
negative, shapes, 71–72; space, 82, 270–271, Fig. 305
Nervi, Pier Luigi and Annibale Vitellozzi, *cupola and dome, Palazzo dello Sport*, Rome, 165, Fig. 179; *dome of Baths at Chianciano*, 216–217, Fig. 244
Neuschwanstein, palace of, 356–357, Fig. 413
neutrals, 120
Nevelson, Louise, *Sky Cathedral*, 194, Fig. 220
Newman, Barnett, Twelfth Station from *Fourteen Stations of the Cross*, 265, Fig. 299
New York, city skyline, 348, Fig. 403; Transportation Authority poster design, 290, Fig. 337
Nivola, Constantino, *Mural Façade of Covenant Mutual Insurance Building*, 111–112, Fig. 140
Noguchi, Isamu, *Cube*, 74–75, Fig. 86
Norton, Dr. Alan, *Fractal Domain of Attraction*, 297, Pl. 30 (p. 292)
Nutcracker, The, Sleigh Ride Scene, 311, Fig. 359

octahedron, 77
Odom, Mel, book cover design, 287, Fig. 330
offset lithography, 284
Op Art, 264, Pl. 17 (p. 125)
Opie, Julian, *Incident in the Library*, 57–58, Fig. 60
opposition, and transition, 196–197, Fig. 222
originality, 192–193, Figs. 216, 217, and 218
Oscar de la Renta, 321–322, Fig. 370
overlapping, 86–87
Owen Christopher, house design, 361, Fig. 418
Ozenfant, Amédée, *Fugue*, 49, Fig. 50

package design, 110–111, Fig. 137; 293–294, Fig. 338
painting, and sculpture, 255–276; attributes, 255–256; casein, 258; contemporary directions in, 260–265, current trends, 265–267; encaustic, 257, Fig. 289; materials

painting, and sculpture (*cont.*) of, 256–257; media, 257–259; oil, 258, Fig. 291; tempera, 256–257, Fig. 288; watercolor, 258, Pl. 27 (p. 210)
Palazzo dello Sport, Rome, Pier Luigi Nervi and Annibale Vitellozzi, 165, Fig. 179
Papavgeris, Athanase, relief panel, 155–156, Fig. 166
paper clip design, 367, Fig. 426
parquetry, 212, Fig. 235
Parr, *Blue Geese Feeding*, 141–142, Fig. 151
Parrott, Alice, *Tapestry*, 232–234, Fig. 264
Parsifal, 187, Fig. 211
Parthenon, 147–148, Fig. 158; 349
patina, 211
Pearlstein, Philip, *Model with Minstrel Marionettes*, 29, Fig. 33
Peine, Otto, *Manned Helium Sculpture from City-thing Sky Ballet*, 59, Fig. 64
perception, 10–12
performing arts, 311–316; costume design, 324–325, Fig. 375; design with lighting, 313; set design, 311–312, Figs. 360–361
Persian Rhyton, 213, Fig. 236
perspective, 90–93; atmospheric (aerial), 91–92, Fig. 108; linear, 90–91, Figs. 106 and 107
Peru, Inca feathered tunic, 103, Fig. 122; terraced farms, 3, Fig. 1
pewter, 213
photograph, as design, 306–308; as document, 304–305, Fig. 350; as symbol, 302–303, Fig. 348; 304, Fig. 349
photography, 300–310; commercial, 305–306; special effects, 308–309, Fig. 357; special techniques, 309–310, Fig. 358
photolithography, 285
photorealism, 266, Fig. 300
photoserigraphy, 285
Picasso, Pablo, *Les Deux Femmes Nues*, 69, Figs. 77, 78, and 79
pigments, 256
Pissarro, Camille, *River-Early Morning*, 134, Pl. 23 (p. 127)
plan for order, 16–17, Figs. 18 and 19
planography, 283–284
plasticity, 207
plastics, 221; methods of working, 221–223; varieties, 221–223
point, 46

Pointillism, 261, 297
Pollock, Jackson, *Number 17*, 264, Fig. 298
Pont du Gard, The, 237–238, Fig. 267
Pop Art, 275, Fig. 311
positive, shapes, 71–72; space, 82, 270–271, Fig. 305
post-and-lintel, 66, Fig. 72; 349, Fig. 404
Post-Modernism, 266–267, Fig. 301
potter's wheel, 228, Figs. 256 and 257
pottery, forming techniques, 227–230; vase, 41, Fig. 44
Powys, Marian, *Lace*, 241–243, Fig. 273
principles of design, 8, 137–204
printmaking, 277–285; processes, 279–285; mechanical processes, 284–285
prism and light, 115, Fig. 143
problem solving, 30–35
proportion, 171–178; and balance, 172; and scale in interior design, 343, Fig. 399; definition, 171; Golden Mean, 172–173; Greek concept, 171, Fig. 186; 172–176
Propylaea, Athens, 105–106, Fig. 128
Pruitt-Igoe housing project, 353, Fig. 409
pyramid, 76, Fig. 88

Raphael, *Madonna of the Chair*, 258, Fig. 290
Rector, Robert, *Charmed Dance*, 71–72, Fig. 83
Red Riding Hood, costume design for *Into the Woods*, 324–325, Fig. 275a
Regardant Feline with Bifid Tail, 215–216, Fig. 243
Regency fauteuil, 334–335, Fig. 388
Regency Park, Cary, No. Carolina, Thompson, Ventulett, Stainback Associates, 161, Fig. 171
relief, bas, 268–270; haut, 268–270; prints, 279–280, Fig. 316
Rembrandt, climactic rhythm, 145; *The Descent from the Cross*, 145, Pl. 24 (p. 128); *The Presentation in the Temple*, 91–93, Fig. 109
Renoir, Auguste, La Première Sortie, 85–86, Pl. 6 (p. 121); *Le Moulin de la Galette*, 200–201, Fig. 226; *Portrait of Louis Valtat*, 283–284, Fig. 326

repoussé, 248, Fig. 281
Richter, Vjenceslav, *Relief Meter*, 194, Fig. 219
Rienzi, stage design, 312–313, Fig. 363
Rigaud, Hyacinthe, *Louis XIV*, 321, Fig. 368
rigidity, 207
riveting, 224, Fig. 250
Rockefeller Plaza, 362–363, Fig. 420
Rodin, Auguste, 18; *Monument to Balzac*, 18–19, Fig. 21, *The Danaïd*, 18, Fig. 20
romanticism, 152, Fig. 161
Rudolph, Paul, reception area of Burroughs, Wellcome & Company, 344–345, Fig. 400
Rutherford, Karen Jenson, *Indiana Wanderings III*, 220, Fig. 248

Sabattini, Lino, silver-plated flower vases, 77, Fig. 90
Saint-Gaudens, Augustus, *William Tecumseh Sherman*, 213–214, Fig. 238
Saint Wulfran façade, 215–216, Fig. 242
Salalua, tapa skirt from Futura Islands, 102, Fig. 121
Salginatobel Bridge, The, 239, Fig. 268
San Ildefonso polychrome jar, 68, Fig. 75
Santachiara, Denis, *Maestrale*, table lamp, 76, Fig. 89
Sargent, John Singer, *El Jaleo*, 154–155, Fig. 164; *The Daughters of Edward Darley Boit*, 244–245, Figs. 275 and 276
saturation, 119
scale, 178–189; as perception, 185–186, Figs. 208 and 209; as symbol, 180, Figs. 201 and 222; diminutive, 185; for devotion, 182–183, Fig. 203; for elegance, 183–184; Fig. 207; for emphasis, 187–188, Figs. 211 and 212; for human ego, 181, Fig. 203; for security, 182–184, Fig. 206; monumental, 181
Schauspielhaus, East Berlin, 163–164, Fig. 176
Scheffer, Victor B., *Green Sea Anemone*, 4, Fig. 3; *Surf at South Point, Island of Hawaii*, p. 144, Fig. 154
Schiele, Egon, *Portrait of Franz Hauer*, 281–282, Fig. 322

Schongauer, Martin, *St. Michael*, 281, Fig. 321
Schwarcz, June, electroformed enamel bowl, 26, Fig. 26
Schwizgebel, C., cut-paper silhouette, 83, Fig. 96
sculpture, and light, 272; and painting, 255–276; and space, 270–271; casting methods, 270; categories, 268–270; contemporary trends, 275–276, directions in, 273–274; freestanding, 268; relief, 268
seeing, psychology of, 9–11
Seeley, J. *Skywire Twins with Chair*, 309–310, Fig. 358
Segal, Barbara, *Shattered Sun*, 249, Fig. 284
Sekimachi, Kay, *Hanging*, 145, Fig. 156
Sekine, Nobuo, *Phases of Nothingness*, 102, Fig. 119
serigraphy, 284, Pl. 29 (p. 292); in fabric design, 252
set design, 311–316
shade, in color, 119
Shaner, David, *Pillow Pot*, 100, Fig. 117
shape, 46, 61–72; abstract, 68–69, Figs. 75–79; and mass, 61–79, 340; geometric, 66–68, Figs. 72, 73, and 74, Pl. 5 (p. 56); in landscape design, 366; natural, 63–66, Figs. 68–71; nonobjective, 70–71, Figs. 80 and 81; relationships, 71–72
Shaw-Sutton, Carol, *Dusk River Crossing*, 53, Fig. 56
Sheraton, Thomas, 337–338, Fig. 393
Shere, Sam, *Explosion of the Hindenburg*, 304–306, Fig. 350
silver, 213
Silverstone residence near Taxco, Mexico, 334, Fig. 387
Simulationists, 267–268, Fig. 302
simultaneous contrast, 130–132, Pl. 20 (p. 126), Pl. 21 (p. 126)
size, in depicting space, 88–90, Fig. 104
Snyder, Joan, *Mourning, Oh Mourning*, 5–6, Fig. 5
softwood, 211
solidity, 211
Sommerburg, Miriam, *Menorah Triptych*, 236, Fig. 266
space, 82–98, 190; actual, 93–96; and light, 91–93, Fig. 108; and line, 46, 340; illusionistic, 86–93;

space (*cont.*)
implied, 83–86, Figs. 98 and 99, Pl. 6 (p. 121); in landscape, 366–367, Fig. 425; manipulation, 331–334; overlapping, 86–87, Figs. 100 and 101; physical, 93; pictorial, 82–83, Fig. 97, 93; positive and negative, 71, Fig. 82; symbolic, 93; tiering, 87–88, Figs. 102 and 103; time and motion, 94–96, Figs. 112 and 113; 237–238
space apparel, 325, Fig. 376
spiral, 174–175, Fig. 190; logarithmic, 174
stage set, parallel, 311–312, Fig. 360; raked, 312, Fig. 361
stamping, 328
Starck, Philippe, *Tippy Jackson*, 340, Figs. 395 and 396
Statue of Liberty, as advertising, 188, Fig. 212
steel, 215
Stella, Joseph, *Skyscrapers*, 15–16, Fig. 17
Stockman, Denison Cash, cover design for *Urban Spaces*, 89, Fig. 104
stone, 215–216
Stonehenge, 66, Fig. 72
Stroud, Virginia A., *Water's Edge*, 129–130, Pl. 18 (p. 125)
structure, and decoration, 235–252; as decoration, 235–237
structural design, 237–243, in architecture, 348–351
structural systems, traditional, 348–349, Fig. 404
St. Peter's Basilica, Rome, 349, Fig. 405
style, 324
stylization, 68
subject, in architecture, 351; in painting, 355; in photography, 301
subtractive principle of color, 116–117, Pl. 9 (p. 122)
subtractive techniques, 224
Sugarman, George, *Kite Castle*, 271, Pl. 28 (p. 291)
Sullivan, Bill, *Niagara Sunset*, 5–6, Fig. 6
Sullivan, Louis, Wainwright Building, 356–358, Fig. 415
Super Swallowtail, 326–327, Fig. 378
support, for painting, 256–257
Surrealism, 263, Fig. 297
symbolism, in space, 93, 245–247,

symbolism, in space (*cont.*)
Figs. 277–279; in surrealism, 263, Fig. 297
symmetry, 162–168; bilateral, 163, Fig. 174; dynamic, 176–177, Figs. 194 and 195; radial, 164–166, Figs. 178–180

Taaffe, Philip, *Yellow, Gray*, 163, Fig. 175
Tacoma Narrows Bridge, 40–41, Fig. 43
tactile, 58; texture, 100–102, Figs. 118–120; 103, Figs. 121–124
Taj Mahal, 183, Fig. 205
Tampan maju, Sumatra, 141, Fig. 149
tapestry, 232–234, Figs. 263–264
tapis, Indonesia, 99, Fig. 116
Tarver, Ron, *The Fireman*, 305, Fig. 351
Tchelitchew, Pavel, *Africa*, 52, Fig. 54
television, 310–311
tempera, 256–257, Fig. 288
Tenniel, John, *Alice After Taking the Magic Potion*, 186, Fig. 210
tensile strength, 207
tesserae, 236, 250
tetrahedron, 77
texture, 99–113; in interior design, 341, Fig. 397; 343, Fig. 398; in landscape design, 366; tactile, 100–104, Figs. 118–124; visual, 104–105, Figs. 125 and 126
Thomas Jefferson State Reception Room, Department of State, Washington, D.C., 164, Fig. 177
tiering, 87–88, Figs. 102 and 103
time, and rhythm, 145–147; in interior design, 345; space and motion, 94–96
tin, 214–215, Fig. 240
tint, 119
Tom's Natural Soap, package design, 293, Figs. 338a, 338b, 338c, and 338d
tonality, 91, 132–134

tone, 119, 133
Torivio, Dorothy, 193, Fig. 218
trademark, 289
Trampas, New Mexico, church, 354–355, Fig. 411
transition, and opposition, 196–197, Fig. 222
Très riches Heures de Jean, Duc de Berry, 201–202, Fig. 227
trumpet shell from Philippine Islands, 96, Fig. 114
truss, 349–350, Fig. 404
trypanosphaera transformata, blown glass model, 165, Fig. 178
Tshimshian clan headdress, 245–246, Fig. 278
Turner, J. M. William, *Dido Building Carthage*, 92, Fig. 108
Turner, Tom, *Bottle Vase*, 249, Fig. 283
Tworkov, Jack, *L. B. Ook #1*, 178, Fig. 197
type design, 286–287, Fig. 329

Unicorn in Captivity, The, 232–233, Fig. 263
unity, 195–204; symbolic, 202–203, Fig. 229; through color, 197, Pl. 25 (p. 209); through line, 198–199, Fig. 224; through repetition, 200–201, Fig. 226; through shape, 199, Fig. 225; through value, 197–198, Fig. 223

value, 117–118, 190; scale, 118, Pl. 13 (p. 123)
van de Bovenkamp, Hans, *Mariner's Gateway*, 94, Fig. 111
van Gogh, Vincent, *Cypresses*, 258, Fig. 291; *Cypresses* (detail), 107–108, Fig. 132
van Hoe, Marc, Ornament Collection, 157–158, Fig. 168
vanishing point, 90
variety, 190–195; through contrast, 190–192; through originality, 192–193; through structure, 194–195, Figs. 219–221

Vasarely, Victor, *KEZDI-111*, 219, Pl. 17 (p. 125); *Painting with Circles*, 67, Fig. 73
veneer, 212
Venus de Medici, 5, Fig. 4
Venus of Willendorf, 270–271, Fig. 304
Versailles, Palace and Gardens, 183–184, Fig. 207
vignette, 12–13, Fig. 14
Voulkos, Peter, catalogue design, 83–84, Fig. 98

Wagner, Richard, climactic rhythm, 145; *Parsifal*, 187, Fig. 211
Weiss, Steven, *Infinity Table*, 59–60; Fig. 63
welding, 224
Wertheimer, Esther, *Madre con Bambino in Circolo*, 11–12, Fig. 13
Westerman, H. C., *The Big Change*, 162, Fig. 173; *Jack of Diamonds*, 224, Fig. 250
West German traffic sign, 68, Fig. 76
White, Minor, *Capitol Reef, Utah*, 190–191, Fig. 213
Widforss, Gunnar, *The Grand Canyon*, 34–35, Pl. 3 (p. 55)
Willis Thornton, *Break Dancer*, 62, Pl. 4 (p. 55)
Winter, Thelma, *Christ and the Apostles*, 176, Figs. 194 and 195
wood, 211; grain, 211, Fig. 234; hard, 211; polychromed, 212, Pl. 26 (p. 210); soft, 211
Wood, Steve, *Untitled*, 275–276, Fig. 312
woodcut, 279, Fig. 317
wood engraving, 279–280, Figs. 318–320
Wright, Frank Lloyd, 296, Fig. 340; 339–340, Fig. 394; Kaufmann House, 350, Fig. 406
wrought-iron lattice, Aachen, 112, Fig. 141
Wyeth, Andrew, *Anna Kuerner* (detail), 255–256, Fig. 288